CHILDREN'S LITERACY DEVELOPMENT

A Cross-Cultural Perspective on Learning to Read and Write

Second edition

Catherine McBride

Routledge
Taylor & Francis Group

LONDON AND NEW YORK

Second edition published 2016
by Routledge
2 Park Square, Milton Park, Abingdon, OX14 4RN

and by Routledge
711 Third Avenue, New York, NY 10017

Routledge is an imprint of the Taylor & Francis Group, an informa business

© 2016 Catherine McBride

The right of Catherine McBride to be identified as author of this work has been asserted by her in accordance with sections 77 and 78 of the Copyright, Designs and Patents Act 1988.

British Library Cataloguing in Publication Data
A catalogue record for this book is available from the British Library

Library of Congress Cataloguing in Publication Data
Names: McBride-Chang, Catherine, author.
Title: Children's literacy development : a cross-cultural perspective on learning to read and write / Catherine McBride.
Description: Second edition. | New York : Routledge, 2016. |
Series: International texts in developmental psychology |
Includes bibliographical references and index.
Identifiers: LCCN 2015024402 | ISBN 9781848722866 (hb : alk. paper) |
ISBN 9781848722873 (softcover : alk. paper) | ISBN 9781315849409 (ebk)
Subjects: LCSH: Literacy. | Children–Writing. | Language arts.
Classification: LCC LC149.M36 2016 | DDC 372.6–dc23
LC record available at http://lccn.loc.gov/2015024402

ISBN: 978-1-84872-286-6 (hbk)
ISBN: 978-1-84872-287-3 (pbk)
ISBN: 978-1-31584-940-9 (ebk)

Typeset in Bembo
by Out of House Publishing
Printed and bound in Great Britain by
Ashford Colour Press Ltd, Gosport, Hampshire

CHILDREN'S LITERACY DEVELOPMENT

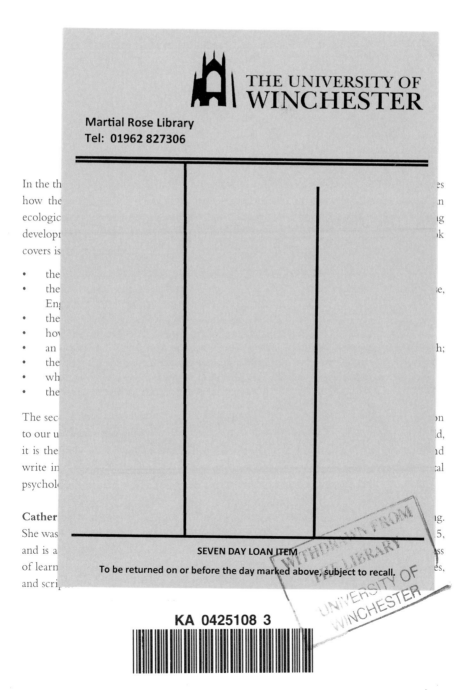

In the th   es
how the   n
ecologic   ig
developr   )k
covers is

- the
- the   e,
  Eng
- the
- hov
- an   h;
- the
- wh
- the

The sec   )n
to our u   d,
it is the   1d
write in   :al
psycholo

Cather   ig.
She was   5,
and is a   ss
of learn   es,
and scri

International Texts in Developmental Psychology

Series editor: Peter K. Smith, Goldsmiths College, University of London, UK.

This volume is one of a rapidly developing series in *International Texts in Developmental Psychology*, published by Routledge. The books in this series are selected to be state-of-the-art, high-level introductions to major topic areas in developmental psychology. The series conceives of developmental psychology in broad terms and covers such areas as social development, cognitive development, developmental neuropsychology and neuroscience, language development, learning difficulties, developmental psychopathology, and applied issues. Each volume is written by a specialist (or specialists), combining empirical data and a synthesis of recent global research to deliver cutting-edge science in a format accessible to students and researchers alike. The books may be used as textbooks that match on to upper-level developmental psychology modules, but many will also have cross-disciplinary appeal.

Each volume in the series is published in hardback, paperback, and eBook formats. More information about the series is available on the official website at: http://www.psypress.com/books/series/DEVP, including details of all the titles published to date.

Published Titles

Child Development: Theories and Critical Perspectives, 2nd edition
By Rosalyn H. Shute, Phillip T. Slee

The Child at School: Interactions with Peers and Teachers, 2nd edition
By Peter Blatchford, Anthony D. Pellegrini, Ed Baines

Children's Literacy Development: A Cross-Cultural Perspective on Learning to Read and Write, 2nd edition
By Catherine McBride

Forthcoming

Aging and Development: Social and Emotional Perspectives, 2nd edition
By Peter Coleman, Ann O'Hanlon

Childhood Friendships and Peer Relations: Friends and Enemies, 2nd edition
By Barry Schneider

To Helmuth, whose warmth, wit, support, insight, and curiosity make life better: LLLL!

CONTENTS

FIGURES

TABLES

PREFACE

It has been eleven years since the first edition of this book, entitled *Children's Literacy Development*, was published. I had a great time writing it then, and revising it for this new edition with a new publisher has also been a pleasure. So many exciting ideas have emerged in the area of literacy research in the last decade or more, and many more studies have emerged from diverse countries than were available then.

Now, as then, I embrace the idea of considering how children learn basic literacy from a developmental perspective. This perspective is important because it incorporates ideas of culture, language, script, age, and educational level all into understanding literacy learning and impairment. Many books on the subject of reading and writing focus primarily on one language (usually English), and I have tried not to do that or at least to keep the reader constantly aware that how children learn to read across the world may be similar in many ways, but there are likely important differences as well. This is a book intended to provide a basic idea of literacy development, and there are plenty of other books written about expertise in reading and writing or about various educational aspects of literacy (usually within a much narrower cultural context) that will be helpful following this introduction for those wishing to delve deeper into the subject. This edition, compared to the previous one, also places more of an explicit emphasis on basic writing skills as well as reading skills.

It is true that this book contrasts English and Chinese as a focal point, and other languages and scripts are discussed in much less detail. This is partly because these are the scripts on which most of my research has been conducted. In addition, however, it is important to note that if one were to try to contrast two scripts for diversity, these two are reasonable choices. Most alphabetic orthographies have many similarities. It is certainly the case that some, such as Spanish and German, are more transparent and easy to read than English, but alphabetic orthographies do have much in common. The system of Chinese character and word recognition truly requires some adjustments in understanding what it means to read if one comes from an alphabetic perspective. Most other scripts, such as Greek, Arabic, Korean Hangul, or the akshara languages of India, such as Hindi, have idiosyncrasies that are very different from Roman script writing, but relatively speaking these are likely to be more minor when compared with Chinese. Thus, although no book can cover reading and writing in every script, this English–Chinese contrast, along with complementary studies in many other languages and scripts, may provide some good basic developmental insight into how literacy develops across cultures.

This edition of the book also includes some suggested references for each chapter. I have tried to keep these mostly at the level of books, because the extensive reference section at the end of the book has many articles that can be accessed if you are interested. The books listed at the end of each chapter are for the most part reasonably new and may give you more ideas on a particular general topic as covered here. There are some recent ones on Hebrew and Arabic in particular that might be of interest to those wanting to know more about these Semitic languages.

I am grateful to many people who helped me directly or indirectly with this edition of the book. First, I am grateful to Peter Smith for suggesting that I embark on writing this book in the first place for the first edition. This was not my idea, but once it was proposed to me, I realized it was the perfect book for me to try to write. Second, for the previous edition, I asked ten people to critique one chapter each, and I learned a lot from all of them. Much of what I say here remains the same or similar in this version. Thus, I wish to thank again reviewers Markéta Caravolas, Nancy Jackson, Che Kan Leong, Iris Levin, Frank Manis, Kara McBride, Fred Morrison, Benjamin Munson, Twila Tardif, and Rick Wagner. Many of these researchers belong to the Society for the Scientific Study of Reading, a society dedicated to understanding reading processes across cultures and languages. I am grateful to the society for serving as a catalyst for generating so much important research in this area.

I also wish to thank the research assistants working in my lab who have helped me in various aspects of editing and referencing. These are Gladys Wing-Sum Lui, Judy Sze-Man Leung, Jamie Sze-Wing Mak, and Bowie Choi-Hin Lau. Xiuhong Tong, a postdoctoral fellow, has also been very helpful in discussions on different aspects of literacy. I am grateful for grants #CUHK8/CRF/13G (the Collaborative Research Fund) and #CUHK402-HSS-12 (Humanities and Social Sciences Prestigious Fellowship), both from the Hong Kong government, which supported some of my time and research for this book.

Great thanks to several people who have generally supported me and made my daily life happier and easier. These include my parents, William and Angela, my children, Claire and Leeren, my sister, Kara, my Aunt Cecilia, and Jonalyn for all of her help. My partner, Helmuth, has been a continuing source of support and inspiration.

Wherever you are in the world or whatever language or script is your native one, I hope that this book serves as a starting point for you to understand how children learn to read and to write from a developmental perspective.

This perspective ultimately can potentially be of use not only to students and researchers but also to clinicians, educational psychologists, and those interested in speech, language, and hearing-related issues. Great strides have been made in expanding this topic across countries and scripts. Thank you for expanding this further.

1

AN ECOLOGICAL APPROACH TO LITERACY DEVELOPMENT

Literacy development broadly depends upon interactions among that which the child brings to the task of reading and writing, the script/language to be learned, and the environment in which this development occurs. Individual and age-related variability across children has been studied extensively in the reading (and writing) literature. Such variability is highlighted throughout this book, as typically developing and disabled readers, younger and older readers, and monolingual and multilingual readers and writers are broadly compared and contrasted. However, *what* children are reading and writing and *how* they are learning to read and write are equally crucial facets of literacy acquisition. In this text, literacy development is roughly and imperfectly defined as reading and writing development.

It is likely that there exist both universals and specifics of literacy development. At some level, the task of every reader/writer is to map oral language onto its written form. This process is, crudely, a universal. Reading and writing specifics depend upon the literacy environment, the language, and the script. (Please note that, throughout this text, the terms *script*, *orthography*, and *writing system* are used interchangeably. They are all taken to mean the way in which the language is represented in writing, including different alphabets or other types of print (e.g. Chinese characters, diacritics/accent marks, spellings with various alphabets, etc.).

There are numerous variations on literacy development, from American monolingual children learning to read a single script, to Swiss schoolchildren learning to read several Indo-European languages, to Berber-speaking Moroccan children learning to read a formal version of Arabic in the Quran. The specificity of these situations is overwhelming for one neat theory of literacy development. Research studies contrasting different situations in which literacy acquisition takes place are also limited; some of these are outlined below.

Understanding children's literacy development first requires a conceptualization of various environments in which children acquire it. These environments involve many institutions, places, and people whose effects on how children learn to read and write are strongly linked. Such environments differ greatly from culture to culture, from city to city, from one child to the next. Bronfenbrenner (1979) articulated what developmental psychologists understand by the term *environment*. His ecological systems, which are useful for understanding various levels of environment affecting children's literacy acquisition, are reviewed later in this chapter. Conceptualizing how environment affects literacy acquisition is particularly important in a book like this, which attempts to understand how literacy develops across cultures.

In direct contrast to this goal of learning about literacy development across cultures, the majority of research studies on children's reading and writing development are focused squarely on the process of learning to read and, to a lesser extent, to write English within an English/western environment. Because this book is a review of relevant research on the development of literacy, it therefore follows that the majority of the research reviewed here will be on how and in what context children learn to read and to write in English.

This, of course, presents a big problem for those interested in understanding how literacy develops across orthographies, languages, and cultures, because English is quite peculiar in some ways (Share, 2008). For example, English is a culturally prestigious language with a history of domination (Baker & Jones, 1998). Learning to read and write in English as a second language brings with it other issues of language learning, such as unfamiliarity with the cultural values of monolingual English speakers, which may differ from native speakers' focuses on reading skills. In addition, English is an irregular orthography, much less clear in its mapping of letters to sounds than are some other fairly common alphabetic orthographies, such as German, Portuguese, or Spanish (Share, 2008). The English script also differs greatly from various non-alphabetic orthographies such as Japanese or Chinese in ways considered explicitly later in this and subsequent chapters.

Although this chapter begins by considering literacy acquisition from the perspective of learning to read English, one purpose of this text is to stimulate discussion and research on the mechanisms by which children learn to read in different cultures and orthographies. I am hopeful that the research presented in the following chapters will arouse your interest in how and where children learn to read and write across the world, both in their native language and in second, third, or fourth languages, whether or not any of these happen to be English.

This book focuses on ten themes of reading and writing acquisition that are applicable across cultures. In this first chapter, we consider the effects of different environmental factors on literacy development. Chapter 2 then focuses on one of the well-researched areas of literacy acquisition: phonological (speech sound) development, from birth onwards. Here, the text covers the developmental aspects of speech perception, phonological sensitivity and awareness, including both segmental and suprasegmental sensitivity, rapid automatized naming, verbal memory, and language learning as they apply to reading acquisition. Chapter 3, 'Building blocks of reading', considers the importance of and extent to which three aspects of children's beginning to read are applicable across cultures. These literacy acquisition fundamentals include home literacy environment, print components (e.g. Roman or other alphabets or Chinese semantic and phonetic radicals, as well as the extent to which the word as a unit makes sense for literacy development understanding cross-culturally), and print automatization.

In contrast to the broader themes of the first three chapters, Chapters 4 and 5 focus exclusively on particular cognitive skills for reading development. Chapter 4, 'The role of morphological awareness in learning to read and to write (spell)', explores the unique contributions of morphemes, or meaning units, to word/character recognition and writing, vocabulary knowledge, and reading comprehension. Chapter 5 highlights the development of visual and orthographic abilities for literacy acquisition across cultures.

Chapter 6 addresses the concept of specific reading disability, or dyslexia. This section covers the cognitive deficits associated with reading problems and the neuroanatomical markers of dyslexia. It also explores approaches to remediation of reading difficulties. Chapter 7 reviews research on reading comprehension in children. This review consists of a broad conceptualization of reading comprehension and then a consideration of motivation and some important cognitive constructs that contribute to its development. Chapter 8 shifts primarily to writing, by reviewing two diverse areas of research – spelling development and composition writing. Models of both are considered. We also briefly consider the issue of dysgraphia, a specific writing difficulty, as a parallel to dyslexia.

Chapter 9 focuses on the ways in which teaching affects children's literacy acquisition. This section reviews the effects of school instruction on literacy, compares whole language and phonics approaches to reading, and explores how particular cognitive skills are influenced by literacy instruction. We also briefly consider the importance of electronic aids, such as computer programs and e-books, in facilitating literacy acquisition. Finally, Chapter 10 focuses on two areas of research into bilingualism and biliteracy. The first is on the transferability of cognitive skills, including phonological and orthographic processing, across languages to print. The second is on reading comprehension in bilinguals. We consider the question of whether it is possible to have reading difficulties in one orthography and not another for those who can read in more than one script or language.

As much as possible, and across the chapters, research on learning to read and to write in orthographies other than English is presented to offer a contrast with research on learning to read English. However, this chapter begins with an explicit consideration of issues related to reading English.

Environmental influences on literacy development in English

Perspectives from different researchers make clear that there are numerous environmental factors affecting how children acquire basic literacy skills in English. Among the most prominent of these include issues of home language spoken (Tabors & Snow, 2001), classroom teaching style (Chall, 1996; Foorman, Francis, Fletcher, Schatschneider, & Mehta, 1998; Treiman, Stothard, & Snowling, 2012), home environment (Whitehurst & Lonigan, 1998), and socio-economic status (Snow, Burns, & Griffin, 1998; Vernon-Feagans, 1996). Beyond the United States, across English-reading countries, additional variables related to English literacy development extend to dialect (Burk, Pflaum, & Knafle, 1982; Kemp, 2009; Terry, 2006; Treiman & Barry, 2000), how alphabet knowledge is taught (e.g. Connelly, Johnston, & Thompson, 1999; Seymour & Elder, 1986; Treiman, 2006), when reading-related skills are taught (Clay, 1998), and culture (Campbell, 1998; Clay, 1998).

Although literacy development is important for most of the information we glean from childhood through adulthood, throughout this book my primary emphasis is on the early years of literacy development, which include *emergent literacy*, defined as the 'developmental precursors of formal reading' (Whitehurst & Lonigan, 1998, p. 12) in children. I have always been particularly fascinated by the transition from a child not knowing how to read to being able to recognize some words in her world. The development of early literacy involves different systems, which interact in complex ways, as discussed below.

Literacy development contrasts: a comparison of Hong Kong Chinese and American monolingual English readers

To illustrate this point, let us consider an issue related to literacy development that I have struggled with in my own research: what are the similarities and differences in comparing reading development across Hong Kong Chinese children, who are learning to read English as a second orthography/language, and American monolingual English-speaking children? These children attend school in very different places, which means that, at the same chronological age, their knowledge of reading and writing varies markedly.

I ask this particular question for several reasons. Practically speaking, it is of interest because I have lived for extensive periods of time in both Hong Kong and the United States. Because my main research area of interest is literacy development, a Hong Kong–American comparison is an obvious one for me personally. Theoretically, this contrast is also of interest because the children from these two regions have such different early literacy experiences (Kail, McBride-Chang, Ferrer, Cho, & Shu, 2013; McBride-Chang & Kail, 2002). This contrast is introduced here to illustrate some striking differences in how children learn to read English across the world. This illustration is intended to focus attention on the fact that, although much has been written about how children learn to read and to write English, the meaning of this achievement cannot be understood outside of that cultural context.

Obviously, the greatest contrast of all is in learning to read and to write English as a non-native versus monolingual English speaker. Yet along with this overwhelming difference follow a host of other, more subtle differences as well.

Typical Hong Kong Chinese children begin learning to read Chinese characters at the age of 3.5 years. They verbally label these characters using Cantonese, their native language. At the same time, they are learning to speak another language, Putonghua (translated in Chinese as 'the common language', and typically referred to by westerners as Mandarin), the dominant/governmental language spoken in China. As they progress through school, their literacy development will focus on learning to read using the grammatical structure and vocabulary of Putonghua, which sometimes differs from the native Cantonese. Along with these language and reading challenges, they also learn to read, write, and speak English at the same age, that is, beginning at 3.5 years old. Both Chinese characters and English words are learned in part via copying of each over and over again several times. Often, English vocabulary is acquired in its oral and written form simultaneously, as regularly occurs for learners of second languages. Reading of both Chinese characters and English words is often accomplished using the 'look and say' method, in which the teacher points to the written referent and pronounces it, after which the children are supposed to repeat the pronunciation. No phonological coding system is introduced to help children learn to decode for Cantonese literacy. In some schools in Hong Kong, letter sounds are still not taught. In many schools, phonics is not taught for English, partly because teachers still are not well versed in phonics; they themselves learned to read English solely via a look and say method. By the age of five, these Hong Kong Chinese children are often one to two years ahead in English reading-related skills, such as letter name knowledge and English word recognition, compared to their American counterparts.

In contrast, most American children are not formally taught to read and write until grade 1, when they are about six years old. Most learn to read English only. Furthermore, the large monolingual English-speaking population in America brings with it a solid oral vocabulary onto which these children can map the single orthography they are taught to read in school. English reading is taught in a variety of ways in the United States, but, typically, children learn some phonics, such as letter sound knowledge and how to put sounds together to form words, in this endeavour. Parental attitudes in America, as compared to those in Hong Kong, differ about the value of education and how best to accomplish the goal of literacy, particularly in their emphases on the relative importance of education and natural ability versus effort (as discussed below). Thus, from a cross-cultural perspective, the number and variety of factors that contribute to children's literacy development are daunting.

Of course, this characterization of what is 'typical' in Hong Kong and American cultures is vastly oversimplified. Within the same city or town, aspects of individual children's backgrounds, including the socio-economic status of the family, the educational background of the parents, the extent to which education is valued in the family, the parents' parenting styles, and children's own pre-literacy experiences, may differ dramatically. Since the first edition of this book came out, many more schools

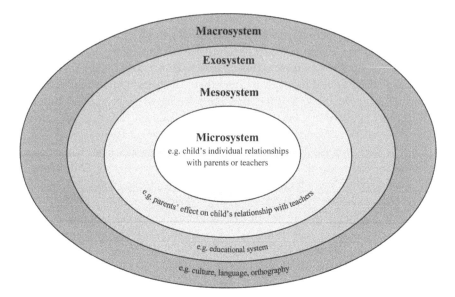

FIGURE 1.1 Bronfenbrenner's (1979) ecological approach applied to children's reading acquisition.

are teaching using Mandarin, rather than Cantonese, as the medium of instruction in Hong Kong. Across the world, conceptualizing literacy development becomes even more complicated, as educational policies and cultural expectations for a literate child are incorporated into a framework for explaining children's literacy development. Culture, language(s) and orthography(ies) to be learned in order to attain literacy, governmental policies on education, parental backgrounds, and attitudes in any given place are all important for understanding literacy development. The remaining sections of this chapter will focus on some of the issues touched on by the Hong Kong–American illustration above, and Bronfenbrenner's ecological approach (see Figure 1.1) is used as a model of the environmental factors affecting children's reading acquisition.

Bronfenbrenner's ecological approach as applied to literacy development

Bronfenbrenner (1979) conceptualized environment as being comprised of at least four systems that interact. These interact within another dimension, which is historical period, or time. At the *macrosystem* level are cultural expectations of achievement, and language(s) and orthography(ies) to be learned. For example, Hong Kong Chinese children live in a society in which there is strong pressure to succeed academically. They also learn to map the traditional Chinese script (taught in Hong Kong and Taiwan, but not in mainland China or Singapore, where simplified characters are used) onto their native Cantonese language. In Hong Kong (but not in other Chinese societies), children are taught both Chinese and English word reading and word writing from age 3.5.

Tibi and McLeod (2014) noted that the macrosystem within the environment of the United Arab Emirates offers many idiosyncrasies that may affect children's literacy development there as well. For example, the language that they learn to read first is Arabic. They learn to read in Standard Arabic, but the form of formal written, or Standard Arabic is different from the language they speak at home with their families. This phenomenon is known as diglossia. In such cases, there is a 'high', or formal, version of the language and also a more colloquial version of the language used for daily life. This occurs for Chinese and sometimes for German as well (e.g. Swiss vs 'high' German in German-speaking Switzerland), among others.

In the United Arab Emirates, there are many different forms of spoken Arabic, and these differ across tribes and families. In addition, many children in the United Arab Emirates are cared for partly by service workers who share different native languages, such as those from the Philippines or Indonesia. These caregivers use different languages to communicate. Children with such caregivers in the early years often have lower word reading and word spelling skills than those without such caregivers, presumably because these language models might confuse them (Tibi & McLeod, 2014). Thus, many culturally determined factors related to language are crucial for literacy development at the level of the macrosystem.

In Bronfenbrenner's (1979) conceptualization, the *exosystem* consists of entities that have a direct one-way effect on how a developing child learns to read. This description suggests that an individual child has no impact on such an entity, but the entity directly affects the child. The educational systems in place in the child's school or the educational department's guidelines on education at the child's level are examples of the exosystem. For example, in the United Arab Emirates, there is a requirement by the Education Department that English language instruction be included alongside Arabic instruction from kindergarten onwards in school (Tibi & McLeod, 2014).

The *mesosystem* consists of the associations among various relationships the child has with others. Thus, whether the child's parents show concern or indifference towards the child or towards each other may affect how the child views her or his teacher(s) at school.

The *microsystem* consists of the child's individual relationships. In reference to learning to read or to write, the child's relationships with both parents are particularly important, because the home literacy environment may affect the child's readiness for literacy learning. The child–teacher relationship is also crucial for reading development.

These four systems continuously interact over time, and the distinctions among them are not always clear. For example, the education system (exosystem) is strongly influenced by the overall culture (macrosystem). These systems are reviewed, in turn, below.

Macrosystem: literacy across cultures

As applied to reading acquisition, the culture, language(s), and orthography(ies) of a society comprise a child's macrosystem. Culture can be conceptualized in many different ways, and a full consideration of its importance is beyond the scope of this book. However, we cannot fully understand the relationship between culture and literacy if we do not at least acknowledge some of the differences in literacy rates for citizens of various countries.

Among those countries with the lowest adult literacy rates are Guinea (25 per cent) and Sierra Leone (43 per cent). Both countries are poor nations, and their respective literacy rates reflect gender discrimination, with males being more likely than females to attend secondary school. In Guinea, these rates are 27 per cent for boys and 17 per cent for girls; in Sierra Leone, these rates are 40 per cent for boys and 33 per cent for girls. Correspondingly, many fewer women than men are literate in each place. Across both countries, basic health care facilities (e.g. access to clean drinking water, access to infant immunizations) are also sparse (UNICEF, 2014). It is difficult to imagine what life is like in certain areas of some countries, where children's very survival is often in question, because of limited access to health care and good nutrition, and the many health-related and family problems that poverty can bring. When life and death are at stake, it may seem strange to focus on the development of literacy as a primary goal for poor families. Yet it is.

As LeVine, LeVine, and Schnell (2000, cited in UNICEF, 2001) argue, relative to those who cannot read, those who can do so enjoy many important lifestyle benefits. Women who are literate are better able to seek care for their babies (pre-natal, immunization), stimulate young children through verbal interactions, and help young children to read themselves. Neighbourhoods even in the same general geographic area (e.g. Philadelphia, Pennsylvania, USA) that have more access to reading materials and resources tend to engage in more reading and have better environments, including both parental and teacher facilitation of reading, for literacy development from early on (Neuman & Celano, 2012). Job opportunities become greater with better reading skills (Searle, 1991), and improved employment ensures an increased income for the family. Knowledge can be a powerful link to a better life worldwide. Poverty and literacy/education are often correlated (Hannum & Buchman, 2005). For example, in 1997 in China, the overall adult literacy rate was 83.6 per cent, but in some provinces, particularly in the west (such as Qinghai and Xizang), the rates were at or below 60 per cent (UNESCO, 2000). Poverty is also much greater in these regions in relation to the rest of China (Yao & Liu, 1998). Worldwide, there are huge disparities across regions in reading development. For example, developing, relatively unstable nations tend to suffer both poverty and low literacy rates as compared to better developed, more stable countries such as Estonia and Denmark, both of which enjoy adult literacy rates of 100 per cent.

As outlined by Olson and Torrance (2001), promoting literacy is not in itself a way to end poverty or other social problems. However, being literate can be extremely helpful when linked to valued resources within society, such as social structures that make use of print to communicate information and to empower learners. Movements towards fostering literacy are likely to succeed only when children have support from parents, schools, and governments that collectively see the value in learning to read. One example is a specific focus on girls, an under-represented group in terms of literacy attainment, by India's National Policy on Education (Rao, Pearson, Cheng, & Taplin, 2013). This body grants some families specific payments over time to keep their daughters in school. In this instance, parents, schools, and the government work together to promote female literacy attainment.

Another aspect of the macrosystem in relation to literacy acquisition is the fact that many children's first experiences in learning to read involve literacy acquisition in a language other than their mother tongue. As eloquently stated by Elley (2001, p. 236), 'Millions of pupils in Africa and Asia are expected to become literate in a language to which they have little exposure, which they have only fragile incentives to learn, and for which many of their teachers provide only indifferent models.' As Matafwali and Bus (2013) observed in relation to Zambian children, 'lack of proficiency in the language of instruction is one of the hallmarks of persistent reading failure' (p. 41). Although the majority of the published research on learning to read focuses on monolingual English speakers (e.g. Adams, 1990), this issue of medium of instruction being a mismatch with one's native language is among the most striking examples of the effects of culture on reading acquisition across the globe.

Macrosystem: explaining achievement

A more specific conceptualization of an element of the macrosystem that affects literacy development involves attitudes towards academic achievement across cultures. Perhaps the best-known comparison of attitudes towards academic achievement is that between western and Asian students. Numerous studies (e.g. Chao, 1994; Chao & Sue, 1996; Feldman & Rosenthal, 1991; Pomerantz, Qin, Wang, & Chen, 2011; Pomerantz, Ng, Cheung, & Qu, 2014; Wang & Pomerantz, 2009) have demonstrated that both parental attitudes and students' attitudes and academic attainment differ between North American and Asian students. Asian students, particularly those from Japanese, Korean, and Chinese societies, tend to show higher academic attainment for their ages than those in the west. Pioneering work on this topic came from Harold Stevenson and his colleagues (for a review, see Stevenson & Lee, 1996), who demonstrated that, relative to urban American children, elementary schoolchildren from both Taipei, Taiwan, and Beijing, in China, were more advanced in reading vocabulary and comprehension and in word/character recognition (see also Lee, Uttal, & Chen, 1995). Reading comprehension tended to be particularly high in Chinese children in a more recent study of fourth graders around the world (Mullis, Martin, Foy, & Drucker, 2011).

Many explanations have been offered for the high academic attainment of Asian students. Here, attribution theory (Weiner, 1985) is the focus, which may have special consequences for reading development. Attribution theory helps us to explain our beliefs about causation, in this case regarding academic achievement. Learning beliefs differ strongly between Chinese and American children and their parents (Li, 2005). For example, if a child performs poorly in a spelling exam, she or her parents might explain this in a variety of different ways, including bad luck, lack of effort, or lack of innate skill. In past studies, there has been a tendency for Chinese parents to focus on educational attainment through hard work; therefore, to them, a poor performance in a spelling test would most likely signal lack of effort. Indeed, Chinese children view academic achievement as relatively changeable, and the more they believe in such changeability, the more likely they are to adopt a proactive approach to schoolwork (Wang & Ng, 2012). Hard work is the key to success.

On the other hand, American parents tend to be more likely to attribute academic performance to ability level. Thus, in this case, American parents might assume that poor performance in a spelling exam signals their child's inherent difficulty with mastering spelling. Of course, individual parents will attribute their own children's performances to a variety of characteristics and events, both internal and external to their children. However, at a cultural level, there tends to be a greater focus on academic achievement through hard work in Chinese societies, and academic achievement through innate ability in American ones (Chen, Lee, & Stevenson, 1996; Stevenson et al., 1990; Li, 2005; Yang & Zhou, 2008).

This effort/ability distinction has advantages and disadvantages for both groups. Americans may inadvertently stunt academic growth in children who would be quite capable of achieving higher levels if extra time were spent mastering schoolwork. Chinese cultures have been praised by educational psychologists around the world for the excellent academic results that a strong academic work ethic has brought to Chinese children.

On the other hand, Americans tend to be more sensitive to those with learning disabilities. For example, they are more willing to devote extra resources (such as special teachers, extra classes, more time for children to complete their work) once children have been diagnosed with a specific learning disability than are the Chinese, who remain, in many regions, sceptical of specific learning problems. (For example, in mainland China, there remains no clear conceptualization of dyslexia as of yet, though dyslexia is recognized in Taiwan and Hong Kong.) Such scepticism might inadvertently create more negative self-concepts in students who perceive themselves as simply not trying hard enough, when they consistently have trouble reading. These perceptions might, in turn, result in considerable frustration and even desperation in these children.

Macrosystem: the privileged and the poor

In addition to these cultural attitudes occurring at a societal level, there are many more cultural differences even within any given society. Perhaps the most obvious ones centre on the socio-economic status and educational level of the family. These, of course, are often confounded. Children from middle- or upper-class backgrounds sometimes have many more literacy experiences than those from lower-class backgrounds (Adams, 1990). For example, regular viewing of *Sesame Street* can help children learn some of the fundamentals of reading and writing. Children who regularly watch television programmes like this, now shown in over 130 countries, may exhibit better progress in early literacy development than those who do not (Fisch & Truglio, 2000). Families of children with relatively high socio-economic status may be more likely to encourage watching such television shows. Indeed, even at the highest of levels, a country's gross domestic product per capita, or GDP, is associated with reading variability, including reading disability (Chiu & McBride-Chang, 2006). Family socio-economic status is also directly associated with reading skills across cultures (Chiu & McBride-Chang, 2010; Chiu, McBride-Chang, & Lin, 2012), presumably because this measure broadly represents family resources, such as access to tutors or reading materials. At the same time, the effects of poverty over time are cumulative and strong in relation to children's achievement as well as other domains (e.g. Conger & Donnellan, 2007; Evans, 2004).

More directly, socio-economic status sometimes determines quality of schools. In the United States, for example, children from higher-income neighbourhoods tend to demonstrate higher academic achievement than those from lower-income neighbourhoods (Leventhal & Brooks-Gunn, 2003). Children from poor neighbourhoods attend neighbourhood schools, the quality of which is often substandard. Poorer families have relatively few tax dollars to maintain the schools. Moreover, these families sometimes suffer other problems that may go hand in hand with poverty, such as lower educational attainment; repetitive, stressful jobs that take time and energy away from child care; cultural preferences rejected by mainstream American society; or limited English proficiency. Thus, it is children from those families which seem to endure more than their fair share of suffering who attend America's poorest schools.

Apart from a comparison of public schools across richer and poorer neighbourhoods, reading scores are also better among American children attending private as compared to public schools (Ogle et al., 2003). Thus, in the United States, the association between socio-economic status and educational attainment is very strong at the level of a school or school district. That is, children from upper-status (richer) schools tend to perform much better academically than children from lower-status (poorer) schools (Snow et al., 1998). On the other hand, within a school, the association between academic achievement and socio-economic status tends to be much less. Thus, within a school, the richer children may be slightly higher in their academic achievement than are the poorer children, but these differences are much weaker than are those across schools.

In China, there are different issues and questions related to poverty and school achievement. One of the most prominent is the fact that there are so many families moving from rural to urban areas in China, in search of a better life. The rules of China's household registration system (called *hukou*) dictate that migrant children in China usually do not have equal opportunities compared to their urban classmates. Migrant children are not registered in the urban areas, so they cannot make a legal claim to the nine years of compulsory education that urban (local) children receive. Their educational opportunities are relatively limited as a result (e.g. Wang, 2008). They still usually go to school, but the schools they attend are typically substandard, with fewer resources, both in terms of a clean and safe place to learn and also in terms of teacher qualifications (Wu, Palinkas, & He, 2011). Around the world, poverty is associated with difficulties in literacy, in both direct and indirect ways (Chiu & McBride-Chang, 2010). For example, children from poor families are more likely to have been born prematurely, a risk factor for subsequent learning disabilities. Poor families are also subject to multiple early risk factors for learning achievement, such as exposure to lead, which is associated with cognitive deficits (Tesman & Hills, 1994).

Poverty is also centrally linked to malnutrition in children (UNICEF, 2001). Malnutrition results in a variety of problems, including inattention, lethargy, and cognitive deficits in children. Children's cognitive functioning suffers not only from the lack of nutrition itself; in addition, close family members or even teachers may not provide as stimulating an environment to malnourished children as compared to well-nourished children, because malnourished children often show little response to such stimulation (e.g. Valenzuela, 1997).

Thus, across the world, poor children who receive some literacy instruction in a malnourished condition may find it difficult to concentrate on their studies or respond appropriately to the new information they encounter.

Macrosystem: linguistic environment

Along with the culture of achievement adopted by a society, constraints of language and orthography also affect children's reading development. Language may affect the reading process in two ways. First, spoken language probably affects the levels at which children attend to a language's sound units. For example, relative to Chinese, English has many consonant clusters (e.g. the *str* in *string*), which may sensitize English speakers to language at the level of the phoneme (Cheung, Chen, Lai, Wong, & Hills, 2001). In contrast, Chinese has almost no consonant clusters. Rather, it may be more appropriate to segment the Chinese language at the syllable level (Chien, Wang, Bai, & Lin, 2000). These linguistic observations correspond to the writing systems of each orthography. English is represented by the Roman alphabet, whereas Chinese is represented by Chinese characters, which are morphosyllabic, representing both a unit of meaning (morpheme) and a syllable (phonological unit) simultaneously.

Language and culture also interact in various ways that may affect the reading acquisition process. For example, in Hong Kong, Chinese students are often accused of poor-quality writing (e.g. Tse et al., 1995). This problem may be attributable to the unique culture of Hong Kong, where people use Cantonese to talk with one another but are expected to read and write in Putonghua, a different Chinese language with a somewhat different structure (Tong et al., 2014). Although the same

Chinese script can be read in different Chinese languages – a special feature of the Chinese writing system (but one similar to Arabic) – there are clear differences in phraseology and grammar across these Chinese languages that may be confusing to students whose mother tongue is not Putonghua. Furthermore, Hong Kong students are learning to speak and read English concurrently. Juggling three different languages and two different scripts from kindergarten through secondary school is certainly a struggle for many Hong Kong students.

The problem of juggling different languages in learning to read is not unique to Hong Kong. Throughout mainland China, Putonghua is mapped onto Chinese characters, though children may speak a different Chinese language at home:

> Therefore access to literacy in China is channeled through (or limited to) the standard language [Putonghua/Mandarin]. This added task of learning to speak the standard language, particularly for children who do not speak the standard at home, puts many Chinese children in a similar position to children in societies with native languages who are forced to use an Indoeuropean language at school.
>
> *(Ingulsrud & Allen, 1999, p. 5)*

Although some Chinese scholars might consider this a rather extreme statement, it is clear that managing multiple languages may complicate literacy acquisition considerably. The same phenomenon occurs in other parts of the world too. For example, in Morocco many children are native Berber-speaking, and many more Moroccans speak Arabic in a dialect that differs substantially from the standard Arabic read by all (Wagner, 1993). As another example, in German-speaking Switzerland children speak Swiss German as their mother tongue but must uniformly use standard, or 'high', German when they learn to read. The diglossia of Arabic, mentioned more extensively above, is perhaps the most famous example of this (Tibi & McLeod, 2014). Diglossia essentially involves use of one or more colloquial forms of language for everyday communication and a 'higher', more literary form for formal schooling. Once again, literacy development requires some children to learn to speak and read a language that is somewhat or very different from their everyday speech (Elley, 2001).

Undoubtedly, the relation of language to culture may affect reading acquisition in even more subtle ways. For example, the extent to which English becomes an international language of communication could conceivably affect when and how both English and the native orthography are taught. In the past few years, Hong Kong has struggled greatly over whether English or Cantonese should be the language of instruction for high-school students. Implicitly, the language/script used to teach school subjects will be better practised as a formal medium of communication, as compared to other languages/scripts, during the course of the child's education. If English subsumes other languages in importance at school, it may eventually subsume other orthographies in output as well, so that fewer noteworthy works of poetry, stories, or scientific articles are written in orthographies other than English. This would be an example of the direct impact of language on culture.

Many regions of the world have attempted to ward off this possibility. Two examples are 'la cause des Quebecois' (Klein, 2010) and Singapore, with its 'Speak Mandarin' campaign (e.g. Montsion, 2014). People of Quebec have historically been strongly opposed to including English as an official language of their province. Their unity as Quebecois is largely defined by their monolingual French language. Singapore's 'Speak Mandarin' campaign was introduced as a unifying force in Singapore, to maintain the 'core' Chinese culture, which is seen as represented by Mandarin (Putonghua), and to ensure that other Chinese dialects do not interfere with effective Mandarin learning in school. There is also some effort to maintain a Chinese cultural atmosphere in Singapore through the use of Mandarin, despite having English as the official language of instruction in the region. Another example is Zambia, which mandated in the year 2000 that children should first be taught to read in their native language or at least a familiar one. Before this legislation was introduced, Zambian children were taught to read first in English, and their literacy skills were relatively poor, probably as a consequence of being relatively unfamiliar with English. The current problem is that in Zambia there are seven official languages, and children in a given classroom might have different mother tongues. Unfortunately, reading achievement has not improved much since the new laws were introduced, perhaps in large part because children's oral vocabulary knowledge in the language of literacy instruction is often relatively limited (e.g. Matafwali & Bus, 2013).

All of these examples illustrate the fact that the process of learning to read occurs within a strong cultural context.

Exosystem: school differences

In many cultures, the timing of reading acquisition is largely dependent upon the norms set up by a particular government. For example, a large number of studies have concluded that part of the key to Chinese children's particular academic success is that they simply spend more time in school (e.g. Chen et al., 1996) relative to their western peers. In addition, they spend more time in academic activities outside of school, such as doing homework. These academic activities are reinforced by schools' requirements.

Different governmental policies related to school achievement have important implications for children's reading acquisition development. For example, by the time a child has finished kindergarten (around age five) in Hong Kong, she or he is expected to have learned approximately 200 Chinese characters and 50 to 100 English words. This pattern is in striking contrast to that of German-speaking countries such as Austria, where no formal education in letters or reading itself is given until children come to primary school at six years old (Wimmer, Mayringer, & Landerl, 2000).

It is not at all clear that early (kindergarten) formal academic tutoring is ultimately beneficial to children. For example, in the 1970s in West Germany, researchers studied the long-term effects of academic kindergartens and play-focused kindergartens on a variety of developmental factors. This was a large-scale study, involving 50 play kindergartens and 50 academic kindergartens. Over a five-year period, relative to those from academic kindergartens, children from the play kindergartens were better off on several dimensions. By the age of ten, play kindergarten graduates were judged to be more creative, better across academic subjects, and more mature socially and emotionally (Darling-Hammond, 1997).

A study of Hong Kong children found somewhat similar results (Opper, 1996). In this research, comparing those who went to academically oriented kindergartens relative to their peers who attended play schools, it was demonstrated that cognitive and language skills, pre-writing and alphabet skills, and knowledge of numbers and arithmetic were consistently similar across groups. However, social interactions and social competence were somewhat more positive in children attending play schools. Educators in Hong Kong have also explicitly recognized other risks of enforced early academic schooling for its kindergarten population (ages three to six), worrying that,

> At this stage when the muscles of the children are not well-developed, and eyes and hands are not well-coordinated, asking them to write too early not only leads to unnatural postures when writing, it also places an undue burden on them and, more seriously, it may stifle their interest.
>
> *(Tse et al., 1995, p. 68)*

Although part of the appeal of early schooling for parents is the desire to boost their children's academic competence as quickly as possible, another impetus for the early schooling movement may be affected directly by the orthography to be learned in school. Chinese is particularly difficult to learn to read because it requires extensive instruction to advance one's knowledge. Each character must be painstakingly introduced and memorized. English, on the other hand, conforms to an alphabetic code. Once this code is mastered (e.g. **K** makes the /k/ sound), children can learn to read new words on their own, often without direct help from the teacher.

However, English is irregular in consistently conforming to the alphabetic code. Exception words, which do not conform to the letter sounds we learn (e.g. that *knew* should be pronounced *kuhnewuh* and *although* should be pronounced *althowguhhuh*), make learning to read English relatively difficult among alphabetic orthographies (Byrne, 1998; Seymour, Aro, & Erskine, 2003). Indeed, English takes about two years longer to learn to read accurately at the word level among children than does German. German, on the other hand, features a very regular orthography. That is, letter sounds map consistently to letters of the alphabet. Of the three orthographies listed above, then, German appears to be easiest to learn to read, English is of middle difficulty, and Chinese is most difficult. It is perhaps reasonable to speculate that difficulty of orthography may be negatively associated with, among other things, the age at which literacy skills are typically introduced. In this example, German literacy skills are first introduced in schools around age six, English skills around ages four to five, and Chinese literacy skills around ages three to five, depending upon region.

Mesosystem: interrelationships among important people and institutions

The mesosystem represents the relations among different individuals with whom the child typically interacts. The best example of a mesosystem in the context of children's literacy development is the parent–teacher relationship. In the educational psychology literature (for a review, see Hoover-Dempsey et al., 2001), it is clear that children tend to be successful learners when their parents take an active interest in their school performance. A nice illustration of this phenomenon comes from a study of sixth-grade Jewish children in Israel who were learning to read Arabic (Abu-Rabia, 1998). Because of the Arab–Israeli conflict, few Jewish parents want their children to learn Arabic, despite the fact that it is an official language of Israel and many Israeli Jews were originally from Arab-speaking nations. However, a minority of Jewish parents encourage their children to learn Arabic. In this study, the strongest predictor of Jewish children's reading skills in Arabic was their perception of their classroom learning environment. Although not a focus of this study, it is likely that those parents who encouraged their children to learn Arabic also indirectly contributed to the positive learning environment of the classrooms, thereby reinforcing students' interests in learning to read in this language.

Lee and Croninger (1994) further distinguish *social capital* (Coleman, 1987) – that is, children's parents being familiar with their children's friends and the parents of those friends – as another influential aspect of the mesosystem in relation to reading development. Pellegrini and Gaida (1998), in their observations of pre-school and early primary school children, also noted clear benefits of having friends share literacy activities together. Such sharing promotes learning. Even among older children across more than forty cultures, friends' enjoyment of reading uniquely explained students' own reading achievement (Chiu & McBride-Chang, 2006) in one study of over 200,000 participants. All in all, the more a school forms a community among parents, teachers, and students, all working towards a common goal of literacy development, the more likely the students are to become excellent readers (see also Serpell, 2001).

How schools handle discrepancies among children with various ethnic, family status (e.g. single-parent vs two-parent families), and socio-economic backgrounds is also crucial in promoting literacy development (Lee & Croninger, 1994). For example, educators have identified a 'middle-class bias' in classrooms and schools (Lott, 2001) that can strongly affect children's perceptions of the values of education and teachers' perceptions of who is likely to do well in school and why American school systems are essentially built for children from middle- to upper-class backgrounds.

Early studies (Rosenthal & Jacobson, 1968) demonstrated that teachers' beliefs about students shape students' performances in the classroom – even if the teachers' ideas about those pupils are incorrect. For example, investigators arbitrarily labelled some children as very bright and others as not too smart at the beginning of first grade for some first-grade teachers. By the end of the year, those children were performing as labelled even though there were no differences between them at the beginning of the year. In other studies, teachers have been found to expect poor or minority-group children, or those from single-parent families, to perform at a lower level than other students (e.g. Ellison, 1979; Levine, 1982; Strong, 1998). It is likely that these expectations are communicated to parents, who themselves may affect their children's academic motivations to succeed. Sorhagen (2013) showed that teachers' inaccurate judgements of first graders' abilities were associated with these students' performances in reading comprehension, among other abilities, at age 15. Collectively, these studies underscore the importance of beliefs of parents, teachers, and the students themselves in affecting progress in literacy development.

School–family partnerships can be difficult to maintain for a variety of reasons. For families in some majority (so-called third) world countries, the decision of whether or not to allow offspring to attend school is sometimes a difficult one to make. Wagner (1993) pointed out that, even when education is free for children, there can be hidden costs. Real costs include incidental fees for school-related activities, clothes, and materials (such as pencils and books). Perhaps most importantly, particularly in rural areas, there is the hidden cost of the loss of child labour income to be considered. For poor families to do without the income that their children might bring in represents considerable hardship. Another major perceived threat of the promise of education for poor families is the possibility of loss of traditional values, particularly when girls are educated. For example, in rural areas of India, parents tend to view basic literacy, rather than higher-level educational aspirations, as the primary goal. For girls a primary goal of school is to have the ability, ultimately, to marry educated men (e.g. Rao et al., 2013).

The developmental consequences of the mesosystem are clear, and have been well articulated previously by Bronfenbrenner (1979). For optimal reading acquisition, the relationships that children have with others should be in harmony. Thus, when parents and teachers agree on educational goals, they can support one another in promoting reading acquisition in the child. For example, in China, teachers view students whose parents give them extra help at home more positively than they do children whose parents do not give homework help (Ingulsrud & Allen, 1999). Similarly, the child benefits when both parents agree on their child-rearing goals and can support their children's literacy development together.

Microsystem: the child's relationships with valued others

The last level of environmental systems is the microsystem. Here, children's individual relationships with others matter most. In adolescence, for example, children who are friends with academically high-achieving peers tend to be high achievers themselves (Chiu & McBride-Chang, 2006). Similarly, peers who are relatively low achievers are likely to associate with one another.

In childhood, one's attachment to one's caregivers may be particularly important for early literacy development. In studies of this association, attachment is typically measured using Ainsworth's 'strange situation' (Ainsworth, Blehar, Waters, & Wall, 1978). Bus and van IJzendoorn (e.g. 1988a; 1988b;1992) have demonstrated that, compared to insecurely attached children, securely attached children tend to show more interest in reading, read more frequently, and are more attentive and need less discipline during story reading.

In a meta-analysis of 33 studies on the effects of parent/pre-school book sharing, Bus and colleagues (1995) found that it predicted about 8 per cent unique variance in reading outcomes, including language growth and reading achievement. This result was not affected by families' socio-economic status. A longitudinal study in Turkey similarly demonstrated that children whose mothers had had mother-focused training in parenting and communication skills when the children were pre-schoolers were more likely to stay in school and to perform better in academic subjects seven years later, compared to those whose mothers had not had such training (Kagitçibasi, Sunar, & Bekman, 2001). Leseman and de Jong (1998) also showed that the socioemotional climate of the home was important in promoting book reading among native Dutch, immigrant Turkish, and Surinamese families. For older (third-grade) children in classrooms, shared book reading combined with a focus on promoting positive socio-emotional functioning appeared to facilitate both reading achievement and socio-emotional skills in one study (Jones, Brown, & Lawrence Aber, 2011). Thus, both parent and teacher focuses on shared reading likely facilitate literacy development and also closer relationships. However, in many cultures, a recognition of the importance of such early literacy activities for subsequent achievement in reading and writing is lacking. For example, many parents and teachers in the United Arab Emirates engage in relatively few book-reading activities and tend to view writing activities as mechanical and unrelated to meaningful early literacy activities such as writing of one's own name (e.g. Tibi & McLeod, 2014).

Interactions among the systems

Results from a study by Li and Rao (2000) illustrate the ways in which Bronfenbrenner's (1979) systems might affect one another. Their study focused on beliefs about and achievement in literacy among pre-schoolers in three large Chinese cities, Beijing, Hong Kong, and Singapore. There are some striking differences across these three societies in all systems. At the macrosystem level, for example, Singapore's linguistic environment stresses English as the medium of instruction in schools, and in business and governmental communication. Therefore, it is not surprising that Singaporean Chinese parents emphasized the fact that Chinese book sharing is important to maintaining their children's identification with Chinese culture. On the other hand, forming a Chinese cultural identity was not of concern to

Chinese parents in Beijing or Hong Kong, where the majority official languages are Mandarin and Cantonese, respectively–both Chinese languages.

The role of the exosystem in literacy development was well illustrated by the importance Hong Kong parents place on reading acquisition as a preparation for primary school performance in this study (Li & Rao, 2000). The Hong Kong Education Department (1996) has actually prepared suggestions for pre-school children's education, implying to Hong Kong parents that even three- and four-year-old children must meet certain educational standards. In contrast, Beijing, for example, discourages the teaching of Chinese characters until primary school. In both cases, the education departments concerned can be conceptualized as part of the exosystem in each culture. The Hong Kong Education Department encourages families to focus on literacy acquisition in pre-school children. The Beijing Education Department officially limits this focus.

One can well imagine how a given mesosystem and microsystem may be affected by both the macrosystem and the exosystem. For example, attitudes about the importance of learning to write Chinese characters from a given culture may be in conflict with parental beliefs. A Taiwanese father was called in to his son's pre-school in Hong Kong to discuss his son's performance in Chinese character learning. The father did not share the belief of his son's teacher that a four-year-old boy who was lax in his character-learning homework was a poor student. From the father's perspective, academic homework for such a small child created too much pressure, and the fact that he was not doing it was unlikely negatively to affect his son's future. For the teacher, a student's low attainment at the pre-school level could mark the beginning of the end of his academic career, because those who fail in kindergarten tend to go to low-quality primary schools and, later, substandard secondary schools. The clash in beliefs between this father and the teacher represents part of a mesosystem.

Harmony across the mesosystem is also common. For example, Ingulsrud and Allen (1999) studied kindergarten attendees in Nanjing, China, and noted that parental participation in the early education process was essential for the optimal development of early literacy in these students. After all, in a single classroom of more than 50 children, any given child needs parental support, including encouragement and direct academic tutoring, for maximal success in learning.

Although the Chinese government is officially opposed to writing instruction for pre-schoolers, teachers and parents are commonly 'co-conspirators' in the race to promote emergent literacy skills in these children. For example, Ingulsrud and Allen often observed teachers introducing new lessons to the children by inviting children to tell what they knew about the lessons already, 'giving the impression that the good student is one who already knows textbook material that the class has yet to cover' (1999, p. 60). Thus, teachers demonstrate high expectations for their pupils, expectations that cannot possibly be met without parents' help. In turn, parents spend much time and effort preparing their children for high academic achievement. For example, it is not unusual for parents to hire extra academic tutors or even to take time off from their own work to help their young children prepare for important examinations. So-called 'cram schools', after-school programmes that teach extra lessons on various subjects, including reading skills, are increasingly popular and prominent in Asia (e.g. Chou, Wang, & Ching, 2012), particularly across Chinese societies, Korea, and Japan. In such instances, parents put a lot of faith in extra teachers for literacy development in their children.

Each microsystem is affected by other systems too. The immigrant experience, common in many places in the world, may be an example of this. A Spanish-speaking mother whose child attends school in the United States may worry about her daughter's academic performance because of the language gap between the child's home and school environments. In this case, the microsystem of a mother–daughter relationship may be strongly affected by the macrosystem of the broader culture in which they live. The anxiety the mother feels may be communicated to her daughter through the mother's insistence that the child work twice as hard as her classmates on the homework assigned each day. However, in the American culture, in contrast to many Chinese cultures, a parent's strong pressure on her daughter to study may be regarded as clashing with cultural norms. The daughter may notice that the pressure she receives from her mother is quite different from the attitudes of the parents of her classmates towards their study habits. In this case, the mother's constant pressure on her daughter may cause mother–daughter conflicts, directly affecting a microsystem.

Another example of multiple pressures in individual relationships affected by the macrosystem is that of mainland Chinese children moving to Hong Kong for the first time. Many of these new arrivals come to Hong Kong without knowing Cantonese, their language of instruction in Hong Kong, or English, which is taught to schoolchildren in Hong Kong from the pre-school years. They sometimes live with only one parent, often the father, because the Hong Kong government limits the number of immigrants to Hong Kong, occasionally prompting separations within the same family for a year or more (Chan et al., 2003). In this new environment, students experience enormous pressure from fathers to do well in school. This pressure may create a father–child relationship that is largely focused on academic achievement, including the quest for literacy, in both Chinese and English.

The purpose of this chapter has been to demonstrate some ways in which culture can affect the development of literacy skills in children from different backgrounds. The importance of culture for mediating and moderating literacy development will continue to be underscored throughout this text. Given the relative paucity of research on learning to read orthographies other than English, understanding precisely what processes are universal aspects of learning to read and what are specific aspects, affected by culture, language, and orthography, is a primary goal of those studying literacy development. With this perspective in mind, the following chapters address some of the most interesting and best-researched areas of reading development. Chapter 2 begins by reviewing the importance of phonological development for literacy acquisition.

Suggested readings

Aram, D., & Korat, O. (2010). *Literacy development and enhancement across orthographies and cultures.* New York, NY: Springer.

Cumming, A. (ed.) (2012). *Adolescent literacies in a multicultural context.* New York, NY: Routledge, Taylor & Francis Group.

Holliman, A. J. (ed.) (2014). *The Routledge international companion to educational psychology.* London: Routledge.

Kucircova, N., Snow, C., Grover, V., & McBride, C. (in press). *International companion to early literacy education.* Oxford: Routledge.

Rao, N., Pearson, E., Cheng, K.M., & Taplin, M. (2013). *Teaching in primary schools in China and India: Contexts of learning.* Abingdon, UK: Routledge.

Wolf, M., & Gottwald, S. (in press). *What it means to read: A literacy agenda for the digital age.* Oxford: Oxford University Press.

2

THE DEVELOPMENT OF SOUND, PHONOLOGICAL SENSITIVITY, AND LANGUAGE FOR READING AND WRITING

This chapter reviews various research studies which suggest that learning to read and write depends in part upon a child's ability to distinguish, attend to, remember, and manipulate sounds, especially speech sounds, from whole to parts. One aspect of phonological sensitivity that has become particularly prominent in the area of research in relation to literacy skills in the last decade or so is suprasegmental phonological sensitivity. This sensitivity is reactivity to sound changes across a word or phrase, including stress in English (e.g. depending on where the stress is placed in the word *refuse*, this segment is two different words, one meaning *garbage* and one meaning *to say no*). Such sensitivity is also important for tonal and pitch languages, which are the majority of languages in the world (about 70 per cent – Yip, 2002) and spoken by over 50 per cent of the world's speakers (Fromkin, 1978), especially in Africa and Asia. A change in tone or pitch constitutes a change in meaning in such languages. Following a brief introduction to sound and reading, a background on suprasegmental phonological sensitivity is presented first, though a focus on phonological awareness, which is segmental phonological sensitivity, dominates. The section on phonological awareness comes from studies that have built on pioneering research (e.g. Bruce, 1964; Calfee, Lindamood, & Lindamood, 1973; Chall, Roswell, & Blumenthal, 1963; Liberman, 1973; Liberman, Shankweiler, Fischer, & Carter, 1974) on the associations of various levels of phonological sensitivity with word recognition and sometimes word writing. A look at this work, accompanied by a discussion of definitions of and ways to conceptualize phonological awareness, forms the bulk of this chapter. Although the section on measurement of phonological awareness is somewhat long, the measurement of phonological awareness, and distinguishing it from other tasks of phonological sensitivity, is important and necessary to our thinking about its development across orthographies.

Other types of phonological processing skills – speeded naming and verbal memory – are then considered. The term 'phonological processing' refers to this group of skills, including phonological awareness, rapid automatized (speeded) naming, and verbal memory (Wagner & Torgesen, 1987). These are collectively referred to as phonological processing skills because they all make use of the sound structure of language.

Following this introduction to phonological processing skills, evidence is then reviewed on infants' impressive abilities to attend to and recall speech, beginning before birth. The chapter then moves on to highlight ways in which both developmental and individual differences in early perception and language skills might be linked to higher-order language skills, such as phonological sensitivity and vocabulary knowledge, which, in turn, may predict early reading skill.

This chapter focuses primarily on consistency, rather than inconsistency, in development. Although there is evidence for both consistency and inconsistency from infant perceptions to emergent readers, I find it particularly exciting to highlight the former. On the face of it, there is little evidence that the behaviours of a baby can predict anything about the abilities of a six-year-old learning to read. Thus, this chapter attempts to consider ways in which some consistency in literacy development may emerge from the first year or two of life. These ideas are indeed controversial. Furthermore, they rely heavily on a merging of ideas across disciplines, including language development, psycholinguistics, and psychology; this merging is itself in its infancy. Nevertheless, a cross-disciplinary approach offers new angles on literacy development.

Sound and reading

In the beginning is the sound. Newborns are exposed to all kinds of sounds and are sensitive to these even before birth. One ongoing debate in research on causes of reading differences, including reading disability, is the extent to which distinguishing sounds, such as a beating drum rhythm or the pitch of a doorbell, might reveal variability in children who subsequently read differently or whether the only sounds that matter for this are speech sounds (e.g. Zhang & McBride-Chang, 2010). While there is no way to settle this issue here, we can at least note that studies of sound variability sometimes do distinguish differences among readers, either concurrently or longitudinally. From birth, babies show divergence in basic auditory sensitivities (Kuhl, 2004), and it is possible that such sensitivities develop into differences in speech sound sensitivities.

Early evidence for sensitivity to nonspeech sounds being associated with subsequent literacy skills comes primarily from studies using an evoked-related potential (ERP) methodology. ERP methods are used to examine how electrical signals in the brain process stimuli, in this case auditory stimuli, even without conscious attention to them. Molfese (2000; Espy, Molfese, Molfese, & Modglin, 2004) showed that the patterns of ERP responses to nonspeech stimuli such as auditory tones in both newborns and those aged one to eight years old were strongly associated with word decoding skills at age eight. Others have shown similar patterns in pure tones, distinguishing Swiss German-speaking kindergartners with and without risk for dyslexia

(Maurer, Bucher, Brem, & Brandeis, 2003) and in Chinese-speaking primary school children with and without dyslexia (Meng et al., 2005).

At least two basic aspects of auditory processing might be important for the development of speech sensitivity and, ultimately, reading. These are rhythmic sensitivity and temporal sensitivity (e.g. Zhang & McBride-Chang, 2010). A series of studies across alphabetic languages has demonstrated that variability in acoustic rhythmic sensitivity is associated with reading variability (Goswami et al., 2002; Goswami, Gerson, & Astruc, 2010 – English; Hämäläinen, Leppänen, Torppa, Müller, & Lyytinen, 2005 – Finnish; Muneaux, Ziegler, Truc, Thomson, & Goswami, 2004 – French; Talcott et al., 2003 – Norwegian). Temporal processing, or ordering, of auditory stimuli, which may involve more attentional processes than does acoustic rhythmic sensitivity (e.g. Zhang & McBride-Chang, 2010), has also been implicated in some studies on reading variability (e.g. Chung, McBride-Chang, Cheung, & Wong, 2013; Hämäläinen, Leppänen, Guttorm, & Lyytinen, 2008; Tallal, 1980). Lyytinen et al. (2005) have suggested that the link between perception and reading may have less to do with a distinction between pure auditory and speech stimuli than with a focus on how demanding the given perceptual tasks are. Such issues remain hotly debated. In one study (Zhang & McBride-Chang, 2014), we found preliminary evidence for an association of nonspeech auditory stimuli with both segmental and suprasegmental speech processing, leading ultimately to word recognition, in Chinese children. Some research has, thus, established a link, either direct or indirect, between basic sound sensitivity and early literacy skills.

However, many more studies have more narrowly focused specifically on children's sensitivities to speech sounds. After all, learning to read and to write centrally involves sensitivity to speech sounds, which are ultimately coded into print. In this next section, then, we consider the nature of suprasegmental processing, after which segmental processing, which has been most thoroughly researched in the area of phonological sensitivity, is considered.

Suprasegmental processing

Recent work has highlighted the fact that prosodic abilities are independently associated with word reading and sometimes spelling and higher-order reading skills such as reading comprehension. Prosodic abilities are said to include 'intonation, rhythm, tempo, volume, and pauses' (Holliman et al., 2014, p. 469). Whereas phonological awareness is sometimes referred to as segmental (focused on speech sounds within a word), prosodic sensitivity refers to suprasegmental awareness (focused on speech sounds across a word or phrase) (Zhang & McBride-Chang, 2010). To measure children's sensitivity across a word, children might be asked, for example, 'Which sounds right? SOfa (with stress on the first syllable) or soFA (with stress on the second syllable)?'. They might also be asked whether the pattern of sounds in the title of the book *Cinderella* matches better with *Sleeping Beauty* or *Wizard of Oz*. Here, all three titles contain four syllables, but the pattern of stressed and unstressed syllables of *Cinderella* is more similar to that of *Sleeping Beauty*, which stresses the third syllable, than *Wizard of Oz*, which stresses the final syllable. Children who are more attuned to stress, as in these examples, or intonation or rhythm or timing, often tend to be better readers.

Why does sensitivity to overall prosody, or word patterns, independently explain word reading in young children? A special issue on this topic published in the *Scientific Studies of Reading* (e.g. Wang & Arciuli, 2015) examined the association of suprasegmental processing to word reading in Italian (Sulpizio, Burani, & Colombo, 2015), where stress is only occasionally marked in print, Spanish (Calet, Gutiérrez-Palma, Simpson, González-Trujillo, & Defior, 2015), where stress is occasionally marked, Greek (Anastasiou & Protopapas, 2015), where stress is consistently marked, and English (Wade-Woolley & Heggie, 2015), where stress is not marked in print. It is likely that sensitivity to prosody, which is multi-faceted, interacts with segmental phonological awareness to highlight certain syllables in language and even in print (e.g. Cutler, 2005; Sulpizio et al., 2015) and to predict certain aspects of morphology within multi-syllable words (e.g. Wade-Woolley & Heggie, 2015). For example, stress patterns sometimes correspond to features of a word, such as whether it is a verb, adjective, or a noun. In addition, stressed syllables tend to be easier to spell than are unstressed syllables (e.g. Treiman, Berch, & Weatherston, 1993).

In tonal languages, lexical tone is an important concept to be explored in relation to word reading and writing for some of the same reasons as is stress in languages that make use of stress. Lexical tone is the part of Chinese that Indo-European foreigners are famous for getting so wrong. Like stress, lexical tone influences the processing of the whole word. Sometimes, lexical tones also change with syllables that precede or follow others. For example, in Mandarin, when '一' (yi1, which means *one*) precedes a syllable with tone 4, its lexical tone changes from 1 to 2, thus, '一' in '一切' (yi2 qie4, which means *all* or *everything*) is pronounced with tone 2 instead of its original tone 1. These are called sandhi rules. Several studies have shown that sensitivity to lexical tone distinguishes dyslexic from nondyslexic Chinese children (Cheung el al., 2009; Liu, Shu, & Yang, 2009; Zhang et al., 2012) and also that lexical tone sensitivity is a unique correlate of word reading in Chinese (McBride-Chang, Tong et al., 2008). Without accurate tone perception, meaning is lost in print.

Because this issue of phonological sensitivity is a relatively new area, we will stop here, having highlighted that this area is a burgeoning one in the field of literacy development in children across languages. Far more research has been done for far longer on phonological awareness, perhaps because much of the research in phonological sensitivity emerged in English, a phonologically relatively arbitrary and complicated writing system. For researchers or teachers interested in understanding what underlying aspects of phonological sensitivity explain early word reading and writing, I recommend including a focus on both suprasegmental and segmental aspects. We now turn to these segmental aspects, typically referred to as phonological awareness. There are many critical questions about which aspects of phonological awareness are most important, why, and for whom. We address these questions in the following section.

Speech and the alphabetic principle

The phonological structure of language is psychologically divisible. That is, we as speakers can perceive segments in speech. Sentences can be divided into words, for example. More importantly for learning to read, words can also be subdivided into syllables, onsets and rimes, and phonemes, or single speech sounds. For example, the word *printer* can be divided into various units. These units include syllables (*prin-ter*) and onsets (*pr*) and rimes (*inter*). Because *inter* is a rhyming segment of speech (e.g. it is contained in both the words *printer* and *winter*), it is referred to as a 'rime'. *Printer* could also be divided into individual speech sounds, called phonemes. In the word *printer*, each speech sound is denoted by a single letter (/p/-/r/- etc.). Most children process speech fairly easily with development. At the same time, many speakers are largely unaware of these units of speech. Indeed, dividing words into fine-grained segments such as phonemes is largely a result of school learning. Why is it important that the phonological structure of language can be divided into different phonological units? How do different phonological units of language relate to reading development?

In the early 1970s, researchers interested in English language and literacy (Calfee et al., 1973; Liberman, 1973; Liberman et al., 1974) began to explore the idea that learning to read requires the ability to reduce whole words to their corresponding phonemes, or individual speech sounds. The alphabetic principle is a relatively consistent mapping of written letters to their respective phonemes. Thus, for example, in English *C* can represent two phonemes, /k/ and /s/. Two consonant letters written together, *SH*, also represent a single phoneme (a phoneme is defined as a single speech sound). Learning the intricacies of the alphabetic principle is not necessarily straightforward, however. As Shankweiler elegantly stated, 'speech is not an acoustic alphabet; successive segments are coproduced in such a way that they overlap' (1999, p. 114). In other words, the phonemes that we map onto letters are by no means an accurate reflection of the actual speech sounds comprising our words. In countries in which English literacy is taught, for example, it is not uncommon for some teachers to teach letter sounds with fairly standard mappings. *B* makes the *buh* sound, *A* makes the *ae* (short *a* as in *sad*) sound, and *G* makes the *guh* sound. Given these mappings, some children may mistakenly identify the printed word *bag* as *buh-ae-guh*, underscoring the fact that speech is not an acoustic alphabet. Speech units overlap. Indeed, any alphabetical representation of speech is, in some ways, flawed.

In addition, speech is variable. The ways in which you utter a given word might differ from those of your various male and female, old and young friends, or a given foreign student learning to speak your language. All speakers vary somewhat in their pronunciations. Even the way in which you yourself utter a given word varies from one pronunciation to the next.

Because of the overlap across phonemes and variability in speech, some children may have difficulty deriving phonemes from spoken words. In fact, most children (and adults) without some explicit reading-related training cannot manipulate the individual phonemes in a word, particularly those that do not comprise the onset of a word. Children who can explicitly isolate phonemes in a spoken word tend to be older and are at an advantage in learning to read. For example, English-speaking children who are skilled in phoneme manipulation tend to have an easier time learning to read English than those who are not (Adams, 1990; Brady & Shankweiler, 1991; Pressley, 1998).

For children of different ages and in different cultures, the ability to perceive and divide speech into different language units – including syllables, onsets and rimes, and phonemes, all facets of phonological awareness – may be important for reading. Indeed, there is strong consensus among researchers that phonological awareness is associated with reading (e.g. Shankweiler, 1999; Stanovich, 2000), even for beginning readers of regular orthographies such as German (Wimmer, 1996) and Italian (Cossu, 1999) and for non-alphabetic languages such as Chinese (Ho & Bryant, 1997b). Other studies show that training in phonological awareness promotes better reading of English (Cunningham, 1990), French (Casalis & Louis-Alexandre, 2000), Hebrew (Bentin & Leshem, 1993), Norwegian (Lyster, 2002), and Dutch (van Goch, McQueen, & Verhoeven, 2014), among others.

What is phonological awareness?

Phonological awareness is typically defined as *awareness of and access to the sound structure of a language*. It has been measured in a myriad of ways. For some examples of measures of phonological awareness in English and Chinese, see Table 2.1.

Presumably, all these tasks demand the child's ability to reflect on the speech sounds comprising a particular language. The focus of all phonological awareness tasks should primarily be on the sound, rather than the meaning, of language. For all examples, you must understand that the child being tested on such an item will be given the speech segment (usually a word or nonsense word) aloud. That is, children taking part in phonological awareness tasks are consistently presented with stimuli orally, either by an experimenter who says the word aloud during testing or via a recording played for the child. By definition, phonological awareness involves awareness of speech sounds, rather than of print.

In phonological awareness, as in many other aspects of reading development – and, indeed, most aspects of developmental psychology – children differ in at least two overarching ways. First, phonological awareness skills improve and become more refined as children get older (Snow et al., 1998). On average, three-year-old children show less phonological awareness than six-year-olds. Second, in any single age group of children, there is individual variability in phonological awareness. Thus, some five year olds may be relatively skilled at a given task of phonological awareness, whereas others may be relatively weak at the same task.

TABLE 2.1 Examples of measures of phonological awareness in English and Chinese (Cantonese).

Syllable level

English: Ans: *dog*

Say *hotdog*. Now say *hotdog* but don't say *hot*.
Cantonese:

請講出小朋友 *(siu2 pang4 yau5)*,
宜家講出小朋友 *(siu2 pang4 yau5)* 但係唔洗講小 *(siu2)*。 Ans: 朋友 *(pang4 yau5)*

Onset level

English: Ans: *up*

Say *cup* without the /k/ sound
Cantonese: Ans: 衣 *(i1)*

講詩 *(si1)*但係唔洗講開頭嘅音

Rime level

English: Ans: *chair*

Which word rhymes with *bear*? *Chair* or *fish*?
Cantonese: Ans: 天 *(tin1)*

邊個字同煙 *(yin1)* 字押韻? 花 *(fa1)* 字定係天 *(tin1)*字?

Phoneme level

English: Ans: **frip**

Say *frimp* without the /m/ sound
Cantonese:

No clear equivalent in Cantonese (Chinese)

Measurement of phonological awareness: general issues

The issue of precisely how to define and measure phonological awareness is non-trivial, and various researchers have addressed this question (e.g. Adams, 1990; Anthony et al., 2011; McBride-Chang, 1995; Stahl & Murray, 1994; Stanovich, 1987). There are two primary dimensions on which tasks of phonological awareness vary. These are types of responses required and levels of representation. *Types of responses* focus on the extent to which children have to come up with an answer themselves or are given a forced choice from which they must select a single given answer. Generally, forced-choice responses, which are subject to effects of guessing, are easier than response requirements that are open-ended. Gombert (1992) refers to such tasks as epilinguistic. *Levels of representation* are the units of speech involved in the task, e.g. syllable, onset–rime, or phoneme. In general, the more finegrained, or smaller, the unit of speech children are given, the more difficult the task. It is essential to bear in mind these dimensions, types of responses, and levels of representation (shown in Figure 2.1) when thinking about the development of phonological awareness across languages.

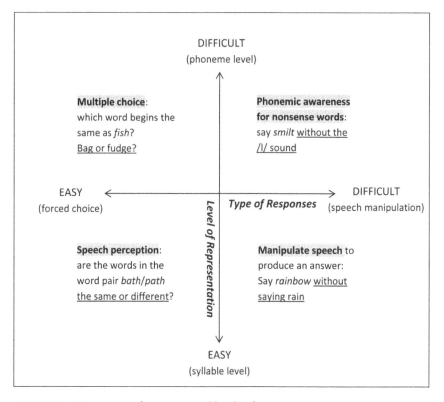

FIGURE 2.1   How types of responses and levels of representation interact to make tasks of phonological sensitivity more or less cognitively demanding in English.

Initially, the importance of phonological awareness was thought to be 'specifically metalinguistic' (Shankweiler, 1999, p. 116). I take this to mean that the major feat of a phonological awareness task was interpreted to involve not merely *perception* of speech, but *manipulation* of it. For example, given the nonsense word *telk* and asked to take away the /1/ sound from it, a phonologically aware child would be able to perform the operation and come up with *tek* as an answer. The child without phonological awareness could not do this. However, in this example, both children were assumed to have *perceived* the initial item (*telk*) correctly; they heard the stimulus as *telk*, rather than as *elk* or *teelk*, for example.

As researchers have explored the construct of phonological awareness more carefully, it has, instead, become increasingly clear that perceptual skills – those explicitly involving sensitivity to speech sounds – may be one fundamental source of variability across phonological awareness tasks. In this view, a phonologically aware child may perceive the linguistic representation of *telk* more clearly than a child who demonstrates poor phonological awareness. In this revised view,

> Phonemic organization of word representations is not a given but the result of a developmental process that undergoes reorganization under the pressure of vocabulary growth. If this view is right, then the emergence of phonological awareness is largely constrained by the development of the underlying representations.
>
> *(Shankweiler, 1999, p. 116)*

In this quote, the term 'underlying representations' refers to the ways in which we perceive words and, over time, the ways in which they are psychologically divisible (e.g. into phonemes, onsets and rimes or codas and final onsets (as in Korean), and syllables). This idea, that perception of oral language might be important for phonological awareness, introduces a whole new dimension to the concept.

At this point, it is necessary to review some tasks that have been used to test both ideas, focusing primarily on the perception of speech sounds and on phonological awareness in previous studies. With this review, you should bear in mind that *measurement* of phonological awareness is the primary issue in studies of literacy development. The *type of response* required and the linguistic *level of representation* involved for these tasks are particularly important areas of consideration in relation to development. A six-month-old, for example, can be tested on perception of speech sound contrasts (e.g. whether the words *bog* and *dog* are perceived as the same or different) but not on a task of phonemic awareness requiring an open-ended response (e.g. 'How do you say *trick* without the /r/ sound?'). For developmental comparisons beginning in infancy, we include all tasks that broadly measure phonological knowledge, beginning with a new concept, important for considering a speech perception–phonological awareness connection: that of *phonological sensitivity*.

Measurement of phonological sensitivity and phonological awareness: specific tasks

Phonological sensitivity is an all-inclusive term for tasks that make use of individuals' sensitivities to speech sounds (Stanovich, 1987). Broadly, I consider all tasks involving forced-choice types of responses to be measures of phonological sensitivity. Thus, phonological sensitivity covers even the easiest tasks involving perceptual skills. For example, Messer (1967) measured three- to seven-year-old children's abilities to select which of two nonsense words presented sounded more like a real English word. In this task, given the choices of *tlop* and *krat*, the correct answer is *krat*, because no English words begin with the *tl* consonant cluster, though both items are pronounceable. The interesting thing about this task is that it requires no conscious understanding of the phonological properties of linguistic stimuli presented. Participants are merely required to select the item that sounds better, based on their fundamental experiences with their native language. The unit of language tested in this task is the word level, and it is a forced-choice measure; thus, it is relatively easy for young children. Other simple speech perception tasks might also fall into the category of phonological sensitivity. In some such tasks, across trials, children are given two choices, such as *bath* and *path*, and must indicate, using one of two buttons, when they hear *bath* or *path*. Such tasks measure children's perceptions across a continuum of speech segments differing on a dimension (e.g. the transition of voice from the /b/ to the /p/ sound in the *bath/path* contrast). Speech perception tasks can often distinguish nondisabled from disabled readers (e.g. McBride-Chang, 1995). However, these tasks are only weakly associated with English word recognition in children without particular reading problems (McBride-Chang, 1996).

Investigators agree that speech perception and phonological awareness or supra-segmental tasks are distinct, based on their abilities to predict subsequent reading (e.g. Snow et al., 1998). Tasks of speech perception are often poor indicators of reading skills, whereas tasks of phonological awareness and of prosodic sensitivity are sometimes good indicators of reading ability. However, there is overlap among the constructs of speech perception and phonological awareness or prosodic sensitivity. Indeed, as mentioned at the beginning of this chapter, even pure auditory vs speech perceptual tasks have considerable overlap vis-à-vis reading in studies of children (e.g. Lyytinen et al., 2005). Underlying perceptual representations of orally presented stimuli may influence performances across all types of tasks.

Practically speaking, speech perception tasks are extremely simple to perform. There is little room for variability when a child's only task is to press one of two buttons to indicate one of two words presented. Even if the word is misperceived, in a forced-choice paradigm such as this, a child may do well on the task just by guessing. Indeed, in one study of reading disabled and normally reading children, the groups did not differ in their behavioural responses (button presses) to stimuli. However, these children's electrophysiological responses (measures of event-related potentials from the brain) to the stimuli clearly demonstrated diminished sensitivity to speech contrasts among the reading disabled children (Bradlow et al., 1999). These results suggest that, even when children's behavioural performances in speech perception tasks do not differ, the underlying perceptual representations of these stimuli may differ among children. Speech perception tasks are among the simplest measures of phonological sensitivity.

A somewhat more complicated phonological sensitivity paradigm that involves a forced-choice response is auditory matching. In this paradigm, children are given a target word (e.g. *hat*) or nonsense word, and asked to choose from two other options the one that sounds most similar to the target item. In this case, given the choices of *cat* and *leaf*, the correct answer would be *cat*, because it rhymes with the target stimulus. Collectively, these tasks may require analytical skills. They introduce a comparison element not required in the speech perception tasks described above. However, as in the speech perception tasks, there is also a risk that children are merely guessing the answers for forced-choice items in such matching tasks. These sorts of tasks successfully predict reading development in young children (e.g. Ho & Bryant, 1997b); they typically tap children's onset–rime awareness.

One of the most remarkable studies on the importance of sound play for promoting subsequent reading in young children was carried out in England. Bryant and colleagues (1989) looked at knowledge of nursery rhymes among 65 three year olds. Over the next two years, they measured these children's sensitivity to rhyme using a test called Odd One Out. In this test, children are asked to choose the word that does not belong, based on the phonology of the words. For example, in the set *fin-win-get*, the word *get* does not belong – it is the odd one out because it does not rhyme with either of the other words in the set. In contrast, the first two words in the set rhyme with each other. These researchers found that children's knowledge of nursery rhymes was strongly related to their sensitivity to rhyme, and to reading, three years later, even after effects of IQ and educational level of the mother were statistically controlled. This is an impressive result, because it tells us that sensitivity to speech sounds is a relatively stable ability and is linked to word recognition.

Phonological awareness tasks involving metalinguistic skills are of a greater level of difficulty than those previously mentioned. In these tests, children are required to change a given stimulus in some way. This manipulation may require that the child add a sound (e.g. *cow* + *boy* = *cowboy*), take a sound away (e.g. *flit* without the /l/ sound is *fit*), or 'count out' sounds (e.g. phonemes in the word *steal* are /s/-/t/-/i/-/l/, a total of four). Another complicated phonological awareness task might be to substitute one sound for another. For example, in the nonsense word *frit*, one could substitute the /f/ sound for a /k/ sound (to get a new nonsense word, *krit*). It should be clear from these examples that all of them require that the child not just perceive and evaluate the stimulus presented, but also change it in some way, either by isolating its components or adding, subtracting, or substituting them. However, the tasks may vary in the language unit to be manipulated. These are the tasks most commonly and collectively referred to as reflecting phonological awareness.

Development of phonological awareness across linguistic units

Levels of linguistic representation are also developmentally important across languages and orthographies. Phonological sensitivity, in the form of phoneme discrimination (Molfese, 2000) or change discrimination (e.g. Leppänen et al., 2002), at the whole-word level can be measured in infancy. Later on, children's awareness of syllables emerges, for some children as early as two years old (e.g. Lonigan, Burgess, Anthony, & Barker, 1998). Another linguistic unit is the onset–rime distinction. Finally, phonemic awareness (e.g. *plan* without the /l/ sound is *pan*) develops latest among English speakers (Treiman & Zukowski, 1991). In other languages, such as Chinese, this type of phonemic awareness may not develop at all because it is not necessary in order to read. In Korean, one of the most common phonological divisions is body and coda. If we were to practise this in English, we might divide *cat* into *ca* as one unit and *t* as the other (Kim, 2007). Thus, there is some evidence that the sequence of phonological awareness acquisition is not invariant (Christensen, 1997). Although there is evidence that both syllable awareness and onset–rime awareness may develop to some extent in the absence of explicit teaching (e.g. Morais, Bertelson, Cary, & Alegria, 1986), phonemic awareness within words is very strongly linked to explicit reading instruction itself (e.g. Huang & Hanley, 1995). Therefore, it is not surprising that in some studies, both of Chinese adults (Holm & Dodd, 1996; Read, Zhang, Nie, & Ding, 1986) and children (Huang & Hanley, 1995), phonemic awareness is low or non-existent. Those who have not been explicitly taught phonemic awareness rarely manifest this skill. Different aspects of phonological awareness have different developmental trajectories. Some units, such as syllables, are naturally occurring. That is, they are clear to all native speakers of the language at an early age, regardless of whether they have had formal instruction in recognizing or manipulating them. To put it simply, 'All languages are syllabic' (Boysson-Bardies, 1999, p. 45). Children are capable of manipulating spoken syllables relatively early. In contrast, other units, such as phonemes, are not obvious to native speakers without explicit training (Bowey & Francis, 1991). Few, if any, children can identify individual phonemes in the natural speech stream without explicit teaching. Perhaps the best way to characterize the relation between phonological awareness and emergent literacy is to say that phonological awareness is bidirectionally associated with reading development (Bryant & Goswami, 1987; Ehri & Wilce, 1985; Perfetti, Beck, Bell, & Hughes, 1987). Children who are naturally more skilled in identifying speech segments tend to be relatively skilled in learning to read. At the same time, reading instruction promotes growth in phonological awareness, particularly in phonemic awareness.

Phonological awareness across languages and scripts

Many studies have demonstrated the utility of phonological awareness for predicting reading (e.g. Byrne, Freebody, & Gates,1992; Catts, 1991; Wagner & Barker, 1994; Wagner et al., 1997) and spelling (Ball & Blachman, 1991; Bradley, 1988; McBride-Chang, 1998), and for distinguishing reading disabled from non-reading disabled children and adults (Pennington, van Ordern, Smith, Green, & Haith, 1990; Pratt & Brady, 1988). The vast majority of these studies have focused on English. Nevertheless, an explosion of recent studies on phonological awareness in other orthographies has revealed an association between phonological awareness and reading or spelling in Norwegian (Hoien, Lundberg, Stanovich, & Bjaalid, 1995), French (Alegria, Pignot, & Morais, 1982; Courcy, Beland, & Pitchford, 2000), Italian (Cossu, Shankweiler, Liberman, Katz, & Tola, 1988), Swedish (Lundberg, Olofsson, & Wall, 1980), Danish (Lundberg, Frost, & Petersen, 1988), Hebrew (Share & Levin, 1999), and Chinese (Ho & Bryant, 1997b; Lei et al., 2011), among others (for a review of some studies, see Branum-Martin, Shao, Garnaat, Bunta, & Francis, 2012; Melby-Lervåg, Lyster, & Hulme, 2012). However, the precise association between phonological awareness and reading is changeable based on at least two factors, apart from explicit teaching itself.

First, the correspondence between units of language and orthographic units differs across cultures. Orthographic units refer to representations of print, such as the Chinese character or a letter of the alphabet. For example, the associations of letters of the alphabet and their sounds is more opaque in English than in other orthographies, such as German (Wimmer et al., 2000), Turkish (Oney & Durgunoglu, 1997), or Spanish (Goyen, 1989), which are relatively regular. In English, for example,

G sometimes makes a soft sound, as in *giant*, and sometimes a hard sound, as in *golf*. Thus, it is inconsistent. In other scripts, such as Spanish, the correspondence of a letter and its sound is more consistent. In more regular scripts, the importance of phonological awareness for predicting subsequent reading may be relatively little once children reach primary school. Perhaps regular scripts encourage children to learn sound–grapheme rules quickly, facilitating their phonological awareness. In Chinese, characters map onto syllables only – not phonemes.

Second, language itself may affect phonological awareness (Branum-Martin et al., 2012). For example, Cheung et al. (2001) found that Chinese children without literacy training were poorer in terms of phonemic awareness than English-speaking children without literacy training. These authors asserted that this difference in performance was attributable to native language differences between the groups. In particular, relatively speaking, the English language contains many consonant clusters, whereas Chinese has few or none. Therefore, it is possible that English-speaking children may become better sensitized to the phoneme as a unit of speech than are Chinese-speaking children. Others have demonstrated superior phonemic awareness in both Italian (Cossu et al., 1988) and Czech (Caravolas & Bruck, 1993) children relative to English-speaking children, and attributed these results in part to the structure of these languages. Thus, the phonological characteristics of the language can, themselves, affect phonological awareness.

To summarize our review of phonological awareness across languages, phonological awareness at some level is linked to the beginnings of literacy development (Branum-Martin et al., 2012; Melby-Lervåg et al., 2012). This appears to be a universal of reading acquisition. However, the importance of phonological awareness for reading differs greatly from orthography to orthography, and depends upon script, language, and teaching practices themselves (i.e. how and when is phonological awareness taught?) across cultures.

Wagner and Torgesen (1987) argued that there were three primary phonological processing skills. They are all, collectively, considered to be (at least partly) phonological processing abilities because they all make use of the sound structure of language. However, they involve different focuses of phonological knowledge. The first is phonological sensitivity, reviewed above. The second is speeded naming, or rapid automatized naming. The third is short-term verbal memory. These latter two skills are described in more detail below.

Rapid automatized naming (RAN)

The importance of rapid automatized naming (RAN) was noted four decades ago for its clinical utility in distinguishing good from poor readers, particularly in studies of individuals with dyslexia (Denckla & Rudel, 1976). Typically, a RAN task involves naming a few stimuli presented randomly in different orders across columns. These stimuli could be blocks of colour or pictures or symbols, such as numbers, letters, or simple Chinese characters. Across RAN measures, the child's task is to name orally each stimulus as quickly as possible. Two experimental RAN tasks are shown in Figure 2.2.

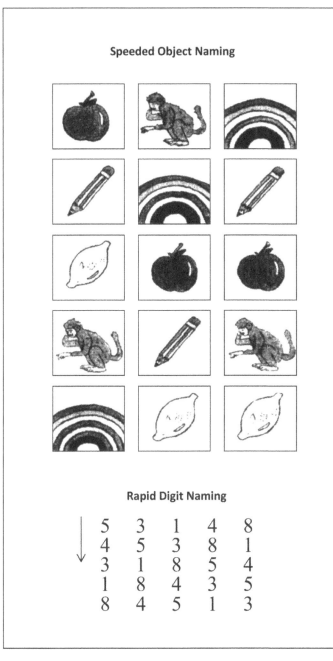

FIGURE 2.2 Examples of RAN tasks. For each task, the child is first asked to identify each of the five stimuli slowly (e.g. objects: *apple, pencil, lemon, monkey, rainbow*); then, the child is asked to name all of the presented stimuli (15 objects; 25 numbers) continuously, from top to bottom across columns, as quickly as possible while the experimenter times the child.

Most early research on the importance of rapid naming for reading was conducted on English-speaking children. For example, Wagner et al. (1997) and Manis and colleagues (1999) separately demonstrated that, in the United States, speeded naming in kindergarten was causally related to subsequent word reading in early primary school. Researchers have extended this to demonstrate the importance of speeded naming for a variety of scripts, including Dutch (de Jong and van der Leij, 1999), Greek (e.g. Georgiou, Papadopoulos, & Kaizer, 2014), Chinese (e.g. Hu & Catts, 1998; Ho & Lai, 1999; Pan et al., 2011), Arabic (Ibrahim, 2015), Hebrew (Bar-Kochva & Breznitz, 2014), and German (Wimmer et al., 2000). There is clear consensus that speeded naming tasks can be useful in distinguishing individual variability in children's early reading acquisition across scripts.

Despite its clinical utility in distinguishing readers of varying abilities, however, the precise nature of RAN has yet to be fully determined. Some argue that the importance of this task is that it involves phonological skills, a key element in the reading process. We are considering this construct here, in a chapter on phonological processing, because of this long-standing assumption. For example, Wagner and Torgesen described speeded naming tasks as comprising 'phonological recoding in lexical access' (1987, p. 192). By this, they meant that, in such tasks, children must recode a visual referent into its spoken form via lexical knowledge. That is, you recode the symbol (e.g. *A*) or picture (e.g. *lemon)* from a visual representation to a spoken one as you engage in such tasks. However, as you examine these tasks, you will recognize that they also tap additional skills. For example, children must visually attend to and identify symbols, and engage in visual sequencing of these symbols. Others note that RAN requires speed to perform proficiently, in addition to pause time and articulation time (Georgiou, Aro, Liao, & Parrila, 2014). Most would probably agree that naming speed is a combination of all of these elements. However, it is still unclear which of these elements is particularly important for learning to read or even whether these components differ by script (Georgiou, Aro et al., 2014).

The evidence that RAN taps phonological ability comes from studies of the associations of RAN with tests of phonological awareness. In most studies including both phonological awareness and RAN measures, the two types of measure are moderately to strongly correlated, suggesting that they share common phonological variance.

From a developmental perspective, there is reason to view speeded naming as fundamentally linked to speech. In my own dissertation study of phonological constructs in relation to reading in English, I found a particularly strong association between constructs of speech perception and speeded naming ($r = 0.67$ with IQ partialled) (McBride-Chang, 1996). I was initially quite puzzled by this association. However, this result is in line with the Motor Theory of Liberman and Mattingly (1985), which argues that speech perception is the sensitivity human beings have for articulatory gestures. In this theory, the purpose of which was to account for the lack of acoustic invariance within and across speakers in the speech signal, speech perception and production are inextricably linked. For example, Morais (1991) summarized several research studies in which individuals were trained in phonemic awareness by focusing on the position of the mouth for articulating phonemes.

Crudely, in my own research, speeded naming could be conceptualized as a timed production task. Speech perception was the other side of the link. The faster the articulation by the child, the better the speeded naming and, equally, the more accurate the child's perceptual skills. Of course, speeded naming does not precisely capture gestural accuracy in children. In addition, others (e.g. Munson, 2001) have not found strong associations of single tasks of speech perception and speeded naming. However, it is true that accuracy and speed tend to be linked in tasks of speeded naming. Fowler, in summarizing the development of reading related skills, noted that 'control over articulation is an important facet of developing stable, and ultimately accessible, phoneme categories' (1991, pp. 108–109).

Apart from the explanation discussed above, that RAN reflects phonological processing, investigators have attempted to explain the theoretical importance of RAN by relating it to other basic cognitive capacities. Manis et al. (1999) suggested that RAN is important for highlighting an 'arbitrariness' factor in reading. That is, such a naming task capitalizes on the fact that symbols and their oral representations are arbitrary. How children learn what to call the letter *W* or the number *5*, for example, depends entirely on their ability to learn the arbitrary print–sound connection. In tasks of reading, some associations are more arbitrary than others. For example, even for children who have internalized the alphabetic principle, many English words have a high arbitrariness factor associated with them. Examples of these include *the*, *have*, or *knew* – exception words. In Chinese, the arbitrariness factor is even greater. Manis et al. (1999) demonstrated that, in predicting exception word reading, as well as other orthographic knowledge, RAN was uniquely important over time – more important than phonological awareness measures, in fact.

Bowers and Newby-Clark (2002) also highlighted the importance of fluency development for becoming a successful reader. As children automatize the symbol knowledge they acquire, they make better use of reading skill at the levels of word, sentence, and paragraph. The arbitrariness factor is not sufficient to explain the importance of RAN for predicting reading variability in German, however, because German is a very regular orthography. Paradoxically, because it is so regular and because phonemic instruction in German is consistent, reading of German is also strongly associated with RAN performance relative to phonemic awareness. The reason for this is that in German-speaking countries, reading tests tap only reading times, rather than reading errors, because after the first couple of years of school, German poor readers rarely show reading errors. However, they remain distinguishable based on their slow decoding (Wimmer et al., 2000). In this case, lack of fluency can still impair reading acquisition.

Verbal memory

The third type of phonological processing skill typically measured in studies distinguishing readers or predicting reading is verbal short-term memory (Wagner

& Torgesen, 1987). Verbal memory can be measured in a variety of different ways, from basic memory capacity, involving recalling in order a list of random words, to sentential memory (see e.g. Waters & Caplan, 1996). Across many studies of various languages and orthographies, less skilled readers tend to exhibit poorer short-term verbal memories than skilled readers. Similarly, short-term verbal memory is correlated with reading skill in young readers (e.g. Wagner et al., 1997).

However, the problem with considering verbal memory as a predictor of reading skill is that the unique importance of this construct relative to the two reviewed above – phonological awareness and speeded naming – is small. Few studies have included this phonological processing skill along with phonological awareness and speeded naming to predict reading simultaneously. When all are included in the same study, whether it is a one-time correlational study or a longitudinal study, verbal short-term memory is not uniquely predictive of reading (Caravolas et al., 2012).

The reason that verbal short-term memory tends not to be uniquely predictive of reading under these circumstances is probably connected with the nature of phonological awareness tasks. At any level, phonological awareness tasks require a participant to remember one or more speech stimuli. What happens after that (whether a judgement of same/different is required, whether a phoneme or syllable must be synthesized with or deleted from it, etc.) differs. However, invariably, memory for the stimulus or stimuli is required. Therefore, verbal memory might better be conceptualized as a secondary, rather than a primary, phonological processing skill in relation to word recognition.

On the other hand, from the perspective of very early development, in the pre-natal period through toddlerhood and the pre-school period, verbal memory may be a primary predictor of phonological awareness itself. Verbal memory is also essential for RAN tasks, which require automatic retrieval of stimulus names. Thus, verbal memory is likely to be subsumed in the growth of phonological awareness and RAN tasks. The importance of verbal memory for early phonological development cannot be overstated. As reviewed below, phonological memory begins even before a child is born.

Earliest language learning

This section highlights some aspects of early language development that may be linked, ultimately, to subsequent reading development. In some ways, it may seem ridiculous to be considering linguistic abilities such as speech perception – which is apparently automatic to infants who can hear – in relation to skills as obviously demanding and deliberately learned as reading. However, given the primacy of phonological processing skills for reading, it is not unreasonable to consider early phonological links, or even pure sound itself, to subsequent reading. The more critical question may be this: where in development does reading acquisition begin? I begin with an overview of pre-natal and newborn capacities, and will then review evidence for continuity in early phonological and language development with subsequent literacy acquisition.

The developmental origins of first-language development can be traced to the maturing foetus before birth. One experiment had mothers-to-be read the same prose aloud in the last six weeks of pregnancy. After they were born, the infants showed a preference for hearing that passage over a new passage read to them, using a sucking paradigm in which regulation of sucking rate determines which passage is heard. This preference held whether the stories were read by their mothers or by strangers (DeCasper & Spence, 1986). In a second experiment, making use of differences in infants' heart rates to infer discrimination, the same authors demonstrated that infants showed a preference for a familiar over an unfamiliar poem even when they were still in utero. The implication of this is that babies enjoy and recognize language from the very beginning.

Infants are also skilled at language recognition. For example, even one-month-old children can distinguish simple speech contrasts that differ by a single initial phoneme (e.g. *ba-pa*) (Trehub & Rabinovitch, 1972). By about six months, infants can detect familiar speech segments embedded in passages (Jusczyk & Aslin, 1995). Infants are skilled in distinguishing speech contrasts regardless of the quality of voice of the speaker – and whether they be male or female, adult or child – by the age of three months (Marean, Werner, & Kuhl, 1992).

Perhaps one of the most amazing discoveries in modern developmental psychology is that infants, regardless of their parents' ethnic or linguistic backgrounds, are biologically predisposed to perceive many speech contrasts from any language. For example, it is clear that native Japanese speakers often confuse the /r/ and /1/ sounds of English. Similarly, if you ask Japanese adults to discriminate these sounds in an experiment, they cannot do it. Non-native speakers often have particular difficulty perceiving tones in tonal languages such as Mandarin or the retroflex/dental in Hindi (Werker & Tees, 1984). Babies, however, turn out to perceive many of these differences in both their native and other tongues. This phenomenon is quite clear in infants aged six to nine months.

At the same time, however, infants demonstrate strong and immediate learning of their native tongue. By one week of age, infants show a preference for the sounds of their native language over other languages (Moon, Cooper, & Fifer, 1993). By 12 months, children have lost much of their ability to distinguish speech contrasts in other languages. Thus, over their first year of life, human infants attend strongly to the sounds of their own language and tune out those of others (Boysson-Bardies, 1999). A primary task of infancy is to attend to and focus on a native language.

In conjunction with speech perception, infants' other major linguistic task is, ultimately, the production of language. Initially, their vocal apparatus makes speech production per se impossible. In the first two months, various types of crying are the sounds most commonly made. From two to five months, however, cooing becomes more common. Cooing consists of vowel sounds only. During this period, infants can make these speech sounds only while lying down. An infant's increasing muscle control makes babbling possible around the age of six or seven months. Babbling consists of various vowel–consonant combinations. All infants, including those who are deaf, babble. Thus, babbling appears to occur naturally with maturation. Initially, babbling includes speech sounds that are not part of the native language. However, as babies become aware of the sounds of their native language, babbling changes. For example, although the babbling of babies in different countries (and therefore exposed to different languages) is indistinguishable at five months, by eight to ten months the babbling of infants of Cantonese-, Arab-, and French-speaking parents can be distinguished (Boysson-Bardies, de Sagart, & Durand, 1984). In addition, babbling in deaf infants occurs several months later than babbling in hearing infants, suggesting that infants' babbling is influenced by their perceptual abilities. Babbling sounds may, thus, be a starting point for the production of syllables, which comprise one's native (oral) language. The syllable has been described as 'the basic rhythmic unit of natural language' (Boysson-Bardies, 1999, p. 45).

We cannot definitively establish that babbling is a necessary prerequisite for language development. However, the parallel between speech perception and babbling, both initially inclusive of speech sounds from a variety of languages and gradually focusing only on the native language, is striking. From very early on, not only are infants concentrating their listening skills on language, but they are also honing their speech production skills. These speech capacities may have a fundamental importance for language development (see e.g. Werker & Tees, 1999) and, ultimately, for reading itself.

We will now consider how children's language development may affect subsequent reading development.

From whole to parts: reading development from birth

Although, within the first months of life, infants can clearly distinguish speech segments differing by only a single phoneme, their abilities to distinguish these speech segments are implicit and do not reflect particular attention to the phoneme level. That is, infants do not appear to be focusing on phonemes per se. Rather, they are distinguishing syllables in which these phonemes are embedded. In some ways, infants' capabilities to distinguish phoneme contrasts within a syllable reflect basic auditory sensation. They can perceive an acoustic difference across syllables differing by a single phoneme. However, infants only begin to assign meaning to these different speech units later in development, perhaps around the ages of six months to a year, with vocabulary acquisition. In the pre-school years, vocabulary grows rapidly.

According to the lexical restructuring model (Fowler, 1991; Metsala & Walley, 1998), growth in vocabulary is a fundamental determinant of phonological representation. As children learn more words, they must become more adept at distinguishing between them based on finer and finer phonological discriminations. In support of this, Metsala (1997; 1999; Metsala & Walley, 2013) has demonstrated that children are more skilled at distinguishing among words with more dense, as compared to sparse, phonological neighbourhoods. Words with dense phonological neighbourhoods are those such as *bat* or *pin*, where there are several other words with similar-sounding overall word structures. For example, *pin* includes the words *sin*, *spin*, *pen*, and *tin* in its neighbourhood. In some sense, to distinguish these words from one another, children may have to attend closely to individual phonological features of each of these members of the neighbourhood. In a word like *choice*, in contrast, there are few phonological neighbours (only *voice* and *chase*). Thus, children may process this in a more holistic fashion. Munson (2001) demonstrated a similar phenomenon in children aged three to seven. Both receptive and expressive vocabulary predicted children's oral word-recognition scores. In an overview of ongoing research, Goswami (2002) also noted that children make better rhyme judgements for words in dense as compared to sparse neighbourhoods. Theoretically, what begins as a very holistic approach to vocabulary production tends to become increasingly segmented and specific with development. This theory can explain both age-related differences in phonological awareness and individual variability in phonological awareness. Metsala (1997) argued that children with specific reading problems may have more holistic phonological representations than those without such problems. Elbro's (1996) phonological distinctiveness hypothesis similarly argues that poor readers lack the fully specified phonemic representations typical of good readers.

The literature on children's early language development demonstrates some parallels to these findings. In particular, it appears that children are not initially consistent in how they produce new words. Werker and Tees (1999), reviewing some studies of children's early word production, noted that they sometimes use incomplete information to produce words. For example, young children may label a dog as *gog* in one situation, suggesting that they cannot accurately pronounce the /d/ sound, but call a *truck* a *duck* in another situation, demonstrating that they can, in fact, produce a /d/ sound. The authors concluded that such 'variability suggests that when first learning words, infants may not "represent" all the detail found in adult speech. Indeed, it has been suggested that they may only represent sufficient information to contrast the words in their own lexicon' (1999, p. 525). This early developmental phenomenon of 'decline in phonetic detail seen in the initial stages of mapping words to meaning' (1999, p. 531) has been demonstrated in research studies. For example, Edwards and colleagues (2002) showed that pre-school children's discrimination of words was associated both with receptive vocabulary knowledge and articulatory accuracy. Vocabulary size is also associated with language sensitivity in younger children (Graf Estes, Edwards, & Saffran, 2011). The better children's production and perception of words, the better their vocabulary knowledge. Early language sensitivity might, therefore, predict, in respective temporal order, subsequent vocabulary growth, phonological awareness, and word recognition. Among Finnish children, for example, early language ability at age one was positively predictive of phonological awareness at age four (Silven, Niemi, & Voeten, 2002).

Infant researchers have gone further with the argument that speech representation predicts subsequent reading by demonstrating that newborns' brain responses to speech stimuli are distinguishable based on their risk of suffering from reading problems (Leppänen et al., 2002; Molfese, 2000). Leppänen et al. (2002) demonstrated that those six month olds with a family history of dyslexia differed from those with no history of oral language problems in their event-related brain responses to consonants. Based on newborn event-related potential measures in response to speech stimuli, Molfese (2000) could, with substantial accuracy, distinguish those children who would suffer reading-related difficulties eight years later from those who would not. These early tasks made use of infants' memories for stimuli because they require that infants implicitly compare old and new stimuli. The role of memory in such tasks is fundamental.

These findings collectively suggest some association between early speech sensitivity and subsequent reading, perhaps even basic auditory sensitivity, speech sensitivity, and subsequent reading. However, the developmental mechanisms through which these relations emerge are far from clear. As mentioned earlier, the first year of life represents a gradual honing of native-language speech skills, so that infants are, at birth, better able to detect certain speech–sound discriminations than they are months later. It is possible, and perhaps likely, that there is individual variability in newborns' capacities to discriminate speech stimuli and that these differences also affect the acquisition of native language phonological representations (Graf Estes et al., 2011). The way in which this occurs, however, is something of a mystery.

The mystery lies, primarily, in the paradox of early speech perception and later phonological development. On the one hand, infants are good at distinguishing speech; on the other, there is strong evidence that phonological development is largely a result of vocabulary knowledge (e.g. Goswami, 2002; Metsala & Walley, 1998). Speech perception and phonological awareness tasks are often correlated (e.g. Foy & Mann, 2001; McBride-Chang, 1996). However, they are clearly different. Whereas phonological awareness tasks are very good predictors of reading ability (Snow et al., 1998), speech perception tasks are not. How can this be?

The answer lies perhaps in the differences in functions of speech for infants and older children (e.g. Zhang & McBride-Chang, 2010). In infants, phonemes can be discriminated, but the discrimination is not linked to meaning. Perhaps distinguishing phonemes and more general auditory cues are, therefore, much the same. That is, for very young infants, distinguishing a speech sound such as /k/ or /m/ may be similar to perceiving any other sound, such as running water or fingers clicking. The speech sounds have not yet taken on special linguistic meaning. For older children, speech-sound knowledge is more strongly related to their knowledge of their native language. For example, a /b/ sound for an older child may be recognized as a part of a familiar word that they have encountered previously many times before, e.g. *bat*. Alternatively, they may perceive phonemes in words such as *bap* (which aren't necessarily familiar to them), or nonsense words such as *bab*. Here again, though, children have formed an understanding that changes in phonemes signal changes in both language sound *and meaning*. Within a developmental framework, then, very simple speech discrimination tasks call upon minimal auditory sensitivity skills. However, infants may differ even in this sensitivity (Kuhl, 2004). Moreover, subsequent vocabulary growth and phonological awareness may, in part, build upon this early sensitivity. With experience, speech sounds acquire meaning and become more integrally related to subsequent reading ability. We turn now to developmental studies of how early language skills, apart from speech perception, predict subsequent reading.

Early language skills as predictors of subsequent reading

Up to this point, the primary emphasis has been on how phonological processing skills predict reading. The basic idea behind this research is that speech-sound sensitivity affects children's abilities to perceive, manipulate, and articulate speech sounds accurately. Early speech sensitivity may then affect vocabulary growth and later influence phonological awareness. On the other hand, there is limited longitudinal evidence for this developmental progression. Few researchers, with the notable exception of Molfese (2000), have traced infants' speech perception through pre-school language skills and phonological awareness to reading. However, there is stronger evidence for pre-school language measures as predictors of subsequent reading skill. We turn to this evidence now.

Studies which suggest that the range of skills predictive of reading may extend beyond the phonological realm to include other basic language abilities are focused primarily on children who are 'at risk' for reading problems or who may have early language difficulties. For example, Scarborough (1990) followed groups of American children, aged from 24 to 48 months, at six-month intervals and then tested them again at 60 months of age. The children in her study were all from middle-class backgrounds. One group of children was included as an 'at risk' group. These children had at least one parent who had a reading disability (i.e. poor reading relative to normal IQ). The other children were from families where there was no history of reading problems. Of the children in the 'at risk' group, 22 of the original 34 children had reading problems in grade 2. In this study, those who became disabled readers had both poor phonological processing and relatively weak syntactic skills at 30–48 months of age. Escarce (1998) followed very young children from a somewhat different population and found similar results.

Snowling and colleagues (2003) additionally found evidence that language tasks, including expressive language and vocabulary skills at age three, uniquely predicted subsequent reading-related skills. Nash, Hulme, Gooch, and Snowling (2013) also showed that children with a family risk for dyslexia who subsequently manifested reading problems themselves tended to have early language difficulties. They tended to have some difficulties with non-word repetition, articulation tasks, and grammatical inflections (at the earlier ages).

Weak language skills have been specifically implicated in early reading problems in other studies too (Bishop & Adams, 1990; Butler, Marsh, Sheppard, & Sheppard,

1985). For example, those diagnosed with specific language impairments tend to have reading difficulties as they enter school (Aram & Hall, 1989; Magnusson & Naucler, 1990). In a study of 75 Norwegian children tested at ages four, six, eight, and nine, selected measures of syntax and semantic knowledge distinguished poor from average and good readers, particularly at age nine (Hagtvet, 1998). These studies suggest that the source of reading variation in early development may not be phonological processing only. Rather, overall subtle language problems or general symbol learning may explain, at least in part, reading differences in development (e.g. Fowler & Scarborough, 1999). In general, those young children who manifest both a broader language deficit and a more specific difficulty in phonological skills tend to show the greatest risk for reading difficulties over time (Nash et al., 2013). Studies of Chinese children (e.g. Lei et al., 2011; McBride-Chang, Lam et al., 2008; 2011; Zhou et al., 2014) show a similar phenomenon. In particular, morphological awareness, vocabulary knowledge, and rapid automatized naming can be good early clinical indicators of subsequent risk for dyslexia in Chinese children, for example.

Conclusion

This chapter has outlined some important aspects of phonological processing that are predictive of reading. Across orthographies, there is evidence that reading acquisition demands access to phonological skills, though at different levels and perhaps for different reasons. Basic auditory skills themselves may also matter for later reading. Suprasegmental processing, including stress and lexical tone, focuses on aspects of prosody and speech and has emerged as a unique correlate of word reading in a variety of orthographies. Segmental processing, focused on awareness of individual speech sounds, has been explored as a core ability for learning to read across scripts for many years. In English and other alphabetic languages, children must learn to use an alphabetic code to synthesize phonemes in order to read. Other units in English and other alphabetic orthographies, including the rime and the syllable, can also be helpful in reading development. In Chinese, phonemes are not necessary to learn to read; however, reading acquisition demands that Chinese characters be mapped onto syllables. Different levels of phonological units, or grain sizes (Ziegler & Goswami, 2005), are linked in different ways to reading. Rapid automatized naming (RAN) is also an important skill in learning to read. In regular orthographies such as German, among older children, speed of reading is particularly important because the rules for mastering the alphabetic code are so consistent that they are acquired relatively early. In irregular orthographies such as Chinese, the characters to be read are quite inconsistent in pronunciation. General skill in mastering symbol–sound arbitrary correspondences may, thus, be most helpful in learning to read. RAN tasks are useful for tapping such a skill. Verbal memory, which is important to all phonological processing, typically does not emerge as a proximal skill, or unique correlate of reading and writing of words in children, but it is a distal skill for all, an essential component of all abilities necessary for learning to read.

The development of phonological processing skills probably begins very early in development with perception of basic sounds and speech and, later, with babbling. In the lexical restructuring hypothesis, children's vocabulary growth affects subsequent phonological awareness and, ultimately, reading. Other general language skills may also predict subsequent reading. Understanding of how and whether early speech and language skills predict subsequent reading ability is limited but growing.

Suggested readings

Fellows, J., & Oakley, G. (2010). *Language, literacy and early childhood education.* South Melbourne, Victoria: Oxford University Press.

Gillon, G. T. (2012). *Phonological awareness: From research to practice.* New York, NY: The Guilford Press.

Hougen, M. C., & Smartt, S. M. (2012). *Fundamentals of literacy instruction and assessment, pre-K-6.* Baltimore, MD: Paul H. Brookes Publishing Co., Inc.

Wendling, B. J., & Mather, N. (2009). *Essentials of evidence-based academic interventions.* Hoboken, NJ: John Wiley & Sons.

3

BUILDING BLOCKS OF READING

The process of learning to read builds on a child's developing oral language skills. This chapter reviews research on how specific literacy experiences may map onto subsequent language- and literacy-related abilities. Here, we consider three distinct aspects of literacy fundamentals. First, research on the home environment in relation to reading development and then to writing development is reviewed; the concept of emergent literacy and its implications is also discussed. Second, we will examine what is known about specific aspects of orthographies that help mark sound and meaning in literacy development. For example, knowledge of the letters of the alphabet contributes to early word recognition in many Indo-European languages in distinct ways. We will then compare how phonetic and semantic radicals – which together form the majority of Chinese characters – contribute to the child's recognition of Chinese characters. In fact, the concept of what a word is and what it is not is important for this issue of early word reading and word writing. The way in which Korean Hangul is taught and used will serve as one contrast. Finally, the role of the automatization of learning for reading growth is reviewed.

Home environment and emergent literacy

First experiences with print for many children occur in the home. Children who have families that make literacy development a focal point of home activities via shared reading are at an advantage later on in school for literacy development (Adams, 1990; Snow et al., 1998). At the same time, a variety of factors, including cultural beliefs, socio-economic status, parenting style, and parental beliefs, may affect children's language and literacy development (e.g. McBride-Chang, 2012; Reese, 2012). Moreover, establishing directional causality among these factors is difficult.

It is also difficult to disentangle the effects of children's genetic make-up from the effects of these children, by temperament or learning abilities, on their biological parents. Although parents' motivations, enthusiasm, and willingness to read are behavioural influences on their children, their effects may be minimal relative to a child's own wants and needs. Parents who read a lot to their children may primarily be responding to the fact that their children are interested in reading. Such an influence is, at least in part, genetically determined. Similarly, parents who read little to their children may be responding to their children's lack of interest or to the fact that, genetically, both parents and children find reading-related activities boring or difficult. Children's genetic attributes strongly influence how their parents interact with them (Scarr & Ricciuti, 1991) as well as many other aspects of the literacy acquisition process (e.g. Harlaar, Trzaskowski, Dale, & Plomin, 2014; Olson, Keenan, Byrne, & Samuelsson, 2014). Given the confounds of parents' behaviours with the family genetic make-up, experiments on parent–child shared reading are perhaps the clearest evidence thus far that home environment can affect reading-related skills.

Experimental intervention studies consistently indicate a positive effect of shared parent–child reading. The concept of book sharing echoes one of the fundamental principles outlined by Vygotsky (1978) of the zone of proximal development. The idea is that children are often capable of better learning at a higher level of engagement when they are learning with capable others compared to when they are learning alone; parents can support their children in the learning experience. Ideally, parents effectively connect children's experiences and interests to the book they read together. In various book-sharing studies, children's language skills were enhanced through shared-reading interventions (e.g. for a review see Mol, Bus, de Jong, & Smeets, 2008; Sénéchal, LeFevre, Thomas, & Daley, 1998; Whitehurst et al., 1994).

Part of this enhanced skill comes from specific techniques parents are taught in intervention studies to boost children's language production and comprehension. One of the best known of these techniques is called dialogical reading (Zevenbergen & Whitehurst, 2003). Using this technique, children are encouraged to engage actively with the text they are reading. They are gradually introduced into the story-telling process as caregivers draw upon the children's varied experiences to make the story meaningful, often with discussions of various aspects of the story.

As described by Bus, in using this technique, 'children's active participation and learning strongly depend on the parental ability to bridge the discrepancy between the child's world and the world of the book through careful choice of pictorial images and language' (2001, p. 183). As parents stimulate children's extended comments about the text, children's vocabularies expand (e.g. Hargrave & Senechal, 2000), and their interest in book sharing sometimes increases (Ortiz, Stowe, & Arnold, 2001). These positive effects of early shared reading may have long-term consequences for reading development (e.g. Wells, 1985).

On the other hand, this is not always the case (e.g. Reese, 2012). For example, Whitehurst and colleagues (1999) found that the initial positive effects of dialogical reading for Head Start pre-schoolers faded over time. Bus (2001) found that individual parental responsiveness, conceptualized as a secure attachment of children to their parents, may mediate the process of storybook reading. For example, parents who are able to engage children in stories by asking questions about them and supporting their answers may be more successful in maintaining their interest in and comfort with shared reading than are parents who are less sensitive to children's individual interests. Thus, it is possible that training in the dialogical reading technique has different influences on caregivers with different parenting styles. Other factors, such as cultural background, parents' enjoyment of reading or their own literacy levels, children's ages, and availability of time and books, may also mediate the short- and long-term effects of shared reading (e.g. Mol et al., 2008; Reese, 2012).

Aside from oral language development, through their experiences in sharing reading materials children may come to have some knowledge about print as well. During typical shared book reading, children actually look very seldom at the print on the page itself (Evans & Saint-Aubin, 2005; Justice, Pullen, & Pence, 2008). However, when parents make a point of integrating discussions about print into their reading with their children, children do pay attention; the trick is to make this explicit (Justice, Pullen, & Pence, 2008). Sometimes, reading with parents is associated with better broad print skills across cultures (e.g. Chow & McBride-Chang, 2003; Crain-Thoreson & Dale, 1992).

Knowledge of print initially emerges at a global level. For example, children begin to distinguish print from pictures around the ages of two to four, depending upon their experiences. In perhaps the most famous test of print concepts – the Concepts About Print observation task – Clay (1998) measured a variety of skills related to print knowledge. These included the direction of the script, book orientation, and the purpose of the print (as opposed to the pictures) on the book cover and in the text itself. It is likely that across cultures increased storybook sharing enhances children's broadest concepts about print.

However, print concepts vary, depending upon contextual factors. For example, Clay's test had to be adapted differently for children learning to read Spanish and Hebrew, for a variety of reasons, including how the scripts appear and their orientations on the page. Thus, children learning to read in two languages may need to alter their print concepts accordingly depending upon the language in question. My own two children could clearly distinguish printed English from printed Chinese very early, for example, because they were regularly exposed to stories and print in both languages.

Apart from the effects of culture and home environment, concepts of print are also strongly affected by schooling. For example, in one cross-sectional research study (Schmidt, 1982, cited in Clay, 1998) of children aged five to eight, Danish and American children scored similarly on the Concepts About Print test. However, American children scored significantly higher on this test at ages six to seven because American children begin formal literacy instruction around age six, while Danish children begin formal reading instruction about a year later.

Why are these initial steps into print important? From a developmental perspective, concepts of print are among the earliest indicators of children's conscious interest in and understanding of reading and writing. Researchers find a modest but stable association between global concepts of print and subsequent reading (e.g. Snow et al., 1998). Some experimental studies have also demonstrated improvement in children's concepts of print (e.g. Bus et al., 1995; Whitehurst et al., 1994), in addition to improvement in oral language skills, following shared storybook-reading interventions. Such studies are supportive of the concept of emergent literacy.

The term *emergent literacy* is itself politically charged, because it implies that there is a natural developmental progression from language to print (Stanovich, 2000). In fact, reading is not natural – in the sense that children almost never learn to read or to write in the absence of explicit teaching and long, focused practice (e.g. Geary, 1995). On the other hand, early reading and writing development do seem to make use of children's basic cognitive skills, particularly those related to speech and language. Therefore, although reading is fundamentally 'unnatural', I continue to use the term *emergent literacy* on occasion to reflect the belief that developing cognitive abilities are related to literacy acquisition.

As reviewed earlier, researchers have demonstrated that both language and literacy skills can be influenced by experimental interventions. However, it is equally clear that the development of language- and literacy-related skills are differently affected by caregivers. Specifically, general language skills develop naturally via parental interaction. As long as the child is talking and turn-taking with a caregiver, she may be expanding her language knowledge base. In reference to home literacy interventions, books serve as a focal point for discussion. However, language interactions in other contexts might, presumably, be just as effective in stimulating language growth (e.g. Reese, 2012). On the other hand, print skills must be explicitly taught. In this case, books are important tools for developing knowledge of print. Children who learn print skills through storybook sharing are learning them because their caregivers are explicitly teaching these.

An interesting example of these separate effects comes from a study by Aram and Levin (2002). In this study, different Israeli mothers both read to and encouraged writing skills in their pre-school children. Results demonstrated that the mothers' explicit writing mediation was directly linked to the children's early writing and reading skills. In contrast, storybook reading was associated only with children's language skills. Aram and Levin (2004) further demonstrated that mothers' maternal mediation skills with their kindergartners in Hebrew-speaking families with relatively low incomes was longitudinally associated with literacy skills in these children 2.5 years later.

Apart from a clear storybook-reading orientation, their paradigm (Aram & Levin, 2002; 2004) for examining mothers' writing mediation was very clever. Researchers gave mothers pictures of words that their kindergartners should have known or been able to identify orally and named each picture for good measure. Mothers were then asked to help their children to write each word 'as they saw fit'. Mothers had many different techniques for getting the children to write. Some wrote out the words and asked their children to copy them exactly. Some actually wrote the words using dotted lines and asked children to connect the dotted lines. Some even held the child's hand in her hand and directed all hand movements!

What Aram and Levin and colleagues found in terms of mothers' behaviours that tended to be positively associated with independent word reading and writing for children was a focus both on giving children autonomy to write themselves and a focus on the critical elements of word writing, which in most orthographies has to do with letter–sound correspondences. For example, a parent who would say something like 'Now we have to write the word "bike". What sound starts the word "bike"? /B/, /b/ – what letter do you hear?' would be facilitating children's thinking about how to write *bike* in English. It is slower to ask children to go through each step in the learning process, from thinking about sounds to how to write each to putting them altogether in a word. However, this technique was associated with children's maximal literacy skills. Similar results have been obtained in Spanish (Levin, Aram, Tolchinsky, & McBride, 2013), Arabic (Aram et al., 2013), and Chinese (e.g. Lin, McBride-Chang, et al., 2012). For Chinese, however, the technique was modified quite a bit. Mothers tended to focus their scaffolding of their children much less on phonological representations in print and much more on representations at the semantic radical or character (i.e. morpheme) levels, showing a preference for a meaning- over a sound-based focus. Other studies conducted in English (Bindman, Skibbe, Hindman, Aram, & Morrison, 2014) and Chinese Pinyin (Pinyin is a phonological coding system used to transcribe Chinese – it is not reading of Chinese but it looks like a simple alphabetic orthography and is transparent, represented using the Roman alphabet) (McBride-Chang, Lin, et al., 2012) have obtained similar results. What is particularly special about this line of research is that, like some of the shared book-reading research (e.g. Justice et al., 2008; Reese, 2012), it highlights the important role of parents in promoting early literacy skills.

Promoting maximal interest in literacy at home

Given the importance of early literacy skills for subsequent school performance, teaching children the joys of print is widely advocated (e.g. Clay, 1998; Snow et al., 1998; Whitehurst & Lonigan, 1998). In particular, children who are constantly being made aware of print as a part of daily life are at an advantage when they enter school. When children see that mum reads the newspaper, dad reads an interesting book, a shopping list must be made before going to the grocery store, and sending and receiving (e)mail are part of daily life, they want to get involved in literacy acts as well. Goodman and Goodman (1979) highlight three important elements in creating a reading-ready child:

1. fostering an environment of literacy
2. incorporating literacy into play
3. reading for a purpose.

Although they discussed these ideas primarily in relation to classroom practice, the concepts are also sensible in relation to the home environment. Thus, when a home is filled with reading activities, there may be a natural acceptance on the part of the child of literacy as a way of life. Reading need not be a foreign concept learned formally only at school. Reading is a part of real life. This attitude is in stark contrast to the attitude of children for whom literacy is mainly introduced at school. For them, it takes much longer to realize the importance of learning to read. Specific literacy activities within the home might include note writing, list making, and internet surfing.

In Israel, Feitelson and Goldstein (1986) found that 60 per cent of the pre-school children in neighbourhoods where children tended to do poorly in school as they progressed through the grades did not have a single book in their homes. Pre-school children in neighbourhoods where children tended to do well in school had families who, on the average, owned 54 books each. Although these statistics say nothing about causality, they clearly illustrate some association between the value parents place on literacy and the performance of their children in school. In a study of 43 cultures using PISA (Program for International Assessment) data, Chiu and McBride-Chang (2006) showed that among 15 year olds, with a long list of country, school, and family related variables statistically controlled, number of books in the home was uniquely associated with individual adolescents' reading comprehension scores. While correlation is not causation, this finding nevertheless suggests that home environment continues to be important for children's literacy attainment with development.

Many families also plan a special place in the home to be devoted to reading. For example, approximately 60 per cent of parents surveyed in Beijing, Hong Kong, and Singapore had created 'reading corners' at home (Li & Rao, 2000). Presumably, having a specific place to read promotes a positive environment for literacy acquisition.

Finally, in Goodman and Goodman's conceptualization, reading is a means to an end. We read for pleasure, for information, and for accomplishing work goals efficiently. Ideally, children should understand why reading is useful, at least implicitly. Parents demonstrate the utility of reading whenever they make use of a shopping list, read a menu at a restaurant, or read food labels at the supermarket. Parents who prepare their children for learning in school by fostering familiarity with reading and reading experiences tend to have children who excel in their early literacy experiences (Adams, 1990).

In many places, the print that children experience in their daily lives and the print they learn at school may differ, perhaps influencing literacy development or motivation (e.g. Kenner & Gregory, 2003). In early childhood, for example, the home language and, by extension, print are products of the home environment. Thus, a Mexican-American pre-schooler living in downtown Los Angeles, where so many signs are printed in Spanish, might see little reason to learn about English print, the orthography most emphasized at school. A Singaporean child growing up in a Mandarin household might feel the same way about English learning. A Moroccan or United Arab Emirates child learning to read in formal Arabic may not see the point of this in their everyday life. Yet much of the time, children show a relatively strong desire to participate in reading and writing activities across languages, using different scripts for different purposes from early on (Kenner &

Gregory, 2003). Some expectations about print may come directly from the family environment. For example, in Morocco or the United Arab Emirates children learning to read formal Arabic will come to understand that this script is integrally linked with their religious beliefs. In this perspective, it is essential to learn this script because this represents the real word of God. This focus and these religious values come primarily from the family.

Thus, while it is clear that general home environment is important for early literacy development, the precise effects of home environment on learning to read and to write must always be considered within a larger cultural, contextual framework. The next section focuses more specifically on print itself. What clues does print offer for readers to facilitate direct and indirect access to language sounds and meaning?

Fundamental building blocks of print

Across orthographies, connected text is comprised of smaller units. In English and other alphabetic languages, text is made up of words, which are comprised of letters or other graphemes. The letters often have names that are unique from, though associated with, the sounds that they represent in text. For example, *B* makes the /b/ sound. Although there is some commonality between letter names and their sounds in English and other languages (e.g. French, Spanish, German, Hebrew, Russian, Korean), the relations among them are not systematic. Consonant letters vary in the association of the letter name to its sound (e.g. in English, both *C* and *G* make two different sounds; *W* has no name–sound connection). Vowels are also quite variable in their name and sound relations. In Maori, in contrast, letter names are the letter sounds themselves (Clay, 1998).

In Chinese and Japanese, text is represented very differently. In Chinese, text is formed from characters, which are created from phonetic and semantic radicals, clusters of strokes that act as constituent units. Thus, while the smallest unit of writing in the English alphabet is an individual letter, the smallest unit of meaningful Chinese writing is the radical. Writing in Japanese text is comprised of kanji, which are Chinese characters, and kana syllabaries (*hiragana* and *katakana*). These building blocks of print may influence children's reading development in different ways. The importance of the alphabet for learning to read is reviewed first below, followed by the utility of semantic radicals and phonetics and even holistic characters for Chinese reading. I also review a bit about Korean Hangul, a script that is unique in structure and appears to be particularly efficient. Following this, I highlight the fact that reading at the word level is not necessarily obvious or easy for everyone.

The ABCs of the ABCs

All of us who are taught to read English or another alphabetic orthography have some experience of learning the letters of the alphabet as an important feature of our emergent literacy. To English speakers, the 'ABC' song is particularly salient.

Knowing the letters of the alphabet is clearly helpful in learning to read English (Evans, Bell, Shaw, Moretti, & Page, 2006; Snow et al., 1998) and other alphabetic languages as well (e.g. Hebrew: Levin, Shatil-Carmon, & Asif-Rave, 2006). What are some ways in which letter knowledge facilitates reading development?

Treiman and colleagues have elegantly demonstrated that the names of the letters themselves can facilitate learning to read to a greater or lesser extent (Treiman & Broderick, 1998; Treiman & Rodriguez, 1999; Treiman, Sotak, & Bowman, 2001). This is clearest in the case of consonants, which Treiman has distinguished into three categories: consonant–vowel, vowel–consonant, and no association letters. Consonant–vowel letters are those that, in a given culture, are named such that the sound they make is the initial sound of the name of the letter. Thus, for example, *V* makes the /v/ sound and *J* makes the /j/ sound. The correspondence between the letter name and its sound is consistent in American English for these two examples. These can be contrasted with vowel–consonant letters, of which *F*, *L*, and *R* are good examples in English. In this case, the sound made by the letter falls consistently at the end of the letter name. There are other letters for which there is no obvious correspondence between the letter name and letter sound. Perhaps the best example of this is *W*. In several studies of these letter-name categories, there has emerged a clear trend among young children to learn the letter sounds made by consonant–vowel letters most quickly and no association letters least quickly. Vowel–consonant letters tend to be of medium difficulty for children to learn (McBride-Chang, 1999; Treiman, Tincoff, Rodriguez, Mouzaki, & Francis, 1998).

These results are consistent with previous research on phonological awareness concerning how English-speaking children focus on words as onset–rime units. English-speaking children tend to notice the beginnings of words first, the ends of words next, and the middles of words last. Much of this focus on words is not conscious; rather it is partly an implicit tendency among children that seems to facilitate understanding in alphabet learning. As testament to this phenomenon, children frequently assume that *W* makes the /d/ sound and that the letter *Y* makes the /w/ sound because of the name–sound correspondence rules they have internalized.

There may, of course, be variations across English-speaking regions in this pattern. Some may affect letter name–letter sound learning, and some may not. For example, *H* is pronounced with no initial /h/ sound in American English. However, in Ireland, it is pronounced *hAch*. This difference in pronunciation suggests that American speakers learn the connection between *H* and its letter sound /h/ more slowly than Irish speakers. However, the fact that Americans say *zee* for *Z* and British people say *zed* is not important for this connection, because the initial sound of the letter *Z* is retained in both cases.

Another issue in alphabet learning concerns the actual ordering of letters in the alphabet (McBride-Chang, 1999; Worden & Boettcher, 1990). Those that appear first (A, B, C) are learned earlier than those that appear last (W, X, Y, Z). In English-speaking places, this phenomenon can be partially attributed to the 'ABC' song. Parents and teachers tend to begin at the beginning, so the salience of A, B, and C is greater than that of other letters. Justice and colleagues (2006) further explored letter name knowledge in pre-schoolers. They confirmed some effects of type of letter and ordering of letter in the alphabet. Not surprisingly, they also found that children tended to know letters that were in their own name, particularly an initial of their name, much better than those that were not. Finally, they showed that letters representing sounds that tend to be learned early phonologically in English (e.g. M, N, B) are sometimes mastered earlier than those that are learned later in language development (e.g. L, R, and S). That is, certain speech sounds in English are mastered earlier than others. Some young children might have difficulties in pronouncing /f/ or /s/, for example, at older ages, but the earliest and easiest ones such as /m/ and /n/ also happen to correspond to letters that are often more efficiently learned.

Taken together, research suggests that letters that are less used and less salient either developmentally or by some other quality such as letter–sound correspondence (e.g. W) should receive more attention in school than those that are relatively well known (e.g. B); letters in the middle of the alphabet should perhaps receive more attention that those that come at the beginning or end of the alphabet. (Note that I am assuming that teachers will teach both the letter names and letter sounds to their pupils. However, in many schools, this is not the case. For example, American schools are more likely to focus on letter names and British schools tend to focus more on letter sounds in initial literacy instruction (Ellefson, Treiman, & Kessler, 2009).)

What might a developmental model of early alphabet learning entail? It is likely that repetition of common components of script initially occurs in many alphabets and languages. Cultural variation in this phenomenon is overwhelming, however. For example, the 'ABC' song commonly sung in the UK or the United States does not occur in Chile or Israel. Nevertheless, repetition of the alphabet or some components of it is not unusual across cultures. From a cognitive developmental perspective, repetition in some form is useful, because young children of the age at which literacy skills are normally taught (roughly ages three to seven worldwide) are relatively concrete in their thinking. They do not generally work well with abstract concepts. Unfortunately, letters and their sounds are relatively abstract concepts. They are symbols. Unlike words, which are linguistic symbols and therefore at least potentially interesting, letters do not stand for anything meaningful. Yet Byrne (1998) has demonstrated that children's initial approach to print is based on meaning alone. Children expect script to represent whole words. The idea that letters have no meaning in and of themselves may be initially confusing to young children.

The English 'ABC' song helps to give these letters more reality to English speakers. Letters become something children know, because they know the song. As with language, children seem to learn the song from whole to parts. Initially, the primacy effect (the idea that we tend to remember the first bit of new material presented better than we do material presented subsequently) is evident, because even the youngest children learning the song begin confidently with the first letters mentioned: 'ABCDEFG'. There is also a recency effect to song learning, so children quickly become adept at ending the song confidently too; Z is salient.

However, much of what is sung in the middle is a fog. It is not immediately clear how many elements are represented by the articulation, often tentatively grouped together, 'LMNOP', for example. With increasing experience with the song, and with increasing support from parents and teachers, children eventually learn to distinguish each letter name as a distinct element.

In their increasing familiarity with the 'ABC' song, children become more comfortable with letter names and, ultimately, letter-sound recognition. This familiarity may also spark an interest in print in general and in writing one's own name in particular (Treiman & Broderick, 1998). Furthermore, in spelling words other than their own names, pre-school children tend to use more letters from their own first names as compared to other letters, which suggests that children's letter-name knowledge depends on their own individual experiences with letters (Treiman et al., 2001).

In places other than the United States or Canada, simple repetition of letter names or emphasis on particular letter names or sounds may be more common. For example, in the Netherlands the letters are simply repeated in order but not set to music. In South America, in contrast, school children are often taught to focus on vowel pronunciation. Parents' concerns with vowel pronunciation are evident in the numbers and varieties of vowel songs they teach their children. One example from Mexico is this:

> How does the 'A' laugh?
> Ha ha ha ha
> How does the 'E' laugh?
> He he he he

The song continues through all of the vowels, until it finally concludes with:

> How does the 'U' laugh?
> He doesn't laugh because the donkey is smarter than you!
> (No te rías porque ¡el burro es más inteligente que tù!)

In Israel, one children's song links letter names with words, e.g. Gimel (G) with Gamal (*camel*), perhaps making the consistency between letter names and their sounds more consistent (Levin, Patel, Margalit, & Barad, 2002).

Once children have acquired knowledge of letter names through repetitions, rhymes, songs, and the spelling of their own names, they may use their letter-name knowledge to derive letter sound knowledge. Children with knowledge of even a few letter names use their knowledge to learn to recognize novel stimuli. For example, children will find it easier to remember that *JN* spells *Jane* than that it spells *John* or *Rex*. Treiman and colleagues have demonstrated in a number of studies that children with even a small amount of alphabet knowledge find it easier to link new stimuli to letter names than to visual cues (Treiman & Broderick, 1998; Treiman & Rodriguez, 1999; Treiman, Sotak, & Bowman, 2001). For example, *JN* certainly looks unusual and might be memorized simply by virtue of its distinctive look, but if you compare how difficult it is for children to remember that this strange-looking letter combination, compared to an alternative choice of the normally written *bo*, says 'ba' (in an experimental setting), children who know the letter B will typically find that the latter example is easier because of the B link to the /b/ sound. Children with more alphabet knowledge (typically those who know about 20 letter names or more) also find it easier to learn to read stimuli that can be linked to letter sounds (e.g. *JN = John*) rather than to visual cues. This appears to be true not only for monolingual English speakers but also for Hong Kong Chinese children learning to read English as a second language (McBride-Chang & Treiman, 2003).

Similar results were found by Levin et al. (2002) in a study of pre-school children learning Hebrew. Relative to those of English, Hebrew letter names are longer (often multisyllabic). Nevertheless, they influence developing spellers' spelling and reading patterns. Partial letter names, which never occur in English, also affect reading and spelling patterns, though less strongly than full letter names. Thus, children appear to make name–sound connections in alphabets consistently. Such connections are sometimes helpful and sometimes a hindrance in learning to spell and read correctly (Levin et al., 2002).

It should also be noted that most of the research on letter-name/letter-sound knowledge focuses on the consonants, rather than the vowels, of an alphabet. The great variability in the sounds made by English vowels may make it more difficult for children to recognize the connections between letter names and sounds consistently. In Hebrew also, children have more difficulty with vowel as opposed to consonant spelling. This relative difficulty may be attributable to the fact that there are few reliable name–sound cues in Hebrew vowels.

To summarize, in alphabets, letter names can be made salient through repetition and song. They are then linked particularly to children's own experiences. For children, the letters of their own names are important, especially the first letter. The first letters, and sometimes the last letters, of the alphabet are also striking. With time, children come to link letter names with letter sounds, often implicitly. This link, to a greater or lesser degree, depending upon the individual alphabet, is probably universal. However, children may learn names or sounds first (Ellefson et al., 2009) and the errors they make in confusing letters might be phonologically, shape, or frequency based (Treiman, Levin, & Kessler, 2007). Understanding these patterns of letter names and sounds may facilitate subsequent spelling and reading.

Clearly, this summary is too simplistic to cover letter learning across all alphabets. For example, in some alphabets, such as that of the Maoris in New Zealand, the letter-name/letter-sound distinction is unnecessary; they are identical. In this case, initially learning how to spell and read might take less time and effort, because children are not bogged down with their efforts to understand the precise relation between the names and sounds of letters.

Nevertheless, there is one pattern here that is likely to be generalizable across orthographies; this is that children are analytic learners. They are skilled in discovering patterns across symbolic representations. These patterns are most easily discovered when they are related to things that are meaningful to the children themselves, such as their own names. Among alphabetic learners, letter names and sounds are quickly linked based on children's insights as to the connections between them. Analytic learning patterns are quickly discovered and implemented across orthographies, including Chinese. This is the subject of the next section.

Chinese radicals and emergent literacy

Although it is beyond the scope of this book to explore the building blocks of every script, I would like to consider the building blocks of reading the Chinese script as being in particularly sharp contrast with an alphabetic one. The majority of Chinese characters (over 80 per cent, according to Chen, Lau, & Yung, 1993) are comprised of two distinct components, namely, a phonetic and a semantic radical. Approximately 72 per cent of those Chinese characters taught in mainland China's primary schools are of this type, and are sometimes called semantic phonetic compounds (Shu, Chen, Anderson, Wu, & Xuan, 2003).

Semantic radicals often give some clues to the meaning of these compound characters. There are approximately 200 in Chinese (Hoosain, 1991). In the analysis of school Chinese by Shu et al. (2003), the position of the semantic radical was fixed in 57 per cent of the compound characters and variable (i.e. it could appear in more than one position) in 43 per cent of these characters. Semantic radicals are most likely to appear on the left side of the character. An example of a semantic radical meaning mouth and its association in meaning to different characters is given in Figures 3.1 and 3.2.

Phonetics, of which there are some 800 in Chinese, can sometimes give an indication as to the pronunciation of the character. In the analysis of school Chinese, 83 per cent of compound characters had phonetics that varied in position, and 17 per cent of the phonetics were of a fixed position. The reliability of the phonetic depends, in part, upon the Chinese language onto which the Chinese script is mapped (Chen, 1996). For example, in Hong Kong written Chinese is mapped onto Cantonese. In contrast, in Singapore, Taiwan, and China written Chinese is mapped onto Putonghua in school. Because Cantonese pronunciation is substantially different from Putonghua, sound information communicated in Chinese characters can differ across Chinese languages. One study of children's use of phonetic information in learning to read compared children from Guangzhou, China, who learned Putonghua at school but spoke Cantonese as their mother tongue, with native speakers of Putonghua from Beijing. Children from Guangzhou were less proficient in applying phonetic information to learning the pronunciations of new Chinese characters in Putonghua than their monolingual counterparts in Beijing (Anderson, Li, Ku, Shu, & Wu, 2003). This result suggests that Putonghua native speakers may have an advantage in mapping phonetic information as they learn to read.

Both semantic radicals and phonetics are composed of strokes. Strokes are individual complete movements of a pen on paper. They can be dots, lines, or curves. The visual complexity of Chinese characters is defined simply as the number of

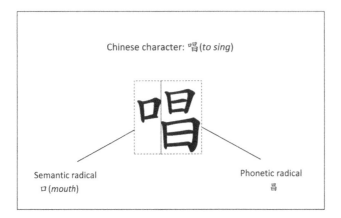

Chinese character: 唱 (*to sing*)

Semantic radical
口 (*mouth*)

Phonetic radical
昌

FIGURE 3.1 In the above character, the left part (semantic radical) of 唱 (*to sing*) is 口 (*mouth*), which gives some clues to its meaning, i.e. the mouth part is involved.

吹 吹   吃 eat   叫 shout

blow   eat   shout

FIGURE 3.2 Other characters that include the 口 (*mouth*) radical; again, the meaning of each character has something to do with the mouth.

strokes composing them. However, strokes by themselves are of little interest in analysing Chinese character learning, except perhaps from the perspective of early visual recognition. That is, Chinese character recognition, measured either via pronunciation or meaning, relies only on phonetic and semantic radicals. Just as the long line in a capital B is not helpful in distinguishing the sound that *B* makes, so strokes are not, by themselves, particularly helpful in communicating sound or meaning information in characters.

Across both simple and compound characters, each character generally represents both a morpheme and a syllable. Thus, Chinese characters are sometimes referred to as morphosyllabic. There are proportionally fewer compound characters

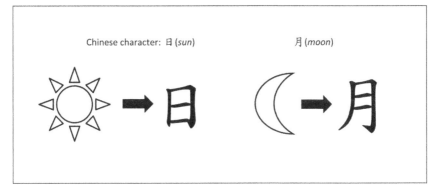

Chinese character: 日 (*sun*)   月 (*moon*)

FIGURE 3.3   Two Chinese pictographs, sun and moon, were originally pictorial symbols of these; note the stylized resemblance.

taught in primary schools as compared to total existing characters (e.g. in estimates of characters necessary for newspaper reading in adults) because character teaching in the early grades entails a focus on simple, non-phonetic characters. Many of these characters are pictographs, which were originally direct representations of meaning. For example, the characters for sun and moon (see Figure 3.3) were originally pictorial representations of these.

Through the years, their character representations have become more stylized, so that one might not recognize these characters as direct representations. Characters introduced early tend to be relatively simple visually and relatively unsystematic in terms of pronunciation and meaning. In addition, such characters tend to be high in frequency. In the current mainland Chinese school system, low-frequency characters, introduced more often at higher grade levels, tend to require more strokes and to be more regular. Regularity means that the phonetic is somehow associated with the pronunciation of the character. This is similar to patterns found in English. For example, the word *have* is irregular but frequently used. In contrast, less frequently used words, such as *grave* or *pave*, more often represent a regular spelling pattern.

The way in which language is mapped onto script differs enormously between English and Chinese. In English, 26 letters are combined to make approximately 44 phonemes and thousands of possible syllables. In Chinese, on the other hand, the number of Chinese characters used regularly is approximately 4,600 (Liu et al., 1975, cited in Chen, 1996), and the number of possible syllables is only about 400 (Cheng, 1982). Therefore, homophony in Chinese occurs much more than it does in English. Although English has some homophones (e.g. *no/know; blue/blew; through/threw*), these are much more common in Chinese. It has been estimated that each Mandarin syllable has at least five unique meanings (Li, Anderson, Nagy, & Zhang, 2002). Figure 3.4 demonstrates four meanings of the spoken syllable pronounced *ma* with all four different tones in Mandarin.

The development of Chinese character recognition is sometimes implied to rely primarily on rote memory processes (e.g. Chan & Wang, 2003), because the

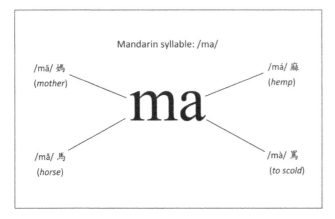

FIGURE 3.4 An example of a single Chinese syllable with four unique meanings, depending upon which of the four Putonghua (Mandarin) tones is used to pronounce it.

association between a character's pronunciation and its phonetic or between a character's meaning and its semantic radical have been assumed to be fairly opaque. In some Chinese regions, the relation of phonetics to pronunciation or semantic radicals to meaning of the character is not explicitly taught by the teacher, because the reliability of these associations is so tenuous. Schools generally rely on repetition in writing and recognition to teach children how to identify new characters. However, despite the fact that the associations of phonetic and semantic radicals are rarely explicitly taught to children, children appear to pick up on the associations fairly quickly.

There is now a strong body of evidence that Chinese children are able to capitalize on their knowledge of the structure of compound characters to recognize characters, to learn new characters, and even to identify novel words, with symbols serving similar functions to semantic radicals and phonetics in various experiments. For example, Ko and Wu (2003) showed that children from Taiwan up to grade four made use of both semantic radicals and phonetics in character decision-making tasks. They also observed that children's knowledge of phonetic information was a bit more advanced than their knowledge of semantic radicals, particularly in second- and third-grade children. Children in both Hong Kong and Beijing also demonstrated increasing knowledge of phonetics and semantic radicals in a study of pseudo-word processing. Again, children's knowledge of phonetic information tended to surpass their understanding of semantic radicals, and strong developmental differences emerged, with older participants demonstrating greater accuracy in making use of both types of character information. Children's understanding of the structure of Chinese characters also emerges relatively early (e.g. Blöte, Chen, Overmars, & van der Heijden, 2003; Tsai & Nunes, 2003). Children seem to understand by about first or second grade at least when fundamental aspects of a character's structure (e.g. position as top/bottom or left/right) are correct and incorrect (e.g. Liu, Chung, McBride-Chang, & Tong, 2010). Anderson and colleagues (2013) further demonstrated that by about the beginning of second grade, Chinese children make clear use of character components (including radicals) to the extent that they can replicate (via a delayed copying task) characters that they have just seen but do not know but that are comprised of familiar components almost as well as they can reproduce characters that are familiar to them overall.

Children's early character-recognition skills thus involve a number of processes. Much of this is sound–sight repetition. Just as alphabetic readers initially spend time repeating the letters of the alphabet, Chinese readers learn characters via repetition.

As children become more sophisticated in their Chinese character recognition, however, they appear to become more sensitive to an implicit structure of compound characters. Their analyses of these characters may aid their learning of new characters, particularly those that contain phonetics, semantic radicals, or both. Statistical learning, that is, discerning certain patterns in print based on increased exposure, facilitates such early learning, even in pre-school children (e.g. Tong & McBride-Chang, 2014).

On defining reading units

One additional issue specifically related to Chinese 'building blocks' of reading that is worth briefly mentioning here is the relations among radicals, characters, and words. Most words in Chinese are comprised of two or more characters, though some single characters can indeed serve as individual words as well. Characters are mastered via radical and other character component sensitivity (Anderson et al., 2013). Words comprised of two or more characters are likely mastered in part via compounding knowledge based on the characters. When several words share the same character, as shown in Figure 3.5, children might use their character knowledge to read them. However, such character knowledge can be incomplete. A child may know only one of the two characters, for example, but guess the meaning based on the position of the character and oral language knowledge. An example in English might be that a child knows the morpheme *ball* but has not learned to read *basketball*, *football*, *ballpark*, or *ballgame*. A child's full knowledge of the word *ball* and partial knowledge of other words in English containing *ball* might help him to guess at the word *football* (begins with *f*; contains *ball*), for example. Some work (Li & McBride-Chang, 2014; Wang & McBride, 2015) has demonstrated, in support of this, that Chinese children of various grade levels read Chinese characters embedded in words more accurately than they read the same characters in isolation. They have further suggested that learning to recognize Chinese characters relies on somewhat different skills, particularly orthographic knowledge, than does learning to read words, which may involve vocabulary knowledge and lexical compounding/morphological awareness more specifically. To summarize, one building block of word reading in Chinese is character recognition; in Chinese, character and word reading, though strongly overlapping, may not constitute precisely the same process

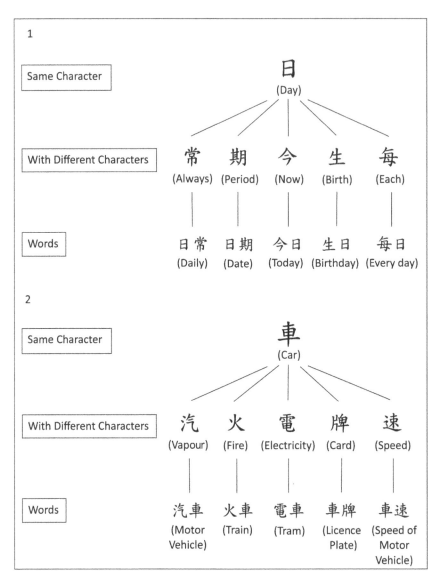

FIGURE 3.5 Two examples of how a single Chinese character paired with different characters forms different Chinese words.

(Figure 3.6). Figure 3.6 shows two examples of how radicals contribute to individual characters and characters, in turn, contribute to two-character words.

More broadly, there are some keys to learning to read in different orthographies that may be special. We simply do not know how important they are yet. The character vs word distinction of Chinese is one example. Another is the fact that Thai children first learn to read words that are delineated with space in between when they begin first grade. Only later do they begin, from the end of first grade, to read

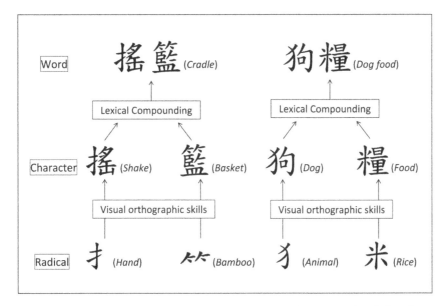

FIGURE 3.6 Chinese character reading may rely on visual-orthographic skills, whereas Chinese word reading may rely on morphological awareness in the form of lexical compounding. For example, when the character '搖' (*shake*) combines with '籃' (*basket*), it becomes the word *cradle* (搖籃) and indicates a basket (bed) which can be moved back and forth literally. Since the motion 'shake' involves the hand, the semantic radical of '*shake*' (搖) in Chinese is *hand*(扌); while a basket is made up of bamboo and therefore the semantic radical of the character '*basket*' (籃) is *bamboo*(⺮). In another example, the word *dog food* (狗糧) is made up of two Chinese characters, '狗' (*dog*) and '糧' (*food*) respectively. The character '*dog*' (狗) contains an *animal* radical (犭) while the character '糧' contains a *rice* radical as rice is the staple food of Chinese people.

with no spaces. This means that the concept of word reading is a bit ambiguous here, as in Chinese (McBride-Chang, Chen et al., 2012). In other orthographies, like the Semitic ones of Arabic and Hebrew, expert reading means that vowels are dropped from words in print. This phenomenon implies a period of adjustment in understanding how vowels are represented and how to incorporate their absence into word reading and writing. Finally, in some orthographies, words can be very long. For example, words of 50 letters or so in length are not uncommon in Finnish, where a single word might have, with all possible derivational and inflectional variations, up to 2,000 or so separate orthographic representations (Niemi, Laine, & Tuominen, 1994). The extent to which such a length requires children's cognitive adjustments is not clear. Finnish is a very regular orthography so in that sense it is easy to read. Each of these variations implies some deviation from word learning in the more typical Indo-European languages, such as Spanish, German, French, or English, that have been most widely researched thus far. Building blocks of reading may, therefore, comprise a variety of adjustments related to early word recognition.

One final example of building blocks of reading is the Hangul system for Korean. This system is of particular interest for at least two reasons. First, unlike most scripts in the world, Hangul was invented through the efforts of one small team, presided over by Korean emperor Sejong the Great, in a very short time. Introduced in 1446, Korean Hangul was created in order to facilitate reading by the common people who had been, up until that time, largely illiterate. Hangul consists of letters, each of which is a simplified picture to indicate positions of the mouth, teeth, and tongue, when pronouncing a given sound. Second, this system is known as an alphasyllabary (e.g. Taylor & Taylor, 1995). This is because, although there are 14 consonants and 10 vowels in this system, unlike languages depicted using the Roman alphabet, these letters are combined into syllables, as shown in Figure 3.7. These syllables have an appearance closer to Chinese than to most other scripts in the sense of taking up space both at the levels of left and right but also from the top and bottom. Interestingly, children are often taught this system first via a syllable chart, in which they memorize 140 syllables that are the basic combinations of 14 consonants and 10 vowels (this does not include compound vowels). Only later do they break the syllables into individual phonemes (Cho, 2009). This is an example of how memorization is emphasized first in literacy learning, and only then does a more focused analysis take place.

Variability in cognitive development: the overlapping waves model

Children learn to capitalize on any clues present in the orthography itself to make sense of it. However, although children tend to use such clues more efficiently with age, I do not mean to imply that they do so in a clear, stage-like fashion. Children likely use multiple strategies simultaneously to learn reading fundamentals. Like the rest of us, children are fundamentally opportunists. They tend to use the strategies they find helpful in solving various learning problems; these strategies may differ from item to item to be read/decoded.

To date, perhaps the best model for children's varied strategy use is the overlapping waves model (e.g. Siegler, 2000). As ably expressed in a study applying this model to learning to spell in English, 'Within the overlapping waves model, abundant variability, adaptive choice, and gradual change are fundamental features of cognition at all points in development' (Rittle-Johnson & Siegler, 1999, p. 332). A study of this model requires that learning individuals' strategies be carefully and closely monitored. When the model has been applied to learning in a variety of different domains (see Siegler, 2000, for a review), children's performances have been demonstrated to improve very gradually. Rather than indicating stage-like progression by age, as has typically been assumed in some research on reading-related skill development, this model stresses individual variability as a key to learning.

Applying this model to reading development, we can expect gradual change in reading skills among all children learning to read. In addition, we can anticipate

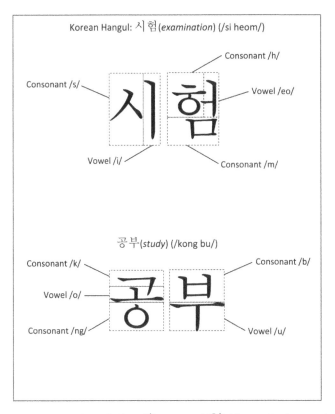

FIGURE 3.7 The syllables '시' (/si/) and '험' (/heom/) take up a left-right structure and left-right-bottom structure respectively. The word '시험' (/si heom/) means *examination* (*above*). The syllables '공' (/kong/) and '부' (/bu/) both take up the top-bottom structure. The word '공부' (/kong bu/) means *study* (*below*).

that strategy choices for reading development will depend both upon children's age and educational attainment, and upon their individual differences. In the overlapping waves model, changes come about through at least four different processes.

First, children learn new, increasingly advanced, strategies. For example, understanding that one can make analogies between previously learned words and those that we subsequently encounter may facilitate word recognition. Knowing the pronunciation of the English word *rough* may help a child to identify new words, such as *tough* and *enough*. In Chinese, understanding the meaning of the semantic radical for *mouth* may help in recalling the identity of the characters for *kiss* and *sing* (see Figure 3.8).

Second, more advanced strategies are more likely to be implemented as children learn. This implies that, as children become more experienced readers, their

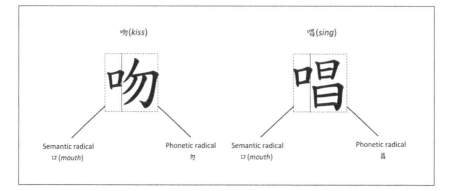

FIGURE 3.8 Both the Chinese characters for *kiss* and *sing* make use of the mouth, and the semantic radical '口' can assist children in remembering their identity.

reliance on analogy in identifying a new word will increase. In contrast, in English, a strategy focused purely on combining individual letter sounds will be implemented less often. Similarly, Chinese children will be more likely to make use of semantic radical or phonetic information to get some clues as to the meaning or sound, respectively, of a new character as they become advanced readers. In contrast, their reliance on parents and teachers alone to identify characters may diminish.

Third, children will become increasingly adept at executing the strategies they learn. For example, their overall implementation of strategies will be more efficient (i.e. quicker). Efficiency in the form of automatization in learning is discussed in more detail in the next section. One indication of this is that spelling/dictation becomes less laborious over time.

Finally, as children's knowledge increases, they will tend to select strategies that are more adaptable to the task at hand. For example, when an individual is confronted with a long but fairly regular English word such as *antidisestablishmentarianism*, an adaptive strategy for figuring out how to pronounce it may be to break it into orthographically sensible units (e.g. as adults, we can distinguish some units we have encountered before in this word, such as *anti*, *dis*, or *establish*). In a different word with a fairly irregular structure, such as *menarche*, a more effective strategy for learning its pronunciation might be simply to look it up in the dictionary. (We might similarly distinguish these words in terms of morphological units to gain some understanding of the meanings of these words.)

In Chinese, children may similarly change their strategies in response to the difficulties of various characters. For example, in deciding how to recognize a new character, children may use at least two different strategies (Chan & Wang, 2003). First, children may understand it using an analogy to some other character that contains the same meaning component (see Figure 3.8). Second, they may attempt to pronounce the character directly based on a pronunciation of its phonetic component (see Figure 3.9).

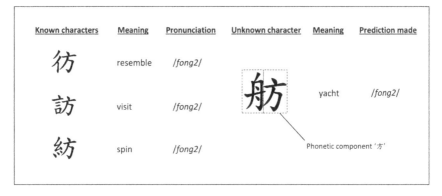

FIGURE 3.9 Children can use the Chinese characters they know to guess the pronunciation of an unknown but similar character, as in this case. The phonetic component '方' is pronounced identically across all characters presented above; thus, a child can make an analogy between characters already known and a newly encountered character to predict its pronunciation. In this case, the prediction of the pronunciation is correct, though there are many exceptions to this across characters.

It is possible that children might be more likely to use the strategy of analogy as their knowledge of Chinese characters becomes greater.

Although strategies may differ for developing readers, depending upon orthography learned, the idea that children make use of multiple strategies as they acquire literacy skills has also been supported in studies of children learning to read Hebrew. In analysing their findings among five-year-olds in Israel, Share and Gur (1999) found little evidence for a stage theory of reading development. Rather, among five-year-old children exposed to Hebrew, there was evidence of contextual reading, logographic reading, partial-alphabetic reading (relying on one or two letter sounds to guess the whole word), and alphabetic reading. Some children even demonstrated use of a strategy not recognized in other orthographies, which they termed *visuographic reading*. In this method, children seemed to focus on multiple visual cues throughout a word string. These varied strategies occurred 'not only across but also within participants . . . Indeed, most 5-year-old children evinced use of more than one strategy' (Share & Gur, 1999, p. 208). Thus, across orthographies, children learn to read (e.g. Elbro, 2013) and also to spell (e.g. Critten & Pine, 2009; Farrington-Flint, Stash, & Stiller, 2008; Sharp, Sinatra, & Reynolds, 2008) based on whatever information is available to them. Although there are general trends for children across orthographies to use more sophisticated reading strategies with experience, there is little evidence that children learn to read or to spell in a strict stage-like progression.

A key element to children's strategy use in learning to read is that their overall task processing becomes more efficient with time. This efficiency is largely attributable to a construct sometimes known as automaticity (e.g. Adams, 1990). The importance of automaticity is discussed below.

The key to growth in reading: automatizing the process

The automatization of word recognition is among the most important achievements for early readers. The faster we can blend together phonemes, the faster we can name a word comprised of those phonemes. If this process is too laborious (*street* = /s/+/t/+/r/+/i/+/t/), a child may forget the initial phonemes in the word before getting to the ones at the end. Similarly, in Cantonese, reading the phrase *two children* requires a child to know five characters:

1. *two* (a pair)
2. a measure word for *friends* (sort of analogous to *the* or *a* in English)
3. the character meaning *small*, which is the first morpheme in *children*
4 & 5. the other two morphemes together meaning *friends*.

See Figure 3.10 for this example.

In this case, a child beginning to read may forget part of the phrase before getting to the end of it. Yet, with practice, the word or phrase can be recognized holistically. And, with more practice, an entire sentence that makes use of a word or phrase (e.g. *The man walked down the street*, in English) can be encoded for meaning. As this process becomes easier, children begin to encode entire paragraphs or whole stories for meaning.

What is this automatization process? The answer to this question remains largely unresolved and has historical origins in several theories in psychology (Wolf & Katzir-Cohen, 2001). Clearly, an important part of automatization is the division of our visual or auditory memory units into larger and larger segments. Thus, memory capacity increases with experience (Case, 1985). As children become better able to divide up units of information into chunks, they can redirect their attentional capacities away from labour-intensive 'lower-level' skills, such as identifying a word by its spelling, which involves each individual letter, to 'higher-level' skills, such as learning to read new words by analogy (e.g. LaBerge & Samuels, 1974) and, ultimately, reading comprehension (Lai, Benjamin, Schwanenflugel, & Kuhn, 2014). At the word level, *pat* may be read as a new word given that a child already knows how to read *sat*, *fat*, and *cat*. In this case, children's knowledge of a rime pattern, *at*, speeds up the process of learning to read new words, because *at* can be processed as a unit, rather than as *a* + *t* separately. Similarly, children learning to read Chinese may make use of the knowledge they have of phonetics or semantic radicals, much of which is derived implicitly through exposure to different characters, to learn new characters (e.g. Chan & Wang, 2003). If one can remember that the semantic radical meaning water represents *water*, then one can perhaps remember other characters that contain this radical (e.g. *river*, *sea*, *lake*, *pond*) more efficiently (see Figure 3.11).

Much of the process of automatization can be explained by development itself. As children get older, they become faster in their handling of a variety of cognitive tasks, even into adolescence (Kail & Ferrer, 2007). This speeding up is a result of brain maturation, and children become faster with life experience. Speed of

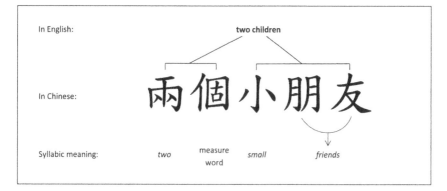

FIGURE 3.10   The phrase *two children* in Chinese has five characters; when children identify each of these characters quickly, it facilitates their reading and understanding of the phrase.

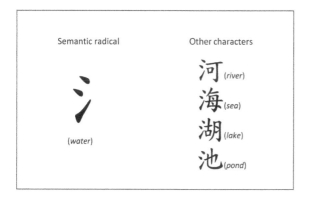

FIGURE 3.11   Knowing that 氵 means *water* can aid in learning the meanings of 河 (*river*), 海 (*sea*), 湖 (*lake*), and 池 (*pond*).

processing is likely attributable to some genetic and some cultural factors, as well as their interactions (Kail, 1991; Kail, McBride-Chang, Ferrer, Cho, & Shu, 2013). Automatization has specifically been applied to reading-related skills in a number of studies.

For example, Rittle-Johnson and Siegler (1999) found three sources of increased speed in spelling among English-speaking children from first to second grade. First, as compared to their performances in first grade, second graders were more likely to make use of one particular spelling strategy that was among the fastest and most accurate. This strategy was the direct retrieval of a particular spelling. Second, children tended to make less use of the slowest strategy, of sounding out words letter by letter while making greater use of faster strategies, such as rule use or drawing analogies. Finally, children generally became quicker to execute all strategies.

This study links automatization to distinct processes related to spelling. Thus, it is not enough to say that children become faster over time. This study actually identifies the sources of this increased speed. In another study applying the ideas of automatization to reading, McBride-Chang and Kail (2002) examined children's Chinese character/English word recognition and demonstrated the importance of speed for very early reading. However, this was a modelling study, in which the exploration of speed of processing was limited to tasks measuring global speed. In this model, the primary predictor of speed of processing itself was children's age. At the same time, along with age-related automatization changes, there are also individual differences in automatization, as highlighted by the overlapping waves model. Just as fluency is considered a crucial element of intelligence (e.g. Horn & Cattell, 1966), it may explain, in part, reading ability. Results of McBride-Chang and Kail's modelling study of early reading indicated that speed of processing was strongly linked to all reading-related skills, which in turn predicted reading itself. Thus, speed of processing strongly affected the cognitive abilities most associated with both English word and Chinese character recognition.

A useful example of the way in which both age and individual differences predict speed of processing in relation to reading skill is outlined in Carver's (1997) rauding theory. In this theory, both age and cognitive speed aptitude explain naming speed level and, ultimately, reading rate – a primary predictor of reading achievement. This model underscores a fundamental focus across cognitive developmental studies: both individual variability and age-related differences are important when considering automatization.

Distinguishing the various nuances of automatization is beyond the scope of this book; moreover, these distinctions are far from clear to educators and psychologists themselves. As Wolf and Katzir-Cohen stated in an article on reading fluency development and intervention possibilities, 'There is no consensus concerning how we use such basic terms as rate, automaticity, speed of processing, temporal processing, dynamic processing, or precise timing, much less fluency' (2001, p. 233). Nevertheless, the importance of basic automaticity for reading, as for all cognitive capacities (e.g. Horn & Cattell, 1966; Kail, 2000), is clear.

Similarities and differences

The focus of this chapter has been on the building blocks of reading. In a comparison across orthographies, it seems reasonable to reflect on the extent to which these building blocks have similar or different functions for different scripts. To begin with, at the environmental level, the stage must be set for reading to develop. Governments and schools must prioritize reading acquisition, of course. Furthermore, home environment can be more or less conducive to fostering reading development. Supportive and interested parents who value reading and have the sensitivity towards their children to support their interest in print at their level, to scaffold them, are likely to have more eager and advanced readers across cultures.

At the individual level, across orthographies, certain general cognitive skills are particularly important to literacy development. First, children must learn some basic components of words by rote learning to facilitate learning. The role of rote learning should not be minimized. Everyone needs a great deal of practice to recognize that the letters *sh* together are pronounced in a very different way to that required when they appear individually. In Chinese, we may need to learn several characters before we understand that the semantic radical roughly meaning *plant* helps us to identify the meanings of many other characters. The Hangul syllable chart must be completely memorized. Automatization is also essential for learning to read across scripts.

Finally, the ability to generalize newly learned information to new contexts requires the ability to learn linguistic information effectively. This basic level of analytic linguistic skill has been demonstrated across orthographies. Siegler's overlapping waves model is important here for explaining how children learn to read for the first time in any script. Across orthographies, we simultaneously make use of multiple strategies in consolidating the information we learn via print. All of these similarities focus on basic cognitive developmental skills and may not be specific to the reading process. These are the generalities of literacy acquisition.

Differences are perhaps more readily apparent than similarities in thinking about learning to read across scripts. Differences in learning to read begin with the languages to which orthographies are mapped and the linguistic units they emphasize. The units of print interact with these language units. Thus, letter-sound learning is essential for reading English, an understanding of phonetics and semantic radicals is important in learning to read Chinese, an appreciation for how both phonemes and syllables are represented in Hangul is required, and a sense of how text can be decoded and understood in both vowelized and unvowelized contexts is important for Hebrew and Arabic. How these are taught and integrated with other primary language and visual skills into a richer conceptualization of language and reading comprehension is discussed in subsequent chapters.

Suggested readings

Justice, L. M., & Sofka, A. E. (2010). *Engaging children with print: Building early literacy skills through quality read-alouds*. New York, NY: Guilford Press.

Neuman, S. B., & Dickinson, D. K. (eds) (2011). *Handbook of early literacy research, vol. 3*. New York, NY: The Guilford Press.

Shanahan, T., & Lonigan, C. J. (eds) (2013). *Early childhood literacy: The national early literacy panel and beyond*. Baltimore, MD: Paul H. Brookes Publishing Co., Inc.

Wasik, B. H. (ed.) (2012). *Handbook of family literacy*. New York, NY: Routledge.

4

THE ROLE OF MORPHOLOGICAL AWARENESS IN LEARNING TO READ AND TO WRITE (SPELL)

This chapter focuses on how an understanding of morphemes contributes to literacy acquisition. In order to grasp the concept of morphological awareness, we begin with an overview of morphology. Morphology is the study of the relational components of word structure. Although morphology can largely be understood using other concepts, such as syntax, phonology, or the lexicon, it is separable from these as the study of morphological units of meaning, or morphemes (Pounder, 2000). Morphemes are the smallest units of meaning in a given language. Morphology is particularly focused on inflections, derivations, and compounding in words.

Inflections are word endings denoting meanings such as case, gender, or syntax. For example, there are two morphemes in the word *houses*. *House* is the one-morpheme root word, and *s*, signalling plural form, is the inflection of the root word *house*. Another example of an inflection is *ed* in the word *waxed*, denoting the past tense of *wax*.

Derivations make use of prefixes and suffixes. For example, in the word *unstoppable*, *un* constitutes a prefix and *able* is a suffix for the root word *stop*. Thus, *unstoppable* consists of three morphemes, two of which represent derivations.

Compounding, another aspect of derivation, involves combining words to form new concepts. For example, *treehouse* is a compound word consisting of the morphemes *tree* and *house*. Inflections, derivations, and compounding are all important concepts in understanding the role of morphological awareness in literacy acquisition.

The importance of morphological awareness for reading development is increasingly recognized, as reflected in the definitions of morphological awareness. Carlisle defined morphological awareness as a focus on 'children's conscious awareness of the morphemic structure of words and their ability to reflect on and manipulate that structure' (1995, p. 194). In considering adults, Koda (2000) stated that morphological awareness represents 'a learner's grasp of morphological structure (i.e., the ways in which morphemes are conjoined in words) as well as his or her capability of using this knowledge during morphological processing in visual word recognition' (p. 299). Both of these definitions are indeed helpful in conceptualizing the nature of morphological awareness. Yet, from a developmental and cross-cultural perspective, both may require fine-tuning.

This chapter first delves deeper into a definition of morphological awareness, including the central notion of morphological productivity. The development of various types of morphological awareness, specifically in relation to reading, is then considered separately in alphabetic and Chinese languages. Next, the focus is both on the ways in which morphological awareness predicts reading, and the extent to which reading affects subsequent morphological awareness and vocabulary skills in developing readers.

Considering morphological awareness across cultures

A particularly inclusive definition of morphological awareness, parallel to that of phonological awareness, is *awareness of and access to the meaning structure of language*. This may be helpful in Chinese, where the concept of 'word' is more elusive than in most alphabetic orthographies (Packard, 2000). From a developmental perspective, this definition is also easier to apply than is that of Koda (see above), whose definition really focuses more on what individuals learn about morphemes from reading than on how children's morpheme knowledge may facilitate reading. The majority of studies tend to focus on the importance of applying morphological structures in known words to the learning of new words among older primary- and secondary-school students (e.g. Adams & Henry, 1997). However, an understanding of morphemes may also help young children learn to read.

Across cultures, morphological awareness is relevant to reading because of the productivity of morphological systems. Productivity has been defined as a language's capacity for 'morphological coining' (Bauer, 2001, p. 99). Morphological coining basically means that new morphological formations, most often words, can be created using morphemes. As an example, think of an adjective to describe an individual who can use a computer mouse with either hand. At a lecture I attended by Professor C. K. Leong, I learned that *ambimousetrous* is the correct terminology for this concept. This new concept is best described using this new word. However, one can clearly note that the prefix *ambi* (meaning two) and the suffix *ous* (making the word an adjective as in *lustrous* or *luscious*) were crucial morphemes in structuring this word. Other new words include *chillax* (combining *chill out* and *relax*), *sexting* (from something about *sex* and *texting*), and *upcycle* (meaning to *recycle* something to make it into a better, more *upscale* product than it had been).

Different scholars may conceptualize morphological productivity somewhat differently. For example, Bauer (2001), a linguist, asserts that morphological productivity requires repetition in a language and consensus in usage across speakers. In this interpretation, a single individual coining a new term, such as *unterminate*, to indicate halting a process of stopping something, as in *unterminate* the contract (ultimately meaning do not not honour the contract), would not constitute morphological productivity. Others consider morphological productivity to allow individuals creativity in producing new concepts based on their linguistic knowledge. However, creativity is not the primary consideration here. Rather, understanding of morphemes and how they can be transferred in order to derive or understand words is the focal point of morphological productivity. Thus, the most important point to note about morphological productivity is that speakers of a language quickly gain knowledge about its morphemes and ways in which they can and cannot be combined. This knowledge, whether implicit or explicit, may be useful for both beginners' and more advanced scholars' reading and writing development. Every year, dictionaries are updated with the results of such productivity.

In many ways, the concept of implicit–explicit morphological awareness has important parallels with the same dichotomy in phonological awareness measurement. Recall that levels of phonological awareness are distinguishable based both on type of response and level of representation. In the same way, morphological awareness can be measured either with implicit (also termed epilinguistic) or explicit (also referred to as metalinguistic; both terms appear in Gombert, 1992) tasks, to gauge different types of response (see also Carlisle, 1995; Casalis & Louis-Alexandre, 2000). Morphological awareness can also be measured at different levels of representation, primarily those tapping either derivation or inflection.

An example of an implicit morphological awareness measure is one in which children are asked to select, from among four given options, the best answer. Casalis and Louis-Alexandre (2000, p. 311) gave French children such a task in which children were shown a picture of *enrouler* (to roll up) from among the choices of *derouler* (to unroll), *rouler* (to roll along), *rouleau* (roller), and the target item itself, *enrouler*. Because children do not have to generate answers themselves in this task (as in speech perception tasks, where there is a forced choice, e.g. *bath/path*), the task is implicit, or epilinguistic.

An explicit morphological task is one in which children must demonstrate awareness of roots in words. Casalis and Louis-Alexandre tested this by having children pronounce two parts of a word based on its morphemes. For example, *breakable* is comprised of two morphemes, *break* and *able*. This task also requires distinguishing phonological and morphological knowledge, because division by syllable could yield a different answer than division by morphemes, as in this example. Indeed, literacy instructors of English typically focus on teaching syllable-level information first and only later focusing on morphological information when the syllable and the morpheme conflict (another example might be the *under* in *understand*; *under* could be divided syllabically but this would undermine the importance of the morpheme *under* in this particular example).

Thus, in contrast to the acquisition of phonological awareness, which theoretically focuses on speech sounds, using either nonsense or real words, attaining morphological awareness requires that children attend simultaneously both to the sound and meaning of language (Nagy & Anderson, 1999). Sound can be confounded with meaning, as is sometimes the case in English. For example, although *know* is a route word of *knowledge*, the syllable *know* is pronounced differently by itself and in the noun representing it. Sound can also be identical across meanings. For example, in Putonghua, the *shu* in *shubao* (meaning *backpack*) is pronounced identically in other words with different meanings. For example, the *shu* in *shubao* means *book*, whereas an alternative meaning for the same syllable is *uncle*. This can also occur in English. For example, the meanings and spellings of the first syllable in *Sunday* and the second syllable in *grandson* differ, though they are pronounced identically.

Most of the work on morphological awareness in alphabetic languages focuses on the complexity of morphemes in relation to grammar, prefixes, or suffixes. In English, some of the earliest attainment of morphological awareness centres on verb tense. Children must learn about how to change verbs in order to reflect meaning changes (e.g. *go/goes*; *walk/walked*; *buy/bought*), which, as these examples demonstrate, are often inconsistent. Although it may sometimes be unclear how to distinguish morphological awareness from syntax, the important difference between them to bear in mind is that morphological awareness focuses on the word level, whereas syntax knowledge is demonstrated at the sentence level.

Other salient morphological problems include how to make nouns plural (*plant/plants*; *box/boxes*) and how and when prefixes and suffixes are related to words (*unclear* = *un* + *clear*; *undone* = *un* + *done*; *understand* is not *un* + *derstand*). In French, inflectional morphemes are also required to mark the masculine or feminine case for nouns (e.g. *bon/bonne*).

The developmental trajectories of inflectional and derivational morphology differ, at least in some alphabetic languages. According to Casalis and Louis-Alexandre, 'In general, major principles of inflectional morphology are acquired before and at the beginning of learning to read. This is not the case for derivational morphology' (2000, p. 306). To sum up, inflectional morphology involves primarily grammatical suffixes that mark case, number, gender, tense, and person. In contrast, derivational morphology in some Indo-European languages includes prefixes, suffixes, and compound words.

Arabic and Hebrew are two orthographies that make strong use of different inflectional and derivational markers for word reading and writing. Person, number, gender, and time are reflected by inflections which can appear as either prefixes or suffixes in Arabic (Abu-Rabia, 2007). There are a variety of derivational forms for nouns and verbs as well. Tasks of morphological awareness in Arabic or Hebrew often require children to identify root words in the face of inflected and derived forms (Abu-Rabia, 2007; Ravid & Schiff, 2006). For the most part, inflectional morphology is learned earlier than derivational morphology in Hebrew as well (e.g. Levin, Ravid, & Rapaport, 2001).

Indeed, most inflectional morphology is mastered by young children as they learn to speak their native tongue, between the ages of two and six years. Pre-schoolers who mistakenly say that they have two *foots* or that they *goed* to the store demonstrate their immersion in the ongoing learning of inflectional morphology.

In contrast, high-school students preparing for SATs in America, and focusing on Latin and Greek root words, continue to develop their knowledge of derivational morphology. For example, learning that *micro* means *small* or that *hydro* means *water* may help in learning to remember the meanings of words such as *microscope*, *microphone*, *hydrogen*, or *hydrostat*. Although struggles to master inflectional and derivational morphology occur across languages, there may be important differences in the difficulties associated with these from one language to another.

In Chinese, for instance, there are relatively few grammatical complexities to word forms. For example, the verb of a sentence remains unchanged in form whether the subject is singular or plural. However, there are other ways in which morphological awareness is essential for competence in both the writing and speaking of Chinese. First, because Chinese has more homophones than other languages, an important task for children is to determine which particular meaning of a given homophone or homograph is represented within a word or phrase. (Again, I say word or phrase because, particularly in Chinese, there is relatively little consensus on what constitutes a word (Packard, 2000; Perfetti & Tan, 1999).)

Thus, although the sounds of many Chinese syllables are the same, their written forms differ. In the case of Chinese, then, learning to read may help clarify meaning differences across homophones because these homophones are represented by different characters. Although learning to read may be useful for distinguishing homophones, it may be equally important for children to learn to distinguish among homophones or homographs as a task of reading acquisition. (Homographs are words that sound and are spelled the same but have different meanings. For example, the word *bat* can mean either a flying mammal or an instrument used to play baseball.) Children must bear in mind the meaning distinctions among various syllables that sound identical in order to comprehend spoken language. Distinguishing among these syllables will also be helpful for mapping them on to new characters in the process of reading acquisition.

A second aspect of Chinese that makes morphological awareness particularly salient for early reading is that it is an analytic language. By this I mean that more complicated vocabulary concepts can be built from simple morphemes. Some literal translations of English words to Chinese include defining computer as *electric + brain*, *adult* as *big + person*, and read as *see + book*. In all of these examples, simple morphemes are compounded to form a different meaning. Morphemes learned by themselves or in these contexts can then be applied to new words. For example, *telephone* is defined as *electric + speech*, *university* as *big + study*, and *backpack* as *book + pack*. The transparency of these morphemes may direct children's attention to them in ways that are not as clear in Indo-European languages.

A third aspect of Chinese relative to English, or various European languages, which may be relevant in considering morphological awareness in relation to reading is that, in Chinese, there is almost a perfect one-to-one correspondence between syllables and morphemes. This clear association may be particularly useful in helping children to focus on meaning in language. In contrast, the associations among syllables and morphemes are often obscure in English. For example, the word *brought* is a single morpheme, although the past tense of many other verbs (e.g. *walked*) are explicitly marked with a morpheme indicating past tense (e.g. *ed*) in addition to the original verb (e.g. *walk*). In other examples from English, single morphemes consist of two or more syllables (e.g. *brother, lettuce*). For fostering explicit early morphological awareness, then, the one-to-one syllable-to-morpheme mappings of Chinese may be particularly helpful.

From this overview, it is clear that there are several aspects of morphological awareness. Furthermore, the importance of morphological awareness, how it is measured in relation to literacy acquisition, and the aspects of morphological awareness that are most relevant probably differ across languages and their corresponding orthographies. In English, for example, grammatical tense and prefixes and suffixes are essential markers of morphological awareness. In contrast, compounding (i.e. putting together two morphemes to form a new word, as in *rainbow, cowboy*, or *houseboat*) may be relatively unimportant for measuring morphological awareness in English, because compounding occurs relatively infrequently in this language. In Chinese, grammatical markers, prefixes, and suffixes are relatively uncommon. On the other hand, compounding is essential for Chinese language learning. Thus, compounding may be a major focus of morphological awareness in Chinese. In Arabic and Hebrew, inflections and derivations are important given that so many derivations of some base words, both nouns and verbs, are possible with different morphological changes. The next section explores, first in some alphabetic languages and then in Chinese, the extent to which morphological awareness is important for early literacy acquisition.

Early development of morphological awareness

Demonstrating young children's competence in morphological awareness has been described as difficult (Derwing & Baker, 1979); however, the extent to which this is true depends in large part on the definition of morphological awareness used, the tasks used to measure it, and the language in which this idea is tested. It is clear that children do evidence early morphological awareness. What is the evidence and how does this relate to reading acquisition?

A classic study of morphological awareness was conducted by Berko (1958). Although, as a language development researcher, she explored only developmental trends in morphology, rather than associations of morphological skill to word reading, it is informative to consider her findings in light of subsequent research on morphology and word recognition. Berko asked children, aged four to seven, various questions related to nonsense words in story form. For example, one of her most famous items was, 'This is a wug [this example was accompanied by a bird-like picture]. Now there is another one. There are two of them. There are two __.' In this case, children were expected to demonstrate their knowledge of plural by saying *wugs*. Other examples focused on children's knowledge of past tense, derived adjective (e.g. a *quirking* dog), third person singular, and possessive. Children showed much variability on these items, but for every item except one, more than 10 per cent of pre-schoolers answered correctly.

Across children, there was some flexibility in the demonstration of skills in applying prior knowledge to new situations to demonstrate grammatical knowledge. For example, when asked what to call a man who *zibs*, 11 per cent of children answered a *zibber*. An additional 11 per cent answered a *zibbingman*, and an additional 5 per cent called him a *zibman*. (Other responses included no answer (35 per cent) or real words, e.g. *clown* or *acrobat*. These real words were sensible because they fitted the picture accompanying the story.) The range of responses given indicates that children can be creative, or productive, with morphological knowledge from an early age.

Berko also asked children about compound words in order to study their knowledge of derivational morphology. Her format was consistent in these queries, saying, 'Why do you think a __ is called a __?' This appears to be quite a difficult type of question to answer, and, indeed, across ages, only 13 per cent of answers were classified as etymological. However, this etymological classification required that children identify both aspects of the word and identify the important features of each. For example, 'Thanksgiving is called Thanksgiving because the pilgrims gave thanks' (1958, p. 169). However, children did appear to demonstrate sensitivity to certain salient features of *part* of the word fairly often. For example, 72 per cent of children explained that the name of a *fireplace* comes from the idea that 'you put fire in it' (1958, p. 169). Although Berko did not consider these types of answers to be technically correct (etymological), they do reflect children's growing competence in understanding morphology and in making sense of the words to which they are exposed.

Berko also identified other words for which explanations of derivation were incorrect, but reflected a personal attempt to identify meaning. For example, 'Friday is a day when you have fried fish'; 'an airplane is called an airplane because it is a plain thing that goes in the air' (1958, p. 170). These reflect children's approach to language as meaning-based in a clear, productive sense. Perhaps the next question to ask, then, is whether individual variability in understanding of morphology as originally measured by Berko might be associated with reading development and, if so, why.

How morphological awareness predicts early literacy development

One reason that morphological awareness might be useful for reading is that, initially, children often assume print is a direct indication of meaning. Thus, the task of reading is one of mapping meaning on to symbols. If this is the case, a child who is more explicitly aware of meaning may find it easier to make connections among oral and printed morphemes than one who is not.

One particularly interesting illustration of children's bias towards approaching print as mapping directly to meaning comes from Byrne (1996), who conducted a series of studies to distinguish children's morphological and phonological knowledge. His focus was on contrasting a single morpheme with a single phoneme, both of which can be represented by a single letter – the almighty *s*. To test children's understanding of *s*, a letter that clearly marks plurality in most English words, he taught children to read word pairs – *hat/hats* and *book/books* – until the children reached a criterion of six trials for which both words in the pair were correctly identified. He then tested children on various other singular–plural pairs, such as *cup/cups* and *pot/pots*, as well as pairs requiring phonemic but not morphemic sensitivity to word pairs (e.g. *bug/bus*). Across trials, he found that children conceptualized *s* as marking plural (so that the singular and plural versions of the words could be distinguished at well above chance levels) but not as representing the /s/ sound. Thus, children performed at chance levels on word pairs based on phonemic contrasts only (e.g. *bug/bus*). He used these results to argue that children appear to be more sensitive to the fact that script represents meaning than sound in early literacy development among native English speakers.

Casalis and Louis-Alexandre (2000) also discussed the importance of morphological awareness for learning to read. They noted that individuals' complete word knowledge in the mental lexicon is often organized according to morphemes. From a young age, children begin to demonstrate knowledge of both inflections and derivations.

Second, citing Gombert (1992), they argued that readers must attend to explicit cues in words that indicate morphological relations. Reading requires explicit attention to cues in a way that language processing does not, because the many contextual cues evident in everyday conversations do not occur in text. For example, the sentence 'Please understand that I am unhappy' might be easy for a child to comprehend as part of a conversation based on the speaker's facial cues, body language, and tone of voice. Emotional cues might be more salient in this case than the words themselves. However, reading this sentence without these cues forces the reader to attend closely to the words, particularly in distinguishing the *un* unit, phonologically identical twice in the sentence but morphologically meaningful as a separate unit only in the latter case (*un-happy*). Thus, both because we are naturally prone to organize language according to morphology and because reading may force us to focus more carefully on morphology to facilitate comprehension than we do in speaking, morphological awareness is, according to these authors, important in reading development.

Casalis and Louis-Alexandre demonstrated the importance of morphological awareness in a longitudinal study of 50 French children followed from kindergarten through to second grade. Using a variety of tasks, tapping both explicit and implicit levels, and including both inflectional and derivational morphology, these researchers found that morphological awareness accounted for unique variance in reading by grade 2. Using stepwise regression, they showed that measures of derivational morphology accounted for unique variance in both word decoding and reading comprehension, even controlling for the age, IQ, and vocabulary knowledge of the children. Whereas phonemic awareness was the best predictor of reading in first grade, by second grade, tasks of morphological awareness were more strongly associated with reading than were measures of phonological awareness. The authors suggested that the stronger influence of derivational, as compared to inflectional, morphology on reading may be attributed to the developmental trajectories of these abilities. Because inflectional morphology develops relatively early and derivational morphology involves ongoing linguistic understanding, it may be particularly strongly associated with subsequent reading.

Mahony and colleagues (2000) also demonstrated the importance of derivational morphological awareness for decoding skill in English-speaking children in grades three to six. Their test of morphological awareness was a forced-choice one in which students were asked to determine whether or not each item in a pair of words was related to the other. For example, word pairs *deep/depth*, *relate/relation*, and *bomb/bombard* are associated, but *let/letter*, *ear/earth*, and *comb/combination* are not. With vocabulary and phoneme awareness controlled, this morphological awareness task, even administered orally, predicted unique variance in children's word recognition.

Another study of morphological awareness in young Chinese children (McBride-Chang, Shu, Zhou, Wat, & Wagner, 2003) looked at the importance of morphological awareness relative to phonological and speed of processing skills for learning to read in Chinese. Two tests of morphological awareness were administered – morpheme identification and morphological construction – along with others to kindergarten and second-grade Hong Kong Chinese children. Morpheme identification required children to distinguish the meanings of homonyms (see Figure 4.1), and morphological construction required them to build meanings from morphemes (see Figure 4.2).

In this study, the morpheme identification task predicted unique variance in Chinese character recognition for pre-school children only. Li et al. (2002) had demonstrated a similar phenomenon in a previous study of first-grade Chinese children. In that study, oral homophone selection predicted character recognition.

Perhaps more interesting, for all children, our own morphological construction task (McBride-Chang, Shu, et al., 2003) was a unique correlate of character recognition. Thus, among Chinese children, morphological awareness explained unique variance in character recognition even statistically controlling for other abilities previously demonstrated to predict reading, such as phonological awareness, speeded naming, and speed of processing. Subsequent studies have demonstrated similar phenomena, especially in predicting those who will and will not have particular difficulties in word reading in primary school based on pre-school performances in morphological awareness (Ho, 2014; Lei et al., 2011; McBride-Chang, Lam, et al., 2011; Wong et al., 2012). Although not every study finds this pattern when statistically controlling for other measures, morphological compounding is useful enough for distinguishing variability longitudinally in early reading that it has become one of the standard measures used to screen pre-school children in Hong Kong for risk for reading difficulties.

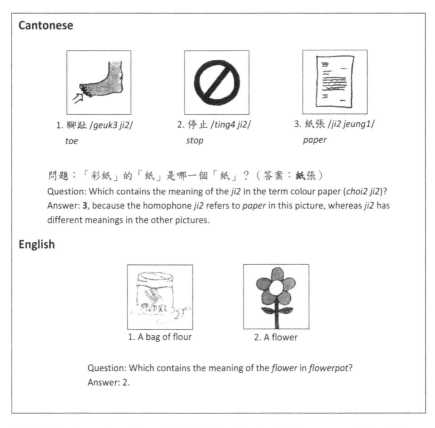

FIGURE 4.1 Examples of morphological identification in Cantonese and English.

Because learning to read requires, universally, that language be mapped onto its representation in print, it seems likely that certain aspects of morphological awareness do play a role in early reading and writing development in several or possibly most languages and orthographies. Recall also from Chapter 2 that several studies specifically linked early problems with syntax to subsequent reading difficulties. Some of these tasks might be considered measures of inflectional morphology. Overall, the ultimate goal of reading is to read for understanding; without understanding meaning in language, reading cannot effectively take place.

Studies of morphological awareness in relation to reading in very young readers often focus on word recognition. In addition, the studies reviewed above involved primarily orally administered morphological awareness tasks. If morphological awareness is developmentally predictive of early reading, it must be the case that oral, rather than written, versions of these tasks are used. At the same time, with increased reading experience, it is possible that reading and morphological awareness are bidirectionally related. A similar case might be made for morphological

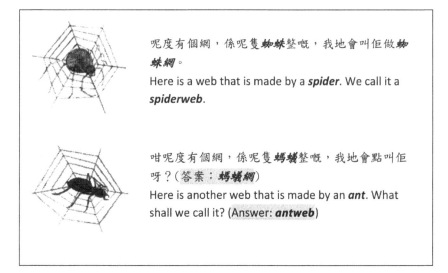

呢度有個網，係呢隻**蜘蛛**整嘅，我地會叫佢做**蜘蛛網**。

Here is a web that is made by a *spider*. We call it a *spiderweb*.

咁呢度有個網，係呢隻**螞蟻**整嘅，我地會點叫佢呀？（答案：**螞蟻網**）

Here is another web that is made by an *ant*. What shall we call it? (Answer: *antweb*)

FIGURE 4.2 Example of an item from the morphological construction test that is applicable in both Cantonese and English.

awareness and writing. The association of morphological awareness to literacy skills in more advanced readers is considered next.

Morphological awareness in developing readers

Experience with print probably helps children to develop their morphological awareness in several ways. First, reading may help to clarify morphemic boundaries. Carlisle (1996) gave the example of identifying *of* and *course* as two separate morphemes in the phrase *of course* for a boy who had previously represented it in his writing as *ofcors*, demonstrating an initial assumption that this phrase was a single morpheme. Seeing *of course* in print helped him to understand that this was a phrase consisting of separate morphemes. In Chinese, too, the one-to-one correspondence between syllables and morphemes may become more explicit as children learn to read and write characters. Second, seeing print may highlight certain aspects of language as morphemes. For example, the apostrophe marking possession in English might underscore the importance of *'s* as a morpheme. Changes in spelling for masculine and feminine in French might have a similar effect (e.g. *bon* vs *bonne*). Third, reading may facilitate children's understanding of morphological structure. For example, once children see *ed* representing the past tense across texts, they may become more likely to identify this as a consistent marker of it. In contrast, among younger children, this marker may not be as clear, because it can be pronounced different ways (e.g. /d/, /t/, or /ed/), although it is consistently spelled as *ed*. We write *walked*, rather than *walkt*, despite the fact that one could arguably present this word accurately purely vis-à-vis phonology, but not morphology, in both ways. Bilingual children learning French and English in Canada also were shown to make use of morphological awareness (in the form of inflections for past tense) to learn to read longitudinally in grades 1–3 as well. This was true within and to some extent across languages (Deacon, Wade-Woolley, & Kirby, 2007). A subsequent research study demonstrated a bidirectional association between word reading and morphological awareness in English (Deacon, Benere, & Pasquarella, 2013). Pittas and Nunes (2014) showed that a combination of inflectional and derivational morphological awareness in Cypriot Greek children was uniquely associated with word reading as well, with other variables typically associated with word reading, including time 1 word reading, verbal IQ, and phonological awareness, statistically controlled.

Correlational evidence that various tasks of morphological awareness are important for a variety of literacy-related skills is growing. For example, Leong (2000) demonstrated that fourth- to sixth-grade children's knowledge of derivational morphology was associated with spelling skill. This was true whether the children were assessed using measures of accuracy or speed on the tasks of morphology. Rispens, McBride-Chang, and Reitsma (2008) found that morphological awareness in the form of derivational morphology was associated with both word reading and spelling in grade 6 Dutch children. Carlisle (2000) showed that morphological knowledge was strongly associated with reading comprehension in children in grades 3 to 5. The association of morphological awareness to reading comprehension was stronger in fifth than in third graders, but significant in both. Furthermore, in typically developing Arabic speakers, morphological awareness was uniquely associated with reading comprehension in children in grades 3 through 6 (Mahfoudhi, Elbeheri, Al-Rashidi, & Everatt, 2010). Windsor (2000) also looked at 10–12-year-old children's knowledge of derivational morphology in relation to reading. She found that derivational morphological awareness contributed unique variance to both word recognition and reading comprehension in these children, some of whom had language-learning disabilities. Moreover, she noted that children's performances on opaque derivations predicted substantially more variance in reading than did performance on transparent ones. Opaque derivatives are those in which the pronunciation of the base word changes with the derivative (e.g. *hero/heroism*; *actual/actuality*), whereas the base word pronunciation remains the same for transparent derivatives (e.g. *allow/allowable*; *diet/dieter*). Windsor interpreted her results as suggesting that some of the importance of derivational morphology for reading may be associated with phonological processing.

In Chinese and Japanese, studies of morphological awareness have focused on ways in which young readers use word structures to understand the meanings of words. The structure of both Chinese characters and kanji, the Chinese characters used to represent Japanese, are helpful in giving children clues to the meanings of both familiar and unfamiliar words (e.g. Hatano, Kuhara, & Akiyama, 1981; Shu & Anderson, 1997; Shu, Anderson, & Zhang, 1995). This phenomenon is due, at least in part, to the fact that approximately 80 per cent of Chinese characters are comprised of a semantic radical in addition to a phonetic. As highlighted in the previous chapter, the semantic radical often gives some clue to the meaning of the word. For example, the semantic radical representing mouth is found in other words related to *mouth*, including *drink*, *sing*, and *kiss* (Nagy & Anderson, 1999). In Japanese, which can be represented orthographically using both kanji and kana, which is a sound-based (syllabary) system, children find it easier to access word meanings using the former, more clearly morphologically based system.

Shu and Anderson demonstrated the importance of semantic radicals for children learning to read Chinese. They found that third and fifth graders clearly made use of semantic radicals to read unfamiliar characters. In addition, children judged to be relatively better readers by their teachers tended to use semantic radical information for reading more than those who were not as proficient in reading. Similar results have been obtained in Hong Kong, Beijing (Chan & Wang, 2003), and Taiwan (Tsai & Nunes, 2003). In these studies, children began to use semantic radicals systematically to read pseudo-words from the ages of seven to nine years. Tong and McBride-Chang (2010) further demonstrated that for second graders radical awareness is a unique skill, separable from morphological awareness, though it overlaps with morphological awareness in fifth graders. These studies demonstrate that radical awareness is important to consider for reading and writing in Chinese children.

Another aspect of morphological awareness in more sophisticated readers is its reciprocal association with vocabulary knowledge. As we become more sophisticated readers, vocabulary is gained through reading. For example, Nagy and Anderson (1984) estimated that American children may learn up to 3,000 words per year from third to twelfth grade. Many of these vocabulary words are comprised of patterns of morphemes that are recognizable and can give clues to the meanings of these words. Wysocki and Jenkins (1987), for example, demonstrated that fourth and eighth graders were able to generalize morphological knowledge in identifying new words. For example, if they had learned a word such as *anxious*, they were more likely to figure out the meaning of the word *anxiety*. The authors termed this ability 'morphological generalization'. If you have ever had any coaching in how to improve your score in a college entrance exam that tests vocabulary knowledge, for example, you may have been coached in the art of morphological generalization.

In fact, it has been estimated that, in approximately 60 per cent of new words students learn, morphemes that can help them to understand their meanings can be identified; moreover, only a small percentage of vocabulary words gained (perhaps 200–300 per year) are attributable to direct instruction (Nagy & Anderson, 1984). Thus, much of our developing vocabulary probably depends on reading and reading experience. Stanovich reviewed evidence for a reciprocal association of vocabulary knowledge and reading comprehension. Although his focus was on more general processes of reading and reading development rather than on morphological awareness per se, his conclusions are applicable here: '[overall], children who are reading well and who have good vocabularies will read more, learn more word meanings, and hence read even better' (2000, p. 184).

One study of American children (McBride-Chang, Wagner, Muse, Chow, & Shu, 2005) demonstrated that our tasks of both morpheme identification and morphological construction (see Figures 4.1 and 4.2) uniquely predicted vocabulary knowledge in pre-school children and second graders.

The complicated relations among morphological awareness, vocabulary knowledge, and reading comprehension have also been demonstrated. For example, Ku and Anderson (2001) gave an experimental test of incidental learning of new Chinese characters to fourth graders in Taiwan. They found that children's reading of passages facilitated knowledge of new characters. In addition, children's knowledge of semantic radicals was strongly related to their vocabulary acquisition test scores in this experiment. Kieffer and Box (2013) showed in both native English speakers and in Spanish-speaking children learning to read English as a second language that morphological awareness (in English) was associated not only with reading comprehension but also with vocabulary knowledge. Thus, reading fosters greater vocabulary knowledge. Partly as a consequence, it can also stimulate morphological awareness.

Given the strong association of morphological awareness to reading, explicit teaching of morphological awareness may be extremely useful in facilitating later reading skills (Adams & Henry, 1997; Leong, 2000). Indeed, Leong noted that such instruction is particularly important for children who have reading difficulties. A focus on morpheme patterns in any given orthography will probably be useful, because children tend to benefit from the explicit teaching of rules of their script.

In English, for example, 'With approximately 25 prefixes, 40 suffixes, 50 Latin roots, and 50 Greek roots creating many thousands of words, teaching these forms to all children makes excellent sense' (Adams & Henry, 1997, p. 434). Others (e.g. White, Power, & White, 1989) have argued likewise that, within an appropriate linguistic framework, morphological instruction will be quite helpful in facilitating students' vocabulary knowledge and, ultimately, their reading comprehension. Explicit morphological training is further recommended to improve children's spelling skills as well (Apel & Werfel, 2014).

In Chinese, explicitly teaching semantic radicals has already been tested as part of an experimental instructional reform in approximately 160 first and 160 fourth graders (Wu, Anderson, Li, Chen, & Meng, 2002). Students whose teachers explicitly linked semantic radicals to meaning in the characters performed better in morphological awareness tasks at the conclusion of the study, of possible long-term benefit in promoting reading. Zhou and colleagues (2012) further demonstrated that a focus on lexical compounding training over a few weeks helped to improve Chinese children's word reading.

Morphological awareness is, then, multi-faceted. Its measurement and its importance change across languages and with literacy development. Among older children in particular, teaching of morphological awareness is likely to focus fairly explicitly on orthographic patterns across scripts, such as using *ed* to represent past tense, whether it sounds like /t/ as in *walked* or *ed* as in *waited*. What orthographic skills entail and how they develop is the topic of the next chapter.

Suggested readings

Bauer, L., Lieber, R., & Plag, I. (eds) (2013). *The Oxford reference guide to English morphology*. Oxford: Oxford University Press.

Fábregas, A., & Scalise, S. (eds) (2012). *Morphology: From data to theories*. Edinburgh: Edinburgh University Press Ltd.

Lieber, R., & Stekauer, P. (eds) (2009). *The Oxford handbook of compounding*. Oxford: Oxford University Press.

Lieber, R., & Stekauer, P. (eds) (2014). *The Oxford handbook of derivational morphology*. Oxford: Oxford University Press.

Ravid, D. D. (2012). *Spelling morphology*. New York, NY: Springer.

Saiegh-Haddad, E., & Joshi, R. M. (eds) (2014). *Handbook of Arabic literacy*. London: Springer.

5

VISUAL AND ORTHOGRAPHIC SKILLS IN READING AND WRITING

In this chapter, I consider the importance of early visual and orthographic skills in learning to read. Compared to the vast literature on phonological awareness in relation to early reading, there is relatively little research on visual and orthographic predictors of literacy development. Historically, this lack of interest is attributable both to a relative lack of data supporting a link between visual skills and reading, and to a plethora of data demonstrating a clear and strong association between phonological processing skills and reading.

Nevertheless, interest in both basic visual and orthographic skills is evident and has emerged from those with diverse theoretical focuses, including Chinese reading development (e.g. Ho & Bryant, 1999; Lee, Stigler, & Stevenson, 1986), alphabetic reading (e.g. Berninger, 1994; Franceschini, Gori, Ruffino, Pedrolli, & Facoetti, 2012), and dyslexia (Lovegrove & Williams, 1993; van der Leij et al., 2013). I will begin by distinguishing and relating visual and orthographic knowledge to literacy development. After that, I will discuss visual information in relation to reading alphabetic and Chinese orthographies. Both visual and orthographic skill development are influenced by cognitive maturation and experience with print, as detailed next. I will also review studies on the effects of visual skills and orthographic abilities on reading development and, equally, the potential effects of reading on pure visual skills. Finally, I will briefly highlight some research studies on visual-motor skills in relation to literacy outcomes.

Visual and orthographic knowledge defined

Although both visual and orthographic knowledge are considered in this chapter, they often represent diverse literatures in reading research. They are sometimes considered together because, crudely, reading across orthographies involves print,

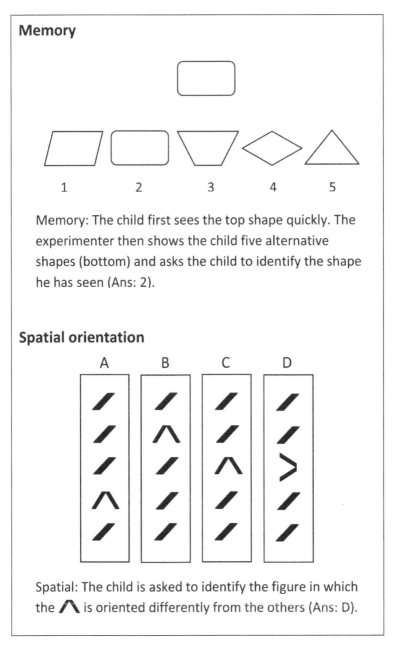

Memory

Memory: The child first sees the top shape quickly. The experimenter then shows the child five alternative shapes (bottom) and asks the child to identify the shape he has seen (Ans: 2).

Spatial orientation

Spatial: The child is asked to identify the figure in which the ∧ is oriented differently from the others (Ans: D).

FIGURE 5.1   Two examples of visual skills.

which is visually perceived. Thus, both visual and orthographic knowledge make use of what is written on the page. Let me begin by offering some definitions of terms used in this chapter. As you will recall from your reading of Chapter 1, I use the terms *orthography* and *script* interchangeably to mean the print system used to write words in a language. In this chapter, I use the terms *visual skills* or *visual abilities* to refer to those abilities that make use of visual information not related to print. For example, remembering the shape of a two-dimensional object and figuring out which shape differs from the others in spatial orientation (see Figure 5.1) are two examples of visual skills.

In contrast, the terms *orthographic skills* and *orthographic knowledge* both refer to an understanding of how graphemes (units of print, such as letters or Chinese radicals) are written correctly in a given orthography. An example of orthographic knowledge is the understanding, either implicitly or explicitly, that English words cannot begin with double consonants (*bb*, *cc*, or *vv* never begin a word in English). We might demonstrate such knowledge simply by acknowledging that a word starting this way 'looks wrong'. Another example of orthographic skill is the understanding that, although both *eat* and *eet* share the same pronunciation in English, only the first word is a correct orthographic representation of the word.

Pure visual skills are of interest for understanding reading and spelling development precisely because they do not involve reading itself. Visual tasks, including perception and recall of pictures or shapes, are often used to measure young children's visual skills. Such visual skills have also been administered to different readers to determine whether they differ in these skills with age or reading experience. Demonstrating a link between visual skills and reading might suggest a developmental progression from basic visual processing to word recognition, which involves visual detection of specific orthographic patterns. In other words, visual skills might later help children to recognize patterns of their script, such as the fact that every English word must contain a vowel (e.g. *chr* and *bmt* are not possible words).

Orthographic knowledge, though defined in various ways, is consistently measured with print itself (e.g. Wagner & Barker, 1994). Definitions of orthographic processing vary both in their specificity (e.g. sometimes orthographic ability is defined in terms of letter units, a problem for orthographies such as Chinese, which do not have such units) and in how confounded orthographic and phonological skills are considered to be. It is likely that orthographic and phonological knowledge are associated across orthographies (e.g. Berninger, 1994), but the degree to which they can be distinguished may vary across scripts. For example, adult Chinese readers can pronounce characters they have never seen before only about 40 per cent of the time (Hung & Tzeng, 1981), whereas some clue to the pronunciation of English words is consistently available. Thus, recognition of unfamiliar words is easier in English than it is in Chinese because there is a stronger overlap between orthographic and phonological information in English than in Chinese.

There are a few studies that demonstrate some connection between visual skills and orthographic skills. For example, Lavine (1972, cited in Berninger, 1994) found that young non-readers tended to distinguish print from pictures. By age five, English-speaking pre-readers were 100 per cent accurate in identifying letters in Roman or Hebrew as writing but only 20 per cent accurate in categorizing Chinese characters as writing. Thus, prereaders aged three to six appear to be engaged in a gradual appreciation of the basic features of print (e.g. Chall, 1983). This distinction applies to children learning a variety of orthographies, including Chinese (Chan & Louie, 1992), Hebrew (Levin, Korat, & Amsterdam, 1996), and English (Adi-Japha

& Freeman, 2001). Not surprisingly, what children are clearest in defining as print is the print to which they have substantial exposure. Perhaps this marks the transition from visual to orthographic skills.

These writing system examples are good illustrations of the connection between visual and orthographic skills. Although children at this level often cannot yet read anything, they have become aware that print is distinguishable from other stimuli. There are certain perceptual features of each script that may affect the relation of visual and orthographic skills to reading development in specific orthographies. For example, in Ehri's (2005) four-phase theory of reading development, the first phase is called the pre-alphabetic phase. In this phase, children learn to recognize a word based on a distinct visual feature of it. For example, *yellow* has two sticks in the middle of it and can be recognized for this reason. Presumably, Chinese characters offer many salient visual cues through which to recognize each as well.

Much of this review of visual skills in relation to reading focuses on print itself. How does this differ from orthographic skill? When I discuss visual skill in relation to reading, the visual skill focuses only on global understanding of print in space and orientation rather than on specific orthographic patterns of print. In contrast, orthographic skill focuses on children's knowledge of specific print patterns. Such patterns require some inherent ability to identify and understand the functions of words or characters, or their parts, as such.

Visual skill development in English

In alphabetic orthographies such as English, each word is distinguishable from the next because it is represented by a string of letters surrounded by blank space on the page. In English or German, words are of varying lengths – some quite short, such as *I* (*Ich*) or *me* (*Mich*) and others quite long, such as *butterfly* (*Schmetterling*). Thus, children learning to read an alphabetic orthography can make use of this spacing to distinguish among words.

In fact, young children often assign special physical meaning to alphabetic words of varying lengths, demonstrating their early sensitivity to this spatial cue. In particular, they tend to view long words as symbolizing big things and short words as symbolizing small things. Thus, in this view, *train*, a big thing, would require more letters than *caterpillar*, a small thing. A similar phenomenon has been demonstrated in Spanish and Italian children (Ferreiro, 1988, cited in Bialystok, 1997). Thus, the layout of the text may affect young children's understanding of it and this often leads to initial confusion.

Research on visual skills in relation to alphabetic reading has a long history (Orton, 1925). In particular, early research on the source of reading disabilities focused on visual deficits as the central explanation for these problems. For example, poor readers often appeared to reverse letters in their writing and even reading (e.g. mistaking *b* for *d*, and so on). Vellutino and colleagues (1977) did much to dispel this idea that dyslexia is a visually based problem. In a series of studies they demonstrated that poor readers are able to copy unfamiliar scripts (in this case, Hebrew given to non-Hebrew-speaking children) about as well as typically developing readers. At least some of the visual reversals of letters of the alphabet observed in reading-disabled older children and non-reading-disabled younger children are, therefore, attributable to the children's inexperience with print. Children who spend time with print will become more knowledgeable about many aspects of print relative to those who do not spend so much time with it (Stanovich, 1986). Script orientation is one of the central aspects of print.

Experience and age are often strongly associated in development, and both are important for perceptual development of script. Early research (Gibson, Gibson, Pick, & Osser, 1962) showed that children become more proficient in distinguishing letter-like forms with age. Bornstein and colleagues (1978) demonstrated that, although infants often distinguish some rotations (e.g. top/bottom) of objects as different, they tend to perceive left–right reversals as similar. They asserted that, because left–right reversals generally occur in the environment as mirror images of each other (representing the same thing), infants naturally view such reversals as representing the same object. This tendency to view mirror images as representing the same object might explain some of children's early letter reversals (e. g. of *b* and *d*, or *p* and *q*) (For a longer discussion of this point, see Dehaene (2009).)

Although these examples focus on young children, I have seen first-hand how inexperience with print can cause perceptual confusion in an adult. Outside my university building, a Hong Kong Chinese street painter, who did not know any English, was working on painting a bilingual street sign to alert pedestrians to oncoming traffic. (All signs in Hong Kong are posted in both Chinese and English.) The Chinese sign had been painted the night before, and the painter had just finished painting the English sign when I saw him. He clearly knew that there was an error in the sign, as he stood looking at his painting, which said 'KOOL RIGHT →', and scratched his head. However, it was equally clear that he was confused as to what the precise error he had made was. I was impressed by this error, because it so nicely illustrates the perceptual difficulties we all have in making sense of unfamiliar print. Perhaps the fact that the sign was on a street, so that it could be viewed from various angles, made it more confusing than a sign posted in an upright position, which can only be viewed from one direction. It was probably unclear to this man whether, for example, the *L* or the *K* was incorrectly positioned as a mirror image of itself or whether, as was actually the case, these letters were themselves positioned in correct spatial orientations but incorrectly placed on opposite ends of the word they were forming. Inexperience with an orthography leads to simple perceptual representational errors. Conversely, experience is crucial in developing perceptual accuracy in that script (Miller, 2002).

Although learning to recognize graphic symbols is part of the early reading process (Gibson & Levin, 1975), relatively little work has been done on the early development of visual skills and reading. In particular, there are few longitudinal studies of changes in visual skills and reading over time. Most studies of visual skills and reading focus on comparing visual skills among children (or adults – e.g.

Kolinsky, Morais, & Verhaeghe, 1994) with different reading proficiency levels. Tasks tapping visual skills include those of visual memory, figure–ground distinctions, spatial orientation skills, and discrimination of pattern similarities from differences. The central issue in these sorts of studies is whether those who are skilled in learning or using visual information are better readers than those who do not make use of such information (or, alternatively, whether better readers have better visual skills). Such studies cannot demonstrate a causal connection between visual skills and subsequent reading (Willows, Kruk, & Corcos, 1993).

However, these studies do demonstrate that differences in visual skills are associated with reading ability and age. For example, Willows et al. (1993) found developmental differences in visual perception between reading-disabled and typically developing English-reading children. Younger reading-disabled children were slower and less accurate than non-disabled children in identifying whether two unfamiliar visual stimuli (Hebrew letters for non-Hebrew speakers) were the same or different, using a computer presentation. Such visual perceptual difficulties appear to be most prominent in younger children (aged six) and to disappear by around age eight. Vellutino, Scanlon, and Chen (1994) also noted that older children tend to perform consistently better across visual tasks than younger children, regardless of reading skill. Given this short overview, we turn now to ways in which visual skills and reading are linked in Chinese.

Visual skill development in Chinese

There are two overarching ways in which alphabetic orthographies differ from Chinese. These are spatial orientation in the reading process and visual information contained within the script. Spatial orientation includes aspects of print such as how print and space are alternately displayed on a page, and the orientation of print in reading it. Each Chinese character, representing a single morpheme, is allotted the same square space on a printed page. Thus, in Chinese, whether a word or concept is comprised of four characters or only one, a developing reader is provided with no clue by the page layout of Chinese text as to where one word or concept ends and another begins.

The fact that each Chinese character takes up an identical amount of space on the page also means that Chinese text can be read flexibly, typically in a left-to-right, top-to-bottom, or even right-to-left orientation (Chen & Chen, 1988). Other scripts vary from English in orientation. For example, Hebrew is read in a right-to-left orientation. However, Chinese may be unique in having more than one orientation permissible in reading.

Attention to visual detail may also be particularly important in reading Chinese, as compared to alphabetic orthographies, because of the very fact that each Chinese character is contained within an identical square space on the page. More visual information is contained within Chinese characters than within English words (Chen, 1996). Although all of English writing is comprised of letter strings of varying lengths made up of different patterns of 26 letters, Chinese readers must master over 4,500 characters, with different visual stroke patterns, in order to read fluently. This difference in visual information presented across orthographies has prompted several observations that both skilled and developing Chinese readers make greater use of visual and spatial skills in reading as compared to American readers (Tzeng & Hung, 1988). Leek and colleagues (1995) also demonstrated that, among adults, the recognition of single characters was primarily based on visual information. Thus, visual perceptual skills may be important for reading development in Chinese. Unfortunately, empirical evidence to support this hypothesis is modest.

In early Chinese character acquisition, left–right spatial reversals sometimes occur, as they do in English (Bornstein et al., 1978; Gibson et al., 1962). For example, Lu and Jackson (1993, cited in Geva & Willows, 1994) found that pre-readers in Taiwan had difficulty with mirror-image rotations of Chinese characters, though their ability to distinguish characters in a right-side-up versus upside-down orientation was good. This natural perceptual focus changes only with experience with one's script.

Miller (2002) demonstrated this clearly in a comparison of Chinese and English monolingual four- and five-year-olds in Beijing, China, and Champaign-Urbana, Illinois, USA, respectively. The American children were significantly better, in comparison to the Chinese children, at distinguishing the spatially reversed alphabetic words (real words in both Pinyin, the alphabetic coding system used in China, and in English) from the nontransformed words. In contrast, the Chinese children were significantly better than the American children at identifying the spatially transformed (reversed) Chinese character from among three Chinese characters. As Miller (2002) summarized, 'Children show an awareness of the visual structure of their writing system before formal reading instruction. This understanding is limited to the orthography they see around them' (p. 25).

Substantial research on visual skills in relation to Chinese reading development has surfaced in the last 20 years or so. A number of these studies have demonstrated a positive association between various visual skills and Chinese character recognition (e.g. Huang & Hanley, 1995; Lee et al., 1986; McBride-Chang & Chang, 1995; Siok & Fletcher, 2001). Other studies have not found significant associations of visual abilities with Chinese reading (e.g. Ho, 1997; Hu & Catts, 1998; Huang & Hanley, 1995; 1997; McBride-Chang & Ho, 2000b). Overall, the correlation between pure visual skills and word reading in Chinese appears to be moderate and to be stronger in younger as compared to older Chinese children (for a review and meta-analysis, see Yang et al., 2013). However, the research paradigm adopted by most of these studies was to examine whether visual skills predicted unique variance in Chinese character recognition once other reading-related skills were statistically controlled. Thus, in many studies, various visual skills are, themselves, positively and significantly correlated with Chinese character recognition. However, these associations are not of particular interest unless they are uniquely predictive of reading. What is striking about these studies is that a variety of visual skills were tested in different ages of children, with mixed results. There is as yet no clear pattern of particular visual skills uniquely and consistently predicting Chinese reading.

However, although the history of reading research is fairly long, relatively little attention has been paid to the role of visual skills in reading. Furthermore, most attention to visual skills in reading has focused on the field of reading disability, rather than on typical reading development (Stanovich, 1993). There has been little time or effort devoted to understanding the types of visual skills that might best predict early print recognition. There has been even less effort devoted to exploring, theoretically, what visual skills might be expected to predict early reading based on the orthography to be learned. One notable important exception to this comes from a cross-cultural longitudinal study carried out by Ho and Bryant (1999).

In this comprehensive study of how visual skills predict reading development, the researchers tested visual skills in children who were not yet reading and found that children's early sensitivity to shape constancy uniquely predicted later Chinese character reading. They also examined how visual skills were related to early English reading development. Among English readers, they found that different visual skills, spatial orientation sensitivity, and figure–ground distinctions were longitudinally predictive of English reading skill. Lee et al. (1986) obtained similar results for their first-grade English-reading sample; spatial orientation was particularly associated with the children's reading skills. These findings support those of Miller (2002), who focused on the importance of the specific orthography to be learned in relation to visual skills. Among young Chinese readers, distinguishing among strokes of different types and sizes may be key in learning to recognize Chinese characters. In contrast, among English readers, awareness of the correct orientation of the letters that begin words, such as *p*, *b*, or *d*, is necessary to ensure that a word is correctly identified. The varied graphic features of Chinese and English scripts may require sensitivity to different visual aspects of print. As children make use of visual skills to learn to read in their respective orthographies, different abilities may serve to facilitate reading differently in different orthographies.

At the same time, as in so much of development, perhaps as children learn to read their orthography, their visual skills are honed in the process. That is, it is likely that visual skills and reading skills are bidirectionally associated. Hoosain (1991) suggested that learning to read might improve certain visual skills in Chinese. McBride-Chang, Zhou, and colleagues (2011) showed that time 1 word reading by itself explained a unique 13 per cent of the variance in pure visual skill among Hong Kong Chinese kindergartners, even with time 1 visual skill statistically controlled. In that study, word reading appeared to be a stronger longitudinal predictor of visual skill than was visual skill of word reading. This study reflected individual variability in visual skills and word recognition within a given group.

However, the issue of how word reading might explain pure visual skill can be explored across groups or scripts as well. Some scripts are more visually dense than others, and this might matter for visual attention or developing of visual skills. For example, Chinese contains the most individual visual units to be memorized, given that individual Chinese characters number in the thousands. Some Indian scripts can also require several hundred unique visual patterns to be memorized. In contrast, alphabets have small numbers of unique visual units, typically around 22 to 30 as letters in most alphabets. Nag (2007; 2011) categorized scripts in terms

TABLE 5.1 Proposed models for the transitional development from visual to orthographic knowledge in English and Chinese. Across writing systems, steps 2–8 are strongly overlapping; these may develop in a different order from that listed or simultaneously. These models await future research studies for support and changes.

	English
	1. Distinguish print from pictures
Overlapping	2. Distinguish English alphabet from other writing systems (e.g. Chinese) but not from other scripts with Roman alphabet features (e.g. Spanish)
	3. Distinguish English words from words in other languages (e.g. Spanish)
	4. Visual cue recognition – word is recognized from its salient context or feature(s)
	5. Letter knowledge (names, sounds)
	6. Elementary word recognition
	7. Distinguish legal from illegal orthographic patterns (e.g. *bb* is not a permissible orthographic unit at the beginning of a word)
	8. Reading and spelling depend upon and predict orthographic skill
	Chinese
	1. Distinguish print from pictures
Overlapping	2. Distinguish Chinese from other writing systems but not from other orthographies using characters (e.g. Korean, Japanese)
	3. Distinguish Chinese from other scripts that make use of Chinese characters (Korean, Japanese)
	4. Visual cue recognition – word is recognized from its salient context or feature(s)
	5. Elementary word recognition
	6. Logographeme knowledge develops and facilitates the learning of new characters
	7. Distinguish legal from illegal orthographic patterns in compound characters (e.g. where and when to use phonetic and semantic radicals)
	8. Reading and spelling depend upon and predict orthographic skill

of visual complexity, from extensive Chinese to contained alphabets. She further argued that more visually confusable or difficult scripts might foster better visual skills. For example, Chinese children tend to manifest better visual skills than do Greek- (e.g. Demetriou et al., 2005) or Hebrew- or Spanish-speaking (e.g. McBride-Chang, Zhou, et al., 2011) children, presumably because learning to read Chinese facilitates their visual attention. We (McBride-Chang, Chow, Zhong, Burgess, & Hayward, 2005) also found that children learning to read the simplified script, which contains about 22.5 per cent fewer strokes, i.e. visual information,

FIGURE 5.2 How font (an aspect of visual skill) can affect word recognition (orthographic skill) for the word *lion*, in English and Chinese, respectively. You may find the same word easier or more difficult to identify depending upon the font in which it is written.

per character as compared to the traditional one, tended to show superior visual skills than did those learning the traditional script in one study. These findings are preliminary but point to the idea that the script that is learned may influence one's visual skills in subtle ways, particularly for children in the beginning stages of learning to read.

Having reviewed some findings on the association of pure visual skills and reading, we turn now to research on orthographic abilities and literacy. An overview of the transition from visual skill to orthographic knowledge is given in Table 5.1. I propose that this transition is different for English and Chinese, with the warning that, for steps 2–8 in each writing system, it is clear that there is overlap. These steps do not, however, necessarily follow each other in a stage-like manner.

Orthographic skills and alphabetic reading

As in the discussion of visual skills and reading above, a review of the association of orthographic skills to reading may best be illustrated by an English/Chinese contrast. The interrelations of visual and orthographic skills are highlighted for both English and Chinese in Figure 5.2, which shows the same word, *lion*, printed in various fonts. It is clear that the shapes of these representations vary in this figure. It is also clear to a reader that all represent the same word. In contrast, a non-reader might fail to see the similarities across each representation.

English is an important orthography to consider when talking about orthographic skills in reading and spelling because it is notoriously difficult for children to learn to read due to its large number of exception words. Exception words represent a core of the top 150 most frequently used words in printed school English and include words like *two* and *through* (Adams, 1990). These are called exception words because they do not represent a regular pairing of letter and letter sound. In addition, both of these examples have homophones (*to, threw*) that are visually quite different from the original two words presented although they are pronounced identically. Letter–sound correspondences can be extremely confusing in English, because its 44 phonemes are represented by only 26 letters (Foorman, 1995).

We are reminded of the confusions of English print letter–sound correspondences when we find ourselves having to explain to pre-schoolers why *cat* is spelled with a C but *kite* is spelled with a K, why *cereal* begins with a C but *sun* with an S, or why *giant* begins with a G but *jelly* with a J. In English print, it is estimated that there are more than 2,000 rules (Venezky, 1970). Children must clarify and internalize these varied and often arbitrary patterns as they develop into expert readers and spellers because merely relying on visual memorization to learn to read and spell will, at some point, strain their capacities for pure visual memorization. A comprehensive study of children learning to read across Europe (Seymour et al., 2003) demonstrated that British children attained the level of proficiency of French children in their native script about two years later in development. At the same time, French children take longer to learn to read than do German or Italian children, because of differences in orthographic transparency across spelling systems.

Thus, children begin to notice at some point rules of their orthography that may help them to remember the growing number of words they are learning. An orthographic cue in English might be using one's knowledge of the word *rough* to read one new word correctly (*tough*) or to read another one incorrectly (*dough*).

A typical English test of orthographic skill is to have students distinguish which of two real English words, homophones of each other, answers a particular question (e.g. 'Which word is a number? *One/won*'). Another such task involves having the students identify which word is a real word from a pairing of two spellings (e.g. *back/bak*) (Foorman, 1995). Those who score higher on such tasks tend to be better readers overall.

Orthographic development and alphabetic reading

Given this overview of orthographic knowledge and alphabetic reading, the development of orthographic skill in relation to reading will now be considered. Willows and Geva (1995) described how pre-school children gradually adapt to the orthographic constraints of their language. First, pre-schoolers begin to distinguish print from non-print. For example, they distinguish pictures from script. Across diverse scripts, including Hebrew, Chinese, and Dutch, children around the age of two appear to distinguish pictures from writing when asked to draw vs write, and adults can also judge with above chance-level accuracy which of these children's productions were intended to be pictures vs writing (for a review, see Treiman & Kessler, 2014). In making this initial differentiation, however, they may not necessarily understand that different languages are associated with different orthographies. Theoretically, any orthography could represent an overall, vague cognitive concept of script for the child. Thus, Spanish, Arabic, or Chinese may be equally representative of print to a Chilean child. Next, pre-schoolers can distinguish very different writing systems from their own. For example, a French Canadian child could distinguish Hebrew or Chinese from French. However, children are easily misled by the physical features of print. In particular, those who know a script with Roman alphabet features may confuse that script with others that have in common a Roman alphabet, e.g. confusing French with English. As children begin to learn to spell and read, they can finally distinguish their own script from those that may initially have looked similar.

Once these distinctions have been made, children's orthographic knowledge may be characterized by some basic visual recognition of a few words. Children may initially recognize alphabetic words based on visual cues rather than based on letter–sound correspondences. Thus, the visual salience of the word is important (e.g. *queen* is distinctive because it has a tail), and letter-name and letter-sound knowledge are not as clearly relied upon (e.g. Ehri, 2005). An early reliance on visual features in print has also been observed in Arabic (Abu-Rabia, 1995). However, researchers debate the extent to which such a phase of reading development distinctly exists and whether it is universal or script-specific (e.g. Bastien-Toniazzo & Jullien, 2001; Sprenger-Charolles & Bonnet, 1996; Wimmer & Hummer, 1990).

Assuming a period in which visual cues are essential for reading, Gough and Juel (1991) noted that the first words recognized by children learning to read an alphabetic orthography have two important characteristics. First, they are often identified before decoding begins, or even before much of the alphabet is learned. Second, these words are sometimes recognized largely through context. For example, a child may read 'McDonald's' every time she passes the golden arches. Similarly, many children learn to read the word 'Coke' on a red can. However, these children can no longer 'read' these same words when they are printed on a piece of paper. Thus, it appears that young children note a particular cue about the word – perhaps something about its placement in context – to associate the printed word with its oral referent.

Gough and Juel (1991) carried out a study with children who could not yet read in order to demonstrate this phenomenon. In this study of American children, four- and five-year-olds learned four words presented on flash cards. One of the cards had a thumbprint in the lower-left corner. This card was learned faster than the other three for every child. However, when the word was presented without the thumbprint, children could no longer identify the word correctly. Thus, the visual cue was the important feature of the word stimulus on which the children were focused.

There is also evidence of cue reading out of context. Young children often recognize a few words that are visually distinctive. *Zoo*, for example, may have a particularly interesting appearance and may therefore be recognized early, even when children are not yet clear about the identities of the letters within the word. This phenomenon of cue reading also explains why developing readers learn dissimilar words better than similar ones but sometimes make overgeneralizations across them (e.g. confusing *cat* for *car*).

Bastien-Toniazzo and Jullien (2001) asserted that, in all alphabetic orthographies, as long as children understand the importance of print as one of encoding meaning, rather than sound, they tend to focus on the visual properties of a word. In alphabetic orthographies, letter order is not important at this phase. Instead, children connect one or a few letter cues to recognize the word. As children learn more words in print, more letters must be recognized in each word in order to distinguish them. Age is not the primary factor in determining early visual discrimination sophistication – rather, experience is. For example, illiterate adults make the same types of errors of early visual word recognition as children do (see the discussion in Bastien-Toniazzo & Jullien, 2001). Based on their research with French five-year-olds, Bastien-Toniazzo and Jullien recognized the great variety of early literacy skills pre-readers have. Some know many letters of the alphabet; some know just a few. The authors summarized the period of visual cue reading as follows:

> The duration of this phase is impossible to determine as a general rule; it most likely depends on how rich the experience of each individual is. One can reasonably assume that it is very brief for a subject living in a stimulating environment, and that it may last quite some time otherwise or in cases where certain disorders are involved.
>
> *(Bastien-Toniazzo & Jullien, 2001, pp. 138–139)*

It may also be reasonable to assume that the phase of cue reading might depend upon the orthography being learned. The consistent correspondences between letter names and letter sounds may facilitate faster word recognition skill development in German or Italian than in French or English, which are relatively less transparent orthographies. Thus, it is possible that the visual cue phase of reading in German or Italian may be very short relative to that in French or English.

A different visual approach to word reading has been noted by Share and Gur (1999). Because Hebrew does not have upper-case letters and each letter is written within a space of uniform size, children learning to read this orthography may be forced to rely on multiple visual cues to recognize words. Although the authors noted that some children do make use of a single visual cue to recognize some words, they also found evidence that many young children could recognize several words based upon several cues within the word. Such a strategy has not been recognized in children learning to read other orthographies. However, identification of this strategy is clearly important in underscoring the dynamic relations among script, environment, and cognitive development in children or, perhaps, anyone learning to read for the first time.

At the same time, recall from Chapter 3 that Siegler's overlapping waves model predicts that children may use several strategies simultaneously to solve problems. Children's use of these strategies is primarily dependent upon how adaptive they are to the problem in hand. As applied to the question of cue recognition, for example, it may be that children often use visual cues to recognize print, but the nature of these cues themselves may vary or might be combined in practice. Globally, context is useful in the environment for distinguishing one's favourite soft drink in a can. As applied to word recognition out of context, children will be most likely to use cues when the print to be recalled is visually distinct. However, when another strategy, say, involving some knowledge of letter names and sounds, is more efficient for recall, children will make use of this alternative either independently or in combination with the original visual cue.

In Chapter 3 it was mentioned that letter-name knowledge tends to be a strong initial predictor of word recognition. Part of the reason for this is that letter names are helpful for making a letter name–letter sound connection, an early initiation into phonological awareness. However, another reason for this connection is suggested by Foorman (1994), who notes the importance of early visual recognition of these symbols, which may be important for distinguishing among words. This again suggests a link between visual and orthographic skills.

With letter-name knowledge and experience with print, sensitivity to orthographic patterns in English words emerges early. As reviewed by Berninger (1994), first-grade children are capable of distinguishing orthographically regular words from both pronounceable and illegal non-words. Children can also code words more easily and quickly than single letters in a comparison (e.g. forced-choice, same/different) task from around the age of six. Orthographic knowledge across scripts may take on a number of important dimensions that remain relatively unexplored thus far (Nag, 2007; 2011). One very striking phenomenon at the group level is that adult native speakers of Arabic reading Hebrew as a second language actually read Hebrew faster than Arabic because of the denser visual information contained in Arabic (Abdelhadi, Ibrahim, & Eviatar, 2011; Ibrahim, Eviatar, & Aharon-Peretz, 2002). The orthography of a language can, thus, influence even expert reading of it.

Thus, unlike visual skills, for which there remains limited evidence of any causal or unique connection with reading skill, the importance of orthographic knowledge for reading is clear across scripts. For example, in a study (Coenen, van Bon, & Schreuder, 1997), Dutch first and second graders demonstrated activation of orthographic knowledge in both spelling and reading. In a separate longitudinal study of the relationship of orthographic skills to word identification from first to second grade, Wagner and Barker (1994) demonstrated a causal association between orthographic skill and subsequent reading. Even after statistically controlling for the effects of word recognition in first grade, verbal ability, and phonological skills, orthographic knowledge uniquely predicted word recognition in second grade.

Stanovich and colleagues (1991) reviewed correlational studies of the use of orthographic skills and reading in both adults and children. Across studies, orthographic skills contributed unique variance to reading skill once phonological processing skills were statistically controlled. Conrad, Harris, and Williams (2013) demonstrated the unique importance of orthographic skills for explaining both word-reading and word-spelling skill beyond phonological processing as well. Although orthographic knowledge is unique, it is also facilitated in alphabetic orthographies by phonological skills (e.g. Ehri, 2014). Thus, although precise measurement of orthographic processing in alphabetic scripts remains somewhat controversial (e.g. Conrad et al., 2013), orthographic skills develop early, are uniquely predictive of reading and spelling, and continue to develop with reading experience (Berninger, 1994; Conrad et al., 2013; Ehri, 2014).

Orthographic knowledge in Chinese

The development of orthographic knowledge in Chinese is described clearly by Ho and colleagues (2003). Their model specifies that, initially, Chinese script is distinguished from pictures but not from other scripts. With experience, Chinese children come to distinguish their Chinese orthography from those with some similar features, such as Hanja in Korean or kanji in Japanese. Eventually, Chinese children become aware that their script is either the simplified one, used in Singapore and mainland China, or the traditional one of Taiwan and Hong Kong. Early ideas about Chinese reading acquisition were that Chinese characters were learned as logograms (Baron & Strawson, 1976), a hypothesis that was subsequently abandoned in the face of much evidence to the contrary. However, it is likely that Chinese children learn their first characters using a visual strategy of recognizing a salient graphic feature of the character (Ho & Bryant, 1997a), as demonstrated for young alphabetic readers (Bastien-Toniazzo & Jullien, 2001). In fact, Chinese characters' visual distinctiveness may foster more visual categorization strategies than do the visual configurations of alphabetic words. Interestingly, McBride-Chang and Ho (2000a) found that English letter name recognition was strongly associated with initial Chinese character recognition among Hong Kong pre-school children. Part of our explanation for this finding was that simple visual skills are important in the initial recognition of both elementary Chinese characters and English letters. For very young developing readers, it is likely that Chinese characters are initially recognized based on a feature of the character, or even on the simple visual distinctiveness of the character. Thus, for example, (fewer) numbers of strokes in a character and symmetry of the character both result in children's facilitated writing of Chinese characters (Yin & Treiman, 2013).

Visual cue recognition may be a strategy used for a longer period of time in Chinese as compared to alphabetic orthographies, because Chinese characters have fewer reliable sound cues than English words. Moreover, Chinese children need to learn a good number of characters before they begin to recognize patterns in the components that make up compound characters (Ho et al., 2003). Unlike children learning an alphabetic orthography, who tend to focus on initial letters in a word, especially their own names, for writing and recognition of it, Chinese children appear to focus particularly on visual characteristics of a given character comprising their names, regardless of its position within the name. Thus, visual properties of characters are quite important for initial learning of them (Yin & Treiman, 2013).

Lau and Leung (2004) hypothesized a stage of logographemic awareness to explain Chinese children's reading development. As children are exposed to Chinese print, they develop knowledge of character subcomponents called logographemes. These logographemes represent units of print that recur across characters. Such units are separable and replaceable, and may represent a character, radical, or single

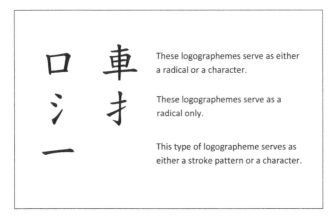

These logographemes serve as either a radical or a character.

These logographemes serve as a radical only.

This type of logographeme serves as either a stroke pattern or a character.

FIGURE 5.3 Some examples of Chinese logographemes. Logographemes represent units of print that recur across Chinese characters, representing a character, radical, and/or stroke pattern.

stroke. They may or may not have a meaning or a pronunciation. Some examples of logographemes are given in Figure 5.3.

Evidence for the existence of logographemes comes from studies in which young children (from kindergarten to lower primary school) showed better recognition of new characters that contained higher-frequency logographemes as compared to non-characters with low-frequency logographemes. These results suggest that young Chinese children make use not only of phonetics and semantic radicals but also of other levels of orthographic information learned in the process of character acquisition. Such orthographic knowledge facilitates subsequent character learning.

With sufficient character knowledge, children make use of both phonetic and semantic radicals as an aid to remembering new Chinese characters. For example, the phonetic meaning to *climb* (pronounced *dang1*), is found in the character *lamp*, which is also pronounced *dang1*. If a child already knows the character *dang1* (*to climb*), this will help her to learn the new character, *lamp* (Ho & Ma, 1999) (see Figure 5.4).

Another analogy that can be made in Chinese is one with a semantic radical, which gives a clue to the meaning of the character. For example, the character or radical (it is used for both) *mouth* is also found in the characters for the words *sing* and *kiss*. Therefore a child recognizing the *mouth* radical may find it easier to remember the meanings of the Chinese characters *sing* and *kiss* (as demonstrated in Figure 3.8). In research on orthographic knowledge in developing and intermediate readers, researchers often test children's abilities to make use of orthographic cues in the reading process.

Early work on orthographic knowledge among Chinese children required them to manipulate both phonetic and semantic radicals in various ways. In some studies, children are asked to distinguish the correct orientation of these radicals from

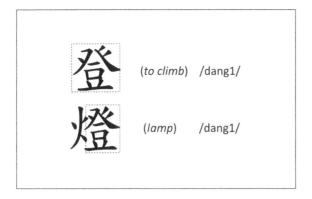

FIGURE 5.4   In Chinese, the pronunciation of 登 is the same as that of 燈. Knowing the pronunciation of the first can help in learning the second because they share the same phonetic radical 登.

those that are backwards, upside down, or positioned in another strange way (e.g. Zhong, McBride-Chang, & Ho, 2002). In other studies, children are asked to make decisions as to whether characters, comprised of radicals in either legal or illegal positions, are real (Ko & Wu, 2003). Orthographic knowledge tends to be associated with reading skills in Chinese. The careful reader will note, however, that, as in alphabetic orthographies, demonstrating such knowledge requires the presence of certain reading abilities, so that it is not always clear whether good orthographic skills actually facilitate word/character recognition or whether they are merely a by-product of solid reading abilities. It is likely that both processes are important.

What is certain, however, is that, despite an absence of explicit teaching of semantic radicals or phonetics across most Chinese regions, children manifest clear understanding of the functions of these character components fairly early (e.g. Yin & McBride, 2015). Some sensitivity to these character components appears at least from the age of about five (Chan & Wang, 2003). At this age, for example, training in semantic radical knowledge facilitated better spelling of Chinese words (Lam & McBride-Chang, 2013). However, complete understanding of radical forms and functions is not completely integrated until approximately ages 10–12 years (e.g. Ho et al., 2003; Ko & Wu, 2003). Sensitivity to the orthographic components of Chinese characters helps children learn new words (Tsai & Nunes, 2003; Yin & McBride, 2015). Moreover, preliminary evidence using an evoked-related potential methodology suggests that Chinese children with dyslexia may fail to make use of radical position effects effectively in character recognition (Chung, Tong, & McBride-Chang, 2012). Collectively, these results suggest some bidirectionality of the associations of orthographic knowledge to reading development in Chinese. For example, with reading experience, children develop sophisticated orthographic knowledge of Chinese characters. At the same time, older children typically demonstrate more sophisticated orthographic knowledge than younger children.

A final aspect of orthographic processing in relation to Chinese is the effect of script itself on processing. Unlike most other orthographies, Chinese can be written either in simplified or traditional characters. Do these different scripts affect orthographic processing during reading? One interesting study, which examined the effects of visual perception in Chinese character recognition, was designed by Chen and Yuen (1991), who hypothesized that visual skills might be more important for distinguishing among simplified, as opposed to traditional, characters. Chen and Yuen (1991) indeed found that those from mainland China tended to use more visually based strategies in their responses as compared to the traditional character users from Hong Kong and Taiwan. The authors asserted that simplified characters tend to be more visually similar to one another than are traditional characters because, in the process of simplification, the numbers of strokes within the characters were substantially reduced. Peng, Minett, and Wang (2010) compared college students reading the same characters (there is an approximate 50 per cent overlap between simplified and traditional characters in common). Half were from the mainland and half were from Hong Kong. They demonstrated that the mainland students showed very early signs of detection of stroke additions or subtractions for the characters presented; those Hong Kong students who read the traditional script did not. They suggested again, similar to Chen and Yuen's (1991) findings, that perhaps learning to read the simplified script might make such readers more sensitive to slight variations in changes within a character. This idea is intriguing, though very tentative.

Visual-motor skills

A final area to consider in relation to literacy development, including both word reading and writing, is a focus on visual-motor skills. An analogy between pure visual skills and learning to read and visual-motor skills and learning to spell seems appropriate here. Vellutino and colleagues (1975) showed that children with reading difficulties did not differ from those without them in copying unfamiliar print (in this case, Hebrew, something that was equally unfamiliar to all the English-speaking children in the study). This was important because it helped establish that reading difficulties in English appear to be less of a visual problem and more of a phonological one. Nevertheless, researchers continue to explore the role of visual-motor skills in reading variability (e.g. Santi, Francis, Currie, & Wang, 2014). Much of the time, they conclude that visual-motor skills are not uniquely associated with literacy skills, though visual-motor skills do tend, individually, to be moderately and positively correlated with reading and spelling skills (e.g. Santi et al., 2014). However, some researchers (e.g. Frith, 1980; Seymour & Porpodas, 1980) have occasionally argued that spelling differences in alphabetic orthographies might be attributable to variability in spatial or sequencing skills. Moreover, Richards and colleagues (2011) showed that those they identified as poor writers made use of more neural regions of the brain in learning to write a novel stimulus, suggesting inefficiency in the visual-motor skills related to writing.

Tan and colleagues (2005) made the case that for Chinese in particular, visual-motor skills in the form of copying might be important for learning to read and write. Chinese has a long history of copying and calligraphy for learning. Especially among younger Chinese children, delayed copying of either characters (Pak et al., 2005; Tan et al., 2005) or other visual stimuli such as shapes (e.g. Tan et al., 2005) is associated with variability in literacy-learning skills. In one study (McBride-Chang, Zhou, et al., 2011), we showed that compared to those without dyslexia, Chinese children with dyslexia were poorer in writing unfamiliar stimuli including Hebrew, Vietnamese, and Korean symbols with which both groups were equally unfamiliar. In a follow-up study of kindergartners from mainland China, we found that such copying of unfamiliar stimuli and also delayed copying of characters were independently and uniquely associated with early Chinese dictation/spelling skills (Wang, McBride-Chang, & Chan, 2014). In another study (Kalindi et al., 2015), we showed that those with dyslexia in Chinese tended to have particular difficulties with pure copying of unfamiliar stimuli. Whether copying continues to be of interest in future work is yet to be determined. Very few studies have examined this across contexts, particularly in relation to reading and spelling development in non-Chinese orthographies. It is not unreasonable to anticipate that the production pattern of pure copying skills (for unfamiliar stimuli) might be bidirectionally associated with learning to spell across scripts, similar to the pattern of visual skill in relation to word reading, which is a purely perceptual/recognition pattern. However, the extent to which visual-motor skills, either in the form of copying or other abilities, emerges as potentially important for spelling in orthographies apart from Chinese remains to be determined.

What's next?

The issue of visual and orthographic skills may be expanded in future work. As researchers focus more on print, such as the akshara languages of India or Chinese, that requires greater visual attention to master both for the purpose of word recognition and word writing, it is possible that greater interest in pure visual skills may emerge. For example, it is still possible that pure visual skills of some sort might serve as important predictors of early literacy beyond phonological and morphological awareness for some scripts; we have not yet exhausted all visual skills or scripts in pursuing this line of research. In addition, some of the most interesting issues in the area of visual and orthographic skills might be related to statistical learning in young children. Rebecca Treiman and her colleagues have carried out important work in this area, showing that children have some sensitivity to their own print very early, and perhaps more could be done with this to understand the process by which children transition from implicit to explicit learning about print. Essentially, how do children go from making use of certain patterns in print without knowing that they know this to making explicit use of such knowledge to learn new patterns? The extent to which there is a link between pure visual skills and orthographic awareness is unclear as well. Should one expect to see that variability in processing of visual stimuli might be associated with variability in orthographic knowledge? How would this process evolve? Finally, how visual-motor skills related to writing and spelling, particularly for young children, develop deserves more exploration. This was a relatively well-researched topic for those interested in English reading and writing many years ago, but since then interest in this area has declined markedly. Again, in some scripts that have many diacritics or many visually easily confusable units, perhaps greater attention to early visual-motor skills could help. Research in these areas is limited and can be expanded with greater attention to multiple scripts.

Suggested readings

Adelman, J. S. (2012). *Visual word recognition, vol. 1: Models and methods, orthography and phonology*. East Sussex, United Kingdom: Psychology Press.

Dehaene, S. (2009). *Reading in the brain: The new science of how we read*. New York, NY: The Penguin Group.

Saiegh-Haddad, E., & Joshi, R. M. (eds) (2014). *Handbook of Arabic literacy*. New York, NY: Springer.

Rayner, K., Pollatsek, A., Ashby, J., & Clifton, C. (2011). *Psychology of Reading, 2nd edn*. New York, NY: Psychology Press.

Stein, J., & Kapoula, Z. (eds) (2012). *Visual aspects of dyslexia*. Oxford: Oxford University Press.

6

DYSLEXIA

A primary goal of many researchers in the field of literacy development is to help those who have reading difficulties to learn to read better. This chapter focuses on those children who have particular difficulties in learning to read. Various labels have been used to describe particular reading problems, including *dyslexia*, *reading disability*, or *specific reading retardation*. Historically, children with apparently specialized problems in reading have been of great interest to clinicians, teachers, and researchers. Early definitions of specific developmental dyslexia focused on three factors that distinguished a dyslexic from a typical poor reader. Dyslexic children were defined (Snowling, 2000) as poor readers who:

1. had had adequate instruction in reading
2. had had ample sociocultural opportunities
3. had normal intelligence.

Other poor readers, whose reading difficulties might be attributed to a host of problems related to poor-quality teaching, sociocultural deprivation, or lower intelligence, were of less theoretical interest. In educational practice, dyslexic children have been defined primarily based on a discrepancy between their IQ and their reading scores (Stanovich, 2000). It is fairly easy for educators to obtain an IQ score for any given child; it is much more difficult to explore a given child's instructional or sociocultural history. Thus, a focus on IQ has been of primary importance for most researchers interested in diagnosing dyslexia.

Although the term *dyslexia* remains popular, a central aspect of its definition – that IQ is important for distinguishing different types of poor readers – appears to be false (Siegel, 1989; Snowling, 2000). Poor readers with different IQ scores tend to perform similarly in tasks of word recognition and have not been distinguished neuroanatomically (Stanovich, 2000). Moreover, there is no evidence that different remediation strategies are implicated for poor readers of varying IQ levels, particularly for promoting basic word-recognition skills (e.g. Scanlon & Vellutino, 1997). The demonstration that poor readers with varying levels of IQ appear to have similar reading skills and reading needs argues strongly against using an IQ-reading performance discrepancy to distinguish among and help children with reading problems.

In fact, there is ample evidence that an IQ-reading performance discrepancy focus in the field of reading disabilities has done more harm than good. An excellent in-depth analysis of the consequences of this focus is offered by Stanovich (2000). From a developmental perspective, the discrepancy notion did a disservice to all poor readers, because, historically, it required students to have been exposed to reading instruction for a fairly long period. One could not officially be diagnosed as dyslexic until the particular reading problem had had time to emerge. Thus, depending upon when formal reading instruction began in a particular location, specific reading disability was unlikely to be diagnosed until at least two to three years following school entry. This presents a practical problem for poor readers: the later remediation for reading problems begins, the less effective it is likely to be (e.g. Adams, 1990). Conversely, early intervention with children with reading difficulties, regardless of IQ, is likely to help prevent them from falling further behind in reading (Foorman, Francis, Shaywitz, Shaywitz, & Fletcher, 1997).

The question of whether IQ and even other abilities are important in diagnosing, understanding, and helping poor readers is important to consider across cultures. Across the world, regions vary in the definitions they use to identify dyslexia. To prepare for a talk I gave several times in 2014 and 2015, I asked friends who happen to know the research in the Philippines, Zambia, Greece, Switzerland, Austria, Korea, Hong Kong, China, and Israel, among others, how dyslexia is diagnosed in each place, respectively. Answers varied widely. For example, probable diagnosis of dyslexia is possible in Hong Kong as early as first grade but not until fourth or fifth grade in Israel. In some places, such as Greece, IQ is measured as part of the diagnosis of dyslexia, and in others, such as Korea, this is not a focal point for diagnosis. The identification of children at risk for dyslexia is sometimes dependent upon teacher selection, as in Greece and Austria, and sometimes dependent upon a broad screening tool, as in Korea. Sometimes instead of a focus on dyslexia, the focus tends to be more broadly on learning disabilities as a whole, such that the concept of attention deficit hyperactivity disorder being part of the overall diagnosis is expected, as in the Philippines. Tests for dyslexia sometimes require untimed word recognition tests, as is typical in English-speaking and Chinese-speaking countries, and sometimes only timed ones, as in German-speaking Switzerland and Austria, places using German, an orthography that is so regular that even dyslexic children ultimately read it accurately, just very slowly.

Indeed, from a global perspective, the concept of dyslexia, in terms of criteria for identification, is not particularly clear. Indeed, even the basic concept of dyslexia has been questioned given a lack of coherence in definitions and a lack of evidence (for a critical review of this issue, see Elliott & Grigorenko, 2014). At a minimum, most researchers expect that dyslexia is defined based on difficulties in reading in the native language. In Zambia and in the Philippines, there are few or no tests given in the native language since children learn English in school quite early and there are many different home languages. In the following research overview, therefore, please keep in mind these anomalies and confusions. Throughout the chapter, the terms *reading disabled*, *poor reader*, and *dyslexic* will be used interchangeably to reflect the concentration on specific reading problems at the word level, including word reading and word writing. This is as clear as we can be at this point in history.

The following text outlines some of the cognitive deficits that have been found to be associated with reading problems in children. Across orthographies, the most striking cognitive deficit among poor readers is in the realm of phonological processing. This evidence will be reviewed first. After that, the chapter considers the evidence for other deficits, including rapid automatized naming and the so-called double-deficit hypothesis (Wolf & Bowers, 1999), in poor readers. Next, the relation between reading disability and biology will be explored. The chapter ends with a discussion of what might be the most effective identification and remediation techniques to use with children at risk of reading problems.

Phonological processing and reading disability

Across alphabetic orthographies, there is a consensus that a fundamental problem shared by the majority of reading-disabled children is that of phonological processing, a topic we covered extensively in Chapter 2. In a variety of tasks involving perception, production, manipulation, and memory for speech segments, dyslexic readers, as a group, perform more poorly than typically developing readers (e.g. Adams, 1990; Blachman, 1997; Snowling & Stackhouse, 2013). What is perhaps most striking is that even as adults, the majority of reading-disabled individuals exhibit some phonological processing deficits. It looks as though, even when they have become adequate readers, in some sense overcoming their reading difficulties, they still have a core deficit, related to phonological processing (Bruck, 1992). For example, adults who were diagnosed as dyslexic in childhood tend to be slower in speeded naming tasks and to have persistent problems in spelling–sound correspondences (Bruck, 1993; Tops, Callens, van Cauwenberghe, Adriaens, & Brysbaert, 2013). Poor readers tend to have difficulties in all of the phonological processing tasks reviewed there. The idea that dyslexics are specifically weak in phonological processing makes the label *dyslexic* clinically appealing. For physicians, clinicians, and educators, dyslexic readers are not having difficulties merely because of lack of experience in reading; rather, they appear to have a specific disorder that impedes reading development. A phonological impairment has been implicated in studies of dyslexic children in a variety of languages, including French (Sprenger-Charolles, Cole, Lacert, & Serniclaes, 2000), Greek (Porpodas, 1999), Chinese (e.g. Ho, Leung, & Cheung, 2011) and German (Wimmer, Mayringer, & Raberger, 1999).

Because alphabetic orthographies differ in the transparency of their grapheme–phoneme correspondences, however, dyslexic children may exhibit phonological problems at different ages in different places. For example, by fourth grade, German children characterized as dyslexic did not differ from their normally reading peers in measures of phonological awareness, though they still exhibited spelling problems, in one study (Wimmer, 1996). German is a relatively transparent orthography to learn to read. That is, letter–sound correspondences are consistent in this orthography. Therefore, it is a relatively straightforward task to master such correspondences, to manipulate them in phonological awareness tasks, or to make use of them to read new words. In contrast, in a study involving French, a relatively inconsistent alphabetic orthography, ten-year-old French dyslexics were deficient in a variety of phonological tasks relative to their normally reading peers (Sprenger-Charolles et al., 2000).

The importance of a phonological deficit for explaining reading and spelling difficulties is highlighted in studies that match reading-disabled students with younger readers of the same reading level. Fundamentally, reading-disabled children have difficulties in a variety of different skill domains. Problems in reading may slow general knowledge and vocabulary acquisition relative to normally reading peers, for example. In addition, dyslexic readers often have difficulties in tasks of rapid naming and sometimes even non-language measures requiring speeded responses (e.g. Nicolson, Fawcett, & Dean, 2001; Sprenger-Charolles, Siegel, Jimenez, & Ziegler, 2011; Zhou et al., 2014). Indeed, as one research team asserted, 'It is difficult to imagine a skill that, when appropriately measured in a sufficiently large sample, will not yield statistically significant differences between dyslexic and normal readers' (Fletcher et al., 1997, p. 101).

To control statistically for some of the cognitive processes involved in reading, a dyslexic group is often compared to a reading-level match control group (e.g. Metsala, Stanovich, & Brown, 1998; Rack, Snowling, & Olson, 1992; Sprenger-Charolles et al., 2011). This younger group presumably has many of the cognitive skills of the dyslexic group, because reading scores do not differ across the two groups. Logically, if word-recognition skills are constant across groups, but particular cognitive deficits emerge in the dyslexic group relative to the reading-matched control group, such deficits may represent especially important characteristics of poor readers. This is because, by definition, younger children often have less sophisticated cognitive abilities than older children. For example, younger children tend to be slower at processing information and to have more limited memory capacities compared to older children or adults. Typically, then, a comparison of an older and younger group should yield overall superior performances by the older group. For poor readers matched to younger reading-matched controls, however, phonological deficits emerge consistently in English (e.g. Manis, Seidenberg, Doi, McBride-Chang, & Peterson, 1996; Stanovich, Siegel, Gottardo, Chiappe, & Sidhu, 1997) and in other alphabetic orthographies (e.g. Sprenger-Charolles et al., 2011). Studies that demonstrate poor phonological skills in poor readers relative to reading-matched controls suggest that their reading difficulties stem in large part from their deviant phonological abilities (Sprenger-Charolles et al., 2011).

Importantly, for learning to read Chinese, since phonemic awareness is unnecessary, sometimes phonological awareness does not emerge as strongly as a prominent correlate of reading difficulty (e.g. Ho, Chan, Chung, Lee, & Tsang, 2007; Shu, McBride-Chang, Wu, & Liu, 2006). Instead, rapid automatized naming and morphological awareness are relatively clear markers of dyslexia in some studies (e.g. Ho, Chan, Lee, Tsang, & Luan, 2004; Lei et al., 2011; McBride-Chang, Lam, et al., 2011; Shu et al., 2006). Orthographic skills, which depend partly on beginning the process of learning to read and to write words, also are important markers of dyslexia in Chinese children (e.g. Chung, Ho, Chan, Tsang, Lee, 2011; Ho et al., 2004; Woo & Hoosain, 1984). Given the many homophones and homographs in Chinese, meaning-related abilities are essential for learning Chinese.

Beyond phonological processing: speed of processing

Across orthographies, slowness in completing tasks of rapid automatized naming is perhaps the clearest 'universal' characteristic of dyslexic readers. As reviewed by Wolf (1997), speeded naming deficits are evident in poor readers of German, Dutch, Finnish, and Spanish. In one study of Chinese dyslexics (Ho, Chan, Tsang, & Lee, 2002), the majority suffered a speeded-naming deficit. Regardless of the phonological demands of the orthography, poor readers tend to be slow. A prominent issue among researchers focusing on children's reading development and impairment centres on the nature of rapid automatized naming. Tasks of rapid automatized naming involve so many of the processes required in fluent reading that it is difficult to isolate a cognitive construct likely to account for the strong association between tasks of naming speed and word or character recognition. Tasks of speed are associated with a variety of cognitive processes (Kail, 1991). Those who are faster at one task tend to be faster and more skilled at other cognitive tasks too.

From this perspective, speeded naming primarily represents fluency. Poor readers are simply slow to automatize a variety of cognitive abilities, including reading itself. Indeed, slowness, even in tasks of motor skill, has been demonstrated in some studies of poor readers (e.g. Nicolson et al., 2001; Nicolson & Fawcett, 2011). The idea that dyslexics' primary difficulty with the speeded-naming task is general slowness is simplistic, however, because poor readers are not necessarily slower in every aspect of a naming-speed task, and this varies across cultures (Georgiou, Papadopoulos et al., 2014).

Because tasks of naming speed involve so many processes, it is likely that other facets of the task are also important correlates of reading. For example, given the prominence of visual/orthographic deficits in Chinese poor readers, the visual sequencing elements of a speeded-naming task may be important in Chinese and possibly other orthographies. The phonological aspect of the task, which requires children to remember and articulate the names of things, is also centrally implicated (Wagner & Torgesen, 1987). Finally, the 'arbitrariness factor' discussed by Manis et al. (1999) in relation to the development of reading may also play a part in poor readers' problems. The idea that, in speeded-naming tasks, children are required to pair a name with a visual stimulus, and that language is used arbitrarily for such pairing, may be crucial for poor readers. In fact, among normal readers, Windfuhr and Snowling (2001) demonstrated that paired visual–verbal associate learning, in which a new visual stimulus was paired with an arbitrary verbal label, was significantly associated with measures of phonological awareness. Moreover, skill in paired associate learning contributed unique variance to reading in these children. Litt and Nation (2014) have also demonstrated that performance in tasks of paired associate learning in which a verbal and a visual stimulus are paired is important for distinguishing children with and without dyslexia. Such paired associate learning distinguishes dyslexic and non-dyslexic children in Chinese as well (e.g. Li, Shu, McBride-Chang, Liu, & Xue, 2009). These findings suggest that flexibility in the ability to match oral with visual referents, primarily a phonological labelling task, may be an additional important factor in explaining why rapid automatized naming tasks are such useful clinical predictors of reading problems across orthographies.

Double deficit?

Along with the interest in the nature of speeded naming, researchers focusing on this particular task have highlighted another apparent factor in reading and spelling problems. This is the link between the number of cognitive deficits evident in poor readers and their relative difficulties with reading itself. In a series of studies (for a review, see Peterson & Pennington, 2012; Wolf & Bowers, 1999) analysing various data sets, there is the suggestion that, in alphabetic orthographies, poor readers who demonstrate a deficit in either speed of processing or phonological awareness alone are less impaired than dyslexic children who have significant deficits in both abilities. This idea has been referred to as the double-deficit hypothesis (Wolf & Bowers, 1999). According to this hypothesis, children impaired in speeded naming may require different remediation efforts to those children who are poor only in tasks of phonological awareness. Those with both deficits have the fewest cognitive resources for coping with their reading problems. These children may require both phonological and fluency training, as reviewed later in this chapter.

Other studies also support the basic premise that children with more than one cognitive deficit will have more severe reading problems than those with a single problem. For example, in their examination of dyslexic Chinese children, Ho et al. (2002) demonstrated that those with more than one cognitive difficulty, including speeded-naming, visual, orthographic, or phonological impairments, tended to be among the poorest readers of the group. Among American readers, those with more than one deficit in reading-related skills, including orthographic processing, phonological processing, or speeded naming, also tend to develop literacy skills more slowly than those with only a single deficit (Stage, Abbott, Jenkins, & Berninger, 2003).

From a practical perspective, the idea that more than one cognitive deficit spells more trouble for poor readers is sensible. After all, having fewer cognitive resources available to an individual to carry out the complex task of reading decreases the probability that efficient processing of print can take place. For example, across many studies of children's reading, correlations of phonological awareness with IQ scores is moderate to high; IQ and reading are similarly associated (e.g. Stanovich, 2000). These associations suggest that various cognitive skills implicated in reading build on one another. From an information-processing perspective, the more cognitive resources an individual has, the easier a task of cognitive processing is; the fewer cognitive resources available, the poorer reading will be.

These ideas have been extended to studies of brain functioning in children with reading difficulties as well (Norton et al., 2014). Norton and colleagues found that compared with those with only difficulties in RAN tasks or with phonological awareness tasks alone, those with difficulties in both kinds of tasks had overall brain activation in specific regions. They had less activation in the fronto-parietal reading network than did those with just a phonological awareness deficit. In addition, compared to those with a RAN deficit only, they demonstrated lower activation in the cerebellum. Children without reading difficulties showed higher activations in both regions, as compared to children with deficits in just a single area.

Dyslexia and biology

As the work by Norton and colleagues (2014) described above demonstrates, reading problems appear to have a neurobiological origin. In studies of poor readers of English (Scarborough, 1989) and Danish (Elbro, Borstmm, & Petersen, 1998), for example, reading problems were more common in those children with at least one dyslexic parent as compared to children whose parents were typical readers. Phonological decoding and phoneme awareness skills were also strongly associated in studies of twins with and without reading problems. Furthermore, there is evidence that there is a genetic heritability component to orthographic skills, at least in English (for a review, see Olson, Wise, Johnson, & Ring, 1997). Overall, dyslexia appears to be substantially heritable. Moreover, dyslexia is more highly heritable in those whose parents have a high level of education, possibly highlighting the biological or genetic underpinnings of dyslexia (e.g. Gabrieli, 2009). This genetic component to reading skill underscores the importance of neurophysiological and neuropsychological investigations of reading impairment. In particular, are there areas of the brain that appear to differ among those with and without specific reading impairments?

Techniques used to examine reading development and impairment in children include the measures with high spatial resolution, such as functional magnetic resonance imaging (fMRI) technology, and measures with high temporal resolution such as the event relation potential (ERP) method. The ERP measure is a technique used to look at readers' processing of stimuli across time, millisecond by millisecond. This technique makes use of individual electrodes on the scalp to record the electrical activity of the brain. The fMRI technique is used to examine which parts of the brain are used in various tasks. It records blood flow to the brain in order to pinpoint specific brain regions. Some researchers are currently attempting to combine methods looking at temporal and brain activations in order to understand fully how reading takes place and, correspondingly, the nature of reading difficulties.

There is some consensus that those who suffer reading problems in alphabetic languages tend to have identifiable variability in brain functioning linked to phonological processing (e.g. Norton et al., 2014). Word recognition appears to be associated in particular with three left-hemisphere neural systems, namely, the frontal, temporoparietal, and occipitotemporal regions (e.g. Gabrieli, 2009; Paulesu, Danelli, & Berlingeri, 2014). In one cross-cultural study, adult dyslexics, relative to normally reading controls, demonstrated low activity in the left temporal lobe while reading (Paulescu et al., 2001). This study, which included disabled readers of Italian, English, and French, showed that the Italians tended to read better than did their English and French counterparts. This was expected because of the nature of the Italian orthography, which is relatively transparent and therefore easier to master because of its consistent sound–symbol correspondences. However, relative to their respective normal reader matched groups, all three dyslexic groups were low-scoring in tasks of both reading and phonological processing. Based on the consistent correspondences between brain functioning and reading and phonological processing, Paulesu et al. (2001) argued that the source of reading difficulties across orthographies is disrupted processing in the left temporal cortex. Similar studies of dyslexic children, varying widely in age from seven to eighteen (Shaywitz et al., 2002; Temple et al., 2001) have demonstrated similar brain patterns. In addition, younger and more reading-impaired children tend to show less brain activation in the left temporal region of the brain compared to those who are older or better readers (Shaywitz et al., 2002). These data fit nicely with behavioural evidence that reading, like most other cognitive processes, is affected both by development, as determined by age, and by individual differences within a given age level.

There is some evidence that Chinese readers make use of some brain regions associated with reading impairment that are slightly different from those used to read alphabetic orthographies. In one study, for example, those with difficulties in reading Chinese showed reduced activation in the left middle frontal gyrus (LMFG) region in comparison to those without dyslexia; however, no differences were found in the activation of the brain in the posterior regions, which are commonly reported to be associated with reading impairment in dyslexia in alphabetic languages (Siok, Niu, Jin, Perfetti, & Tan, 2008). These authors argued that the complex visual-spatial structure of Chinese characters demands detailed visual-spatial computation, and the LMFG is proposed to be associated with the processing of visual-spatial and verbal information as well as to coordinate cognitive resources (Tan et al., 2005; Tan et al., 2003). However, Hu et al. (2010) reported that developmental dyslexics in Chinese exhibited strikingly similar brain patterns to their English counterparts. That is, they found that compared with matched typically developing readers, those with dyslexia in either Chinese or English both showed reduced activation in the left middle frontal gyrus, the left posterior middle temporal gyrus, the left occipito-temporal cortex, and the left angular gyrus. These authors suggested that there is a universal neural origin for both Chinese and English dyslexia. This issue remains up for debate, and more research is clearly needed in this area.

Speeded functioning may also be important for reading and linked to brain functioning (e.g. Christodoulou et al., 2014; Galaburda, 1999; Temple, 2002). The focus of this work is on the processing of information at the millisecond level (Tallal, Miller, Jenkins, & Merzenich, 1997). Tallal and colleagues noted across several studies that children with language-processing problems often have difficulty in distinguishing and sequencing sounds, both tones and stop consonants. Although relatively many studies highlight this difficulty of processing tone, speech, or other auditory stimuli that children with reading problems manifest (for a review, see Goswami, 2011; Zhang & McBride-Chang, 2010; 2014), the difficulties children exhibit in processing speech could also be attributable to an underlying temporal processing deficit that extends to the visual modality too (Farmer & Klein, 1995; Tallal et al., 1997).

Temporal order processing requires one to identify, distinguish, and sequence a series of two or more stimuli that are presented one after another. Across several studies involving discrimination of either visual (e.g. dots, light flashes) or auditory (e.g. tones, rhythms) stimuli, poor readers tend to demonstrate a temporal processing deficit. Farmer and Klein (1995) argued that such a deficit may be causally associated with reading, and with visual-temporal processing problems leading to possible difficulties in orthographic processing and/or lack of exposure to print. Auditory temporal processing would be most strongly associated with deficits in phonemic awareness.

In a correlational study of this model involving 35 children ranging in age from 11 to 18 years of age, and 32 adults, all of whom were poor readers, this idea was tested with measures of visual and auditory temporal order processing tasks and measures of reading (Booth, Perfetti, MacWhinney, & Hunt, 2000). These researchers demonstrated that only temporal auditory processing performance predicted unique variance in non-word reading, a measure of phonological processing in children. Only rapid visual ability was predictive of exception-word reading, a measure of orthographic processing, in children. Thus, among children, different types of temporal order processing were associated differently with reading involving primarily phonological and orthographic abilities. In contrast, in adults, rapid auditory ability was strongly associated with both phonological and orthographic processing; rapid visual skill was no longer predictive of orthographic processing. These results were interpreted as demonstrating that rapid visual skill deficits become less important for reading in adulthood, whereas rapid auditory skill deficits persist throughout adulthood among poor readers (Booth et al., 2000). On the other hand, Ben-Yehudah and colleagues (2001) showed that reading-disabled Hebrew speakers had particular difficulties in processing sequentially presented visual stimuli, relative to normal readers.

It is intriguing to consider the temporal order processing deficit across orthographies for three reasons. First, it explains the clear difficulties of poor readers in alphabetic orthographies. This theory is compatible with a great deal of evidence that the majority of poor readers of alphabetic orthographies exhibit phonological processing deficits (e.g. Gabrieli, 2009). Second, this theory is more inclusive an explanation for deficits among the poorest Chinese readers, many of whom may manifest no obvious phonological deficits (e.g. Ho et al., 2002). Indeed, it predicts that visual difficulties may be evident among poor readers, particularly in early childhood, and this is what has been found in a number of studies of Chinese poor readers, as reviewed above (Ho et al., 2002). Third, it might help explain why poor readers across orthographies are consistently distinguished by a speeded naming task (e.g. Klein, 2002). Tasks of speeded naming involve all of the problems that stand out among poor readers across orthographies: phonological skills, speed, and visual sequencing.

On the other hand, neuropsychological evidence for this deficit remains scant. As is typical of the majority of studies on reading development, most studies of brain functioning in disabled readers rely on correlational analyses, which cannot explain the causal associations of structure and behaviour (e.g. Goswami, 2014). Moreover, a temporal order processing deficit is probably difficult to localize in the brain. This is unappealing for researchers and educators, who spend considerable time with those with obvious reading problems. Such reading problems do not appear to pervade every aspect of life for poor readers. Much of the difficulty is merely to do with core reading skills. Thus, it seems strange that such a pervasive problem in the brain would be so localized in relation to specific reading behaviours.

Another important issue is the extent to which this deficit might be a manifestation of general slowness. Nicolson and Fawcett (Nicolson et al., 2001; Nicolson & Fawcett, 2011) have asserted that poor readers' core difficulties are ones of automatization. They claim that functioning in the cerebellum best explains developmental dyslexia. In this theory, it is not phonological processing that is centrally implicated in dyslexia but a more general cerebellar deficit.

One study that could be used to support either a phonological processing or more general temporal order processing theory of reading impairment stands out methodologically in its focus on both behavioural and brain changes over time in poor readers (Temple et al., 2003). In this study, the brain functioning of children, aged eight to twelve, was examined twice using fMRI, which again is a technique commonly used to look at changes in blood flow to the brain. The children were tested on phonological processing, language, and reading tasks before and after they received remedial language and reading training using a computer training package over about four weeks for about 500 minutes per week. Following training, dyslexic children's reading, speeded-naming, and vocabulary skills improved significantly. The children's brain activity also increased significantly following training, particularly in the left temporoparietal cortex and left inferior frontal gyrus. Moreover, children's phonological blending skills were correlated 0.43 with brain activity following remediation, though other performance measures were not associated with brain activity.

This study is particularly useful in demonstrating a direct brain–behaviour connection. It shows that changes in the brain are directly associated with changes in behaviour, even over a relatively short period of time. The remediation technique used in this study combined tasks of phonological skills with tasks emphasizing speed of processing.

One more aspect of dyslexia that involves some link to speed but also to vision is the so-called M-cell deficit hypothesis (Stein & Kapoula, 2012). Here, M stands for magnocellular cells, those cells in the ventral visual pathway which are particularly large and helpful for motion detection. The ventral visual pathway is responsible for helping us to identify what we see. It can help to recognize texture, form, and colour, and it is implicated in print detection. M-cells are relatively large and carry visual information along the dorsal pathway of the brain to detect motion. They help to control eye movements and visual attention. When these cells are in some way impaired, eye movement control is reduced. Some children with dyslexia complain specifically about visual difficulties when they read, feeling like the print is 'jumping on the page' or that letters become blurry or seem to float around. Children with dyslexia sometimes show lower visual sensitivities in relation to detecting flicker, contrast, or overall motion (for a review, see Stein & Kapoula, 2012). Others have suggested that perhaps such visual deficits actually represent broader categories, such as an inability to form perceptual categories clearly (e.g. Lu, Sperling, Manis, & Seidenberg, 2005) or difficulties with speed of processing (McLean, Stuart, Coltheart, & Castles, 2011). Much more must be done in neuroscience research to understand fully what the biological bases for dyslexia are. At the same time, however, researchers have tried to link some of this important work to identification and remediation of those who are reading disabled or even to those who are at risk for reading disabilities (e.g. Gabrieli, 2009).

Remediation for poor readers

Many studies have sought to help dyslexic readers. A comprehensive approach to helping young children become successful readers encourages instruction in a variety of literacy domains, including comprehension skills such as vocabulary development and meaning construction, writing and spelling experience, a focus on word decoding (Foorman & Torgesen, 2001), including retrieval of words and automaticity in processing them, and orthographic aspects of reading (e.g. Wolf et al., 2009).

At the word level, phonological awareness and orthographic processing skills are both important. Among English-reading children with low word-recognition skills, an emphasis on phonological skills is encouraged (e.g. Foorman et al., 1998). In many programmes intended to promote reading skills in at risk readers, children are also encouraged to note the irregularities of given exception words and to remember these unique patterns. This explicit instruction appears to be particularly important for poor readers, whose orthographic knowledge, apart from core phonological skills, tends to lag behind that of normal readers. In addition, much of the core reading vocabulary we learn in the early stages of reading is composed of exception words (e.g. Adams, 1990). Such words, among the most frequently encountered, include *the*, *of*, and *was*. For exception words, phonological awareness may be only minimally helpful. If these words are not identified consistently, reading comprehension suffers. Thus, automatizing poor readers' identification of exception words is an important focus of their training (Torgesen, Wagner, & Rashotte, 1997). Moreover, promoting general fluency in reading has been emphasized in several successful remediation studies (Foorman & Torgesen, 2001; Wolf, 1997; Wolf et al., 2009).

It is likely that, across orthographies, practice with word or character recognition, identification and fluency will help improve reading. It is essential that educators reveal clues to the code to poor readers because, even when these are sometimes misleading (e.g. *s* is often, though not always, pronounced /s/), children, as analytic learners, benefit from rules that can be applied at least some of the time. Without internalizing the rules of an orthography, children may approach each word or character to be learned as a unique event, without generalizing to the next word or character. This approach can tax either phonological or visual memory skills far beyond what is possible and thus severely restrict reading acquisition. In one study, German-speaking children with spelling difficulties who received an orthographic spelling intervention improved significantly over those with similar difficulties who did not receive the intervention in spelling and reading over 15 weeks (Ise & Schulte-Körne, 2010).

A far more controversial approach to reading remediation comes from Tallal and colleagues (e.g. Tallal et al., 1996; Tallal et al., 1997). These researchers argued that, because language-disabled children and, by extension, dyslexics (Farmer & Klein, 1995) have difficulty with temporal processing, these children should be trained to discriminate speech by elongating short speech sounds such as stop consonants to make them easier to perceive. Tallal and colleagues (1996) did this in a computer package, Fast ForWord, which has been marketed for use by the general public. In addition to its explicit focus on the discrimination of speech sounds, the package emphasizes matching phonemes to word structures and matching words to pictures. Grammatical skills are also taught. It was this package that was used in the study demonstrating clear behavioural and brain correspondences both before and after treatment for reading-disabled children (Temple et al., 2003) discussed above. It therefore appears that this package was useful in helping some children to read better.

What is not clear, however, is the extent to which training in speeded recognition of speech sounds is essential for promoting reading in dyslexic children. After all, this particular package offers training in a variety of explicit phonemic skills demonstrated to be essential for the remediation of poor readers (e.g. Foorman & Torgesen, 2001). Moreover, the package was used extensively over a relatively long period of time. It is likely that any explicit, long-term practice combining phonics and fluency skills could be useful in promoting reading skills, given that the training was attractively presented to children. Temple et al. (2003) argued that their study could in no way isolate what components of this training programme facilitated reading improvement in their study.

Gaab, Gabrieli, Deutsch, Tallal, and Temple (2007) also showed that the same programme used by Temple et al. (2003) was effective in improving skills in language, phonological processing, and auditory processing among those children with dyslexia. Correspondingly, the brain activation of the children with dyslexia showed some changes in the left prefrontal cortex. Specifically, it appeared that the children's brains distinguished rapid and slow transitions in this region in a way that they did not prior to training. However, there was no comparison group in this study of children with dyslexia who did not receive this training.

In fact, the idea that slowing down stimulus presentations and then gradually speeding them up can somehow facilitate children's learning and reading skills is controversial. Few researchers have replicated this claim. For example, Segers and Verhoeven (2002) found that Dutch language-impaired children had difficulties across all speech-discrimination tasks, relative to children without speech and language problems, regardless of whether the speech sequences were presented quickly or slowly. This result suggests that slowness of speech by itself may not promote poor readers' phonological skills. Strehlow et al. (2006) similarly showed that a focus on auditory temporal measures did not improve dyslexic children's performances in reading and spelling skills any more than did a standard training programme focused on these over a one-year period. However, another study of French-speaking children with dyslexia (Joly-Pottuz, Mercier, Leynaud, & Habib, 2008) using similar methods did find that such methods, combined with articulatory skills training, improved phonological and non-word reading skills over a six-week intervention. It is likely that interventions focused on auditory or phonological training are generally somewhat useful in promoting reading-related skills in children with dyslexia learning alphabetic orthographies. However, the distinctiveness of auditory temporal training remains unclear.

Few other studies have examined training for those with dyslexia in relation to changes in the brain. One popular idea, namely that dyslexia may be attributable to difficulties in motor-coordination, associated also with speed and centered in the cerebellum, has prompted certain organizations to create centres focused on training of coordination and motor skills with the goal of remediating dyslexia. There is no empirical evidence that such training can reduce difficulties in those with dyslexia (Bishop, 2007). There is much more to do in this area of neuroscience and dyslexia in relation to training before researchers can understand clearly how particular aspects of training and teaching can influence those with dyslexia both behaviourally and in terms of corresponding changes in the brain.

What's next?

There is good cross-cultural evidence that some children have special difficulties in reading in every orthography. What is not clear is the extent to which phonological processing problems represent the core deficit of reading difficulty across scripts. What is perhaps clearest across orthographies is that speeded naming, though difficult to define as a construct, is a universally good predictor of poor reading, although researchers remain divided as to the theoretical relevance of tasks of speeded naming. It also seems plausible that explicit instruction in reading, emphasizing the tricks of its code and also fluency in that script, is essential to the remediation of reading problems across any script. How the tricks of the code of each script might unfold is a continuing puzzle. More ideas, particularly in the areas of suprasegmental processing (Goswami et al., 2011) and visual word form processing and its development and correlates across scripts (e.g. Maurer et al., 2011), may be important to address by pairing neuroscience techniques with behavioural measures and training in future work.

Suggested readings

Deirdre, M. (2013). *Researching dyslexia in multilingual settings: Diverse perspectives (Communication disorders across languages)*. Bristol, UK: Multilingual Matters.

Ellis, A. W. (2014). *Reading, writing and dyslexia: A cognitive analysis*. Psychology Press.

Hulme, C., & Snowling, M. J. (2009). *Developmental disorders of language learning and cognition*. West Sussex, UK: Blackwell Publishing.

Siegel, L. (2013). *Understanding dyslexia and other learning disorders*. Vancouver: Pacific Educational Press.

7

READING COMPREHENSION

This chapter outlines some of the issues of most importance in understanding reading comprehension development. First, it reviews consensus about how best to conceptualize reading comprehension, as involving text, activity (or purpose), and the reader (Snow, 2002). We will then go on to mention some of the key cognitive skills (along with motivation) thought to contribute to good reading comprehension at an individual level. We will include a short section on poor comprehenders as well. The sociocultural context in which reading comprehension takes place will then be considered in relation to reading development.

A group of scholars, chaired by Catherine Snow, compiled a report available via the internet that sets out a research agenda for reading comprehension teaching and investigation (Snow, 2002). Although its agenda is decidedly based on the needs of children from the United States, its emphasis on sociocultural factors that can affect reading comprehension transfers well to children from all cultures. The researchers assert that reading comprehension involves the text to be understood, the activity for which reading comprehension is taking place, and the reader. It is important to consider the interactions among these as we think about reading comprehension among individuals. For example, imagine a passage devoted to quantum field theory in an introductory college physics textbook. This is neither an inherently difficult nor an easy passage. To an experienced college physics professor, it would be an easy passage to understand and it may require only that she skim the passage once before she is certain of its contents and how to discuss them with her students. To an introductory physics student, particularly one who is not especially interested in or confident about physics, such a passage may be extremely difficult and require several readings before its contents are clear. Similar arguments can be made for children reading a variety of different passages based on their grade level, background knowledge, or purpose in reading a given passage. This chapter thus considers first the text and the purpose of reading before turning to the attributes of the reader and

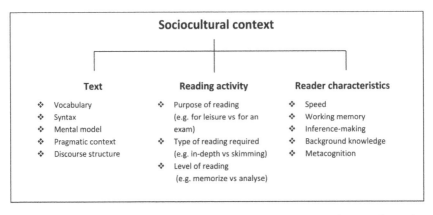

FIGURE 7.1 Reading comprehension involves interactions among the text, the reading activity, and reader characteristics, within a sociocultural context (Snow, 2002).

the sociocultural context in which reading comprehension takes place. Figure 7.1 overviews aspects of reading comprehension as outlined in this chapter.

Reading comprehension and the text

The nature of the text is affected by several factors that may interact at different levels. These include vocabulary, syntactic and propositional properties, and the mental model set forth in the text. Vocabulary is clear to any of us who have read college texts across disciplines. For example, the new physics student may have a poor vocabulary within the discipline of physics, rendering weak his schema for the associations among concepts like *quarks, photons, muons,* or *tau.* The extent to which vocabulary within the text is new will affect the readability of the text. Crudely, the more new vocabulary words are included in the text, the more difficult it is likely to be to read. Vocabulary knowledge is among the most important factors related to reading comprehension in some studies (e.g. Cromley & Azevedo, 2007; Verhoeven & van Leeuwe, 2008).

Another factor affecting the nature of the text is syntax. For example, American Psychological Association style requires that sentences in texts be relatively short, with few clauses. Many philosophy texts, on the other hand, use relatively long sentences with many clauses. Because written text often contains more idea units than oral language, which has a simpler structure, written text may be more difficult to remember and understand without sufficient practice (Snow, 2002). An example of a syntactically complex sentence is this, from Barbara Kingsolver's *The Poisonwood Bible*, in reference to a paste called *fufu*, which, when transformed, is then called *manioc*: 'It comes from a stupendous tuber, which the women cultivate and dig from the ground, soak in the river, dry in the sun, pound to white powder in hollowed-out logs, and boil' (p. 105). Within this sentence, several propositions, or idea units, can be distinguished. The more intricate the syntax of a text, the more difficult the text may be to comprehend. Syntactic knowledge facilitates reading comprehension. For example, in a four-year longitudinal study, Demont and Gombert (1996) demonstrated that syntactic awareness uniquely predicted subsequent reading comprehension among French primary-school children. Other studies have demonstrated the importance of syntax for reading comprehension in other languages such as Chinese (Chik et al., 2012).

The sentence by Kingsolver is also helpful in illustrating the importance of a mental model for reading comprehension. A mental model is one's understanding of the basic topic of the text. For example, if you do not know that manioc is a major food source for people in the African Congo, this may make it more difficult for you to place the activities described in the sentence in terms of context or relevance. This mental model is clearly an interface between the author's powers of explanation in the text and the reader's understanding based on concepts of how the world works. Vocabulary knowledge is also helpful for facilitating a mental model of a given text (Cromley, Snyder-Hogan, & Luciw-Dubas, 2010).

Two other aspects of text are highlighted by Snow (2002). First, the text is written in pragmatic context. That is, the text communicates the level at which the passage should be understood. Some cookbooks, for example, may be written for relative novices. Recipes in these books should be fairly simple, with little room for interpretation. Other cookbooks may include commentary and advice that are optional; such texts are written for more experienced cooks. Most children's books in libraries are organized according to children's developmental levels. Resourceful librarians are skilled at identifying pragmatic contexts that help match reading skills to readers. Thus, a seven year old interested in types of sea creatures may be happy with Dr Seuss's *Wish for a Fish*, a rhyming reader that covers a whole range of them, from the great blue whale to krill, at an entertaining but superficial level. A 15 year old is likely to prefer a more sophisticated science text.

Second, discourse structure is an important aspect of text. Depending upon the type, or genre, of text, a passage will be constructed differently. For example, in literary novels, stories may be told from the past to the future, from the future with flashbacks to the past, or holistically from different individuals' perspectives. These literary works may be particularly distinctive in terms of the descriptive voice of the storyteller. Such variability and richness of description are not typical of science texts. In science texts, summaries of experiments are predictable, beginning with a theoretical introduction, then offering an explanation of the procedure used, followed by experimental results, and ending with a discussion of these results. In addition, science texts feature language that is straightforward and avoid flowery language.

Reading comprehension and reading activity

Apart from the attributes of a text itself, the reason that the text is being read is relevant to an understanding of reading comprehension. Snow (2002) calls this the *reading activity*. Reading comprehension takes place for a variety of purposes. It is important to remember that, with the same text, these purposes can vary markedly. For example, I discussed a (Magic School Bus) storybook about friction with my then seven-year-old son. In the story, a class goes off to a baseball game, held in a magic environment without friction, and must later escape the frictionless atmosphere using their wits. My son's task in interacting with this text was to write a book report on it. Within this, he was asked to identify a main character and explain the main events in the book. This was an interesting story that successfully explained some important concepts about friction to a young audience. A child could equally have read the book for the purpose of understanding friction, learning new vocabulary words, or attempting to apply the structure of the story in order to write his own.

As adults, we have a variety of experiences in reading texts for different purposes. We read instruction manuals in order to assemble things or get them to work. We read cookbooks or magazine articles in order to cook or create works of art. We read newspapers to understand what is going on around us. We read for enjoyment, for our studies, and for our jobs. Along with these different purposes, we may have different approaches to texts. If reading is relevant to our work or studies, we may need to read text carefully, perhaps even more than once. If we have a very vague and hurried purpose, such as finding out whether any major news events have taken place overnight, we may simply skim a newspaper, without even reading it word for word. Children's abilities to change their reading strategies to fit a purpose are, not surprisingly, linked both to age and reading comprehension skills. Younger and poorer readers tend to have more trouble adjusting their reading styles (e.g. skimming text, reading to remember specific materials, etc.) to a particular text (Oakhill & Garnham, 1988).

Bloom (1956) conceptualized learning as potentially occurring at a number of different levels. His taxonomy of approaches as applied to text is useful in understanding how we read. At the lowest level of his taxonomy is *recognition* of content. For example, students often study their textbooks to learn new vocabulary words on which they may be tested; answering a multiple-choice question in an exam by correctly identifying a given definition as matching the word *morpheme* might be an example of this. Recognition is a relatively easy process, even for young children. At a greater level of difficulty is *recall*, which involves retrieving information from memory. For example, if, when asked in an exam to define a morpheme, a student can produce a definition such as 'the smallest unit of meaning in language', she demonstrates adequate recall. *Comprehension* is more difficult still. This involves highlighting information gleaned from the text in one's own words. My son's summary of the main point of his Magic School Bus story as explaining 'how friction works' is one example of comprehension (albeit very vague). *Application*, according to Bloom, is at a higher level of cognitive processing; application is the process of using knowledge gleaned from the text to approach a new problem. For example, once a child has learned to use algebra in several example story problems, she can presumably make use of these skills in tackling new story problems.

At perhaps an equal level of difficulty to application (Snow, 2002), cognitive skills in reading comprehension can include three other processes: analysis, synthesis, and evaluation (Bloom, 1956). *Analysis* involves understanding how different aspects of the text are related. For example, a teacher might ask a child who has read a passage on elephants to analyse the similarities and differences between Asian and African elephants. *Synthesis* requires that readers make use of the text to create a new product. Writing a report on the soft drinks industry, for example, required my then 11-year-old nephew to synthesize information obtained through government documents, business reports, and email messages that asked questions of public relations employees at major cola factories. The report was his synthesis of a variety of texts. Finally, *evaluation* of a text is the process of judging it as compared to a given standard. An example of this might be the section of a child's book report that critiques the book relative to other books she has read during the school year.

Reading comprehension and the reader

Having acknowledged the importance of both texts and the purposes of reading them for reading comprehension, we turn back to individual differences in reading comprehension. Here, the focus is on what the reader brings to the task of reading comprehension. The bulk of this book on literacy acquisition focuses on such individual differences in the form of cognitive skills relevant for reading. Reading comprehension clearly draws upon all of them. Indeed, as noted by Crowder and Wagner, 'Reading is connected with almost all mental activities there are!' (1992, p. 110).

An example of this comes from a paper linking first-grade reading to eleventh-grade reading comprehension (Cunningham & Stanovich, 1997). Both word-recognition and reading-comprehension skills in first grade significantly predicted reading comprehension ten years later. Although these researchers did not test cognitive skills such as phonological awareness or speed of processing in the study, we have seen evidence in previous chapters which demonstrates that these skills are strongly linked to word recognition in early reading. Thus, early reading-related skills are important for subsequent reading comprehension. There is substantial variability in these reading-related skills.

Gough and Tunmer (1986) offered a so-called 'Simple View' of reading. In this view, reading comprehension depends upon both decoding and linguistic comprehension skills. Word decoding has been covered extensively in this book already. Linguistic comprehension skills consist of a variety of abilities that rely on language processing. Language comprehension includes oral language knowledge, such as vocabulary knowledge and verbal understanding of what has been said (typically involving memory and grammatical skills, among others). Without language comprehension, reading comprehension cannot occur. Several recent studies have tested this model and found support for it in Greek (Kendeou, Papadopoulos, & Kotzapoulou, 2013), in Chinese (Ho, Chow, Wong, Waye, & Bishop, 2012), and across English and more transparent orthographies more generally (Florit & Cain, 2011). Moreover, training children in word recognition or language comprehension can promote small to intermediate gains in reading comprehension (Melby-Lervåg & Lervåg, 2014).

Reading comprehension and cognitive skills (and motivation)

This section discusses some of the most prominent aspects of linguistic comprehension that have been related to individual differences in reading comprehension. They include speed of processing and word recognition, working memory, inference-making, background knowledge, and metacognition. As in other areas related to literacy acquisition, the reading comprehension literature boasts relatively few longitudinal studies that might help to suggest a causal association among these variables and reading comprehension. Rather, most studies of children's reading comprehension focus on good and poor comprehenders and demonstrate differences between them. Nevertheless, it is worthwhile considering group differences in reading comprehension in an attempt to understand what cognitive abilities most clearly distinguish readers of different levels. It is also important to consider motivation in relation to reading comprehension, a factor not explicitly included in Snow's (2002) model. Taboada and colleagues (2009) described motivation as an 'energizer' of cognitive skills deployed to read text. Without motivation, such skills are likely to be only minimally developed in service to reading comprehension. For this reason, we focus briefly on motivation as well.

Speed of processing

Speed of processing is strongly related to the acquisition of many cognitive tasks, and its relevance for reading comprehension is clear to anyone who has helped to read a story with a developing reader. Much of the struggle for a new reader lies in the tension between word or character recognition and text comprehension. The problem comes down to a finite short-term memory store. If all of our short-term memory capacity is devoted to individual word units, we have no store left for larger chunks of meaning. As children's word recognition improves, children gain in fluency (Adams, 1990). Words are more often processed automatically. Children can now identify a range of words or characters and identify them without the laborious process of sounding them out. With faster word-identification skills, speed of reading increases.

One aspect of fluency of word/character recognition of relevance here is how we define such recognition. Definitions of word identification based on English generally require that children identify a printed word orally: they 'sound it out'. In English and in other alphabetic orthographies, it is possible to pronounce a word without knowing its meaning. Although this is possible in Chinese as well, as long as children guess at the sound of a character based on a commonly used pronunciation from its phonetic, it is less likely. On the other hand, in Chinese, children can some-times guess at the meaning of a Chinese character, indicating that they recognize its meaning (or at least something about the meaning, for instance, that it may be related to an activity using the mouth), though not its pronunciation. This seems less likely in English. Reading comprehension is limited by word recognition, both as it relates to identifying a word or character by sound and also to grasping its meaning (Oakhill & Garnham, 1988).

In the years to come, this view is likely to be refined in relation to Chinese. Chen and colleagues (2003) have demonstrated that Chinese readers shift from a word or concept level to a character level of reading with age. That is, their eye movements in reading text indicate that they focus less on comprehensive word-level units, e.g. *children* in Cantonese is three characters long (as shown in Figure 3.10), and more on individual characters with development. This pattern may highlight younger children's difficulties with character recognition relative to older children, or their shift towards morpheme recognition with age. Whatever the mechanism explaining these results, it is difficult to consider reading comprehension from the perspective of word level only in light of them.

However, it is likely that, across orthographies, readers tend to develop meanings from (relatively) smaller to larger units. In text, as long as readers recognize individual meanings, they collapse these into composite interpretations. We constantly reconcep-tualize sentences, paragraphs, even chapters, in light of new things we read. According to Adams (1990), being good at this composite interpretation involves both the ease and speed with which individual words are recognized and the ability to recognize the opportunities where recoding and thinking about meaning is best and most appro-priate. In Chinese, the ease and speed with which characters are recognized appears to be the fundamental unit for bottom-up accurate skilled reading comprehension. Across studies, there is evidence that fluency itself is an important correlate of reading comprehension (e.g. Kim, Wagner, & Lopez, 2012; Yildiz et al., 2014).

Working memory

Alongside speed of processing for reading comprehension is the concept of working memory. Working memory involves two primary processes central to reading com-prehension: the storage and processing of verbal information (e.g. Just & Carpenter, 1992). The storage of verbal information involves the ability to retain information. If you are given three colours to remember (e.g. *blue*, *violet*, and *magenta*) can you retrieve them from your memory immediately and repeat them back to me? This is one aspect of phonological processing identified by Wagner and Torgesen (1987). However, verbal memory storage capacity alone is not related to reading compre-hension (Daneman & Merikle, 1996).

Rather, the processing of verbal information required in measures of working memory appears to be crucial to understanding reading comprehension. To tap this ability, Daneman and Carpenter (1980) came up with a working memory task that requires both processing and recall of sentences. This task requires participants to listen to and understand (i.e. process) a series of sentences presented one after another while simultaneously trying to remember the final word of each sentence. An example of this would be that, given the following three unrelated sentences:

1. *I turned my memories over at random like pictures in a photograph album.*
2. *He had an odd elongated skull which sat on his shoulder like a pear on a dish.*
3. *I will not shock my readers with the cold-blooded butchery that followed.*

you recall the words *album*, *dish*, and *followed*, the final word in each of the three example sentences, respectively (from Daneman & Merikle, 1996).

Such tasks of working memory, whether administered orally or in writing, tend to be excellent predictors of reading comprehension and vocabulary knowledge in children and adults (Carpenter, Miyake, & Just, 1995; Daneman & Merikle, 1996; Daneman & Tardif, 1987). A greater working memory capacity may facilitate recall because, as soon as readers are able to, we build on the information in the text. In other words, we interpret the ideas presented as we ourselves best understand them, to form an overall idea of what is being said in the text. We use our own idea, or schema, to take in additional information presented as we read. Read the following sentence as an example: *The big pink cat thought sadly of her former summers in Paris, lounging around the pool, eating large meals of tuna and chicken, and sleeping for many luscious hours in the sun.* Although the creature described above is pink, which is unusual, many of the other details of this cat may have been easy to process and remember, because they fit well with some notions you may have about cats. For example, they enjoy sleeping in the sun and eating tuna. Although you probably would not be able to recall this sentence word for word, many of the ideas presented in it might easily be recalled because, as soon as you understand that this refers to a cat, other details are easily integrated into your overall impression of how the world works, or your schema. Phrases and sentences are easily collapsed to form new meanings in text.

In this way, we easily integrate new information into the structure of the sentence, paragraph, or text we are reading (Just & Carpenter, 1992). Our immediate understanding, influenced by vocabulary and background knowledge, facilitates the processing of text as soon as we encounter it. This idea goes along with speed of processing, as discussed earlier. The faster we can process and recall information, the better we are able to comprehend what we read. Thus, working memory, like speed of processing, is often conceptualized as a capacity that increases with experience and age through adulthood. These capacities influence our sensitivity to syntactic cues, pragmatics, and meaning communicated in the text, as discussed earlier.

Some correlational evidence in adults (McVay & Kane, 2012) and evidence from reading comprehension training in children with special needs (Dahlin, 2011) and in typically developing children (Loosli, Buschkuehl, Perrig, & Jaeggi, 2012), suggests that working memory is important not only for immediate processing of information but also for focusing on that information. Good working memory skill involves focusing on relevant ideas in the text and avoiding distractions, both in the external environment and in one's mind – irrelevant thoughts that take away from processing of text. In line with these findings, Wang and Gathercole (2013) suggested that those with reading difficulties may have a core deficit in the central executive, a part of the memory system that is particularly important for attentional control. A study of adults learning English as a second language (Erçetin & Alptekin, 2013) also demonstrated an important role of working memory for reading comprehension in English because of its role in attentional control.

Inference-making

Researchers (Cain & Oakhill, 1998; Kendeou, Bohn-Gettler, White, & Van Den Broek, 2008; Oakhill & Cain, 2012; Paris, Lindauer, & Cox, 1977; Paris & Upton, 1976) have focused on inference-making as another source of difficulty in the process of reading comprehension in children. Inferences are preliminary conclusions about meaning in text. This meaning may be implied but not explicitly stated. An example of a short text in which some inference must be made is this: *Molly took the carton from the refrigerator, opened it, and took a whiff. The milk was spoiled!* A literal reading of these sentences might bring up several *inferential questions*, such as:

1. *What was in the carton?*
2. *Where was the milk?*
3. *How did Molly know that the milk was spoiled?*

Inferring from the text, a reader might assume that the milk was contained in the carton, and Molly smelled its contents. The smell of the milk in the carton was acrid. Therefore, Molly concluded that the milk was spoiled. *Factual questions* related to this text might be:

1. *Where was the carton? (In the refrigerator),* and
2. *Who opened the carton? (Molly).*

Children's abilities to make inferences differ both by age and by reading ability. Younger children tend to show a larger gap between answering factual and inferential questions about a text; for older children this gap is smaller. Thus, inferential questions are particularly difficult for young children to grasp. Although young children – at least from the ages of four or five years (Lepola, Lynch, Laakkonen, Silvén, & Niemi, 2012; Omanson, Warren, & Trabasso, 1978) – can make inferences about a story, they do so less frequently than older children. In addition, less skilled comprehenders (aged seven to eight years) tend to make fewer inferences in stories than same-age good comprehenders and younger comprehension-age matched controls (Cain & Oakhill, 1998). These differences cannot be attributed to differences across groups in memory, background knowledge, or reading strategies. Rather, poor comprehenders tend to have trouble monitoring their own reading of, and even listening to (Lepola et al., 2012), the text. Similar conclusions have been made for Chinese children. In one study of sixth graders (Chan & Law, 2003), the stronger Chinese children's beliefs about metacognition were in conceptualizing reading as a process of problem solving to be approached actively rather than passively, the better their inferential but not literal comprehension. These results held, even controlling for vocabulary knowledge. At the same time, it is also clear that vocabulary knowledge itself strongly supports inference-making (Currie & Cain, 2015). Children with difficulties in inference-making need help learning when to make these inferences and how to use their knowledge base to make them (Elbro & Buch-Iverson, 2013).

Background knowledge

Knowledge base is another vitally important skill for adequate reading comprehension. Notice that the two short sentences (about Molly and the milk) I made up to illustrate the idea of inferences are also useful for demonstrating the importance of background knowledge to reading comprehension. To make inferences in this example, you need to know that milk is often packaged in cartons in certain parts of the world. This is less true in Hong Kong, where milk is more likely to be in a bottle or a box, than in America, where cartons are frequently used to transport milk. It might also be useful to know, for understanding these sentences, that one can often detect whether or not milk appears to be spoiled by smelling it.

The importance of background knowledge for reading comprehension is broadly related to at least two factors. First, background knowledge promotes reading comprehension because it may facilitate understanding of the ideas via vocabulary in the text (e.g. Lepola et al., 2012). Thus, if you don't understand that *whiff* is an approximate synonym to the word *smell* in the above sentences, you may not infer that Molly understood the milk to be spoiled because she smelled it. The physics professor vs student introduced at the beginning of this chapter are other good examples of individuals differing in sight vocabulary for physics terms, making understanding of an introductory physics text a quite different experience for each. Second, background knowledge is important as it relates to schemas, or mental structures that organize facts about how the world works. For example, from life experience, I might assert that the way to decide whether or not a drink is still palatable depends on the drink. Red wine that tastes too much like vinegar may be described as unpalatable. However, to label a soft drink as old or stale may call upon different skills. A soft drink that, when poured, gives no evidence of carbonation via fizzing might also be described as undrinkable. In contrast, perhaps the best way to test for undrinkable milk is to smell it. There is nothing obvious about these different tests for good taste across drinks; this knowledge comes from experience. Without such experience, it is difficult to infer from the above text that Molly determined the status of the milk as spoiled by smelling it. Without adequate background knowledge, reading comprehension thus suffers. Elbro and Buch-Iverson (2013) devised a training programme for Norwegian sixth graders that made use of the connection between background knowledge and inference-making to help students to do a better job of making inferences in expository texts. Using both graphic models and question prompts, they demonstrated clear positive effects of their inference-making tutorials on students' reading comprehension.

Metacognition

Metacognition is a fifth prominent factor in children's reading comprehension. It refers to the ability to reflect on one's own cognition, one's own thoughts. When we talk about metacognition in reference to reading comprehension, we focus on the ways in which children can reflect on how they are reading and how to comprehend (e.g. Nicholson, 1999). Most adults have had the experience of failing to comprehend as they read. This may have occurred, for example, when you suddenly find yourself three pages further on in a text compared to the last time you remember having processed its meaning. In the interim three pages, you have gleaned absolutely no clues as to what you have just read. There is no sense of comprehension. A reader who *notices* that she has not processed or understood what has just been read demonstrates knowledge about comprehension. She has shown an ability to reflect on her own thoughts in relation to reading. Metacognition in relation to reading may also include ideas about reading. For example, children who view reading as meaning construction are often more successful in reading comprehension tasks than are those who view reading as a task of memorization or production of knowledge (e.g. Chan & Law, 2003). This idea dovetails nicely with the purposes of reading reviewed above. Bloom's (1956) ideas of learning as recall or recognition represent lower-level approaches to text than those of analysis or synthesis, which presumably make better use of constructivism in text.

Children's understanding of how to comprehend is a second aspect of metacomprehension. This aspect of metacomprehension includes the ability to detect errors, notice inconsistencies, and draw conclusions from the text (Nicholson, 1999). An example of an error in the text finding a missing word in a sentence. In this last sentence, if you noticed that the sentence is missing a verb, such as *is*, you have used a metacomprehension strategy to detect an error in print. An inconsistency in the text might be recognizing that, in the story of Cinderella, it is not clear how the glass slippers survived a magical transformation at the stroke of midnight. Why, if all of the rest of Cinderella's fancy clothes and accessories changed back to her former attire of rags, as her fairy godmother had warned, were the slippers spared this fate? Finally, successful secondary-school students learn how to understand the main points of their textbooks by reading and rereading difficult passages and spending more time on the summary sentences (typically at the beginning or end of a paragraph) to aid their comprehension. These are ways of demonstrating metacomprehension by drawing conclusions from a text. In one study of over 158,000 15 year olds across 34 countries, students' metacognitive strategy usage was uniquely and positively associated with reading comprehension, even when many other country-, school-, family-, and other individual-level variables were statistically controlled. Moreover, classmates' use of metacognitive strategies were independently associated with better reading comprehension scores for these students as well (Chiu, Chow, & McBride-Chang, 2007).

Motivation

One aspect of Snow's relatively comprehensive model of reading comprehension that is missing is the idea of motivation. What and how we read likely has a lot to do with how much we wish to do so. The cognitive skills described above are presumably deployed in part because of motivation (Taboada et al., 2009). Researchers have very roughly divided motivation into intrinsic and extrinsic categories (Wang & Guthrie, 2004; Wigfield & Guthrie, 1997). Whereas intrinsic motivation basically refers to genuine curiosity and interest in a given domain, extrinsic motivation implies that one engages in a given activity for instrumental purposes, i.e. to gain some outside reward such as grades in school.

In general, intrinsic motivation for reading results in children who read more in general and who read more broadly (e.g. Lau, 2004; Lin, Wong, & McBride-Chang, 2012; Taboada et al., 2009; Wigfield & Guthrie, 1997). In contrast, extrinsic motivation is typically not positively associated with reading comprehension skills, though instrumental motivation (specifically, motivation to do well in order to obtain good grades in school) was associated with higher reading comprehension in English as a second language for Hong Kong Chinese fifth graders in one study (Lin et al., 2012). A study of 9–11 year olds demonstrated that intrinsic motivation was particularly strongly associated with reading comprehension skills in first-language English for lower-ability comprehenders (Logan, Medford, & Hughes, 2011). Finding ways to increase motivation for reading may be helpful in improving reading comprehension over time (e.g. Archambault, Eccles, & Vida, 2010; Logan et al., 2011; Morgan & Fuchs, 2007). Teachers, parents, and students are all aware of this from the beginning. The challenge is how to find the right text or the right resource for every developing reader so that each child's intrinsic motivation for reading is stimulated from the outset.

This turns out to be a complicated issue, particularly for those who are struggling to read depending upon their developmental level. For example, one challenge for secondary-school teachers in international schools in Hong Kong is how to motivate non-Chinese-speaking children to get interested in reading Chinese. Many of these adolescents are relatively limited in what they can read in Chinese. At the same time, the books or other texts available to those at an elementary reading level are on topics that are of little or no interest to adolescents. Their interests and hobbies are completely mismatched with elementary texts intended for much younger children. This is also likely the case for disabled readers who are reading at levels far below their oral language skills. I appreciate Snow's (2002) model of reading comprehension particularly because it includes some attention to the issues of interactions of reader capabilities, text, and purpose of reading, all within a given cultural context. There are many complications in motivating readers in a given situation.

Poor comprehenders

Apart from those with dyslexia and dysgraphia (touched upon in the next chapter on writing), discussed elsewhere, some researchers have focused on the issue of poor comprehenders as a special group of children who have particular difficulties with reading comprehension. Poor comprehenders have a difficulty in reading that is very different from children who cannot read words. Poor comprehenders typically read words adequately and also perform relatively well in phonological processing skills (e.g. Nation, Cocksey, Taylor, & Bishop, 2010). What they lack, however, are the oral language skills crucial to the Simple View of reading discussed above (Gough & Tunmer, 1986).

The profile of poor comprehenders appears to be one in which they manifest a variety of oral language deficits. For example, morphosyntax was significantly lower in those with poor comprehension as compared to those who were typically developing readers in one study of fourth graders (Adlof & Catts, 2015). Certain morphological awareness skills are sometimes impaired in poor comprehenders as well (e.g. Tong, Deacon, & Cain, 2014; Zhang et al., 2013).

Across several studies, vocabulary knowledge in poor comprehenders was lower than those of typically developing readers, particularly with development (e.g. Nation et al., 2010; Zhang et al., 2013). Indeed, vocabulary skills appear to become depressed in poor as compared to typical comprehenders, over time, perhaps in part because of a bidirectional effect in which less reading stimulates less vocabulary knowledge growth (Cain & Oakhill, 2011; Cain, Oakhill, & Elbro, 2003). Cain, Oakhill, and Lemmon (2004) also showed that poor comprehenders, relative to those who are not poor comprehenders, show a limited ability to make use of context within a given text in order to learn new words.

Finally, some poor comprehenders manifest difficulties in inference-making (Cain & Oakhill, 1999; 2006; Cain, Oakhill, Barnes, & Bryant, 2001). Indeed, even when knowledge base between good and poor comprehenders is equivalent, poor comprehenders appear to have particular difficulties in making inferences (Cain & Oakhill, 1999; Cain et al., 2001).

How can we help poor comprehenders? Some studies have focused explicitly on the extent to which training in inference-making improves reading comprehension (e.g. Elbro & Buch-Iverson, 2013; McGee & Johnson, 2003). Such training does appear to be helpful in facilitating the reading comprehension performance of poor comprehenders. In general, poor comprehenders can improve in reading comprehension when specific oral language skills are targeted and trained. However, different strategies might work differently for different children depending upon their specific difficulties related to oral language. Moreover, training in oral language skills that are integrated with the process of reading comprehension itself, rather than being focused on listening or oral language only in the absence of print, is likely to be maximally beneficial, as demonstrated in one study of 9–11-year-old Italian children (Carretti, Caldarola, Tencati, & Cornoldi, 2014).

Reading comprehension in sociocultural context

We have considered reading comprehension as a dynamic process that involves the text, the purpose of reading the text, and the reader. However, the individual does not read in isolation. Rather, culture and societal expectations also play an important part in the intricate dance of reading comprehension. To illustrate some of the complexities involved in explaining reading comprehension, I will now highlight studies of reading comprehension involving multiple variables across cultures. For example, across cultures, girls tend to outperform boys in reading comprehension overall (Chiu & McBride-Chang, 2006; Chiu, McBride-Chang, & Lin, 2012; Ogle et al., 2003), but this is not the whole story. Texts and their purposes are important factors in explaining reading achievement.

In one in-depth study, data on the reading comprehension of 9 and 14 year olds from 32 countries were gathered by the International Association for the Evaluation of Educational Achievement (Wagemaker et al., 1996). The focus of the research was on similarities and differences in comprehension in girls and boys. The researchers explored three aspects of reading comprehension: narrative passage, expository passage, and document comprehension. This detailed study highlighted the associations among text, reading purpose, and reader.

Results of the research were as follows. Across all 32 countries sampled, girls outperformed boys in narrative passage comprehension at age nine. These passages communicate a story, either fact or fiction, from the point of view of the narrator. In 24 of these 32 countries, nine-year-old girls also excelled significantly in comprehending expository passages. Expository texts are generally intended to inform and are written in a neutral voice. Interestingly, in document comprehension, there were no significant differences between boys and girls in 25 of the 32 countries: girls outperformed boys in six countries, and in one country boys outperformed girls. This domain focuses on 'material that requires the reader to locate information or follow directions' (1996, p. 16). This text often involved deriving information by reading maps, graphs, or other directories. By age 14, there were fewer differences between girls and boys in comprehension. In fact, boys outperformed girls in document comprehension in 18 countries, though girls continued to do better in narrative comprehension in 31 of the 32 countries.

The authors' in-depth analysis of students' performances and item analyses across cultures suggested that, while maturation differences may partially account for comprehension differences between the sexes, the sociocultural context in which reading comprehension is taught and practised accounts for many of these differences as well. The sociocultural context includes how societies value reading for girls and boys, the topics covered in reading materials, and the type of reading engaged in by each sex. For example, the United States tends to conceptualize reading as belonging more to the domain of females; girls are 'naturally' expected to do better in reading comprehension than boys. In Nigeria, on the other hand, boys may be expected to have superior reading skills to girls (Wagemaker et al., 1996).

Topics covered in reading materials may make a big difference in how important or interesting children think they are. Motivation is an important aspect of this. Girls tended to outperform boys on passages of the IEA Study of Achievement in Reading Literacy about human beings or human activities. In contrast, on topics related to science, there were few sex differences. The types of reading material preferred by girls and boys also differ. For example, in the majority of countries sampled, boys preferred to read comics, whereas girls tended to read books.

From this study, it is clear that many aspects of reading affect comprehension. Whether one is a boy or a girl is one aspect of culture. Just as important, even aspects as broad as the culture in which one is raised or the way in which reading comprehension is defined (narrowly, as in narrative texts, vs broadly, to include deriving information from all sorts of printed materials) explain performance differences in it. Snow, for example, noted,

> Researchers working within a qualitative paradigm have found patterns in their data to suggest that adolescents who appear most at risk of failure in the academic literacy arena are sometimes the most adept at (and interested in) understanding how media texts work − in particular how meaning gets produced and consumed.
>
> *(2002, p. 89)*

The internet and variations possible in hypermedia text have expanded the uses and types of text. It becomes ever more complicated to talk about good and poor readers as if they exist in a vacuum. Indeed, it also appears as an even greater complication that use of texting, with all of its divergence from regular writing (e.g. *gr8* for *great*, *u* for *you*), is associated positively with word reading and word spelling in children but negatively with such skills in adolescents (for a review, see Waldron, Kemp, Plester, & Wood, 2015). The technological aspects of culture are becoming stronger and more powerful, along with other variables.

Beyond types of text, there are other factors that might also impact reading comprehension performance. Variables at the country, school, and family levels have all been implicated in reading comprehension (Chiu & McBride-Chang, 2006; 2010; Chiu et al., 2012). For example, generally those with a higher income tend to perform better in reading comprehension, though this association was modified somewhat depending upon culture, in one study of 41 countries involving over 193,000 15 year olds (Chiu & McBride-Chang, 2010). Wealth at the country level also independently explains reading achievement in children (Chiu et al., 2012) and adolescents (Chiu & McBride-Chang, 2006).

Certain characteristics related to school qualities also matter for children's reading comprehension. For example, schools with students with higher reading comprehension tend to foster classmates with better reading skills, perhaps not surprisingly (e.g. Chiu & McBride-Chang, 2006; Chiu et al., 2012). Perhaps more interesting, when peers expressed more interest in reading, classmates' reading comprehension scores were higher in one study of 43 countries with over 199,000 participants, with many other variables at many levels statistically controlled (Chiu & McBride-Chang, 2006). Various qualities of schools related to resources, both in terms of physical (e.g. adequate access to cooling or heating when necessary; books available for reading) and human resources (e.g. access to teachers with particular adequate training in literacy teaching), are also uniquely associated with reading comprehension incomes in children across cultures (e.g. Chiu et al., 2012).

Finally, in these large-scale studies of many cultures (Chiu & McBride-Chang, 2006; Chiu et al., 2012), families emerged as important for reading comprehension as well, in some statistically unique ways. For example, parents who endorsed more strongly statements about the importance of reading tended to have children with higher reading comprehension (e.g. Chiu et al., 2012). In addition, with many other variables at the country, school, family, and individual levels statistically controlled in these large-scale studies, number of books in the home was uniquely associated with children's reading comprehension (Chiu & McBride-Chang, 2006; Chiu et al., 2012). This finding was amazing to me given that these studies focused on children who were in primary and even secondary school, rather than in the early years of literacy development where we might have expected stronger effects based on the presence or absence of books. The value of reading via owning of books still seemed to matter at these advanced ages for reading comprehension.

Indeed, family systems are important for literacy learning at multiple levels and in complicated ways. For example, the role of grandparents in literacy learning is noteworthy across cultures. The ways in which grandparents facilitate literacy acquisition are both directly and indirectly related to reading comprehension because they focus both on early skills such as word recognition and on facilitating children's enjoyment of language skills and storytelling and comprehension, skills that promote ultimate reading comprehension. In one empirical study of thousands of Swedish citizens, Modin, Erikson, and Vågerö (2013), did an extensive (historical) analysis of Swedish grandparents and their children and found that grandparents' skills in Swedish tended to predict their grandchildren's performances in Swedish (all based on school marks) as well, more so for girls than for boys. As another illustration, in qualitative research examining different immigrant and non-immigrant families in Singapore (Ren & Hu, 2013), those with grandparents nearby seemed to have some clear advantages in terms of cultural capital. Grandparents were able to read with their grandchildren and instruct them in various literacy skills in a way in which parents often did not have time to do. African American children in the United States, faced with learning African American English at home and Standard English at school, also benefit in the development of various literacy skills, including storytelling, singing, and reading and writing, from their extended families (Boutte & Johnson, 2013).

Another interesting example of grandparent involvement in literacy skills development for young children, aged three to six, comes from Kenner and colleagues (2007). They found that Bangladeshi grandparents in London helped their grandchildren in several ways in developing school-related skills. The nine families followed in this research spoke various combinations of Bengali, English, and Arabic.

Grandparents sometimes facilitated poetry reading, storybook reading, writing in different scripts (especially in Bengali and English), and reading of the Quran (in Arabic). Interestingly, grandchildren tended to help their grandparents in computer literacy development at the same time that their grandparents helped them to develop various aspects of learning to read and to write. This was a fruitful and enjoyable exchange of skills.

In a study of families in 41 countries, Chiu and McBride-Chang (2010) showed that grandparents also seemed to be important for literacy development. Two-parent families and families in which grandparents did not live together with grandchildren tended to have children who read better at age 15. However, in collectivistic cultures, this effect was not as strong. Fewer siblings in the home was also related to better reading performance, presumably because fewer siblings implies greater adult attention for developing any given child's literacy skills. At any rate, a full focus on sociocultural contexts of literacy development would not be complete without a consideration of the family. Families matter for reading comprehension.

In this text, we have talked more extensively about parent involvement (as compared to involvement by other family members) in literacy development of children in different contexts (e.g. storybook reading, early writing facilitation), but it is equally important to understand that children's literacy skills development depends on multiple family members in many cultures and situations. In a recent dissertation by Kalindi (2015b), for example, fathers and mothers were both likely to help their children in scaffolding literacy skills in second graders in Zambia. However, beyond parents, other adult figures, such as older siblings, grandparents, and even family friends, were also frequently involved in teaching word reading and writing in both Bemba and English.

What's next?

Given the impressive breadth of factors affecting reading comprehension, there are many directions for research expansion in the future. Perhaps most evident when one peruses the many books devoted to literacy development (including this one) is that, considering the broad spectrum of literacy studies, research focused squarely on reading comprehension in children continues to be relatively rare; longitudinal studies are particularly lacking. Snow (2002) complained that there exist only few and narrowly defined tests of reading comprehension, limiting understanding of the development of reading comprehension itself. Such measurement problems also limit understanding of the consequences of reading comprehension. This has improved somewhat in the past ten years but continues to be a problem. Comprehension of documents, expository writing, stories, newspaper headlines, text messages, internet websites, instruction manuals – all are important for modern life, but only a few are typically measured in children.

From the cognitive developmental perspective, it is useful to consider all of the ways in which thinking might be affected by reading. Reading appears to be a strong predictor of vocabulary growth and a solid predictor of general knowledge (see Stanovich, 2000, for a review). However, reading does not appear to predict decontextualized reasoning, once general cognitive ability is controlled. Thus, for example, children's syllogistic reasoning is not strengthened by print exposure. This overall pattern of results has prompted Stanovich to state, 'somewhat sadly, I have tentatively concluded that reading makes you smarter but not wiser' (2000, p. 253). This conclusion is based primarily on studies that view measures of print exposure as a proxy for past reading experiences. This technique – which involves asking participants to distinguish, given a checklist of authors or titles, which they recognize as true and false (some on the list are fakes) – has been among the most successful in predicting unique variance in word recognition or reading comprehension aside from phonological processing skills in school-aged readers.

Ideally, a developmental theory of reading comprehension would examine the types of texts children read; their reasoning, higher-order language, and word-recognition skills; and the interests of the readers, to explain how reading comprehension develops and its consequences. We know from previous studies of cognitive development that interest in a specific area (e.g. dinosaurs) promotes advanced reasoning within this area. Is it also likely that reading within a particular area promotes not only vocabulary building but other metacognitive skills and text-sensitivity development in relation to reading. With more longitudinal studies in the future on reading comprehension compared across texts, ages, and cultures, a clearer pattern may emerge of ways in which particular types of reading comprehension develop relative to sociocultural, cognitive, and motivational factors in children.

Suggested readings

Cain, K. (2010). *Reading development and difficulties: An introduction.* West Sussex, United Kingdom: BPS Blackwell.

Oakhill, J., Cain, K., & Elbro, C. (2015). *Understanding and teaching reading comprehension: A handbook.* London: Routledge.

Rayner, K., Pollatsek, A., Ashby, J., & Clifton, C. (2011). *Psychology of Reading, 2nd edn.* New York, NY: Psychology Press.

8

WRITING

Spelling and higher-order processes

In this chapter, I start by discussing the development of early writing. I then review studies of spelling development, particularly in English, and consider the extent to which the term 'spelling' can apply to children's character writing in Chinese. Invented spelling is an important component to consider in relation to early writing. We consider briefly the issue of dysgraphia in the final section devoted to word writing. Finally, the chapter reviews a global model of writing composition (e.g. Hayes, 1996), which outlines some of the basic processes involved in composing text. Writing composition has received more attention in recent years and appears to be a relatively burgeoning field.

Early writing development

The transition to literacy is a gradual one, marked by children's appreciation for print as distinct from pictures. Young children have been found to separate writing from drawing accurately (Lavine, 1977). Chan and Louie (1992), for example, demonstrated that three-year-old Chinese children could distinguish print from pictures. In addition, Levin et al. (1996) found that Israeli pre-readers typically understood the difference between drawings and writing the word for a given object; their drawings clearly differed from their pretend writing. Chinese pre-schoolers typically use strokes and dots to represent writing; western pre-schoolers use more short strokes in writing than in drawing (for a review, see Adi-Japha & Freeman, 2001). In children's early representations, writing also often tends to be smaller than pictures (Tolchinsky-Landsmann, & Levin, 1985). In contrast, children's drawings typically make use of more circles or smooth curves (Adi-Japha & Freeman, 2001; Chan & Louie, 1992). In one study of Chinese children's writing and drawing (Treiman & Yin, 2011), adults could distinguish children's intended writing as compared to their drawing by the time the children were approximately 2.5 years old. Children appear to be faster in writing than in drawing, and can clearly distinguish their own writing from their drawing by the age of six or earlier.

Children demonstrate writing knowledge in their informal play, as their scribbling is transformed into letters or letter-like forms around the ages of three to four years in American culture (Snow et al., 1998). Random letters placed together are used to represent the printed word, although children are not always confident in the word or words they have 'written' (Clay, 1975). Although children understand from an early age that writing is distinct from drawing, they may initially assume that writing is a direct representation of meaning, rather than sound. Thus, for example, in alphabetic languages, young children assert that big things should be represented as longer words, with more letters, in print, than small things (e.g. Bialystok, 2000). Children also more often represent nouns with print as compared to verbs, presumably because nouns are more 'picturable' and meaningful to them in some languages (Ferreiro & Teberosky, 1982; Landsmann & Levin, 1987). Indeed, in German, nouns are afforded special status because all nouns have an initial capital letter, perhaps highlighting their salience. Verbs are subsequently incorporated into print by children, and grammatical articles are last to be introduced into writing (e.g. Ferreiro, 1978). These are indeed interesting observations about children's understanding of print because they correspond well to the focus of western languages on nouns in early development. Most English- or French-speaking children, for example, demonstrate a noun bias in early language learning (Boysson-Bardies, 1999). Nouns seem logically more concrete than verbs.

However, the extent to which such writing trends among children are found in other scripts awaits future research. In language development, Japanese, Korean (Boysson-Bardies, 1999), and Chinese (Tardif, 1996) children use fewer nouns and more verbs in early speech. One explanation for this phenomenon is that nouns can be dropped as subjects and objects more easily in these Asian languages than they can in many western languages. Additionally, at least in Chinese, a greater variety of verbs are used with young children as compared to verb use in English speakers (Tardif, 2006). Correspondingly, it is not clear that speakers of Asian languages necessarily focus their early writing efforts on any particular grammatical form.

Bialystok (1997), making an analogy between word length in alphabets and stroke number in Chinese, tested the idea that Chinese children assume that character representations of large objects should boast more strokes than those of small objects. She asked children to match Chinese characters with their spoken representations using stimuli with different numbers of strokes. *Mountain*, for example, is represented by a relatively simple character, whereas candy is represented by a relatively complicated one (see Table 8.1). If Chinese children believe that stroke number corresponds to size of object, they might mismatch these types of characters and others like them. However, in Bialystok's experiment, there was little evidence that children actually thought this way about characters.

In contrast, across orthographies, it is likely that children's writing gradually changes from a focus on superordinate to subordinate features of script.

TABLE 8.1 Examples examining whether stroke number corresponds to the size of an object in Chinese. The question here (Bialystok, 1997) was whether a character that represents a large object but has few strokes (e.g. mountain) would be more difficult to pair with its picture than a character with few strokes representing a small object (e.g. mouth) or a character representing a large object with many strokes (e.g. tree).

		Object size	
		Big	Small
Stroke number	Few	山 (*mountain*)	口 (*mouth*)
	Many	樹 (*tree*)	糖 (*candy*)

Tolchinsky-Landsmann & Levin, summarizing findings from a variety of researchers, asserted that

> preschoolers' knowledge of the graphic aspect of the written system undergoes three phases: First, children grasp the superordinate features of form of a written text, common to almost any writing (e.g. linearity); second, they grasp the ordinate features which characterize in general a particular alphabetic system (e.g. Roman vs Chinese); and, third, they get to know the subordinate features of the system, i.e., distinctions between particular letters.
>
> *(1985, p. 321)*

Initially, then, children appear to distinguish writing from pictures at a basic level. Writing implies the use of symbols, including letters or characters from a given script as well as symbols representing numbers or other graphic symbols (e.g. arrows). Another salient superordinate feature of script is that it is unidirectional – that is, produced by going in one direction on a page. However, the direction of print may initially vary from child to child. For example, Hebrew-learning children predominantly represent print as unidirectional from age four but do not settle on the conventional right-to-left representation until age five (Tolchinsky-Landsmann & Levin, 1985).

As in most aspects of children's literacy development, early writing experiences are strongly influenced both by age and individual differences. Children's writing skill becomes increasingly sophisticated from ages three to six (Gombert & Fayol, 1992). At the same time, there is enormous variability across emerging writers (for instance, kindergarten and first-grade students) (e.g. Levin et al., 1996). Although trends in the development of writing are clear across ages three to six, they are much less apparent in narrower age ranges (Levin et al., 1996) (e.g. one and a half years). Thus, as discussed in Chapter 3 in relation to the acquisition of the building blocks of print, there is little evidence for qualitatively different stages of writing in young children (Levin & Korat, 1993). Rather, across pre-school, children gradually make use of different overlapping strategies to represent meaning via print. It is again appropriate to consider Siegler's overlapping waves model here. It is likely that, as children gain knowledge of print, they experiment with using both more and less sophisticated strategies simultaneously.

With experience, children learning alphabetic languages begin to understand that print is primarily a representation of sounds, rather than meaning, in language (Treiman & Bourassa, 2000). In very early writing, children appear to demonstrate awareness of the statistical properties of the script in their writing. For example, they notice patterns of print in their native orthography even before understanding letter–sound correspondences and attempt to reproduce these (Treiman & Kessler, 2013). Moreover, their sensitivity to conventional writing of letter sequences when they are at a pre-phonological stage of writing (that is, before they have learned to associate letter names and sounds in print) predicts their subsequent spelling of words once they become conventional spellers (Kessler, Pollo, Treiman, & Cardoso-Martins, 2013). As children begin to map letters to word representations, their attention is focused on phonemic representations of print. That is, they use individual letters in different configurations to depict words. In Chinese, young children also make use of phonetics and positional regularities of radicals early in development. Their sensitivity to statistical properties of Chinese characters before they have formally learned to read partly explained their writing skills one year later (at age five) in one study (Yin & McBride, 2015).

Perhaps years later, when at school, children might make use of some knowledge of morphology and orthographic units in their attempts to spell. Understanding that morphemes are represented as particular orthographic units sometimes facilitates the correct spelling of new words. For example, *morphosyllabic* is easier to spell if one knows the words *morpheme* and *syllable*. Morphological knowledge can also hinder correct spelling, however. As an example, Adams (1990) noted that she spelled *hierarchy* incorrectly for a long period of time because she had assumed that the word was derived from *heir*.

A preferred framework for discussing spelling development is to emphasize stages, and, again, this emphasis on stages, in thinking about word writing as a series of qualitatively different steps, is inaccurate because children often use several strategies simultaneously when they are learning to spell. At the same time, however, and with development, children exhibit a tendency to move gradually from less efficient to more efficient strategies in spelling (Rittle-Johnson & Siegler, 1999). Such trends will be discussed below, first for alphabetic orthographies and then for Chinese. It is clearly important to distinguish the concept of spelling in alphabets and in Chinese separately, because children's early tendencies to make use of print to represent their ideas may differ considerably across these types of script.

Alphabetic spelling development

Children learning about alphabets may initially experiment freely with letters without concern for their particular contributions to word sounds or meanings. For example, when my daughter was three, she picked up on our occasional family practice of spelling to each other. When my then six-year-old son told me he wanted to drink M-I-L-K for dinner, my daughter let me know that she wanted L-P-O-D-Q (which spells *water*, in case you were wondering). The idea here is that children understand that letters are somehow useful in representing something meaningful. Children can do this orally and in writing. However, when children are just beginning to explore alphabetic spelling, they may or may not demonstrate consistency in how they use letters to represent sound. Early work by Ehri and colleagues (e.g. Ehri & Wilce, 1985) showed that young children with limited letter knowledge had an easier time learning to recognize new spelling stimuli based on visual cues (e.g. WBC, a visually distinctive layout, spells *giraffe*) than on spelling–sound correspondences (e.g. *jrf*, comprised of phonemes that sound similar to the target, spells *giraffe*). In this experiment, children were taught to associate particular letter formations with different words (e.g. *giraffe*). Children's first writing experiences follow a similar course. That is, there is a period during which children understand that letters represent print, which is distinguishable from pictures or shapes. However, in this initial period, these children may not yet understand the relation between letter names and their sounds – termed the *pre-phonological stage* (e.g. Treiman & Kessler, 2013).

Vacca and colleagues (2000) outlined four subsequent stages of spelling development based on previous research on English-speaking children. All four stages focus on children's emerging understanding of the association between printed letters and their sounds. These stages highlight some of the differences in strategies that may be used to spell with age. They are reviewed below with the proviso that these so-called stages might more accurately be referred to as strategies, and these strategies are typically combined with one another in the actual process of spelling.

Vacca et al. (2000) referred to the first stage, or strategy, of spelling as *pre-phonemic spelling*. Using this strategy, many children clearly demonstrate insightfulness about letter sounds by spelling words with letters that correspond to some part of the word, particularly the beginning or ending. In addition, as touched upon in Chapter 3, children are particularly prone to spell with letters that have their names contained within words. Thus, in children's early spelling, *bread* might be spelled with a B, *team* with a T, or *deep* with a D. Words might be even more fully represented, e.g. BN might represent *bean*. Much of this very early spelling demonstrates that children are analytic learners, deriving and making clear use of aspects of the alphabet to communicate. However, at this stage, children do not make use of vowels to represent sound in their writing. Although we are focused on more conventional spelling here, Ehri (2005) also noted a pre-alphabetic phase before this. In this phase, children would not refer to letters but to visual features. For example, *yellow* is *yellow* because it has two sticks in the middle.

In the conceptualization by Vacca et al. (2000) of the next most sophisticated strategy, the *phonemic spelling stage*, children expand their spelling to include vowels. The long vowels are easiest to recognize (BOT for *boat*, CAK for *cake*), and these may appear most frequently. With this technique, children make liberal use of invented spelling if given the opportunity. Invented spelling gives children a way to express themselves relatively freely. With the tools of invented spelling, children may become independent writers. In addition, these spelling experiences may improve subsequent phonological awareness and word recognition (Caravolas & Bruck, 2000; Caravolas, Hulme, & Snowling, 2001). Children's intuitive understanding of linguistics often influences their spelling. For example, spelling *her* as *hre* probably reflects the understanding that *her* is formed with an initial consonant and the syllabic /r/ as the ending (Treiman, 1997). This demonstrates substantial phonological sensitivity. Likewise, this spelling effort is also likely to reflect a transitional incorporation of orthographic knowledge, namely the understanding that all words must contain one or more vowels in English.

During the third stage, a still more sophisticated strategy emerges. This strategy is termed *transitional spelling* (Vacca et al., 2000). During this period, children may pick up on orthographic patterns in spelling the language. Children may have come to recognize that /sh/ is spelled *sh* or that the rime /ir/ is often spelled *ear* (as in *dear*, *near*, *hear*). However, spelling productions such as 'I LIVE HEAR' demonstrate that these rules are often misapplied. In their analysis of the role of morphemes in spelling, Bryant and colleagues (1999) referred to this stage as that of *generalizations and overgeneralizations*. Here, children often use particular endings (e.g. *-ed*) indiscriminately, typically making accurate judgements sometimes (e.g. *kissed*) and inaccurate ones at other times (e.g. *sleped*; *sofed* (for *soft*)).

The ultimate spelling strategy identified by Vacca et al. (2000) is that of *conventional spelling*. As children mature, they are required to conform to the standard spelling rules of a language. Spelling tests may become part of the school curriculum, in order to facilitate children's memorization of various spelling patterns. In reference to morpheme spelling, Bryant et al. (1999) distinguished two stages here. First, children recognize that past-tense rules apply only to verbs. Thus, for example, *kissed* will continue to be spelled accurately, *sleped* also continues to be spelled as it was previously (inaccurately), but non-verbs, such as *soft*, will now be spelled correctly (without using *-ed*). Finally, children ultimately are able to apply *-ed* spellings only to regular verbs; they spell irregular verbs (and non-verbs) accurately.

Treiman and Cassar (1997) and Varnhagen and colleagues (1997) highlighted the limitations of stage theories for understanding alphabetic spelling development. Stage theories imply qualitatively different spellings with development and consistent spellings within a given developmental period. Neither of these emerges consistently in studies of developing spellers. In fact, developing spellers combine knowledge of phonology, orthographic rules, and morphology of words from very early on. The above review of strategies of young spellers focuses mostly on the phonological understanding that they exhibit. Indeed, reviewing a number of studies of young children learning French, German, Spanish, and English, Sprenger-Charolles (2004) argued that children's speech knowledge is the foundation of their reading and spelling knowledge.

Orthographic knowledge emerges as a result of knowledge built up from speech–spelling correspondences over time. However, fairly early on, children are also capable of sophisticated orthographic knowledge, 'so even first graders do not usually produce such errors as BBAL for *ball* or HAAT for *hat*' (Treiman & Cassar, 1997, p. 78). Developing spellers of Kiswahili demonstrate similar knowledge (Alcock & Ngorosho, 2003). Thus, children form implicit ideas about how letters are configured in a particular orthography.

Children also demonstrate some morphological understanding in their early spelling, as highlighted by Bryant et al. (1999) and others. For example, 'Children have some ability to divide *dirty* into *dirt* and *-y*, some notion that spelling represents meaning as well as sound' (Treiman & Cassar, 1997, p. 78). Thus, phonological, orthographic, and morphological knowledge are all important for spelling development. As knowledge in these domains increases, children's spelling gradually becomes more sophisticated.

What is the relationship between spelling and reading? Ehri (2000) pointed out that the term 'spelling' is somewhat ambiguous in reference to alphabetic orthographies. In fact, the act of spelling can encompass (i) writing a word, (ii) checking a word presented to see if it 'looks right' (e.g. is *conciet* the correct way to spell *conceit?*), or (iii) writing a word oneself and checking its spelling. In these examples, reading and spelling may be confounded. Thus, it is perhaps not surprising that, in a variety of correlational studies from first grade to adulthood, spelling and reading scores tend to be highly associated.

At the same time, spelling is distinguishable from reading. Particularly in early development, 'spelling is to a large extent a creative process of symbolizing the linguistic structure of spoken words' (Treiman & Bourassa, 2000, p. 2). Invented spelling is a crucial part of this. Young children's strong desires to communicate in writing sometimes make their early spelling attempts unique yet systematically linked to their analyses of connections between spoken and written language, as discussed above. Although most of us have also undoubtedly tried to sound out unfamiliar words when we read (e.g. how might a novice pronounce *mosquito* upon first inspection?), the notion of creativity in reading at the word level is not equivalent to the creativity demanded by invented spelling. Sounding out an unfamiliar word often yields a sound segment that is meaningless (what is a *MOS-kitoe?*), whereas invented spelling is generally meaningful to the speller.

In addition, sophisticated spelling is more cognitively demanding than reading (e.g. Bosman & van Orden, 1997). To *read* a word, only a single stimulus is generated from memory, 'a pronunciation-meaning amalgam' (Ehri, 2000, p. 24). In contrast, to remember how to *spell* a word, a child must juggle several different ideas about the word configuration simultaneously. For example, when I spell the word *Wednesday*, which, in my midwestern American English I pronounce *Wenzday*, I often consciously remind myself to pronounce this odd word as *Wed-nes-day*. I am conscious that this word sounds one way but is spelled another. The spelling is orthographically distinctive and has been encoded phonologically to represent a unique pronunciation different from the real one. In addition, in this case, we have to keep in mind that this word is a proper name and, as such, must be capitalized. There are fewer issues to contend with in simply recognizing this day of the week in print.

What is perhaps most surprising about the association between spelling and reading is that, although spelling ability appears to influence subsequent reading, early English spelling skills do not necessarily build strongly upon early reading skills. In a three-year longitudinal study following British children beginning in their reception class (at age four to five) through to second grade, Caravolas, Hulme, and Snowling (2001) showed that early invented spelling skills clearly predicted subsequent reading skills. At the same time, however, early reading ability did not predict subsequent invented spelling skill in young English readers.

However, in later stages of spelling development, when children were producing more conventional spellings, reading was an important predictor of spelling. The authors interpreted these results as demonstrating that, while early phonological transcoding skills (i.e. invented spelling) drive reading development, reading skill, in turn, facilitates children's acquisition of orthographic knowledge, required for conventional spelling. Ahmed, Wagner, and Lopez (2014) found similar results using latent change score modelling in a longitudinal study to understand the development of reading and writing (including word writing) among first to fourth graders. At the word level, reading was primarily predictive of writing (but not vice versa) in these English-speaking children.

More research on word recognition in relation to word spelling from a developmental perspective might help researchers understand this association better. A finding that spelling predicts reading is consistent with early work by Carol Chomsky (e.g. 1976), and Charles Read (in Schreiber & Read, 1980), who noted a tendency for children to become capable readers primarily through their writing. Early phonological skills and letter-sound knowledge appear to lay the foundations for both early spelling and reading, in English (Caravolas et al., 2001) and in French (Sprenger-Charolles, Siegel, & Bechennec, 1997). As summarized by Caravolas et al. (2001, p. 771), 'One practical implication of this finding is that encouraging beginner spellers to produce phonologically plausible spellings (along with direct instruction in spelling) may help them to lay the foundations for the development of reading as well as spelling.' This may apply primarily to the very beginning processes of literacy acquisition, however.

The lack of prediction of reading for subsequent spelling in the early stages is equally important, however. In studies of Dutch children, reading skill also tends to be a relatively poor predictor of spelling (for a review see Bosman & van Orden, 1997). These findings, of a relatively limited effect of reading on spelling in young children, underscore the need for direct instruction in spelling production, apart from mere reading practice, in developing spellers.

With development, reading and spelling performance may or may not become more integrally linked. We probably know many people who are adequate readers but lacklustre spellers. In fact, knowledge of spelling can even slow us down in certain language tasks. For example, in one study, Seidenberg and Tanenhaus (1979) presented skilled adult readers with various words. The participants' task was to decide whether or not the words rhymed. Decisions about rhyming status were made faster for words with similar spellings than for those that differed in spelling. For instance, given a target word *clue* and two others, *glue* and *shoe*, skilled readers judged *glue* as a rhyming match more quickly than they judged *shoe*. On the other hand, when spellings were similar but the words did not rhyme (e.g. *bomb* and *tomb*), skilled readers took longer to make negative decisions than when both pronunciation and spellings were different (e.g. *bomb* and *room*). The important thing to bear in mind about this experiment is that all words were presented orally. There was no reading involved.

The implication of this study is that once we reach a level of skill in reading, it also affects our oral language abilities. There is also evidence that any exposure, via reading, to incorrect spellings can adversely affect our subsequent spelling. Thus, if one is asked to select the correct spelling from among alternatives in a multiple-choice test (e.g. *embarrass*, *embarass*, *embaras*), for example, this can promote confusion about the correct way to spell *embarrass* in the future (Bosman & van Orden, 1997). Although there is clear overlap between reading and spelling in development, the precise relations of spelling and reading skills in literacy acquisition, particularly by age and grade level, remain somewhat unclear.

Chinese spelling development

What is the nature of spelling in Chinese? Ho et al. (2003) point out that spelling (and reading) of Chinese may differ from alphabetic spelling in several ways. First, more explicit teaching of each character is required both inside and outside the classroom for Chinese than for alphabetic languages. Second, along with this, more orthographic units must be learned in Chinese compared to alphabets. Finally, there is a weaker correspondence between orthography and phonology in Chinese compared to alphabetic orthographies. In some ways, it seems strange to talk about Chinese spelling because, for some people, the concept of *spelling* itself conjures up images of letter strings.

Nevertheless, the ways in which children combine semantic radicals and phonetics indeed encompass the essential ingredients of spelling as defined by Ehri (2000), including writing a word/character and checking to see that it looks correct. Invented spelling is also possible in Chinese by combining various semantic radicals and phonetics to create new pseudo-characters. Studies of Chinese children's spellings indicate that children make use of both phonetics and semantic radicals from the early grades. Shen and Bear (2000), for example, analysed spelling errors made by children in grades 1 to 6, and found evidence for at least three types of error – phonological, graphemic, and semantic. Younger children tended to make more phonological errors, whereas older children tended to make more graphemic and semantic errors. Tong and colleagues (2009) found more evidence for morphological and orthographic errors, however, so part of this probably depends on how errors are defined. As Treiman and Cassar (1997) said of alphabetic spellers, spelling development is a gradual (not clearly stage-like) process. From early on, spellers across scripts appear to have some sense that meaning, orthographic components, and phonology are all represented in print.

Ho et al. (2003) presented a detailed, thoughtful model of orthographic knowledge acquisition based on observations of Chinese children's spelling and reading skills. This model highlights the importance of knowledge of the learning of semantic radicals and phonetics as well as of their positions across characters. The beginning of orthographic knowledge development in Chinese is termed *character configuration knowledge*. Children at this level clearly distinguish writing from drawing. This ability is a rudimentary orthographic skill, as discussed across scripts earlier in this chapter. With development, children tend to learn each Chinese character as a whole, without breaking it down into its components (Shu & Anderson, 1997).

However, *structural knowledge* (Ho et al., 2003) of characters soon emerges. Structural knowledge is the understanding that compound characters are comprised of two separate constituents. At this point, there is little appreciation of the unique features of these constituents. Nevertheless, structural knowledge development facilitates children's acquisition of radical information. Thus, instead of having to memorize each character as a new, complex visual configuration, children with structural knowledge can break down stroke patterns within characters to approximately 1,000 radicals in various combinations.

With experience, children begin to notice that (i) radicals comprise each compound character, (ii) these radicals are of two types – semantic radicals for meaning and phonetic radicals for sound, and (iii) these radicals are positioned systematically within compound characters. This period of spelling and reading development is described as the acquisition of *radical information and positional knowledge*. Children are often explicitly taught the meanings of semantic radicals in school, at least in Hong Kong, and this facilitates their semantic radical knowledge. In contrast, children are unlikely to be taught phonetic radicals of characters explicitly. However, they are quick to make use of correct phonetic radicals, learned implicitly. For example, in the study by Ho et al. (2003), 68 per cent of pre-school children used appropriate phonetics to write out pseudo-characters.

With increasing learning, children eventually begin to demonstrate *functional knowledge* of both phonetic and semantic radicals, during the functional knowledge acquisition period. This implies that children begin to associate particular phonetics with particular sounds, and particular semantic radicals with specific meanings.

With extensive experience of print across primary school, children advance to an *amalgamation stage* of orthographic knowledge development, according to Ho et al. (2003). At this level, children demonstrate the ability to put together all of the different types of orthographic knowledge about Chinese to spell efficiently. Combined knowledge of the forms, functions, and positions of phonetics and semantic radicals is demonstrated at this period. However, presumably, this knowledge is acquired slowly, in fits and starts. Thus, during this time, children may combine phonetics and semantic radicals accurately to form some characters but combine them inaccurately at other times.

Ho et al. (2003) asserted that a final stage of orthographic understanding, termed *complete orthographic knowledge*, occurs relatively late in spelling development, perhaps in early secondary school or later. At this level, Chinese writers will consistently write real Chinese characters correctly and demonstrate clear logical understanding of semantic radicals and phonetics in writing pseudo-characters.

This model characterizes spelling in many of the same ways that spelling development in alphabets has been discussed (e.g. Ehri, 1997; Treiman & Cassar, 1997). Learning to spell in Chinese is a long process, and, as in English, spelling errors may occur even in expert readers. Although there are clearly many differences between Chinese spelling acquisition and alphabetic spelling acquisition, it is important to understand that spelling across scripts involves an emerging analytical approach to print. Children's abilities to focus on the logical, at least somewhat consistent, aspects of print highlight similarities in writing development.

Dysgraphia

In some societies, the phenomenon of dysgraphia is formally recognized. This is not as common as dyslexia is in terms of understanding its parameters or how to diagnose it. Dysgraphia is a difficulty related to written expression. As with many definitions of dyslexia, which typically attempt to rule out alternative explanations for reading difficulties, dysgraphia is often defined based on the idea that despite adequate learning and intelligence, a child still has substantial difficulties in writing, writing at a far lower level than one would expect based on grade level (e.g. Nicolson & Fawcett, 2011). Handwriting difficulties are the hallmark of this disability. Spatial and motor difficulties are often part of dysgraphia, with students exhibiting generally slow and laboured writing with some unfinished words and other words that lack proportionality (e.g. very cramped small letters and larger letters together). Sometimes the pencil grip looks off in the child with dysgraphia or the hands get cramped very easily. Chinese children with dysgraphia exhibit problems similar to those with dysgraphia writing in an alphabetic orthography. Their writing of Chinese characters is often disproportional and sometimes incorrect in terms of the composition or construction of individual characters (e.g. Chang & Yu, 2005). Often the suggestions for helping children with dysgraphia centre on finding aids to help in the writing process, including using various keyboards or computers to substitute, ultimately, for handwriting (e.g. Berninger & Wolf, 2009; Chang & Yu, 2014). Research in the area of dysgraphia is gradually increasing, and often, but not always, those with dysgraphia also have reading problems. As this disorder becomes more clearly defined and understood, those with this difficulty might be helped with additional interventions.

Writing in older children

Moving away from word-centered writing, we now consider writing composition. Writing in the upper grades inevitably involves multiple processes. This section highlights a model of writing that integrates the environment in which the writing takes place with the cognitive abilities of the writer. This model (Hayes, 1996; Hayes & Flower, 1980) provides a good overview of writing that is useful across cultural contexts. According to Hayes (1996), writing takes place within a social context and involves important aspects of an individual's cognitive processes, affect, and motivation. Hayes, therefore, distinguished two aspects of writing – the task environment and the individual. The task environment consists of the social and physical environments in which writing takes place; the social environment includes the culture of the writers, the audience for whom the writing is undertaken, and the extent to which the writing is a collaborative process. The physical environment consists of the writing medium and the existing text.

Culture is an all-pervasive aspect of this task environment (e.g. Brisk & Harrington, 2000). As Hayes succinctly summarized, 'what we write, how we write, and who we write to is shaped by social convention and by our history of social interaction' (1996, p. 5). When I am asked to write recommendation letters for my Hong Kong undergraduate students applying to graduate school in Hong Kong as opposed to overseas, for example, I write differently because I perceive the cultural contexts as valuing different things. Within Hong Kong, aside from academic qualifications, I emphasize the extent to which the student is cooperative, polite, and friendly. These personality characteristics are more highly valued in academic settings in Hong Kong and the rest of China than they are in the United States or France, say. Culture also influences the topics of a text. Personal accounts of wartime are unlikely to appear in Hong Kong essays but may well emerge in writings by Palestinian, Syrian, or Iraqi children. In contrast, references to typhoons, which are sometimes of great concern in parts of Asia such as Taiwan, Hong Kong, and the Philippines, during the summer typhoon season, are less likely to serve as writing topics for Palestinian or Syrian children as compared to some Asian children.

The audience to whom we write is also an important aspect of the writing environment. In certain western school contexts, for example, a secondary-school student may be more willing to risk expressing her heartfelt emotions about personal events to a trusted teacher than to an entire class of her peers. Thus, if a teacher asks students to write an essay entitled 'My Proudest Moment', students may write a very different paper depending upon whether this essay is likely to be read aloud to the class or only by the teacher.

Finally, writing can be influenced by the extent to which it is a collaborative effort. Group writing is often the norm in Hong Kong universities, where a class report is often the collaborative effort of four to five group members. Groups have members with different motivational levels, areas of expertise, and creative ideas that influence the final product. For example, research on training fourth- to sixth-grade students to revise one another's work has demonstrated improved writing for both learning-disabled and average writers (see Graham & Harris, 1996, for a review).

Apart from the social environment of writing, part of the physical environment important for writing is the writing medium. This medium can vary from pencil and paper to word processing, from text only to interactive internet sites complete with graphics and sounds, and even across multiple languages. The writing medium can influence the extent to which writers reflect on their existing prose – another aspect of the physical environment of writing. In particular, the ease with which we write using word processing packages may lead us to reflect less on our writing as compared to handwritten compositions (Hayes, 1996). Our understanding of who is a good vs poor writer may also differ depending upon medium. For example, some children who are not stellar story writers may, nevertheless, demonstrate outstanding composition skills using interactive media (e.g. Snow, 2002).

Part of the physical environment may also include the language of composition. For example, I remember a first-grade Hong Kong Chinese boy attending an English-speaking school. He excelled in story writing in English, and was anxious to express his ideas through a mixture of correct and invented English spellings. He could not do the same in Chinese, although his oral language expression in Chinese was far superior to his English language skills. (Although it is possible to come up with an invented spelling of a given Chinese character, this is far too difficult and confusing (would require extensive knowledge of radicals that young children simply do not possess) for young children to do on a practical level.) As an alphabetic orthography, English perhaps lends itself better than Chinese to invented writing from early on (Ho et al., 2003; Li & Rao, 2000). As another example, it is easier for many of my Chinese college students to produce their term papers in psychology in English because most of the terminology and concepts they learn about in that subject come from textbooks written in English. In contrast, for many of them, expressing their most personal thoughts, hopes, and dreams is much more easily done by writing in Chinese.

At the individual level, interactions among working memory, long-term memory, motivation, and cognitive processes facilitate writing (Hayes, 1996). Working memory is comprised of phonological, visual/spatial, and semantic memory systems. All three are recognized across scripts as essential elements of spelling development. Indeed, working memory stands out as a strong predictor of writing composition in children of different ages (e.g. Guan, Ye, Wagner, Meng, & Leong, 2014). Long-term memory, on the other hand, is wisdom acquired over time about language, the given topic about which one is writing, and the writing genre. In writing the essay 'My Proudest Moment', for example, knowing several synonyms for *proud* demonstrates linguistic knowledge, recalling a proud moment in one's life demonstrates topic knowledge, and writing in the first person demonstrates an understanding of the narrative genre. Knowing how to complete this task of essay writing (e.g. how to begin writing or how to end an essay appropriately) is another element of long-term memory, according to Hayes's model.

Motivation is also important for writing. It probably influences the enjoyment of writing, time spent on the task, and confidence in writing. For example, learning-disabled primary-school children, for whom writing is difficult, write longer and better-quality essays when they are taught clear goal-setting behaviours (Graham & Harris, 1996), which presumably enhance their writing motivation. In their studies of Hebrew-learning pre-school children, Levin and colleagues (1996) argued that self-efficacy about writing arises from understanding one's system of writing through exploration. Indeed, exploration of writing, enjoyment of writing, and self-efficacy about writing are often strongly associated. In a meta-analysis of writing, Graham, McKeown, Kiuhara, and Harris (2012) showed that several strategies used by teachers to facilitate better writing seemed to work. Many of these facilitated children's feelings of self-efficacy about writing. These included pre-writing activities, allowing peers to help with writing (sometimes using a collaborative technique), and explicit assessment of one's own writing. Merely requesting extra writing was also associated with better writing. These techniques generally facilitate children's goal-setting and goal execution for writing tasks.

The final aspect of individual qualities involved in writing was referred to by Hayes (1996) as cognitive processes. These include skills such as planning and decision-making about how the text should continue, actual text writing, and revisions and interpretations of the text. These skills encompass many aspects of thinking and problem-solving. Across texts, we write with goals in mind, and we take steps to achieve these goals by 'subgoaling'. For example, when my ultimate goal is to write an essay, I must first write an introductory paragraph, then set up my arguments, and finally write a conclusion. Thus, an important focus of writing, for both children and adults, is to take advantage of the strategies relevant to planning and revising text, and to eliminate the problems that may hinder writing (Graham & Harris, 1996). For example, primary-school children who are taught to write stories by planning the setting, characters to be included, goals of the characters, and the ending, tend to write better stories.

Researchers (e.g. Yan et al., 2012; Zhang, McBride-Chang, Wagner, & Chan, 2014) have demonstrated that fluency is among the most important cognitive correlates of writing composition. Handwriting fluency is one of the hallmarks of fluent writing (Wagner et al., 2011). Fluency is important for writing both in one's native language and in a second language (e.g. Zhang, McBride-Chang, Wagner, et al., 2014). Other abilities that stand out as critical for writing composition skills are vocabulary knowledge and knowledge of how to write words (Wagner et al., 2011; Yan et al., 2012). This is clearly important, because a child who does not know how to spell a word is unlikely to include it in an essay. Sometimes children (and their teachers!) appear to value good spelling over good ideas, so spelling knowledge constrains output in writing compositions. A practical implication of this is that teachers of aspiring young writers should offer to provide children with the spellings of given important words within the writing assignment so as to minimize the children's limiting of topics or writing quantity based on fear of word misspellings.

Much of the writing process also involves self-regulation, including monitoring one's own thoughts, or *metacognition*. One part of this is the increasing give and take, with development, between reading and writing skills (e.g. Berninger & Richards, 2002). For example, children are increasingly encouraged to reread what they have written in order to revise it, or to write about what they have read, e.g. in book reports.

This model of writing is quite useful for considering various aspects of the person and the environment that influence a piece of writing. From a developmental perspective, it might also be important to consider the age and training of the writer as additional influences on all aspects of the writing process. (For a more comprehensive developmental review of this process, see Berninger & Richards, 2002.) In childhood, with age, our memory capacities increase and we automatize literacy skills so that writing becomes more fluent and less effortful. Our metacognitive strategies also improve so that we are better able to monitor the flow of our writing. Writing motivation may also change because of age and experience. With age, we become more realistic and less overly optimistic about our abilities (Bjorklund & Green, 1992). It is possible that this realism might dampen our enthusiasm for writing. On the other hand, enthusiastic, mature teachers who foster an interest in literacy in children can perhaps increase their motivation to write (Graham et al., 2012; Levin et al., 1996). The next chapter specifically considers research on the effects of teaching on various elements of early literacy.

Suggested readings

Bereiter, C., & Scardamalia, M. (eds) (2013). *The psychology of written composition*. New York, NY: Routledge.

Berninger, V. (ed.) (2012). *Past, present, and future contributions of cognitive writing research to cognitive psychology*. New York, NY: Psychology Press/Taylor Francis Group.

Fayol, M., Alamargot, D., & Berninger, V. (eds) (2012). *Translation of thought to written text while composing: Advancing theory, knowledge, methods, and applications*. New York, NY: Psychology Press/Taylor Francis Group.

Nunes, T., and Bryant, P. (2009). *Children's reading and spelling: Beyond the first steps*. Chichester: Wiley-Blackwell.

Treiman, R., and Kessler, B. (2014). *How children learn to write words*. New York, NY: Oxford University Press.

9

APPROACHES TO TEACHING READING

In this chapter, we consider how methods of teaching reading and writing affect literacy development. Across different countries, approaches to literacy instruction range from quite eclectic, as in the United States (Snow et al., 1998), to very uniform, as in German-speaking countries (e.g. Mayringer, Wimmer, & Landerl, 1998). Teaching is essential for reading and writing development. Although this may be obvious to you, this chapter begins with a review of studies that demonstrate how teaching facilitates literacy acquisition (and also how it does not) and some skills that have been linked to reading.

Perhaps the best-known comparison of methods of reading instruction comes from proponents of different methods of reading instruction in English: the so-called whole language and phonics groups; the debate between these groups will be considered next. There has been little disagreement over the best ways to teach reading in Chinese or other cultures; however, different methods of teaching reading may have different consequences and these are the chapter's next area of consideration.

Finally, across regions, approaches to teaching reading clearly influence the timing of reading development and the specific aspects of the reading process that are most emphasized by taught pupils. Cognitive skill development is also affected by teaching techniques and even by teaching tools such as electronic books and computer games. Phonological awareness and short-term memory skills are two cognitive abilities that may be particularly influenced by such techniques, as demonstrated in the final section of this chapter.

How teaching affects reading

Although schooling is clearly important for literacy development, not all researchers believe that earlier schooling is clearly beneficial for children. In western countries, academic schooling does not usually begin as early as it does in Hong Kong, where formal literacy instruction typically begins at age 3.5 years. Nevertheless, there remains a question about the effects of schooling on young children. From the perspective of cognitive development, for example, does beginning formal academic schooling at age seven (as is typical in Sweden) as opposed to age five (typical in England) have long-standing effects? This question cannot be answered easily because of the many methodological problems involved in comparing across cultures.

However, Morrison and colleagues (e.g. Christian, Morrison, Frazier, & Massetti, 2000; Morrison, Smith, & Dow-Ehrensberger, 1995; Skibbe, Connor, Morrison, & Jewkes, 2011; Skibbe, Grimm, Bowles, & Morrison, 2012) have looked specifically at the effects of schooling on children's cognitive-linguistic and reading abilities within the American culture. In their research, Morrison and colleagues compared groups of similar ages that differed in whether or not they attended school because of their birth dates. Some children's birthdays fall before a given school cut-off date, whereas others' fall after it. Children whose birth dates come before the cut-off start school the following year; those whose birthdays come after it do not. These groups differ little in age (typically by a few weeks). The important question is the extent to which the schooling of children in these groups, who are essentially the same age, matters.

Across studies, those children who attended school tended to be significantly better in their phonological awareness, letter knowledge, and reading achievement, including reading comprehension (Skibbe et al., 2012), compared to those who did not attend school. Interestingly, Morrison et al. (1995) also demonstrated a significant increase in short-term memory skills among children who attended school compared to those who did not. Schooling did not seem to have a strong effect on self-regulation skills or vocabulary knowledge (Christian et al., 2000; Skibbe et al., 2011; 2012), however. Collectively, these findings demonstrate that schooling is particularly important for growth in both reading itself and specific skills that are essential for decoding such as phonemic awareness and letter knowledge. In contrast, some aspects of learning that are important for school, such as the ability to pay attention or moderate one's behaviour in a classroom (i.e. self-regulation), or general vocabulary knowledge, appear to depend more on individual variability and less on explicit teaching. Other differences across reading and language are examined below, in a comparison of phonics vs whole-language approaches to reading.

The fundamental difference between reading and language

Some who argue in favour of the whole-language approach to reading begin with the assertion that learning to speak and learning to read are essentially analogous (Goodman & Goodman, 1979). For both, the goal is communication. However, while language learning unfolds naturally among children who do not suffer sensory deficits or physical, emotional, or mental difficulties, and who are raised in a social environment, reading does not. This is the fundamental difference between the development of language and the development of reading.

All children, throughout the world, learn language at approximately the same rate. As Chomsky (1968) observed, children seem biologically 'prewired' to do this. Interestingly, explicit instruction or correction in language learning sometimes slows down children's language development, and parents rarely focus explicitly on young children's specific syntactic or grammatical errors. Instead, parents are more interested in communicating to their children the meaning of words. For example, if a child says, 'Doggy have hands', a mother or father is unlikely to say back, 'No, Doggy *has* hands.' Rather, parents more often say something like, 'No. Charlie has hands. Doggy has *paws*.' Parents, like their children, use language to exchange ideas about the world. In this endeavour, concepts are important, grammar is not. Yet every child, though largely uncorrected, uses correct grammar most of the time from early on, prompting Pinker to describe a three-year-old child as a 'grammatical genius' (1994, p. 274).

Not only the ease, but also the rate at which children learn language is remarkable. For example, children generally learn to label objects on the first or second try, a phenomenon known as fast-mapping. A mother points to a cat and labels it *cat*, and her one- to two-year-old usually grasps the concept of it and generalizes the label correctly. She thinks other cats – brown, white, black, or tabby – are all called *cat* too, and that dogs and bunnies must have other names. Only occasionally do children misjudge and label only a particular cat *cat* – so that only the family pet, Fluffy, is called *cat* (an *underextension*) – or call all animals with four legs (including horses and dogs) *cat* (an *overextension*). This is just one example of the accuracy and rapidity with which we learn language. To appreciate the remarkable linguistic prowess of the young child, recall your struggles in learning a foreign language some time in your past. Most of us have had such an experience. For an adult native English speaker like me, the tasks of mastering the grammatical rules of French or German, or the tones of Chinese, are daunting. Yet most young children learn their mother tongue with relative ease.

In contrast, reading development does not unfold naturally. There have been entire societies that have not used writing to express ideas. Currently, many people across the world lead productive lives without being able to read. These are individuals who are of at least average intelligence, with all of their senses intact. They simply cannot read either because they have not been taught to read or they have been taught but have had difficulty learning for any number of reasons (e.g. insufficient motivation, learning difficulties, bad teaching).

Children often vary tremendously in how quickly and accurately they learn to read. Some have life-long problems with reading. In the United States alone, Snow et al. (1998), summarizing results from a variety of studies of reading performance, argued that 'the educational careers of 25 to 40 percent of American children are imperiled because they do not read well enough, quickly enough, or easily enough to ensure comprehension in their content courses in middle and secondary school' (p. 98). A more recent estimate put the figure of adults lacking adequate literacy skills at 90 million, with only approximately 38 per cent of American high-school seniors judged to be at or above proficiency level in reading (Lesgold & Welch-Ross, 2012). To return to our theme, although literacy is far from universal across cultures, language is universal. Therefore, perhaps the clearest difference between learning language and learning reading is one of instruction. Whereas language learning requires no explicit instruction or specific practice, literacy acquisition requires both.

There has been a long debate (Adams, 1990; Chall, 1996; Tunmer, 2014) about where the focus of literacy teaching should be, particularly among beginning readers. Those who emphasize the non-shared aspects of reading and language acquisition tend to argue that phonics instruction is essential for successful reading acquisition. These parents, teachers, and researchers advocate that early alphabetic reading instruction must include some explicit training in sound–spelling correspondences and patterns. Those who concentrate more on the similarities of language and literacy development often emphasize the importance of learning to read through connected text. In this philosophy, children are not given explicit training in letter–sound correspondences, because reading for meaning, rather than for decoding practice, is the central philosophy of this method, which is called whole-language instruction.

Whole language and phonics: a comparison

Although explicit school teaching of phonics promotes reading of English, not everyone receives such instruction. Nevertheless, many children learn to read anyway. However, phonics training clearly helps children learn to read more quickly, and it is essential for some children who may have particular difficulties with reading, at least in English (Snow et al., 1998). Stanovich (2000) noted that children who receive relatively little home literacy immersion are most at risk of reading difficulties if they do not receive explicit phonics instruction. These children suffer most.

In contrast, other children are likely to learn to read regardless of instructional method. Stanovich stated:

> In short, when explicit teaching of the components of the alphabetic code is short-changed in early reading instruction, the middle-class children end up reading fine because they induce the code through their print-rich home environments and/or explicit parental tuition.
>
> *(2000, p. 363)*

Thus, middle-class children who enjoy some home literacy experiences often learn to read no matter how they are taught in school. This idea was echoed by Byrne (2005) when he talked about a division of labour between the learner and the environment, and by Tunmer (2014) who highlighted the fact that some children simply come into literacy learning situations with more literacy capital, or personal resources that can be used to learn to read and write.

As discussed in Chapter 2, teaching children to 'crack the code' of alphabetic conversions to word reading, particularly in a non-transparent orthography like

English, is fundamental to learning to read. Phonics tutoring that efficiently teaches children to decode words ultimately leads to better reading comprehension too (Stanovich, 2000). After all, if children cannot identify the single words that make up a sentence, paragraph, or story, and keep these in memory long enough to process their meaning, how can they enjoy or learn efficiently through reading?

The traditional way in which English phonics has been taught was through the names and sounds of the alphabet. From there, words were identified by synthesizing letter sounds. For example, although it is possible that you have never read the nonsense word *kem* before, you can easily pronounce it by blending the sounds made by the *K*, *E*, and *M* into a single (nonsense) word. In the traditional phonics approach, many worksheets intended to get children used to understanding simple writing and reading of words were produced. The types of stories available for children to read at early levels of language development tended to be relatively uninspiring because of their limited vocabulary words.

Whole-language proponents have rightly pointed out that, historically, some children have been turned off by phonics and have needed to be brought back to the more exciting aspects of reading, which include its status as a method of communicating meaning. Children's motivation to read for learning depends upon this inspiration. For whole-language teachers, learning that begins by presenting children with stories to read offers the best way of learning to read. Traditionally, this approach has encouraged children to read words as whole units, sometimes relying on visual recognition (Seymour & Elder, 1986). Whole-language teachers may also occasionally make a link between letter names, sounds, and words (e.g. *pumpkin* begins with a /p/ sound), but systematic phonics teaching is not part of the curriculum (Snow et al., 1998). The basic assumption behind this teaching method is that children's primary task is to derive meaning from print; they acquire phonics knowledge implicitly through experience with print (e.g. Goodman & Goodman, 1979). In this respect, a lack of explicit phonics teaching is analogous to the way in which Hong Kong children have traditionally been taught to read both English and Chinese – through the 'look and say' method (Holm & Dodd, 1996).

Reading for meaning, without the benefit of explicit letter-sound knowledge to help crack the alphabetic code, may encourage children to generate their own hypotheses about what will happen next in the story. After all, many of the main consumers of this method, monolingual American English-speaking children, come to school with a solid grounding in vocabulary and substantial background knowledge, and so should be able to draw on their considerable resources in this area to engage with the text fully. One review (Graham & Harris, 1994) concluded that, compared to phonics learners, whole-language learners tended much more fervently to view the fundamental task of writing as meaning, rather than skills, based.

Thus, whole-language learners may approach literacy from a top-down, rather than a bottom-up, perspective on reading-related skills. Whole language proponents warn that the fundamental danger faced by aspiring readers taught with the phonics approach is one of burnout. These children may be totally 'turned off' by the purely mechanical way in which reading is taught, where they read colourless materials – isolated words, very simple sentences, dry stories (eventually) – because they are limited by the simplicity of the words they can initially read.

In contrast, phonics proponents argue that a much more serious problem in native English speakers learning to read English is that there exist many children who simply cannot master the alphabetic code. These may be the 10 to 20 per cent of children we label reading disabled, dyslexic, or simply poor readers (Stanovich, 2000). For these children, letter–sound correspondences often cause much perplexity. In fact, Siegel and colleagues (1995) found that reading-disabled children actually recognized exception words better than did children without reading problems. Exception words, as we have seen, include *busy* or *dough*, words that one cannot recognize purely on the basis of regular letter–sound correspondences. For children with special reading problems, the ways in which whole-language learners initially learn words, by sight, may, at first, actually be easier than the traditional phonics method of sounding words out.

At this point, it is important to point out that employing a visual strategy to recognize print severely limits one's capacity for learning words. Our memory for unconnected information, such as different word patterns, is limited. We need to recognize some method in print to help us remember more words. Thus, it is impossible to maintain a purely visual strategy, so reading suffers (Gough, Juel, & Griffith, 1992).

The ways in which whole-language and phonics-taught children traditionally initially learn to read words are fundamentally different. One study, by Seymour and Elder (1986), looked at the kinds of mistakes made by children who had been taught using the whole-word method of reading words for the first year in school. They tended to read words as logograms, much like a Chinese character might be read: as a whole. It was striking that children taught using the whole-word method sometimes read words in front of them as completely different in sound, or phonology, from what they saw. However, these words tended to have similar meanings to the correct words. For instance, they would read *white* as *green*; *lions* as *tigers*, and so on, reflecting their attention to meaning over phonology. They were also quite at a loss when presented with new words. They had no tools with which to tackle them. Readers who had been taught phonics, on the other hand, tended more often to make phonological errors. For example, they might say *mouth* for *mouse* or *boy* in place of *toy*. These phonological errors are precisely the mistakes one would predict for children learning to read using a phonics code.

As whole-language proponents argue, phonics readers may be good word readers, but is word recognition what reading is fundamentally about? These children may be bored with reading in general and less aware of, say, story structure. There are several studies, particularly in educational psychology, that point out the lack of motivation in many students who are being taught traditional phonics with numerous drills and worksheets for practice. Indeed, those trained using a whole-language approach to develop early literacy appear to enjoy reading more than those trained using a traditional phonics approach (Stahl & Murray, 1994).

What is the empirical evidence on differences across instructional methods relative to children's literacy skills development? Problems in designating classrooms as specifically 'phonics' or specifically 'whole language' are many, because classrooms vary greatly in their emphases on different aspects of reading instruction (Snow et al., 1998). Many educators value an eclectic approach to reading instruction because literacy acquisition is so multi-faceted (Adams, 1990). Many argue that most researchers and teachers now agree on this eclectic approach and provide many different types of support for early literacy classrooms aimed to focus on both phonics and whole language needs (e.g. Tunmer, 2014). In existing reviews of classrooms primarily oriented towards phonics versus whole-language instruction, it is clear that some systematic phonics instruction is necessary for children to learn to recognize words most efficiently. Compared to their peers receiving whole-language instruction, phonics-trained students are also more accurate spellers of English (Bruck, Treiman, Caravolas, Genesee, & Cassar, 1998). Other studies on children learning to read Danish (Lundberg et al., 1988), Norwegian (Lie, 1991), and German (Schneider, Kuspert, Roth, Vise, & Marx, 1997) have also consistently demonstrated that training in phonological awareness facilitates optimal word recognition in beginning readers.

Another study of first and second graders in America compared children's reading growth in response to three instructional strategies. These strategies were phonics-trained (in which children are given systematic practice in making letter–sound correspondences), embedded phonics (which focuses on directing children's attention to similar patterns of printed and spoken words – e.g. *sight, night, flight*), and whole language (Foorman et al., 1998). Results of the study indicated that word reading was significantly better among the phonics-trained children compared to those in the other two groups, which did not differ. However, the whole-language-trained children differed in having a significantly more positive attitude to reading than the other groups. This finding is important, because those who are more interested in reading may persist with it longer. Greater experience with reading is, in turn, associated with better reading achievement (Stanovich, 1986).

Variable responses to instruction?

Researchers have also begun to highlight the importance of individual variability in early reading development. Comparing across the training groups described above, Foorman et al. (1998) noted that, among phonics-trained students, those who benefited most from such explicit training were the children lowest in reading-related skills at the beginning of the study. Similar conclusions about the particular importance of explicit training in phonics for children with relatively low-level reading skills were drawn by Juel and Minden-Cupp (2000). These researchers observed four classrooms using different instructional practices in relation to the performances of first-grade students across classrooms. Within each classroom, children were divided into groups based on reading ability. Among students with low phonological awareness and reading skill, those who received more explicit phonics training demonstrated the greatest improvement in word recognition by the end of first grade. In contrast, those with relatively good word-recognition skills benefited most from reading instruction that emphasized vocabulary development and independent reading. Similar results were demonstrated in other studies of first graders (Connor, Morrison, & Katch, 2004), second graders (Connor, Morrison, & Underwood, 2007), and pre-schoolers (Connor, Morrison, & Slominski, 2006). Collectively, these studies suggest that children with different literacy skill levels benefit from different types of teaching. Those with low-level decoding skills require more phonics- and print- (especially letter knowledge) based explicit instruction, whereas those with relatively good decoding skills need more emphasis on meaning- and comprehension-related literacy activities (Morrison, Connor, & Hindman, 2010).

The idea that literacy instruction, particularly for younger children, should be targeted to a child's individual existing skills is becoming more popular (Connor et al., 2009). Some researchers also advocate following a child's progress and intensifying literacy skills teaching for the minority of children (typically 20 per cent or less) who appear to need more training in order to develop adequate literacy abilities (e.g. Haager, Klingner, & Vaughn, 2007). This idea is somewhat in parallel with the idea of more individualized instruction above, though here the focus can also be on older children who might be more at risk for reading difficulties. Although there are different core skills that appear to be important to target for maximally enhancing early reading and writing skills in English (e.g. phonics; letter sound knowledge) and in Chinese (e.g. morphological skills; orthographic skills), for example, this targeted response-to-intervention approach is advocated by some researchers for both languages (e.g. Haager et al., 2007; Ho et al., 2012). One study from Finland (Nurmi et al., 2013) did show also that first-grade teachers focused their reading and writing skills instruction more on those children who had weaker literacy abilities in kindergarten; those teachers with less experience in teaching actually did more individualized instruction than did those with more experience.

The overall conclusion of this research may well be exactly what most good teachers will tell anyone about their own classrooms: children acquire literacy skills on a variety of levels. Therefore, it is important for teachers to teach children on all of these levels, including help with word recognition, background knowledge, reading comprehension, and metacognition. All phonics and no whole language may indeed make Jack a dull boy. All whole language and no phonics may well be disastrous for Jack's word recognition development, particularly if he is at risk of reading failure from the outset (e.g. Lundberg, 1994; Snow et al., 1998). Thus, the so-called 'reading wars' are over from the point of view of science. Phonics instruction and a print-rich environment are both essential ingredients for fluent readers.

Teaching effects across cultures

Despite the clear scientific evidence that phonics instruction promotes reading in alphabetic orthographies, the idea that most children can eventually learn to read given any type of ongoing, explicit instruction is supported across cultures (e.g. Ho et al., 2012). Most children who are taught to read eventually acquire basic word-recognition skills. There are even those who explicitly argue that teaching type makes little difference to reading development for most children. For example, in Lundberg's (1999) consideration of Scandinavian countries, he noted that the effects of teaching are far outweighed by home and community factors. In thinking about reading achievement, he stated (1999, p. 166):

> In most countries, the variation between classrooms is small in relation to the variation that exists between students within classes. In the Nordic countries and some others, variation between classrooms accounts for less than 10 percent of the total variations. This means that there is almost no scope for teaching factors to operate in the explanation of student variation.

However, this does not mean that all methods of instruction are equally good. In fact, methods of instruction may be particularly important for those children who have the most difficulty in learning to read. For example, teaching students phonemic awareness facilitates reading among poor readers in practically important ways (e.g. Williams, 1980; Wise & Olson, 1995). For children who require extra help with reading skills, instruction in the code being used is necessary. In studies of English-speaking children learning to read English, poor readers benefit from clear, explicit instructions on letter–sound correspondences and other aspects of word decoding (e.g. Blair, Rupley, & Nichols, 2007; Foorman et al., 1998).

Thus, as the comparison of whole-language versus phonics instruction above demonstrates, the few systematic published studies of different approaches to reading instruction yield different consequences for specific aspects of literacy development, including interest in reading and decoding skills. This is probably generalizable across languages. For example, de Melo (1997, cited in Rego, 1999) demonstrated that, with explicit instruction in and reflection on one particularly difficult spelling rule, the digraph *rr*, children mastered the rule significantly better than children receiving traditional instruction in Portuguese spelling. In traditional classrooms in Brazil, 'the emphasis has been on memorizing the correct spellings of words or on the repetition of spelling rules by rote' (Rego, 1999, pp. 86–87). No explicit reflection on spelling rules is institutionalized. 'As a result most children take a lifetime to discover the more intricate conventions of spelling in Brazilian Portuguese' (Rego, 1999, p. 80). This theme seems to echo that from the whole-language critics. In Brazil, as in the United States, children learn basic word-recognition and spelling skills better when they are explicitly, rather than implicitly, taught.

Studies of Chinese reading also suggest that children's learning of reading-related skills is better when they are explicitly taught. Li, Corrie, and Wong (2008) have suggested that, given the nature of Chinese in all of its complexity, early explicit instruction in Chinese literacy may be important for subsequent reading and writing success. There are also some critiques of Chinese literacy instruction. In particular, 'Drill-and-practice predominates in the teaching of characters' (Wu, Li, & Anderson, 1999, p. 585). Children are subject to a great deal of repetition in order to learn characters, both as the teacher teaches new characters and as the student practises writing them at home. The problem with this is that children do not receive much explicit attention to meaningful aspects of the character. Children at risk of reading problems might benefit most from such explicit, meaning-based instruction, because, according to Wu et al. (1999, p. 585), these children 'tend not to make discoveries about structure unless prompted by the teacher'. Indeed, meaning-based instruction, focused both on semantic radicals within characters and patterns of repetitions of characters across words in mothers teaching their pre-schoolers to write in Chinese tends to be associated with children who are more highly skilled in word reading and word writing (Lin et al., 2012). In contrast, rote copying is associated with lower literacy skills in Chinese pre-schoolers (Lin et al., 2009).

Given the success of meaning-based instruction and some perceived problems with copying by itself, a common suggestion among Chinese academics is that children should be taught characters in groups based on some structural characteristics (Tse et al., 1995). This approach may be fairly flexible, but the basic point is that, rather than being taught in a random order, characters can be grouped to facilitate recall. For example, a small but important minority of characters are pictographs, derived directly from pictures or symbols. If these characters are taught together, children may have a fairly easy time remembering them because of their resemblance to the pictures with which they are paired to facilitate recall.

Similarly, characters that share the same semantic radical might be taught in the same few weeks of lessons to give students a way of remembering them that is based on their common component (e.g. *flower* and *tea* share the semantic radical *grass*). Likewise, characters that share a similar (e.g. same syllable but different tone) or the same (same syllable and tone) phonetic may be grouped to facilitate students' more efficient recall of these characters. Such explicit techniques might prove helpful for beginning learners.

In addition, the organization of Chinese dictionaries is based either on semantic or phonetic radicals (characters can be looked up using either strategy). This technique of grouping characters based on radicals would be useful in getting students familiar with thinking about characters not only holistically but also based on their radical components. In fact, Wu et al. (2002) have demonstrated that an explicit focus on the components of Chinese characters can facilitate various aspects of reading in primary-school children, particularly with regard to their morphological awareness.

Secondary effects of literacy instruction: phonological awareness and associated skills

Although successful Chinese literacy instruction is particularly highly associated with morphological skills and radical knowledge teaching (e.g. Ho et al., 2012), most Chinese learners also make use of some kind of phonological coding system to learn Chinese as well (Pinyin in mainland China and Zhu-Yin-Fu-Hao in Taiwan). It is clear that those who learn to use a phonemic system to represent characters are significantly better in terms of phonological awareness than those with no such training, despite equivalent levels of literacy in Chinese character recognition itself (Holm & Dodd, 1996; Huang & Hanley, 1995; Leong, 1997; Read et al., 1986). Thus, explicit training in phonemic awareness fosters better phonological awareness in Chinese students. In one longitudinal study of mainland Chinese, young children's excellent knowledge of Pinyin was also associated with better Chinese character recognition, even five years later (Lin et al., 2010; Pan et al., 2011), with other early literacy variables, including early Chinese character recognition itself, statistically controlled.

Phonemic awareness also transfers to reading English as a second language. Holm and Dodd (1996) compared mainland Chinese learners of English with Hong Kong Chinese English learners. Although the groups were comparable in reading and spelling real words, the Hong Kong group had much more difficulty than the mainland Chinese group in phonological awareness, or spelling or reading of non-words in English. Although Hong Kong pre-school children are implicitly capable of making use of letter names and letter sounds in learning new English word forms (McBride-Chang & Treiman, 2003), these children have traditionally not been explicitly taught any phonemic coding system in either Chinese or English. Lack of explicit teaching may be particularly problematic when these students encounter unfamiliar words. Without a coding system, it is more difficult to figure out how to pronounce new words. Pinyin knowledge can facilitate word reading in English as well (Pan et al., 2011). Some educators (Tse et al., 1995) have suggested that Hong Kong try a coding system such as mainland China's Hanyu Pinyin, to facilitate reading in young children, but as yet no such coding system has been adopted.

Perhaps the greatest advantage of teaching a coding system to help children learning to read Chinese is that it facilitates comprehension. Children can easily refer to the coding to learn a new character when it is introduced in a textbook. Otherwise, children need to rely on the help of an adult to recognize it. Of most benefit is that such coding 'helps students with composition and helps them to read more elaborate and interesting stories than would otherwise be possible' (Wu et al., 1999, p. 580). These coding systems in Chinese societies are quite helpful in facilitating children's boot-strapping of their own knowledge of Chinese to learn more. Pinyin familiarity likely fulfils a self-teaching function (e.g. Shahar-Yames & Share, 2008) in that Pinyin letter patterns are quickly mastered. These Pinyin patterns are then decoded to learn pronunciations of unfamiliar characters in textbooks.

A theme from studies throughout the world that focus on the explicit teaching of script is the fear that certain reading-related rules, if followed consistently, may mislead children. Internalized rules about the sounds that *K* or *P* make will be a hindrance when learning to read exception words such as *know* or *psychology*, for example. Underscoring this point in a different script, Levin et al. (2002) noted, 'In Israel there is a long tradition of objecting to the instruction of letter names prior to the mastery of basic reading' (p. 294). Some programmes of English literacy instruction also emphasize letter sounds to the exclusion of letter names. However, the available evidence seems to argue that it is better to learn rules that work some of the time than to learn to read in the absence of any rules at all. Children implicitly pick up on many commonalities in their orthographies quickly. Why not teach them?

In alphabetic scripts, for instance, although letter-name knowledge may in fact mislead children in spelling and reading some words, the benefits of this knowledge probably outweigh the problems. When children learn letter names, they may come to recognize them concretely. They are also fitting their graphic to their oral representations of these symbols. Furthermore, children's learning of letter names helps parents and teachers support children's literacy learning. Letter labelling gives everyone a common way of sharing ideas about writing and reading. These benefits prompted Levin et al. to conclude, 'It appears that the view against promoting letter knowledge should be reconsidered' (2002, p. 294). Similarly, although both phonetic and semantic radical information contained in compound Chinese characters are reliable only some of the time, they nevertheless facilitate the reading process better than rote memorization (Anderson et al., 2003; Chan & Wang, 2003; Ko & Wu, 2003; Shu et al., 2003; Wu et al., 2002).

What about teaching aids?

One area of interest from parents and teachers related to teaching practices is the extent to which new electronic technology can be helpful for facilitating literacy skills in children.

Some researchers have focused on the use of e-books, or electronic books that can be downloaded onto tablets or computers, for reading. Do children benefit more from books in this format as compared to the regular, static paper format? The answer appears to be that, for children, there are generally no differences in word recognition (Huang, Liang, Su, & Chen, 2012) or reading comprehension (Wright, Fugett, & Caputa, 2013) across formats for independent reading. Thus, Daniel (2013) has suggested that increased motivation for reading afforded by electronic media might well be the most important reason for parents or teachers to encourage e-book exploration for elementary school children and adolescents. For primary-school children, e-books probably are not harmful, but their positive effects are also unclear.

For younger children, however, interactive media books can be helpful in certain contexts. In a meta-analysis comparing young children's independent interactions with a multimedia book as compared to a traditional book, the multimedia book context appeared to yield better vocabulary knowledge and story comprehension (Takacs, Swart, & Bus, 2014), and even phonological awareness (Shamir, Korat, & Fellah, 2012). However, multimedia books read alone as compared to traditional books read with an adult yielded no significant outcome differences (Takacs et al., 2014). When interactive books serve in some way to prompt young children to answer questions or focus on aspects of the story that are currently being introduced, children appear to benefit (Bus, Takacs, & Kegel, 2014). Those aspects of interactive books that most facilitate learning appear to be animated pictures, music, or interactive questions related to the book; in contrast, games designed to complement the stories are often cognitively distracting for overall story comprehension (Bus et al., 2014). Children at risk for language or reading difficulties might benefit particularly from multimedia e-books (e.g. Bus et al., 2014; Plak, Kegel, & Bus, 2015; Shamir et al., 2012), though some at risk groups, such as those from families who have relatively little education, often miss out on such opportunities (van Dijken, Bus, & de Jong, 2011).

Apart from books, to what extent can multimedia games designed to improve reading-related skills facilitate literacy learning? Here, the focus is on games specifically designed to focus on skills development, such as letter knowledge or phonemic awareness. A meta-analysis of such games (Wouters, van Nimwegen, van Oostendorp, & van Der Spek, 2013) has demonstrated that these are indeed effective for enhanced learning (though not necessarily for motivation). One of the greatest success stories in relation to such games comes from something called graphogame (Ojanen et al., 2015). This game was created originally in Finnish, which has a very consistent orthography. There, it was initially given to children who were at risk for reading difficulties. It is now available online for free to all Finnish children. It is a simple electronic game involving matching of letters (presented visually) and letter sounds, and it can be administered on a computer or even a mobile phone. Young children encouraged to play this game show strong effects of improved reading and spelling skills in both Finnish (Saine, Lerkkanen, Ahonen, Tolvanen, & Lyytinen, 2011) and English (Kyle, Kujala, Richardson, Lyytinen, & Goswami, 2013), one of the languages for which graphogame has been adapted for use, even over time, and even in comparison to traditional literacy instruction. This game has also been adapted for some African languages, in particular a Bantu language called ciNyanja. Some teachers and parents speaking ciNyanja themselves sometimes had difficulties in mapping letter sounds to their names (Ojanen et al., 2015). Graphogame in ciNyanja has not only helped children to learn these correspondences, but it has also helped the adults to scaffold these children's learning so as to be better teachers because they are clearer on these associations through the use of this game, which is often played on a mobile phone, a more common medium than computers on which to play in the African world. Based on results from this graphogame in Zambia, an institute was created in Finland to train teachers in Zambia, Namibia, Kenya, and Tanzania about basic literacy skills, especially phonological awareness and letter knowledge (Ojanen et al., 2015). This is perhaps one of the best examples worldwide of how electronic media can reinforce literacy learning for children, because the electronic media here acts as a complement to and a reinforcer of teacher expertise on early literacy learning.

Parents and teachers should be cautious when exploring the effects of electronic games and other tools that are commercially advertised as facilitating literacy learning, however. The two outstanding aspects of graphogame are that many published, peer-reviewed studies have demonstrated its effectiveness, and, equally, it is free to all worldwide; there is no profit-making aspect to this software. There are other games designed by researchers that have been pegged as effective but also are sold to consumers, so that researchers might have a vested interest in promoting them for profit. One such example is Fast ForWord, mentioned previously in the chapter on dyslexia (e.g. Tallal, 1980; Tallal et al., 1996). This game is based on the idea that those with reading difficulties (and also those with speech difficulties) may have a core deficit in perceiving rapidly presented speech. Part of the purpose of this game is to encourage children to listen to speech in faster and slower presentations in order to improve their temporal processing of speech. One estimate from 2007 was that approximately 570,000 children were using this game in the United States, and others use the game as a form of intervention in Canada, the UK, and Australia (Strong, Torgerson, Torgerson, & Hulme, 2011). A meta-analysis of studies that tested Fast ForWord in children, either against a control group that did nothing or that had some other type of academic intervention (Strong et al., 2011), showed no effect of Fast ForWord on literacy skills. This is important because it illustrates some issues of conflict of interest between research and industry. A single licence for this software may cost hundreds of (US) dollars, and the efficacy of this program is hotly debated, both in research circles and by the public more broadly.

Parents and teachers seeking to enhance literacy teaching for children with electronic media should consider several factors. First, when the media are engaging, they may be motivating (e.g. Daniel, 2013). Therefore, for children who struggle with literacy for whatever reason, if a book or game is targeting literacy skills and can do so in a way that is appealing, electronic media might be a nice option. Second, such media should focus on given skills and not be distracting. Use of electronic media for enhancing literacy skills should indeed be targeted at particular skills, such as vocabulary building, letter name–letter sound correspondences, memory skills, phonological awareness, or story comprehension (e.g. Bus et al., 2014; Ojanen et al., 2015). Games that do not target important skills may be more distracting than helpful (Bus et al., 2014). Third, there should be research available to back up claims made in support of any programs that assert that they enhance reading or writing skills. In the short term, electronic media may be more interesting to children who are struggling than are static books. However, it is important to understand the theory and logic behind electronic media designs so that one can be sure that they make sense to use. Happily, there are many electronic books and programs available that do this very well, in many cultures around the world.

Effects of rote memorization

One alternative to targeted skills-based teaching is rote memorization. Thus, another question involving the debate about bottom-up/top-down approaches to reading that the initial phonics vs whole-language controversy from the west introduced is what happens when literacy development involves primarily rote memorization. In English, some memorization of words must take place, particularly for exception words such as *busy* or *know*. However, the potential for memorization based on teaching techniques in Chinese may be greater.

A common way for instructors to teach early reading of Chinese is to have the class recite Chinese stories in unison (Wu et al., 1999). My son learned to read Mandarin/Putonghua this way daily at school when he was in early primary school. The consequences of this technique in the short term were clearly different from his approach to reading English, however. In Putonghua, his holistic memorization of the story meant that, often, he could not recognize many of the characters. The only way in which he could identify individual characters was to recite the story, syllable by syllable, allotting one character to each syllable. In this way, he could eventually identify a single character, when he got to it (using his finger as a guide!). Perhaps in some ways analogous to the reader of English taught using a strict whole-language method, he was interested in and engaged in the stories and poems he read. He thoroughly enjoyed his Chinese class. At the same time, however, his character-identification skills were limited – guessing was sometimes his only strategy for identifying a given character.

Wagner's (1993) study of children's early reading development in Morocco provided a unique perspective on the consequences of whether learning to read is primarily a 'parts to whole' (e.g. English phonics approach) or 'whole to parts' (e.g. whole-language) process. One pedagogical issue relating to Arabic schooling is how Quranic schooling, compared to modern schooling, might affect children's literacy learning and other cognitive abilities. Quranic schooling focuses children's attention primarily on memorizing the Quran, the religious text that forms the foundation of the Islamic faith. Memorization of the entire Quran is a mark of achievement and religious faith (e.g. Moore, 2011).

Because the Quran is considered to be the actual word of God, it cannot be altered or simplified for children's ease of comprehension. The Quran, presenting ideas in ways that are very abstract, is also written in classical Arabic, which most common people find very different from their everyday spoken or written language. Therefore, it is likely that children from Quranic schools can recall entire pages, or even chapters, of the text without comprehending much of what is being said. Here, literacy takes on a new dimension. We often think of literacy as communicating ideas through print, so that early readers derive meaning from reading. In this case, children can decode and recite a text, sometimes with little awareness of meaning. Moreover, the first language of the child in a Quranic school may be quite different from Arabic, as, for example, is the case for children in Cameroon, whose first language is Fulfulde (Moore, 2011).

Wagner tested the effects of Quranic schooling versus modern secular schooling on Moroccan children's academic performance by comparing children who had attended one of these types of pre-schools for one to two years before beginning primary school. Overall, he demonstrated that children trained in Quranic pre-schools demonstrated significantly better serial memory skills than those trained in secular pre-schools. That is, children with greater experience in memorizing the Quran tended to be able to remember longer strings of numbers and names. However, the two groups of children did not differ in their memory for meaningful sentences, picture location, or a test of embedded figures.

Wagner concluded that, although the two types of schooling had no effects on most cognitive skills, Quranic learning does seem to promote enhanced serial memorization. These results are in line with those of Scribner and Cole (1981), who found superior incremental memory skills in Liberian adults who, as children, had attended Quranic as opposed to other schools. As in the studies of English teaching techniques and their effects on children, Wagner's results demonstrate that particular teaching styles can have very specific consequences for children's literacy skills.

Literacy teachers

One final note we should make about teaching in relation to literacy learning is that the quality of the teachers seems to matter. One reason uniformly touted for Finland's excellent world rankings in reading comprehension as well as other subjects is that the Finnish people widely support and appreciate their teachers (Sahlberg, 2011). Likewise, one of the main reasons cited for lower than expected rankings in literacy development based on government policies in Zambia is lack of teacher training (e.g. Kalindi et al., 2015). At an extreme, teaching is difficult when the language of the teacher is different from the language of her or his students, as is sometimes the case in Zambia where there are seven official languages and many more dialects and languages that are not official government languages (e.g. Kalindi et al., 2015).

Absenteeism is sometimes a problem of teachers as well (Kalindi, 2015a). In addition, researchers have demonstrated that one aspect of teaching is a lack of knowledge of phonological and morphological skills necessary for early literacy training (Binks-Cantrell, Washburn, Joshi, & Hougan, 2012; Ojanen et al., 2015). More broadly, teachers' training in literacy-related skills is associated with early childhood outcomes (Mashburn et al., 2008). In-service training of teachers, mentoring, and requiring professional degrees of teachers might all facilitate better teaching (Mashburn et al., 2008). Thus, although the main focus of this chapter has been on how the act of formal teaching might influence children's literacy skills as a general factor, we cannot forget the fact that individual variability in teaching can also matter in important ways for how quickly and how well children learn to read and to write.

This chapter ends with two 'take-home messages' about the effects of instruction on literacy development. First, because literacy acquisition is a multi-faceted process, optimal teaching should focus on multiple facets of reading and writing simultaneously. Whether children are learning to read in China, Norway, or Morocco, they should receive some explicit instructions about the orthography they are learning. How are words or characters related? How can character or word recognition be facilitated? What are the tricks of the code? Second, at the same time, an overemphasis on rote memorization, dictation, and word/character recognition can only serve to stifle children's interest in literacy acquisition. Thus, daily demonstrations that reading and writing are vital means of communication are equally important for the successful classroom. Students' vocabularies, imaginations, knowledge of syntax, and knowledge bases can all be stimulated by systematic sharing of stories and texts. In this way, the bottom-up and top-down approaches to reading can, together, foster literacy development in the young reader. These can sometimes be supplemented by electronic media. Clearly, solid literacy development is facilitated by motivated, well-informed, and well-qualified teachers.

Suggested readings

Bus, A. G., & Neuman, S. B. (eds) (2014). *Multimedia and literacy development: Improving achievement for young learners.* New York, NY: Routledge.

Li, H. (2015). *Teaching Chinese literacy in the early years: Psychology, pedagogy and practice.* Abingdon, UK: Routledge.

Pressley, M., & Allington, R. L. (2015). *Reading instruction that works: The case for balanced teaching,* 4th edn. New York, NY: The Guilford Press.

Wyse, D., Andrews, R., & Hoffman, J. (2010). *The Routledge international handbook of English, language and literacy teaching.* Abingdon, UK: Routledge.

10

BILITERACY AND BILINGUALISM

It is probably still true (as I said in the first edition of this book) that the majority of books on literacy acquisition focus on the process of learning to read English from the perspective of a native English speaker. Bilingual children's reading development may involve a variety of cognitive, social, and contextual elements that monolingual children do not face, as highlighted elsewhere (e.g. Bialystok, 2000; Datta, 2000; Kenner, 2004). Worldwide, bilinguals are clearly in the majority. Thus, models of reading development derived from monolingual English-speaking children learning to read and to write are not sufficient to explain fully children's literacy development.

This issue is further complicated by the fact that, for many bilinguals, learning to read is not simply learning to read and write first in one's mother tongue and then in one's second language. Instead, literacy acquisition may occur first in a second language. What percentage of the world's population of children learns to read for the first time in a second language? This situation applies to children of immigrants throughout the world, who must adapt to the orthography used in their schools. It applies to some areas of sub-Saharan Africa, where children's home languages differ strongly from their postcolonial school languages of English, French, Spanish, or Portuguese, and South Africa where, despite boasting 11 official languages, English is the medium of instruction in the vast majority of schools (Tsui & Tollerson, 2003).

Second-language reading is also required in much of India, where English is the language taught in the greatest number of schools and across all states. Hindi also serves as a second language of instruction for many children of India with different regional and local home languages, such as Bengali, Tamil, or Gujarati (Datta, 2000). Indeed, there are 211 languages that are recognized as part of India officially, and 18 of these are used as the medium of instruction in some primary schools (Rao et al., 2013). Second-language reading is expected in large portions of the Middle East, Asia, and South America too, sometimes at different times. The issue of diglossia, with a higher, formal, written version of a language in addition to the lower, more colloquial, everyday version which might differ substantially from it and often has no written form, should also be considered in this mix. Arabic speakers find themselves in this situation (for some examples, see Saiegh-Haddad & Joshi, 2014), as do many Chinese speakers. Once educational and sociolinguistic policies are considered worldwide, it is clear that many children's first experience with literacy is that of learning to read in a second or foreign language. Although I have not found any published estimate of precisely how many children this applies to, I once consulted with three experts on literacy and bilingualism: Ellen Bialystok, Catherine Snow, and Daniel Wagner. They concurred in their estimation that approximately 50 per cent of all children learn to read for the first time in a second language.

Note that this half of the world's population of children is only a portion of those who are to some extent bilingual. In modern society, most countries expect an educated person to be one who is fluent in more than one language. In many countries, then, children learn to read more than one script, perhaps simultaneously, as in Hong Kong, or perhaps over a span of years of education, as in most of Europe.

This chapter considers the possible effects of bilingualism on literacy development. First, research explicitly focused on transfer of reading-related skills across orthographies will be reviewed. Next, I will consider some recent research focused on whether it is possible to have reading difficulties in one language or script but not the other. Following this focus on word-recognition skills, I will turn to bilingualism in relation to context and culture, particularly as it relates to reading comprehension. Finally, the chapter will return to evaluate the implications of the research presented for the 50 per cent or so of all children learning to read for the first time in a second language.

Before turning to this discussion, however, I would like to offer a cautionary note regarding definitions of bilingualism. For the purpose of researching literacy in development, it is important to define bilingualism clearly. However, this is a difficult task, particularly for young children who, relative to adults, have not yet fully mastered a single language system with all of its semantic and syntactic nuances.

Bilingual learners develop at very different levels. At one extreme are those who speak two or more languages effortlessly, with no trace of foreign accent and with native-like fluency in all aspects of each language. My nephew, whose command of both Putonghua (Mandarin) and English is flawless, fits this definition. At the other extreme might be the average Hong Kong Chinese child, who learns English only in school and speaks Cantonese at home. This student rarely uses English to communicate. Rather, English is learned primarily as a series of words to be memorized in school. Moreover, the words that are memorized are read and written but rarely spoken in the context of a conversation.

This contrast is a meaningful one to me in relation to literacy, precisely because there can be a mismatch between word identification patterns and oral language levels attained. At one point, my then sixth-grade nephew, whose oral Chinese was excellent, read Chinese only at a third-grade level, because he attended a public school in Los Angeles, where Chinese was not taught. He learned to read Chinese only by attending classes for a few hours per week outside his regular school pro-gramme. In contrast, the Hong Kong student, whose oral English is often relatively poor, can read aloud English words at a level higher than a typical American reader of the same grade (e.g. McBride-Chang & Kail, 2002).

This oral/written language contrast is useful for conceptualizing bilingual read-ing development. Word decoding among bilinguals depends upon the scripts to be learned, the reader's reading-related skills, the extent to which the reader can draw upon previous literacy experiences in learning to read a new script, and the kinds of instruction in reading received. For bilinguals with adequate school sup-port, word recognition is the easy part. In contrast, skilled reading comprehension requires wide-ranging cultural support and motivation, often difficult to sustain for any group of children but especially for second-language learners. Thus, skilled reading comprehension poses the greatest challenge for bilinguals (Datta, 2000). These ideas are expanded below.

Transfer of reading-related skills across orthographies

Across studies, there is good evidence for the transfer of phonological process-ing skills across scripts. In many of these studies, children are typically fluent in two languages and read in both. Investigators then test the children on a variety of reading-related tasks and on reading itself, and look at the associations across measures. These associations are generally moderate to strong. For example, one correlational study compared pre-school children with a variety of home lan-guages – including, among others, Japanese, Tagalog, Arabic, Hindi, and Punjabi – to monolingual English speakers (Chiappe, Siegel, & Gottardo, 2002). In this study, English phonological processing skills, including multiple measures of phonological awareness and one task of rapid automatized naming (RAN), were similarly predict-ive of reading ability across groups.

A one-year longitudinal study, focusing primarily on phonological awareness in both French and English, demonstrated their strong overlap (Comeau, Cormier, Grandmaison, & Lacroix, 1999) in children at grades 1, 3, and 5. Overall, phono-logical awareness in either language among these children, all of whom were native English speakers learning French as a second language, was as strongly associated with reading in French as in English. Furthermore, phonological awareness in both languages predicted French word decoding one year later. Based on the results of this study, Comeau et al. asserted that 'phonological awareness is a general (not language-specific) cognitive mechanism' (1999, p. 40). This paper clearly demon-strates that phonological awareness is easily generalized from one's native language to a second language.

Not only has generalization of phonological processing been found between Indo-European languages, but it has also been found in languages as diverse as Chinese and English. In one study, measures of phonological processing in Chinese and English were positively associated, and both contributed uniquely to English word recognition (Gottardo, Yan, Siegel, & Wade-Woolley, 2001). Here again, phonological skill appears to be at least partly a stable aspect of cognitive processing. Such findings of Chinese–English phonological transfer were demonstrated even across a one-year period (Luo, Chen, & Geva, 2014).

The above-mentioned studies focused primarily on comparing phonological processing skills across languages and examining their utility for predicting reading in a single orthography. Other studies have highlighted the importance of first-language learning and literacy acquisition for facilitating reading in a second language. For example, a study of bilingual Urdu–English and monolingual English-speaking children (Mumtaz & Humphreys, 2001) focused on transferability from native- to second-language phonological processing and reading. Urdu is a phonologically regular orthography, whereas English is relatively irregular in its phonological associations. In this study of seven- to eight-year-olds, those with an Urdu background outperformed their monolingual English-speaking peers in tasks of verbal memory, phonological awareness, non-word repetition, and reading of regular words and non-words in English. Mumtaz and Humphreys interpreted these results as demonstrating a facilitating effect of Urdu on second-language learning and reading in English. They argued that cracking the alphabetic code of Urdu was fairly simple for the bilingual group. Once the children understood this relatively easy code, they transferred their knowledge of reading to a more difficult coding system in a second language. Because of its many phoneme–grapheme inconsistencies, English is not, initially, a simple language to read. Thus, for monolinguals who only knew English, learning to read English was more difficult without the benefit of the more straightforward code that the Urdu–English bilingual children had had.

Similar results were obtained in two studies of nine- to thirteen-year-old bilingual children as compared to their respective age- and reading-matched monolingual English-speaking comparison groups. That is, the bilingual children were significantly better than their monolingual peers at pseudo-word reading and spelling. Again, these results may be attributable to the shallow orthographies learned by the bilingual children. These orthographies, Portuguese (Da Fontoura & Siegel, 1995) and Italian (D'Angiulli, Siegel, & Serra, 2001), may have facilitated literacy skills in English, a more difficult orthography to decode. As in the previous Urdu example, both Portuguese and Italian alphabetic codes are transparent as compared to the English one. Therefore, learning to read in a shallow orthography helped the bilingual children learn to read the deeper English one.

There is other evidence that bilingualism itself may facilitate phonological awareness. For example, several studies of kindergarten and first graders (Bruck & Genesee, 1995; Campbell & Sais, 1995; Kang, 2012; Rubin & Turner, 1989; Yelland, Pollard, & Mercuri, 1993) found bilingual relative to monolingual children had some advantages in phonological awareness. However, it may be that this facilitating effect depends on the level of similarity across languages. For example, in a study of bilingual Chinese–English children (Bialystok, Majumder, & Martin, 2003), the bilinguals performed significantly more poorly than their monolingual English-speaking peers in tasks of phonological awareness. These tasks focused on phonemic awareness rather than on larger linguistic units of phonological awareness. What accounts for these results? It may be that in some alphabetic languages, children are sensitized to phonemic units of language. On the other hand, in Chinese the syllable is the basic linguistic unit. Thus, when bilingual Chinese–English-speaking children are asked to perform tasks of phonemic awareness, they may have difficulties because they have less experience with phonemes as compared to native English speakers. As discussed in previous chapters, English children are sensitized to the phonemic nature of English, whereas phonemes are relatively unimportant for learning Chinese (Cheung et al., 2001). Similarly, because Chinese emphasizes syllables, whereas English emphasizes phonemes, syllable awareness may be facilitated in young Chinese children, even in a second language. For example, in one study, Hong Kong Chinese children's syllable awareness in English, their second language, was better than monolingual English speakers' English syllable awareness (e.g. McBride-Chang & Kail, 2002). These studies suggest that native language affects phonological awareness in a second language. In a meta-analysis precisely focused on bilingual phonological awareness, Branum-Martin and colleagues (2012) demonstrated that both language and psycholinguistic grain size (including phoneme, rime, and syllable comparisons) strongly influence how phonological awareness manifests itself in bilingual children.

Perhaps even more important than the inherent characteristics of a language in determining an individual's level of phonological awareness is the effect of direct instruction in phonemic awareness. For example, Hong Kong college students at least in the past were strikingly poor in English phonemic awareness relative to comparable students from China, Vietnam, or Australia, all of whom receive some phonemic instruction in their first language (Holm & Dodd, 1996). Without learning any phonemic coding system to aid their reading, Hong Kong adults and children (Huang & Hanley, 1995) had poor phonemic awareness, despite adequate reading of real words in English. In contrast, Chinese children taught the Pinyin or Zhuyin-Fuhao coding systems to facilitate Chinese reading tend to have well-developed phonemic awareness. Bringing the data together, we might infer that, when phonemes play a major role in the writing system and/or reading instruction of the child's first language, this may facilitate enhanced phonemic awareness in the child's second language. In contrast, when phonemes play a minimal role in a bilingual child's literacy acquisition in the first language, this may have an inhibitory effect on the development of phonemic awareness in the second language.

There is less evidence for transfer of morphological awareness or orthographic skills, but there is a little bit, some a bit surprising given the diversity of languages and corresponding morphemes. How to define transfer across languages is not always clear. Researchers often assume that a moderate to high correlation between tasks purportedly measuring the same construct (e.g. morphological awareness) in different languages indicates some transfer effect. Perhaps stronger evidence comes from studies in which morphological awareness in one language explains unique variance in reading in the other language, with other important reading-related variables statistically controlled. Lexical compounding (i.e. creating compound words) is one skill that can be tested in both Chinese and in English. Although English has relatively fewer compound words, it has enough such that the principle is clear. Thus, it was quite interesting that Zhang and colleagues (2010) demonstrated that fifth graders who were trained in lexical compounding in Chinese were able to use such training to improve their lexical compounding skills in English. In contrast, only the academically better students were able to make use of their lexical compounding training in English to demonstrate higher levels of lexical compounding in Chinese. Another study of Chinese children showed that morphological awareness in English was a unique correlate of reading comprehension in Chinese among Chinese children, with other reading-related skills statistically controlled (Wang, Cheng, & Chen, 2006). In another study by Wang, Ko, and Choi (2009), morphological awareness in either Korean or English explained unique variance in reading in the other language. Among English (L1)–Arabic (L2)-learning children in Canada, children's morphological awareness in Arabic explained variance in their reading in English (Saiegh-Haddad & Geva, 2008) as well. However, importantly, the tasks of morphological awareness in Arabic and English were not significantly correlated. All of these studies are interesting particularly because they show some evidence of some transfer, loosely defined, across different orthographies. In scripts that share a Roman alphabet, such as French–English (Deacon et al., 2007) and Spanish (L1)–English (L2) (Ramirez, Chen, Geva, & Kiefer, 2010), some evidence of morphological awareness transfer has been demonstrated as well. The mechanisms by which such transfer might take place remain relatively unclear at this point, but, as with phonological awareness, it appears that there is some overlap in understanding or processing of meaning units across languages and that this may facilitate reading skills in bilinguals.

So far, there is less evidence for orthographic transfer across scripts or languages such as Chinese–English (e.g. Keung & Ho, 2009; Wang, Park, & Lee, 2006; Wang, Perfetti, & Liu, 2005). Akamatsu (2003) did, however, demonstrate in college students that some alterations of text using CaSE sensITive script like this was more difficult to read for Chinese and Japanese readers as compared to Persian readers, presumably because the Persian students were used to reading in an alphabetic script and had experienced more diversity and variability in doing so, so they could adjust to this challenge. In this way, orthographic knowledge of one script might sensitize or desensitize a reader in another. Moreover, some research suggests some overlap between orthographic sensitivity, especially in two scripts that both make use of the Roman alphabet (Deacon, Wade-Woolley, & Kirby, 2009; Sun-Alperin & Wang, 2011). Because such studies typically involve correlational research, again, the precise mechanisms by which such transfer takes place have yet to be well understood. Nevertheless, it is interesting to contemplate the possibility that even in sensitivity to how words look and the rules of how they are written, some transfer might be possible.

Apart from the importance of general cognitive-linguistic skills – such as phonological processing, morphological awareness, and orthographic processing, as

discussed above – studies demonstrate that script-specific knowledge is also crucial to learning to read in a second language (e.g. Geva & Siegel, 2000; Geva &
Wade-Woolley, 1998). In particular, the extent to which an orthography is relatively
regular (shallow) or irregular (deep) in correspondences between orthographic units
(e.g. letters, characters) and speech sounds affects children's reading in that script.

One example can be found in the case of Farsi (Persian), which has a shallow
orthography for reading but an opaque one for spelling. That is, each grapheme (letter) of the Persian script has a single pronunciation. Thus, reading using these consistent letter–sound correspondences is straightforward. On the other hand, spelling
Persian is more difficult because some phonemes can be represented by more than
one letter. For example, the sound of /z/ can be represented by one of four different letters. Thus, in a study of second- and third-grade Iranian children living in
Canada, only Persian orthographic processing skill (spelling recognition), but not
Persian phonological ability (pseudo-word reading), predicted spelling in Persian
(Arab-Moghaddam & Senechal, 2001). In contrast, these children's English spelling
was uniquely predicted by their performances in both orthographic and phonological processing tasks – parallel to the Persian ones administered – in English. The
authors suggested that the Persian orthography may encourage reliance on orthographic skills in a way that English does not. They speculated that differences in
grapheme–phoneme correspondences for reading and spelling in Persian may have
prompted children to use different strategies to learn these skills. Strategies for word
recognition may well focus on learning letter–sound correspondences and applying
them. In contrast, spelling strategies may encourage children to memorize word
spellings, promoting orthographic strategies.

Mumtaz and Humphreys (2001) put forward a similar argument about Urdu/
English differences. Here, English is compared to a language, Urdu, that has a more
regular orthography. Among seven- to eight-year-old Urdu–English bilinguals, recognition of irregular English words was significantly poorer than that of monolingual English speakers. This result was in striking contrast to the same bilingual
children's significantly better performance in reading regular words and non-words
as compared to their monolingual peers, as reviewed above. These contrasting results
suggest that, in comparison to a regular orthography such as Urdu, orthographically deep English demands greater attention to orthographic cues in reading. Those
who have learned to read Urdu are relatively inexperienced at making use of orthographic cues to read English words, because orthographic processing was not particularly important in reading in their first language; rather, Urdu readers could
rely on consistent grapheme–phoneme associations for both reading and spelling.
In contrast, native English readers are forced to focus on orthographic units to read
words (such as *conceit, feat,* or *feet*), the equivalent sounds of which (in this case, the
long E sound) may be represented with different spellings.

Chinese–English bilinguals make extensive use of orthographic skill in learning to spell. Compared to their monolingual English-speaking peers, second-grade
Chinese–English bilinguals were found by one study to be significantly better at
spelling both real words and irregular English pseudo-words (Wang & Geva, 2003).

These results were interpreted as suggesting a greater reliance on visual and orthographic information in learning to spell among the bilinguals, most of whom had begun learning to read Chinese using a 'look and say' method typical in Hong Kong from the age of four. This 'look and say' method, emphasizing the holistic visual memorization of characters, may have been applied to English word learning as well. An emphasis on orthographic knowledge in learning to read Chinese is sensible given the relatively unreliable phonological cues of Chinese as compared to alphabetic scripts. A modelling study by Leong and colleagues (2005) lent further evidence to this idea by demonstrating a much stronger association of orthographic as compared to phonological abilities in relation to word reading in English as a second language among Hong Kong Chinese children aged 10–12.

Overall, studies of bilingual readers demonstrate that deep orthographies require a wider variety of orthographic strategies in literacy acquisition than shallow ones. In addition, shallow scripts tend to be more accurately read as compared to deeper ones (Geva & Siegel, 2000). These results highlight both the importance of general cognitive skills that transfer across orthographies and the significance of specific orthographies for tapping specific reading-related skills.

Bialystok and colleagues (Bialystok, 1997; Bialystok et al., 2000) investigated two other aspects of literacy development among bilinguals. First, they explored the extent to which children understand that print itself represents a word that, regardless of the picture with which it is paired, remains the same. This is the idea of the *invariance* of a printed word. Second, they tested the extent to which children understand the arbitrariness of a word's size relative to its meaning in a given orthography. For example, the words *bus* in English or *shan* (mountain) in Putonghua are short words (and a simple character in Chinese print), even though they represent large objects. Meanwhile, many small objects, such as *butterfly* in English or German (*Schmetterling*), are represented by words with more syllables and which are relatively long or complicated in print. Given that children initially assume that print represents meaning (Byrne, 1998), these examples often confuse young children. Relative to monolinguals, then, do bilinguals differ in their performances on tasks measuring these concepts?

On the invariance task, bilingual children consistently outperformed their monolingual peers, regardless of the languages tested (for a summary, see Bialystok, 2002). It appears that, because of their extensive experience in different languages, they understand that an object's label within a language remains constant. They further apply this concept to print. In one study, pre-school bilinguals were given a task in which they were initially shown two printed labels (e.g. *king* and *bird*) correctly paired with their corresponding pictures. When these pictures were subsequently switched (e.g. a *king* label with a *bird* picture, and vice versa), they correctly identified the labels approximately 80 per cent of the time. In contrast, monolinguals correctly identified such labels only about 45 per cent of the time (e.g. Bialystok, 2002).

In contrast, in the word-size task bilinguals outperformed monolinguals only if they were familiar with two different writing systems. Thus, Hebrew–English and Chinese–English bilinguals outperformed both monolinguals and French–English bilinguals, whose orthographies share the same alphabet, in this task (Bialystok, 1997; Bialystok et al., 2000). In this task, experience with different types of script appears to have sensitized children to the arbitrariness of the relationship between a word's length or complexity and its meaning. In contrast, children learning two alphabetic orthographies, such as French and English, were no clearer about the association between a word's written form and its meaning than were monolinguals. Inherent in Chinese are some iconic features (i.e. pictorially similar to the objects they represent) of certain characters, and children seem to master learning of associations between these characters and their oral referents more quickly than characters that are not iconic. Thus, Bialystok and Luk (2007) argued that although matching print to oral referents is a universal aspect of learning to read, script itself might affect how quickly such associations are learned.

Thus, across the studies considered in this section, related to phonological processing, reading and spelling skills, and early concepts about the nature of print, the effects of bilingualism must be qualified. Bilinguals appear to have a relatively easy time with phonological processing across languages, for example, but this depends upon the individual languages and scripts learned, as well as the method of instruction to which learners are exposed. Learning to read in a second language also depends particularly upon the idiosyncrasies of the 'second' script to be learned. Finally, although bilingualism appears to facilitate children's understanding that print labels invariantly refer to a single object, a bilingual advantage in understanding the arbitrary relationship between a word's size in print and its meaning may be partly script-dependent.

Is it possible to have difficulties in reading of one orthography but not another?

I occasionally get invited to give talks to parents in Hong Kong on research related to literacy. Sometimes the parents have children in local schools, where the children learn their subjects primarily in Chinese but study English as a subject in class. Other times, the parents have children in international schools. In these schools, the medium of instruction is English but Chinese is studied as a subject in school. All of my academic life, I have operated from the basic principle that of course it is better to learn school subjects in one's native language, whatever that might be. Imagine my surprise, then, when I found parents asking me literacy-related questions that even challenged that fundamental belief. Here are two that parents actually have asked me (more than once): 1) 'If a child has dyslexia in English, will he/she have an easier or a harder time in learning Chinese?' 2) 'Should I send my child to international school? We are a Chinese-speaking family, but learning to read in Chinese is too hard.'

Such questions stimulated me to ask whether, given all of the solid evidence for transfer across languages and orthographies reviewed above, it might also be possible to have difficulties in word reading in one orthography but not the other. Case studies had previously indicated that some individual patients did manifest reading difficulties in one orthography but not another (Wydell & Butterworth, 1999; Wydell & Kondo, 2003) – in this case a Japanese/English contrast. However, generalizing to populations from individual examples such as that one is notoriously difficult. What about group studies? One research study on Spanish-speaking children learning English found that for those who had learning difficulties in English, the chances of them being classified as having reading difficulties in Spanish was 55 per cent (Manis & Lindsey, 2010). This overlap seems relatively high. Yet another study on scripts all representing Japanese (Uno, Wydell, Haruhara, Kaneko, & Shinya, 2009) found that reading difficulties were very rare in hiragana, medium in katakana, and relatively high in kanji, among children reading in all three. Perhaps it is script-related variations that might affect whether and how children learn to read.

Evidence for a discrepancy in difficulties in word reading across orthographies would theoretically be more likely to emerge in scripts that are more diverse and that are taught differently. We tested this idea in studies comparing reading of Chinese and English in the same children. When we compared the bottom 25 per cent of readers of Chinese and then separately of English from the same large and representative sample of children from Beijing and Hong Kong, respectively, we were interested in the extent to which this bottom 25 per cent would be the same. That is, what percentage of children who were in the bottom 25 per cent of readers in Chinese was also in the bottom 25 per cent of readers for English? In Beijing, the overlap was about 40 per cent, which was statistically significant (McBride-Chang, Shu et al., 2013), but in Hong Kong, the overlap was not significant at 32 per cent. We had expected such a result because in Beijing, Pinyin, an alphabetic phonological coding system, is used to teach Chinese, so there is some mediation of an alphabetic system in teaching both English and Chinese there. In contrast, in Hong Kong, children use no phonological coding system to learn Chinese. Our results hint at the fact that it might be possible to have reading difficulties in one orthography but not the other, depending upon how 'reading difficulty' is defined.

Another question we asked in a series of studies on Chinese children learning to read both Chinese and English (Kalindi et al., 2015; McBride-Chang, Shu, et al., 2013; McBride-Chang, Lam, et al., 2011; Tong, Tong, & McBride-Chang, 2013) was whether those who are poor in reading in Chinese only, in English only, or in both, differ from one another in any of the cognitive abilities typically tested. So far, in different samples, we have found that phonological awareness tends to be somewhat lower across all three groups of poor readers, though there is some tendency for those who are poor in reading English (either poor only in English or in both Chinese and English) to have lower phonological sensitivity than do those who are poor only in reading Chinese (Tong et al., 2013). Those who are poor in reading Chinese tend to have difficulties in Chinese morphological awareness tasks and in pure copying tasks; poor readers of English do not (Kalindi et al., 2015; McBride-Chang, Shu, et al., 2013). Finally, those who are poor readers in both Chinese and in English are extremely slow in rapid automatized naming tasks. Indeed, they are significantly slower than their peers, who are poor only in reading one orthography at this task (Kalindi et al., 2015; McBride-Chang, Shu, et al., 2013). Biliteracy, thus, shows not only some overlap but potentially some differences as well. Given that Chinese is relatively unreliable phonologically and manifests the most different visual-orthographic patterns of any orthography, and that English word reading is based on the alphabetic code, these results seem reasonable.

What are the practical implications of this work? If it is possible for children to have difficulties in reading in one orthography but not another, this implies that children who are learning to read in two scripts might benefit from having access to screening for reading problems in both scripts. It is not always necessary to give remedial help to a child who is dyslexic in his first language in the second language. This may be needed, but this is not a given by any means. By the same token, learning to read words in a second orthography may pose unique challenges not covered in L1 literacy training. For example, as more foreigners learn to read Chinese, more strategies targeted specifically to the special skills required for Chinese learning should be offered. Given the popularity particularly of learning English and Chinese as second languages throughout the world, researchers and teachers should be aware that some different types of skills may be required for each. These are important at the word level. We now turn to the greatest challenge of bilingual reading of all, reading comprehension.

Bilingualism and reading comprehension

Children's two primary difficulties in second-language literacy acquisition are in accessing the meaning of text and communicating meaning through writing (Datta, 2000). In Gough and Tunmer's (1986) 'Simple View' of reading, reading comprehension requires both word decoding and language comprehension skills. While many research studies demonstrate adequate or superior word-recognition skills among bilingual children, their oral language skills, critical in building meaning for understanding, tend to lag behind those of their monolingual peers (e.g. Droop & Verhoeven, 2003). Although word recognition may be difficult for some bilingual readers, meaning construction at every level is the primary concern of both bilingual students and their teachers.

A lag in oral language skill development is particularly worrisome among those termed at risk bilinguals (Tabors & Snow, 2001). At risk bilinguals are those who speak primarily in a language other than their mother tongue. This phenomenon is especially likely to occur in the children of immigrants. In such cases, larger society often makes use of a language other than the one used at home, and parents are anxious to encourage their children's learning of this dominant societal language because they believe this will help children to do better in the new society. The problem with such communication is that these children may fail to develop fully their vocabularies, concepts, and thoughts about how the world works because of a lack of support in any language. The result is that some children never learn either language sufficiently (e.g. Wong-Fillmore, 1992).

One example of this might be minority-group Turkish children in the Netherlands. These children's parents may perceive that their primary responsibility is to facilitate their children's Dutch development for better school performance. At the same time, however, the Turkish parents' command of Dutch may not be good enough to promote sophisticated linguistic development in that language. In this case, the children receive limited language stimulation from their parents, who are strong in Turkish and weak in Dutch, and often purposefully limit Turkish linguistic input to their children. The result may be that children learn some Turkish and some Dutch but neither with the richness necessary to develop the sophisticated semantic knowledge built up with extensive home and societal linguistic support.

Much of the richness of language comes from vocabulary development. Interestingly, development of vocabulary is often somewhat delayed in young developing bilinguals relative to monolinguals, simply because the amount of language input they receive in either language will be less than the total received by a monolingual speaker. At the same time, however, bilinguals' total vocabulary knowledge across languages is usually greater than that of the monolinguals in a single language.

Early literacy development not only depends upon knowledge of a language; it is also facilitated by experience with print, particularly through shared story reading (e.g. Snow et al., 1998). In the situation described above, immigrant parents may read very little with their children in either Turkish or Dutch because of lack of support. There may be few Turkish reading materials available, and parents are reluctant to emphasize reading in Turkish for fear that this will compromise their children's Dutch development. On the other hand, parents' Dutch proficiency may not be sufficient to stimulate their children's interest in Dutch reading.

Weak language skills at pre-school age are often associated with difficulties in literacy at primary school. The relationship between language skills and literacy is reciprocal. As Tabors and Snow put it, 'Much of the more sophisticated vocabulary and more complex syntax that adult speakers of a language know comes from exposure to literacy in that language; after about third grade, oral language development derives from and depends on literacy' (2001, p. 172). Droop and Verhoeven (2003) have demonstrated that Dutch reading comprehension among primary-school children learning Dutch as a second language depends upon a variety of higher-order language skills, including understanding of syntax and meaning, vocabulary knowledge, and oral comprehension of Dutch. In addition, among the best predictors of reading comprehension is previous reading comprehension, underscoring the importance of early linguistic comprehension for subsequent reading comprehension. These results highlight the bidirectional association of language skills and reading *within* a given language.

In addition, language skills *across* languages build upon one another to promote literacy. For example, vocabulary development is crucial to reading comprehension across languages. In one study, Carlisle and colleagues (1999) demonstrated that primary-school native Spanish speakers' Spanish vocabulary knowledge was a good predictor of their English reading comprehension. In another study of Dutch children learning to write in English, eighth graders' writing skills in the two languages were highly correlated with one another (Schoonen et al., 2003). These studies highlight the importance of knowledge of a first language for literacy development in a second. However, studies (e.g. Gottardo & Mueller, 2009; Nakamoto, Lindsey, & Manis, 2008) of Spanish (L1)-English (L2) learners also have demonstrated that children's English reading comprehension is fully explained by their English abilities. That is, English word recognition and oral language skills fully explain English reading comprehension in statistical models; although these Spanish L1 children's reading comprehension in L2 English was associated with Spanish word reading and oral language abilities, once English word reading and oral language abilities were included in the models, the Spanish skills were no longer unique correlates of reading comprehension in English. Such results suggest that although there is some transfer from L1 to L2 for reading comprehension, at least for languages that are relatively similar in alphabetic structure, L2 reading-related skills may be ultimately more important for L2 reading because they are closer to what is actually required for L2 reading to take place. This idea has not been explored extensively in the context of cognitive skills related to reading comprehension, but it is a central topic for researchers interested in explaining biliteracy from a cultural perspective (e.g. Kenner, 2004). Overall, it is possible and even likely that some vocabulary and some particular topics lend themselves more to one language or another, and this culture-specific knowledge reinforces cognitive skills required for reading comprehension.

Because literacy acquisition builds upon (and is reciprocally related to) vocabulary knowledge, reading development may also be slower in some bilingual children. This problem is particularly striking among at risk bilinguals, whose language comprehension is relatively weak in both languages. Therefore, Tabors and Snow (2001) strongly recommend that parents use their home language to communicate with their children consistently. In addition, literacy development will be facilitated if parents also read with their children in the home language. It is clearly easier for children to transfer ideas developed in a language they know well to a second language than it is for children to learn two languages simultaneously but weakly (e.g. Moll, Diaz, Estrada, & Lopes, 1992). Children's concepts about print are similarly transferable, provided that these concepts are well developed in a primary language.

The research reviewed above has important practical implications. For example, in the United States, in Massachusetts, bilingual education has been outlawed. Legislators and parents have instead opted for 'English for the children'. In contrast, researchers agree that second (English) language oral and reading proficiency will be greatly facilitated by a solid first language base (Moll et al., 1992; Tabors & Snow, 2001). Thus, outlawing bilingual education is a mistake. Frustration among children because of language barriers is probably, at least in part, the explanation for the fact that, nationally, 13 per cent of Hispanics, as compared to 4 per cent of non-Hispanic whites and 7.5 per cent of blacks, dropped out of high school in the United States in 2012 (US Department of Education, National Center for Education Statistics, 2014). This brief review of bilingualism and reading development emphasizes the potential risks of teaching children a second language before a primary language has been sufficiently developed. The primary risk is that language may not develop enough in either language to facilitate advanced reading development.

Prioritizing one language and/or script over another is a move that has often been attempted for political reasons. For example, some right-wing politicians in Israel have attempted to legislate a move to take Arabic away as an official language of Israel. In the Andes Mountains of Peru, Quechua is the preferred spoken language, though schools only teach reading in Spanish. Here, as in so many different places in the world, children, parents, and teachers are relatively flexible in their use of languages, including code-switching (i.e. changing from one language to another in the course of a conversation), even in the context of biliteracy (Dworin & Moll, 2006). The politics of bilingualism and biliteracy are complicated and require specific cultural knowledge to understand.

However, it is clear that when children are secure in their first language, they can thrive in a multilingual environment (e.g. Kenner, 2004). Datta (2000), for example, described her excitement at listening to Bengali fables, watching Hindi films of tales already learned first in Bengali, and hearing her father tell stories and read the news in English. Her rich language experiences apparently built upon one another such that she became a fluent reader in all three languages. What is perhaps clearest in her personal account of literacy learning and her review of the literature on bilinguals and literacy development is that meaning construction within a cultural context is essential for adequate literacy acquisition. In particular, as children understand a culture better, they are better able to absorb the ideas expressed in that culture's literature. Motivation is an important component of cultural mastery (Datta, 2000). For example, children who are highly motivated to learn a new language – including an expressed desire to master the language, excitement in mastering the language, and effort spent in learning the language – tend to achieve higher grades in their language courses than those who have low motivation to learn (Masgoret & Gardner, 2003).

Baker (1996) reviewed various approaches to meaning construction in literacy with multilingual learners. For example, interaction with exciting books is critical for stimulating children's interest. Thus, fun, developmentally appropriate, and relevant books – part of a so-called *whole-language approach* – should be a central aspect of literacy teaching to young bilinguals.

Moreover, children should be encouraged to interact with the text. They should regularly be prompted to respond to the story and to the ideas. This is referred to as the construction of meaning approach to literacy (Baker, 1996; Datta, 2000). For example, Reyes and Azuara (2008) demonstrated that young Mexican immigrant children living in the south-western United States learned a lot of their literacy skills in both Spanish and in English via exchanges with friends and family in cultural events. One five-year-old who was observed in this study created a bilingual (Spanish–English) prayer book to match her grandmother's Spanish prayer book. She did this in order to facilitate her own thoughts and prayers for her family member who had died, and she did this on her own, without the help of adults, in order to help her understand her own thoughts and feelings.

The idea behind this *construction of meaning approach* is that different children's reactions to any story may vary depending upon their personal experiences and cultural backgrounds. Differences in understanding and reacting to a text are to be cherished and discussed so that students and teachers can learn from everyone participating in the literacy experience. For example, the reading of an English storybook about children alongside their mother who is baking muffins in an oven might bring about different ideas in children. Most Hong Kong households do not have any sort of oven. The idea of baking muffins at home is a strange one. Expatriates in Hong Kong, having often used ovens to cook before arriving in Hong Kong, are more likely to have ovens than are native Hong Kong families. Children with different backgrounds attending any given Hong Kong school might, therefore, find themselves considering the advantages and disadvantages of ovens from various perspectives.

Another critical aspect of literacy development among bilinguals is that children should be facilitated to understand their worlds within their own cultural context (Baker, 1996; Datta, 2000). An enormous part of cultural context is language. Thus, in this *sociocultural literacy approach*, children should read about their culture, read documents particularly relevant to their culture, and read them in the language of their culture (e.g. the Torah in Hebrew or the Quran in Arabic). A strong first language is paramount for excellent reading development (Tabors & Snow, 2001).

A final feature of literacy development in bilinguals that it is important to teach is called the *critical literacy approach* (Baker, 1996). This is the idea that language is political. For example, English functions as a language of domination in many societies, indeed worldwide (Baker & Jones, 1998). Older children need to understand that language and literature are tools. How these tools are used to communicate with others can shape people's perceptions of the world in both striking and subtle ways. Hong Kong secondary-school students, for example, are given school textbooks written in English to learn about physics, chemistry, and mathematics. These texts perhaps communicate to students that English is a language of science and power. Children need to learn to pay attention both to the message and to the language in which the message is delivered, as well as the cultural meaning of the medium. Culture is strongly communicated through language, with its differences in focus, ways of describing things, and writing styles. For example, for non-native speakers of English, English may offer an appropriate way to file a formal complaint with a company but a poor way to communicate personal feelings to a friend.

Reading for the first time in a second language

Given this brief consideration of some primary issues relevant to literacy development, we return to the striking idea that some 50 per cent of the world's children learn to read for the first time in a language other than their mother tongue. As highlighted previously, this is not ideal because of the strong relationship between language and literacy development. To comprehend text well, one needs a solid knowledge base in that language.

On the other hand, the issue is qualified and complicated by reality. For example, many Chinese children learn to read using Putonghua, when their home language is different from this. An advantage of Chinese is that most meaning can be communicated through Chinese writing regardless of the Chinese language spoken (Packard, 2000). Thus, in this situation, children are not learning to read a script that is a complete mismatch with their home language. At the same time, they are mapping script onto an oral language that is not their first language, a form of diglossia. In contrast, in parts of Africa or with some Native American languages (such as Navajo in the United States), the home language may have only a very short history as a writing system. Thus, there are few books or other materials available to read in the mother tongue. With this in mind, Tabors and Snow posed the following question, which is not easily answered: 'Does it make sense . . . to teach a child to read first in Hmong or Haitian Kreyol?' (2001, p. 175). These languages share a very short history of writing systems and parents who are unlikely to read in the mother tongue. If the parents do read, this is more than likely to be in more societally dominant languages, such as Vietnamese for Hmong people or French among Haitians.

These experiences probably interfere with optimal literacy acquisition in children. Reading comprehension will probably be slowed considerably because of the many linguistic and cultural factors related to it, as discussed above. In addition, the domination of a foreign language over children's native language communicates preferences for others' cultural beliefs above their own. This may dampen their motivation to learn (Datta, 2000). As expressed by Tsui and Tollerson,

> The use of a foreign language as the medium of instruction for children who are still struggling with basic expression in that language hampers not only their academic achievement and cognitive growth, but also their self-perception, self-esteem, emotional security, and their ability to participate meaningfully in the educational process.
>
> *(2003, p. 31)*

The issue of bilingual learning and reading development is complicated. It involves aspects of economics and politics that are too far afield from the topic of this book to consider here; however, they clearly affect children's reading development across cultures in direct ways. When English speakers think about children's reading development, they often think first about monolingual English speakers learning to read English and, second, about monolingual speakers of other languages learning to read in their own first languages. However, as I hope this chapter has outlined, it is vital to think about literacy acquisition from multiple perspectives. Developing biliterate children certainly constitute the educational majority. The needs of these children extend to word reading and writing and their correlates at the phonological, morphological, and orthographic levels, such that different writing systems may involve different central skills, and are particularly centred on adequate reading comprehension, the main goal of reading instruction.

Suggested readings

Baker, C. (2011). *Foundations of bilingual education and bilingualism, 5th edn.* Tonawanda, NY: Multilingual Matters.

Chen, X., Wang, Q., and Luo, Y. C. (eds) (2014). *Reading development and difficulties in monolingual and bilingual Chinese children.* New York, NY: Springer.

Clinton, A. B. (ed.) (2014). *Assessing bilingual children in context: An integrated approach.* Washington, DC: American Psychological Association.

Francis, N. (2013). *Bilingual development and literacy learning: East Asian and international perspectives.* Hong Kong: City University of Hong Kong Press.

Grosjean, F., & Li, P. (2013). *The psycholinguistics of bilingualism.* Oxford: Wiley-Blackwell.

REFERENCES

Abdelhadi, S., Ibrahim, R., & Eviatar, Z. (2011). Perceptual load in the reading of Arabic: Effects of orthographic visual complexity on detection. *Writing Systems Research*, 3(2), 117–127.

Abu-Rabia, S. (1995). Learning to read in Arabic: Reading, syntactic, orthographic and working memory skills in normally achieving and poor Arabic readers. *Reading Psychology: An International Quarterly*, 16, 351–394.

Abu-Rabia, S. (1998). The learning of Arabic by Israeli Jewish children. *Journal of Social Psychology*, 138(2), 165–171.

Abu-Rabia, S. (2007). The role of morphology and short vowelization in reading Arabic among normal and dyslexic readers in grades 3, 6, 9, and 12. *Journal of Psycholinguistic Research*, 36(2), 89–106.

Adams, M. J. (1990). *Beginning to read: Thinking and learning about print*. Cambridge, MA: MIT Press.

Adams, M. J., & Henry, M. K. (1997). Myths and realities about words and literacy. *School Psychology Review*, 26(3), 425–436.

Adi-Japha, E., & Freeman, N.H. (2001). Development of differentiation between writing and drawing systems. *Developmental Psychology*, 37, 101–114.

Adlof, S. M., & Catts, H. W. (2015). Morphosyntax in poor comprehenders. *Reading and Writing*. doi: 10.1007/s11145-015-9562-3.

Ahmed, Y., Wagner, R. K., & Lopez, D. (2014). Developmental relations between reading and writing at the word, sentence, and text levels: A latent change score analysis. *Journal of Educational Psychology*, 106(2), 419–434.

Ainsworth, M. D. S., Blehar, M. C., Waters, E., & Wall, S. (1978). *Patterns of attachment: A psychological study of the strange situation*. Hillsdale, NJ: Erlbaum.

Akamatsu, N. (2003). The effects of first language orthographic features on second language reading in text. *Language Learning*, 53(2), 207–231.

Alcock, K. J., & Ngorosho, D. (2003). Learning to spell a regularly spelled language is not a trivial task: Patterns of errors in Kiswahili. *Reading and Writing*, 16(7), 635–666.

Alegria, J., Pignot, E., & Morais, J. (1982). Phonetic analysis of speech and memory codes in beginning readers. *Memory & Cognition*, 10, 451–456.

Anastasiou, D., & Protopapas, A. (2015). Difficulties in lexical stress versus difficulties in segmental phonology among adolescents with dyslexia. *Scientific Studies of Reading*, 19(1), 31–50.

Anderson, R. C., Ku, Y.-M., Li, W., Chen, X., Wu, X., & Shu, H. (2013). Learning to see the patterns in Chinese characters. *Scientific Studies of Reading*, 17, 41–56.

Anderson, R. C., Li, W., Ku, Y.-M., Shu, H., & Wu, N. (2003). Use of partial information in learning to read Chinese. *Journal of Educational Psychology*, 95, 52–57.

Anthony, J. L., Williams, J. M., Durán, L. K., Gillam, S. L., Liang, L., Aghara, R., . . . Landry, S. H. (2011). Spanish phonological awareness: Dimensionality and sequence of development during the preschool and kindergarten years. *Journal of Educational Psychology*, 103(4), 857–876.

Apel, K., & Werfel, K. (2014). Using morphological awareness instruction to improve written language skills. *Language, Speech, and Hearing Services in Schools*, 45(4), 251–260.

Arab-Moghaddam, N., & Senechal, M. (2001). Orthographic and phonological processing skills in reading and spelling in Persian/English bilinguals. *International Journal of Behavioral Development*, 25(2), 140–147.

Aram, D., & Hall, N. (1989). Longitudinal follow-up of children with preschool communication disorders. *School Psychology Review*, 18, 487–501.

Aram, D., Korat, O., Saiegh-Haddad, E., Arafat, S. H., Khoury, R., & Elhija, J. A. (2013). Early literacy among Arabic-speaking kindergartners: The role of socioeconomic status, home literacy environment and maternal mediation of writing. *Cognitive Development*, 28(3), 193–208.

Aram, D., & Levin, I. (2002). Mother–child joint writing and storybook reading: Relations with literacy among low SES kindergartners. *Merrill-Palmer Quarterly*, 48(2), 202–224.

Aram, D., & Levin, I. (2004). The role of maternal mediation of writing to kindergartners in promoting literacy in school: A longitudinal perspective. *Reading and Writing*, 17(4), 387–409.

Archambault, I., Eccles, J. S., & Vida, M. N. (2010). Ability self-concepts and subjective value in literacy: Joint trajectories from grades 1 through 12. *Journal of Educational Psychology*, 102(4), 804–816.

Baker, C. (1996). *Foundations of bilingual education and bilingualism, 2nd edn.* Clevedon, UK: Multilingual Matters.

Baker, C., & Jones, S. P. (1998). *Encyclopedia of bilingualism and bilingual education*. Clevedon. UK: Multilingual Matters Ltd.

Ball, E. W., & Blachman, B. A. (1991). Does phoneme awareness training in kindergarten make a difference in early word recognition and developmental spelling? *Reading Research Quarterly*, 26, 49–66.

Bar-Kochva, I., & Breznitz, Z. (2014). Reading scripts that differ in orthographic transparency: A within-participant-and-language investigation of underlying skills. *Journal of Experimental Child Psychology*, 121, 12–27.

Baron, J., & Strawson, C. (1976). Use of orthographic and word-specific knowledge in reading words aloud. *Journal of Experimental Psychology: Human Perception and Performance*, 2(3), 386–393.

Bastien-Toniazzo, M., & Jullien, S. (2001). Nature and importance of the logographic phase in learning to read. *Reading and Writing*, 14, 119–143.

Bauer, L. (2001). *Morphological productivity*. New York, NY: Cambridge University Press.

Bentin, S., & Leshem, H. (1993). On the interaction of phonologic awareness and reading acquisition: It's a two-way street. *Annals of Dyslexia*, 43, 125–148.

Ben-Yehudah, G., Sackett, E., Malchi-Ginzberg, L., & Ahissar, M. (2001). Impaired temporal contrast sensitivity in dyslexics is specific to retain-and-compare paradigms. *Brain*, 124, 1381–1395.

Berko, J. (1958). The child's learning of English morphology. *Word*, 14, 150–177.

Berninger, V. W. (ed.) (1994). *The varieties of orthographic knowledge: Theoretical and developmental issues*. London: Kluwer Academic.

Berninger, V. W., & Richards, T. L. (2002). *Brain literacy for educators and psychologists*. San Diego, CA: Academic Press.

Berninger, V. W., & Wolf, B. J. (2009). *Teaching students with dyslexia and dysgraphia: Lessons from teaching and science*. Baltimore, MD: Paul H. Brookes Publishing Company.

Bialystok, E. (1997). Effects of bilingualism and biliteracy on children's emerging concepts of print. *Developmental Psychology*, 33(3), 429–440.

Bialystok, E. (2000). Symbolic representation across domains in preschool children. *Journal of Experimental Child Psychology*, 76(3), 173–189.

Bialystok, E. (2002). Acquisition of literacy in bilingual children: A framework for research. *Language Learning*, 52(1), 159–199.

Bialystok, E., & Luk, G. (2007). The universality of symbolic representation for reading in Asian and alphabetic languages. *Bilingualism: Language and Cognition*, 10(2), 121–129.

Bialystok, E., Majumder, S., & Martin, M. M. (2003). Developing phonological awareness: Is there a bilingual advantage? *Applied Psycholinguistics*, 24, 27–44.

Bindman, S. W., Skibbe, L. E., Hindman, A. H., Aram, D., & Morrison, F. J. (2014). Parental writing support and preschoolers' early literacy, language, and fine motor skills. *Early Childhood Research Quarterly*, 29(4), 614–624.

Binks-Cantrell, E., Washburn, E., Joshi, R. M., & Hougan, M. (2012). Peter Effect in the preparation of reading teachers. *Scientific Studies of Reading*, 16, 526–536.

Bishop, D. V. (2007). Curing dyslexia and attention-deficit hyperactivity disorder by training motor co-ordination: Miracle or myth? *Journal of Paediatrics and Child Health*, 43(10), 653–655.

Bishop, D. V. M., & Adams, C. (1990). A prospective study of the relationship between specific language impairment, phonological disorders and reading impairment. *Journal of Child Psychology and Psychiatry*, 31, 1027–1050.

Bjorklund, D. F., & Green, B. L. (1992). The adaptive nature of cognitive immaturity. *American Psychologist*, 47, 46–54.

Blachman, B. (ed.) (1997). *Foundations of reading acquisition and dyslexia*. London: Lawrence Erlbaum Associates.

Blair, T. R., Rupley, W. H., & Nichols, W. D. (2007). The effective teacher of reading: Considering the 'what' and 'how' of instruction. *The Reading Teacher*, 60(5), 432–438.

Bloom, B. S. (1956). *Taxonomy of educational objectives, Handbook I: Cognitive domain*. New York, NY: McKay.

Blöte, A., Chen, P., Overmars, E., & van der Heijden, A. H. C. (2003). Combining phonological and semantic cues in reading pseudocharacters: A comparative study. In C. McBride-Chang & H.-C. Chen (eds), *Reading development in Chinese children* (pp. 127–140). Westport, CT: Praeger Publishers.

Booth, J. R., Perfetti, C. A., MacWhinney, B., & Hunt, S. B. (2000). The association of rapid temporal perception with orthographic and phonological processing in children and adults with reading impairment. *Scientific Studies of Reading*, 42, 101–132.

Bornstein, M. H., Gross, J., & Wolf, J. (1978). Perceptual similarity of mirror images in infancy. *Cognition*, 6, 89–116.

Bosman, A. M. T., & van Orden, G. C. (1997). Why spelling is more difficult than reading. In C. A. Perfetti, L. Rieben, & M. Fayol (eds), *Learning to spell: Research theory and practice across languages* (pp. 173–194). London: Lawrence Erlbaum Associates.

Boutte, G. S., & Johnson Jr, G. L. (2013). Do educators see and honor biliteracy and bidialectalism in African American language speakers? Apprehensions and reflections of two grandparents/professional educators. *Early Childhood Education Journal*, 41(2), 133–141.

Bowers, P. G., & Newby-Clark, E. (2002). The role of naming speed within a model of reading acquisition. *Reading and Writing*, 15(1–2), 109–126.

Bowey, J. A., & Francis, J. (1991). Phonological analysis as a function of age and exposure to reading instruction. *Applied Psycholinguistics*, 12, 91–121.

Boysson-Bardies, B. (1999). *How language comes to children*. New York, NY: Bradford Press.

Boysson-Bardies, B., de Sagart, L., & Durand, C. (1984). Discernable differences in the babbling of infants according to target language. *Journal of Child Language*, 11, 1–15.

Bradley, L. (1988). Making connections in learning to read and spell. *Applied Cognitive Psychology*, 2, 3–18.

Bradlow, A. R., Kraus, N., Nicol, T. G., McGee, T. J., Cunningham, J., & Zecker, S. G. (1999). Effects of lengthened formant transition duration on discrimination and neural representation of synthetic CV syllables by normal and learning-disabled children. *Journal of the Acoustical Society of America*, 106, 2086–2096.

Brady, S. A., & Shankweiler, D. (eds) (1991). *Phonological processes in literacy*. Hillsdale, NJ: Erlbaum.

Branum-Martin, L., Tao, S., Garnaat, S., Bunta, F., & Francis, D. J. (2012). Meta-analysis of bilingual phonological awareness: Language, age, and psycholinguistic grain size. *Journal of Educational Psychology*, 104(4), 932–944.

Bronfenbrenner, U. (1979). Contexts of child rearing: Problems and prospects. *American Psychologist*, 34(10), 844–850.

Brisk, M. E., & Harrington, M. M. (2000). *Literacy and bilingualism: A handbook for all teachers*. London: Lawrence Erlbaum Associates.

Bruce, D. (1964). The analysis of word sounds by young children. *British Journal of Educational Psychology*, 34, 158–170.

Bruck, M. (1992). Persistence of dyslexics' phonological deficits. *Developmental Psychology*, 28, 874–886.

Bruck, M. (1993). Word recognition and component phonological processing skills of adults with childhood diagnosis of dyslexia. *Developmental Review*, 13, 258–263.

Bruck, M., & Genesee, F. (1995). Phonological awareness in young second language learners. *Journal of Child Language*, 22(2), 307–324.

Bruck, M., Treiman, R., Caravolas, M., Genesee, F., & Cassar, M. (1998). Spelling skills of children in whole language and phonics classrooms. *Applied Psycholinguistics*, 19, 669–684.

Bryant, P., Bradley, L., MacLean, M., & Crossland, J. (1989). Nursery rhymes, phonological skills, and reading. *Journal of Child Language*, 16, 407–428.

Bryant, P., & Goswami, U. (1987). Beyond grapheme phoneme correspondence. *Current Psychology of Cognition*, 7(5), 439–443.

Bryant, P., Nunes, T., & Bindman, M. (1999). Morphemes and spelling. In T. Nunes (ed.), *Learning to read: An integrated view from research and practices* (pp. 15–42). London: Kluwer Academic.

Burke, S. M., Pflaum, S. W., & Knafle, J. D. (1982). The influence of black English on diagnosis of reading in learning disabled and normal readers. *Journal of Learning Disabilities*, 15, 19–22.

Bus, A. G. (2001). Joint caregiver-child storybook reading: A route to literacy development. In S. B. Neuman & D. K. Dickinson (eds), *Handbook of early literacy research* (pp. 179–191). New York, NY: Guilford Press.

Bus, A. G., Takacs, Z. K., & Kegel, C. A. (2014). Affordances and limitations of electronic storybooks for young children's emergent literacy. *Developmental Review*, 35, 79–97.

Bus, A. G., & van IJzendoorn, M. H. (1988a). Mother–child interactions, attachment, and emergent literacy: A cross-sectional study. *Child Development*, 59, 1262–1273.

Bus, A. G., & van IJzendoorn, M. H. (1988b). Mother–child interactions, attachment, and emergent literacy: A longitudinal study. *Journal of Genetic Psychology*, 149, 199–210.

Bus, A. G., & van IJzendoorn, M. H. (1992). Patterns of attachment in frequently and infrequently reading mother–child dyads. *Journal of Genetic Psychology*, 153, 395–403.

Bus, A. G., van IJzendoorn, M. H., & Pellegrini, A. D. (1995). Joint book reading makes for success in learning to read: A meta-analysis on intergenerational transmission of literacy. *Review of Educational Research*, 65, 1–21.

Butler, S. R., Marsh, H. W., Sheppard, M. J., & Sheppard, J. L. (1985). Seven-year longitudinal study of the early prediction of reading achievement. *Journal of Educational Psychology*, 77, 349–361.

Byrne, B. (1996). The learnability of the alphabetic principle: Children's initial hypotheses about how print represents spoken language. *Applied Psycholinguistics*, 17(4), 401–426.

Byrne, B. (1998). *The Foundation of Literacy*. Hove, UK: Psychology Press Ltd.

Byrne, B. (2005). Theories of learning to read. In M. J. Snowling & C. Hulme (eds), *The science of reading: A handbook* (pp. 104–119). Malden, MA: Blackwell Publishing.

Byrne, B., Freebody, P., & Gates, A. (1992). Longitudinal data on the relations of word-reading strategies to comprehension, reading time, and phonemic awareness. *Reading Research Quarterly*, 27(2), 140–151.

Cain, K., & Oakhill, J. (1998). Comprehension skill and inference-making ability: Issues of causality. In C. Hulme & R. M. Joshi (eds), *Reading and spelling* (pp. 329–342). Mahwah, NJ: Lawrence Erlbaum Associates, Inc.

Cain, K., & Oakhill, J. V. (1999). Inference making ability and its relation to comprehension failure in young children. *Reading and Writing*, 11(5–6), 489–503.

Cain, K., & Oakhill, J. (2006). Profiles of children with specific reading comprehension difficulties. *British Journal of Educational Psychology*, 76(4), 683–696.

Cain, K., & Oakhill, J. (2011). Matthew effects in young readers reading comprehension and reading experience aid vocabulary development. *Journal of Learning Disabilities*, 44(5), 431–443.

Cain, K., Oakhill, J. V., Barnes, M. A., & Bryant, P. E. (2001). Comprehension skill, inference-making ability, and their relation to knowledge. *Memory and Cognition*, 29(6), 850–859.

Cain, K., Oakhill, J. V., & Elbro, C. (2003). The ability to learn new word meanings from context by school-age children with and without language comprehension difficulties. *Journal of Child Language*, 30(3), 681–694.

Cain, K., Oakhill, J., & Lemmon, K. (2004). Individual differences in the inference of word meanings from context: The influence of reading comprehension, vocabulary knowledge, and memory capacity. *Journal of Educational Psychology*, 96(4), 671–681.

Calet, N., Gutiérrez-Palma, N., Simpson, I. C., González-Trujillo, M. C., & Defior, S. (2015). Suprasegmental phonology development and reading acquisition: A longitudinal study. *Scientific Studies of Reading*, 19(1), 51–71.

Calfee, R. C., Lindamood, P., & Lindamood, C. (1973). Acoustic-phonetic skills and reading: Kindergarten through twelfth grade. *Journal of Educational Psychology*, 64(3), 293–298.

Campbell, R. (ed.) (1998). *Facilitating preschool literacy*. Newark, DE: International Reading Association.

Campbell, R., & Sais, E. (1995). Accelerated metalinguistic (phonological) awareness in bilingual children. *British Journal of Developmental Psychology*, 13, 61–68.

Caravolas, M., & Bruck, M. (1993). The effect of oral and written language input on children's phonological awareness: A cross-linguistic study. *Journal of Experimental Child Psychology*, 55(1), 1–30.

Caravolas, M., & Bruck, M. (2000). Vowel categorization skill and its relationship to early literacy skills among first-grade Quebec-French children. *Journal of Experimental Child Psychology*, 76(3), 190–221.

Caravolas, M., Hulme, C., & Snowling, M. J. (2001). The foundations of spelling ability: Evidence from a 3-year longitudinal study. *Journal of Memory and Language*, 45, 751–774.

Caravolas, M., Lervåg, A., Mousikou, P., Efrim, C., Litavský, M., Onochie-Quintanilla, E., . . . Hulme, C. (2012). Common patterns of prediction of literacy development in different alphabetic orthographies. *Psychological Science*, 23(6), 678–686.

Carlisle, J. F. (1995) Morphological awareness and early reading achievement. In L. Feldman (ed.), *Morphological aspects of language processing* (pp. 189–209). Hillsdale, NJ: Erlbaum.

Carlisle, J. F. (1996). An exploratory study of morphological errors in children's written stories. *Reading and Writing*, 8, 61–72.

Carlisle, J. F. (2000). Awareness of the structure and meaning of morphologically complex words: Impact on reading. *Reading and Writing*, 12(3–4), 169–190.

Carlisle, J. F., Beeman, M., Davis, L. H., & Spharim, G. (1999). Relationship of metalinguistic capabilities and reading achievement for children who are becoming bilingual. *Applied Psycholinguistics*, 20(4), 459–478.

Carpenter, P. A., Miyake, A., & Just, M. A. (1995). Language comprehension: Sentence and discourse processing. *Annual Review of Psychology*, 46, 91–120.

Carretti, B., Caldarola, N., Tencati, C., & Cornoldi, C. (2014). Improving reading comprehension in reading and listening settings: The effect of two training programmes focusing on metacognition and working memory. *British Journal of Educational Psychology*, 84(2), 194–210.

Carver, R. P. (1997). Reading for one second, one minute, or one year from the perspective of Rauding Theory. *Scientific Studies of Reading*, 1, 3–43.

Casalis, S., & Louis-Alexandre, M.-F. (2000). Morphological analysis, phonological analysis and learning to read French: A longitudinal study. *Reading and Writing*, 12, 303–335.

Case, R. (1985). *Intellectual development: A systematic reinterpretation*. New York, NY: Academic Press.

Catts, H. W. (1991). Early identification of dyslexia: Evidence from a follow-up study of speech-language impaired children. *Annals of Dyslexia*, 41, 163–177.

Chall, J. S. (1983). *Stages of reading development*. London: McGraw-Hill.

Chall, J. S. (1996). *Learning to read: The great debate, 3rd edn*. Fort Worth, TX: Harcourt.

Chall, J. S., Roswell, F., & Blumenthal, S. (1963). Auditory blending ability: A factor in success in beginning reading. *Reading Teacher*, 17, 113–118.

Chan, C. K. K., & Law, D. Y. K. (2003). Metacognitive beliefs and strategies in reading comprehension for Chinese children. In C. McBride-Chang & H.-C. Chen (eds), *Reading Development in Chinese Children* (pp. 171–182). Westport, CT: Praeger.

Chan, G. W.-Y., McBride-Chang, C., Leung, P. W. L., Tsoi, K. W., Ho, C. S.-H., & Cheuk, C. S.M. (2003). Factors influencing anxiousness/depression among adolescents migrating between Chinese societies: The case of adolescents emigrating from Mainland China to Hong Kong. *Journal of Psychology in Chinese Societies*, 4, 121–140.

Chan, L., & Louie, L. (1992). Developmental trend of Chinese preschool children in drawing and writing. *Journal of Research in Childhood Education*, 6, 93–99.

Chan, L., & Wang, L. (2003). Linguistic awareness in learning to read Chinese: A comparative study of Beijing and Hong Kong children. In C. McBride-Chang, & H.-C. Chen (eds), *Reading Development in Chinese Children* (pp. 91–108). Westport, CT: Praeger Publishers.

Chang, S. H., & Yu, N.Y. (2005). Evaluation and classification of types of Chinese handwriting deficits in elementary school children. *Perceptual and Motor Skills*, 101(2), 631–647.

Chang, S. H., & Yu, N.Y. (2014). The effect of computer-assisted therapeutic practice for children with handwriting deficit: A comparison with the effect of the traditional sensorimotor approach. *Research in Developmental Disabilities*, 35(7), 1648–1657.

Chao, R. K. (1994). Beyond parental control and authoritarian parenting style: Understanding Chinese parenting through the cultural notion of training. *Child Development*, 65(4), 1111–1119.

Chao, R. K., & Sue, S. (1996). Chinese parental influence and their children's school success: A paradox in the literature on parenting styles. In S. Lau (ed.), *Growing up the Chinese way: Chinese child and adolescent development* (pp. 93–120). Hong Kong, China: Chinese University Press.

Chen, C.-S., Lee, S.-Y., & Stevenson, H. W. (1996). Academic achievement and motivation of Chinese students: A cross-national perspective. In S. Lau (ed.), *Growing up the Chinese way: Chinese child and adolescent development* (pp. 69–91). Hong Kong, China: Chinese University Press.

Chen, H.-C. (1996). Chinese reading and comprehension: A cognitive psychology perspective. In M. H. Bond (ed.), *The handbook of Chinese psychology* (pp. 43–62). Hong Kong, China: Oxford University Press.

Chen, H.-C., & Chen, M. J. (1988). Directional scanning in Chinese reading. In I. M. Liu, H.-C. Chen, & M. J. Chen (eds), *Cognitive aspects of the Chinese language* (pp. 15–26). Hong Kong, China: Asian Research Service.

Chen, H.-C., Song, H., Lau, W. Y., Wong, K. F. E., & Tang, S. L. (2003). Developmental characteristics of eye movements in reading Chinese. In C. McBride-Chang & H.-C. Chen (eds), *Reading development in Chinese children* (pp. 157–170). Westport, CT: Praeger.

Chen, M. J., Lau, L. L., & Yung, Y. F. (1993). Development of component skills in reading Chinese. *International Journal of Psychology*, 28, 481–507.

Chen, M. J., & Yuen, J. C.-K. (1991). Effects of Pinyin and script type on verbal processing: Comparisons of China, Taiwan, and Hong Kong experience. *International Journal of Behavioral Development*, 14, 429–448.

Cheng, M. (1982). Analysis of present day Mandarin. *Journal of Chinese Linguistics*, 10, 282–358.

Cheung, H., Chen, H.-C., Lai, C. Y., Wong, O. C., & Hills, M. (2001). The development of phonological awareness: Effects of spoken language experience and orthography. *Cognition*, 81, 227–241.

Cheung, H., Chung, K. K., Wong, S. W., McBride-Chang, C., Penney, T. B., & Ho, C. S. (2009). Perception of tone and aspiration contrasts in Chinese children with dyslexia. *Journal of Child Psychology and Psychiatry*, 50(6), 726–733.

Chiappe, P., Siegel, L. S., & Gottardo, A. (2002). Reading-related skills of kindergartners from diverse linguistic backgrounds. *Applied Psycholinguistics*, 23, 95–116.

Chien, L.-F., Wang, H.-M., Bai, B.-R., & Lin, S.-C. (2000). A spoken-access approach for Chinese text and speech information retrieval. *Journal of the American Society for Information Science*, 51, 313–323.

Chik, P. P. M., Ho, C. S. H., Yeung, P. S., Chan, D. W. O., Chung, K. K. H., Luan, H., . . . Lau, W. S. Y. (2012). Syntactic skills in sentence reading comprehension among Chinese elementary school children. *Reading and Writing*, 25(3), 679–699.

Chiu, M. M., Chow, B. W. Y., & McBride-Chang, C. (2007). Universals and specifics in learning strategies: Explaining adolescent mathematics, science, and reading achievement across 34 countries. *Learning and Individual Differences*, 17(4), 344–365.

Chiu, M. M., & McBride-Chang, C. (2006). Gender, context, and reading: A comparison of students in 43 countries. *Scientific Studies of Reading*, 10(4), 331–362.

Chiu, M. M., & McBride-Chang, C. (2010). Family and reading in 41 countries: Differences across cultures and students. *Scientific Studies of Reading*, 14(6), 514–543.

Chiu, M. M., McBride-Chang, C., & Lin, D. (2012). Ecological, psychological, and cognitive components of reading difficulties testing the component model of reading in fourth graders across 38 countries. *Journal of Learning Disabilities*, 45(5), 391–405.

Cho, J. R. (2009). Syllable and letter knowledge in early Korean Hangul reading. *Journal of Educational Psychology*, 101(4), 938–947.

Chomsky, C. (1976). Creativity and innovation in child language. *Journal of Education Boston*, 158(2), 12–24.

Chomsky, N. (1968). *Language and mind*. New York, NY: Harcourt Brace Jovanovich.

Chou, C. P., Wang, S., & Ching, G. S. (2012). Balanced reading instructions: An action research on elementary cram school students. *International Journal of Research Studies in Language Learning*, 1(1), 3–20.

Chow, B. W.-Y., & McBride-Chang, C. (2003). Promoting language and literacy development through parent–child reading in Hong Kong preschoolers. *Early Education and Development*, 14(2), 233–248.

Christensen, C. A. (1997). Onset, rhymes, and phonemes in learning to read. *Scientific Studies of Reading*, 1, 341–358.

Christian, K., Morrison, F. J., Frazier, J. A., & Massetti, G. (2000). Specificity in the nature and timing of cognitive growth in kindergarten and first grade. *Journal of Cognition and Development*, 4, 429–448.

Christodoulou, J. A., Del Tufo, S. N., Lymberis, J., Saxler, P. K., Ghosh, S. S., Triantafyllou, C., . . . Gabrieli, J. D. (2014). Brain bases of reading fluency in typical reading and impaired fluency in dyslexia. *PloS One*, 9(7). doi: 10.1371/journal.pone.0100552.

Chung, K. K. H., Ho, C. S.-H., Chan, D. W., Tsang, S. -M., & Lee, S.-H. (2011). Cognitive skills and literacy performance of Chinese adolescents with and without dyslexia. *Reading and Writing*, 24, 835–859.

Chung, K. K., McBride-Chang, C., Cheung, H., & Wong, S. W. (2013). General auditory processing, speech perception and phonological awareness skills in Chinese–English biliteracy. *Journal of Research in Reading*, 36(2), 202–222.

Chung, K. K., Tong, X., & McBride-Chang, C. (2012). Evidence for a deficit in orthographic structure processing in Chinese developmental dyslexia: An event-related potential study. *Brain Research*, 1472, 20–31.

Clay, M. M. (1975). *What did I write?* Auckland, NZ: Heinemann.

Clay, M. M. (1998). *By different paths to common outcomes*. York, ME: Stenhouse.

Coenen, M. J. W. L., van Bon, W. H. J., & Schreuder, R. (1997). Reading and spelling in Dutch first and second graders: Do they use an orthographic strategy? In C. K. Leong & R. M. Joshi (eds), *Cross-language studies of learning to read and spell* (pp. 249–269). London: Kluwer Academic.

Coleman, J. S. (1987). The relations between school and social structure. In M. T. Hallinan (ed.), *The social organization of schools: New conceptualizations of the learning process* (pp. 177–204). New York, NY: Plenum.

Comeau, L., Cormier, P., Grandmaison, E., & Lacroix, D. (1999). A longitudinal study of phonological processing skills in children learning to read in a second language. *Journal of Educational Psychology*, 91(1), 29–43.

Conger, R. D., & Donnellan, M. B. (2007). An interactionist perspective on the socioeconomic context of human development. *Annual Review of Psychology*, 58, 175–199.

Connelly, V., Johnston, R. S., & Thompson, G. B. (1999). The influence of instructional approaches on reading procedures. In G. B. Thompson & T. Nicholson (eds), *Learning to read: Beyond phonics and whole language. Language and literacy series* (pp. 103–123). Newark, DE: International Reading Association.

Connor, C. M., Morrison, F. J., & Katch, L. E. (2004). Beyond the reading wars: Exploring the effect of child–instruction interactions on growth in early reading. *Scientific Studies of Reading*, 8(4), 305–336.

Connor, C. M., Morrison, F. J., & Slominski, L. (2006). Preschool instruction and children's emergent literacy growth. *Journal of Educational Psychology*, 98(4), 665–689.

Connor, C. M., Morrison, F. J., & Underwood, P. S. (2007). A second chance in second grade: The independent and cumulative impact of first- and second-grade reading instruction and students' letter-word reading skill growth. *Scientific Studies of Reading*, 11(3), 199–233.

Connor, C. M., Piasta, S. B., Fishman, B., Glasney, S., Schatschneider, C., Crowe, E., . . . Morrison, F. J. (2009). Individualizing student instruction precisely: Effects of child instruction interactions on first graders' literacy development. *Child Development*, 80(1), 77–100.

Conrad, N. J., Harris, N., & Williams, J. (2013). Individual differences in children's literacy development: The contribution of orthographic knowledge. *Reading and Writing*, 26(8), 1223–1239.

Cossu, G. (1999). The acquisition of Italian orthography. In M. Harris &G. Hatano (eds), *Learning to read and write: A cross-linguistic perspective* (pp. 10–33). New York, NY: Cambridge University Press.

Cossu, G., Shankweiler, D., Liberman, I. Y., Katz, L., & Tola, G. (1988). Awareness of phonological segments and reading ability in Italian children. *Applied Psycholinguistics*, 9, 1–16.

Courcy, A., Beland, R., & Pitchford, N. J. (2000). Phonological awareness in French speaking children at risk for reading disabilities. *Brain and Cognition*, 43(1–3), 124–130.

Crain-Thoreson, C., & Dale, P. S. (1992). Do early talkers become early readers? Linguistic precocity, preschool language, and emergent literacy. *Developmental Psychology*, 28, 421–429.

Critten S., & Pine, K. J. (2009). Viewing spelling in a cognitive context: Underlying representations and process. In C. Wood & V. Connelly (eds), *Contemporary perspectives on reading and spelling* (pp. 92–108). London: Routledge.

Cromley, J. G., & Azevedo, R. (2007). Testing and refining the direct and inferential mediation model of reading comprehension. *Journal of Educational Psychology*, 99(2), 311–325.

Cromley, J. G., Snyder-Hogan, L. E., & Luciw-Dubas, U. A. (2010). Reading comprehension of scientific text: A domain-specific test of the direct and inferential mediation model of reading comprehension. *Journal of Educational Psychology*, 102(3), 687–700.

Crowder, R. G., & Wagner, R. K. (1992). *The psychology of reading: An introduction*. Oxford, UK: Oxford University Press.

Cunningham, A. E. (1990). Explicit versus implicit instruction in phonemic awareness. *Journal of Experimental Child Psychology*, 50, 429–444.

Cunningham, A. E., & Stanovich, K. E. (1997). Early reading acquisition and its relation to reading experience and ability 10 years later. *Developmental Psychology*, 33, 934–945.

Currie, N. K., & Cain, K. (2015). Children's inference generation: The role of vocabulary and working memory. *Journal of Experimental Child Psychology*, 137, 57–75.

Cutler, A. (2005). Lexical stress. In D. B. Pisoni & R. E. Remez (eds), *The handbook of speech perception* (pp. 264–289). Oxford, UK: Blackwell.

Da Fontoura, H. A., & Siegel, L. S. (1995). Reading, syntactic, and working memory skills of bilingual Portuguese-English Canadian children. *Reading and Writing*, 7, 139–153.

Dahlin, K. I. (2011). Effects of working memory training on reading in children with special needs. *Reading and Writing*, 24(4), 479–491.

Daneman, M., & Carpenter, P. A. (1980). Individual differences in working memory and reading. *Journal of Verbal Learning and Verbal Behaviour*, 19, 450–466.

Daneman, M., & Merikle, P. M. (1996). Working memory and language comprehension: A meta-analysis. *Psychonomic Bulletin and Review*, 3(4), 422–433.

Daneman, M., & Tardif, T. (1987). Working memory and reading skill re-examined. In M. Coltheart (ed.), *Attention and performance*, vol. 12: *The psychology of reading* (pp. 491–508). Hillsdale, NJ: Lawrence Erlbaum Associates.

D'Angiulli, A., Siegel, L. S., & Serra, E. (2001). The development of reading in English and Italian in bilingual children. *Applied Psycholinguistics*, 22(4), 479–507.

Daniel, E. J. (2013). Effects of ebooks in adolescent struggling readers (Master's thesis). Northern Michigan University, Marquette, MI, United States of America. Retrieved from https://www.nmu.edu/education/sites/DrupalEducation/files/UserFiles/Daniel_Eric_MP. pdf.

Darling-Hammond, L. (1997). *The right to learn*. San Francisco, CA: Jossey-Bass.

Datta, M. (2000). *Bilinguality and literacy: Principles and practice*. London: Continuum.

Deacon, S. H., Benere, J., & Pasquarella, A. (2013). Reciprocal relationship: Children's morphological awareness and their reading accuracy across grades 2 to 3. *Developmental Psychology*, 49(6), 1113–1126.

Deacon, S. H., Wade-Woolley, L., & Kirby, J. (2007). Crossover: The role of morphological awareness in French immersion children's reading. *Developmental Psychology*, 43(3), 732–746.

Deacon, S. H., Wade-Woolley, L., & Kirby, J. R. (2009). Flexibility in young second-language learners: Examining the language specificity of orthographic processing. *Journal of Research in Reading*, 32(2), 215–229.

DeCasper, A. J., & Spence, M. J. (1986). Prenatal maternal speech influences newborn's perception of speech sounds. *Infant Behavior and Development*, 9, 133–150.

Dehaene, S. (2009). *Reading in the brain: The new science of how we read*. New York, NY: Penguin.

De Jong, P. F., & van der Leij, A. (1999). Specific contributions of phonological abilities to early reading acquisition: Results from a Dutch latent variable longitudinal study. *Journal of Educational Psychology*, 91(3), 450–476.

Demetriou, A., Kui, Z. X., Spanoudis, G., Christou, C., Kyriakides, L., & Platsidou, M. (2005). The architecture, dynamics, and development of mental processing: Greek, Chinese, or Universal? *Intelligence*, 33(2), 109–141.

Demont, E., & Gombert, J. E. (1996). Phonological awareness as a predictor of recoding skills and syntactic awareness as a predictor of comprehension skills. *British Journal of Educational Psychology*, 66(3), 315–332.

Denckla, M. B., & Rudel, R. G. (1976). Rapid 'automatized' naming (RAN): Dyslexia differentiated from other learning disabilities. *Neuropsychologia*, 14, 471–479.

Derwing, B., & Baker, W. (1979). Recent research on the acquisition of English morphology. In P. Fletcher & M. Garman (eds), *Language acquisition* (pp. 209–223). New York, NY: Cambridge University Press.

Droop, M., & Verhoeven, L. (2003). Language proficiency and reading ability in first- and second-language learners. *Reading Research Quarterly*, 38(1), 78–103.

Dworin, J. E., & Moll, L. C. (2006). Guest editors' introduction. *Journal of Early Childhood Literacy*, 6, 234–240.

Edwards, J., Fox, R. A., & Rogers, C. L. (2002). Final consonant discrimination in children: Effects of phonological disorder, vocabulary size, and articulatory accuracy. *Journal of Speech Language and Hearing Research*, 45, 231–242.

Ehri, L. C. (1997). Learning to read and learning to spell are one and the same, almost. In C. A. Perfetti, L. Rieben, & M. Fayol (eds), *Learning to spell: Research theory and practice across languages* (pp. 237–269). Mahwah, NJ: Lawrence Erlbaum Associates.

Ehri, L. C. (2000). Learning to read and learning to spell: Two sides of a coin. *Topics in Language Disorders*, 20, 19–36.

Ehri, L. C. (2005). Learning to read words: Theory, findings, and issues. *Scientific Studies of Reading*, 9(2), 167–188.

Ehri, L. C. (2014). Orthographic mapping in the acquisition of sight word reading, spelling memory, and vocabulary learning. *Scientific Studies of Reading*, 18(1), 5–21.

Ehri, L. C., & Wilce, L. S. (1985). Movement into reading: Is the first stage of printed word learning visual or phonetic? *Reading Research Quarterly*, 20, 163–179.

Elbro, C. (1996). Early linguistic abilities and reading development: A review and a hypothesis. *Reading and Writing*, 8(6), 453–485.

Elbro, C. (2013). Literacy acquisition in Danish: A deep orthography in cross linguistic light. In R. M. Joshi & P. G. Aaron (eds), *Handbook of orthography and literacy* (pp. 31–46). Mahwah, NJ: Lawrence Erlbaum Associates.

Elbro, C., Borstmm, I., & Petersen, D. K. (1998). Predicting dyslexia from kindergarten: The importance of distinctness of phonological representations of lexical items. *Reading Research Quarterly*, 33(1), 36–60.

Elbro, C., & Buch-Iverson, I. (2013). Activation of background knowledge for inference making: Effects on reading comprehension. *Scientific Studies of Reading*, 17, 435–452. doi: 10.1080/10888438.2013.774005.

Ellefson, M. R., Treiman, R., & Kessler, B. (2009). Learning to label letters by sounds or names: A comparison of England and the United States. *Journal of Experimental Child Psychology*, 102(3), 323–341.

Elley, W. B. (2001). Literacy in the present world: Realities and possibilities. In L. Verhoeven & C. E. Snow (eds), *Literacy and motivation: Reading engagement in individuals and groups* (pp. 225–242). London: Lawrence Erlbaum Associates.

Ellison, E. (1979). Classroom behavior and psychosocial adjustment of single- and two-parent children. Paper presented at the Biennial Meeting of the Society for Research in Child Development, San Francisco, CA.

Erçetin, G., & Alptekin, C. (2013). The explicit/implicit knowledge distinction and working memory: Implications for second-language reading comprehension. *Applied Psycholinguistics*, 34(4), 727–753.

Escarce, M. E. W. (1998). Toddlers with specific expressive language impairment: Reading outcomes to age 8. *Dissertation Abstracts International, Section B: The Sciences and Engineering*, 58(8-B), 4490.

Espy, K. A., Molfese, D. L., Molfese, V. J., & Modglin, A. (2004). Development of auditory event-related potentials in young children and relations to word-level reading abilities at age 8 years. *Annals of Dyslexia*, 54(1), 9–38.

Evans, G. W. (2004). The environment of childhood poverty. *American Psychologist*, 59(2), 77–92.

Evans, M. A., Bell, M., Shaw, D., Moretti, S., & Page, J. (2006). Letter names, letter sounds and phonological awareness: An examination of kindergarten children across letters and of letters across children. *Reading and Writing,* 19(9), 959–989.

Evans, M. A., & Saint-Aubin, J. (2005). What children are looking at during shared storybook reading: Evidence from eye movement monitoring. *Psychological Science*, 16(11), 913–920.

Farmer, M. E., & Klein, R. M. (1995). The evidence for a temporal processing deficit linked to dyslexia: A review. *Psychonomic Bulletin and Review*, 2, 460–493.

Farrington-Flint, L., Stash, A., & Stiller, J. (2008). Monitoring variability and change in children's spelling strategies. *Educational Psychology*, 28(2), 133–149.

Feitelson, D., & Goldstein, Z. (1986). Patterns of book ownership and reading to young children. *Reading Teacher*, 39, 924–930.

Feldman, S. S., & Rosenthal, D. A. (1991). Age expectations of behavioural autonomy in Hong Kong, Australian and American youth: The influence of family variables and adolescents' values. *International Journal of Psychology*, 26(1), 1–23.

Ferreiro, E. (1978). What is written in a written sentence? A developmental answer. *Journal of Education*, 160, 25–39.

Ferreiro, E., & Teberosky, A. (1982). *Literacy before schooling*. New York, NY: Heinemann.

Fisch, S. M., & Truglio, R. T. (2000). *'G' is for growing: 30 years of research on children and Sesame Street*. New York, NY: Lawrence Erlbaum and Associates.

Fletcher, J. M., Morris, R., Lyson, G. R., Stuebing, K. K., Shaywitz, . . . Shaywitz, B. A. (1997). Subtypes of dyslexia: An old problem revisited. In B. A. Blachman (ed.), *Foundations of reading acquisition and dyslexia: Implications for early intervention* (pp. 95–114). Mahwah, NJ: Lawrence Erlbaum Associates.

Florit, E., & Cain, K. (2011). The simple view of reading: Is it valid for different types of alphabetic orthographies? *Educational Psychology Review*, 23(4), 553–576.

Foorman, B. R. (1994). Phonological and orthographic processing: Separate but equal? In V. W. Berninger (ed.), *The varieties of orthographic knowledge*, vol. 1: *Theoretical and developmental issues* (pp. 321–357). London: Kluwer Academic.

Foorman, B. R. (1995). Practiced connections of orthographic and phonological processing. In V. W. Berninger (ed.), *The varieties of orthographic knowledge,* vol. 2: *Relationships to phonology reading and writing* (pp. 377–419). London: Kluwer Academic.

Foorman, B. R., Francis, D. J., Fletcher, J. M., Schatschneider, C., & Mehta, P. (1998). The role of instruction in learning to read: Preventing reading failure in at-risk children. *Journal of Educational Psychology*, 90(1), 37–55.

Foorman, B. R., Francis, D. J., Shaywitz, S. E., Shaywitz, B. A., & Fletcher, J. M. (1997). The case for early reading intervention. In B. Blachman (ed.), *Foundations of reading acquisition and dyslexia* (pp. 243–264). London: Lawrence Erlbaum Associates.

Foorman, B. R., & Torgesen, J. (2001). Critical elements of classroom and small-group instruction promote reading success in all children. *Learning Disabilities Research and Practice*, 16, 203–212.

Fowler, A. E. (1991). How early phonological development might set the stage for phoneme awareness. In S. A. Brady & D. P. Shankweiler (eds), *Phonological processes in literacy: A tribute to Isabelle Y. Liberman* (pp. 97–117). Hillsdale, NJ: Erlbaum.

Fowler, A. E., & Scarborough, H. S. (1999). Reading disability. In D. A. Wagner, R. L. Venezky, & B. Street (eds), *Literacy: An international handbook* (pp. 54–59). Boulder, CO: Westview Press.

Foy, J. G., & Mann, V. (2001). Does strength of phonological representations predict phonological awareness in preschool children? *Applied Psycholinguistics*, 22, 301–325.

Franceschini, S., Gori, S., Ruffino, M., Pedrolli, K., & Facoetti, A. (2012). A causal link between visual spatial attention and reading acquisition. *Current Biology*, 22(9), 814–819.

Frith, U. (ed.) (1980). *Cognitive processes in spelling*. London: Academic Press.

Fromkin, V. A. (ed.) (1978). *Tone: A linguistic survey*. New York, NY: Academic Press.

Gaab, N., Gabrieli, J. D. E., Deutsch, G. K., Tallal, P., & Temple, E. (2007). Neural correlates of rapid auditory processing are disrupted in children with developmental dyslexia and ameliorated with training: An fMRI study. *Restorative Neurology and Neuroscience*, 25(3), 295–310.

Gabrieli, J. D. (2009). Dyslexia: A new synergy between education and cognitive neuroscience. *Science*, 325(5938), 280–283.

Galaburda, A. M. (1999). Developmental dyslexia: A multilevel syndrome. *Dyslexia*, 5, 183–191.

Geary, D. C. (1995). Reflections of evolution and culture in children's cognition: Implications for mathematical development and instruction. *American Psychologist*, 50(1), 24–37.

Georgiou, G. K., Aro, M., Liao, C. H., & Parrila, R. (2014). The contribution of RAN pause time and articulation time to reading across languages: Evidence from a more representative sample of children. *Scientific Studies of Reading*, 19(2), 135–144.

Georgiou, G. K., Papadopoulos, T. C., & Kaizer, E. L. (2014). Different RAN components relate to reading at different points in time. *Reading and Writing*, 27(8), 1379–1394.

Geva, E., & Siegel, L. S. (2000). Orthographic and cognitive factors in the concurrent development of basic reading skills in two languages. *Reading and Writing*, 12(12), 1–30.

Geva, E., & Wade-Woolley, L. (1998). Component processes in becoming English–Hebrew biliterate. In A. Y. Durgunoglu and L. Verhoeven (eds), *Literacy development in a multilingual context: Cross-cultural perspectives* (pp. 85–110). Mahwah, NJ: Lawrence Erlbaum Associates.

Geva, E., & Willows, D. (1994). Orthographic knowledge is orthographic knowledge is orthographic knowledge. In V. W. Berninger (ed.), *The varieties of orthographic knowledge, vol. 1: Theoretical and developmental issues* (pp. 359–380). London: Kluwer Academic.

Gibson, E. J., & Levin, H. (1975). *The psychology of reading*. Cambridge, MA: MIT Press.

Gibson, E. P., Gibson, J. J., Pick, A. D., & Osser, H. (1962). A developmental study of the discrimination of letter-like forms. *Journal of Comparative and Physiological Psychology*, 55(6), 897–906.

Gombert, J. E. (1992). *Metalinguistic development*. Chicago, IL: University of Chicago Press.

Gombert, J. E., & Fayol, M. (1992). Writing in preliterate children. *Learning and Instruction*, 2, 23–41.

Goodman, K. S., & Goodman, Y. M. (1979). Learning to reading is natural. In L. B. Resnick & P. A. Weaver (eds), *Theory and practice of early reading*, vol. 1 (pp. 137–154). Hillsdale, NJ: Erlbaum Associates.

Goswami, U. (2002). In the beginning was the rhyme? A reflection on Hulme, Hatcher, Nation, Brown, Adams, and Stuart. *Journal of Experimental Child Psychology*, 82, 47–57.

Goswami, U. (2011). A temporal sampling framework for developmental dyslexia. *Trends in Cognitive Sciences*, 15(1), 3–10.

Goswami, U. (2014). The neural basis of dyslexia may originate in primary auditory cortex. *Brain*, 137(12), 3100–3102.

Goswami, U., Gerson, D., & Astruc, L. (2010). Amplitude envelope perception, phonology and prosodic sensitivity in children with developmental dyslexia. *Reading and Writing*, 23(8), 995–1019.

Goswami, U., Thomson, J., Richardson, U., Stainthorp, R., Hughes, D., Rosen, S., & Scott, S. K. (2002). Amplitude envelope onsets and developmental dyslexia: A new hypothesis. *Proceedings of the National Academy of Sciences*, 99(16), 10911–10916.

Goswami, U., Wang, H. L. S., Cruz, A., Fosker, T., Mead, N., & Huss, M. (2011). Language universal sensory deficits in developmental dyslexia: English, Spanish, and Chinese. *Journal of Cognitive Neuroscience*, 23(2), 325–337.

Gottardo, A., & Mueller, J. (2009). Are first- and second-language factors related in predicting second-language reading comprehension? A study of Spanish-speaking children acquiring English as a second language from first to second grade. *Journal of Educational Psychology*, 101(2), 330–344.

Gottardo, A., Yan, B., Siegel, L. S., & Wade-Woolley, L. (2001). Factors related to English reading performance in children with Chinese as a first language: More evidence of cross-language transfer of phonological processing. *Journal of Educational Psychology*, 93(3), 530–542.

Gough, P. B., & Juel, C. (1991). The first stages of word recognition. In L. Rieben & C. A. Perfetti (eds), *Learning to read: Basic research and its implications* (pp. 47–56). Hillsdale, NJ: Lawrence Erlbaum Associates.

Gough, P. B., Juel, C., & Griffith, P. L. (1992). Reading, spelling, and the orthographic cipher. In P. B. Gough, L. C. Ehri, & R. Treiman (eds), *Reading acquisition* (pp. 35–48). Hillsdale, NJ: Lawrence Erlbaum Associates.

Gough, P. B., & Tunmer, W. E. (1986). Decoding, reading, and reading disability. *Remedial and Special Education*, 7, 6–10.

Goyen, J. D. (1989). Reading methods in Spain: The effect of a regular orthography. *Reading Teacher*, 42, 370–373.

Graf Estes, K., Edwards, J., & Saffran, J. R. (2011). Phonotactic constraints on infant word learning. *Infancy*, 16(2), 180–197.

Graham, S., & Harris, K. (1994). The effect of whole language on children's writing: A review of the literature. *Educational Psychologist*, 29, 187–192.

Graham, S., & Harris, K. R. (1996). Self-regulation and strategy instruction for students who find writing and learning challenging. In C. M. Levy & S. Ransdell (eds), *The science of writing: Theories, methods, individual differences and applications* (pp. 347–360). Mahwah, NJ: Lawrence Erlbaum Associates, Inc.

Graham, S., McKeown, D., Kiuhara, S., & Harris, K. R. (2012). A meta-analysis of writing instruction for students in the elementary grades. *Journal of Educational Psychology*, 104(4), 879–896.

Guan, C. Q., Ye, F., Wagner, R. K., Meng, W., & Leong, C. K. (2014). Text comprehension mediates morphological awareness, syntactic processing, and working memory in predicting Chinese written composition performance. *Journal of Educational Psychology*, 106 (3), 779–798.

Haager, D. E., Klingner, J. E., & Vaughn, S. E. (2007). *Evidence-based reading practices for response to intervention*. Baltimore, MD: Brookes Publishing Company.

Hagtvet, B. E. (1998). Preschool oral language competence and literacy development. In P. Reitsma & L. Verhoeven (eds), *Problems and interventions in literacy development* (pp. 63–80). London: Kluwer Academic.

Hämäläinen, J., Leppänen, P., Guttorm, T., & Lyytinen, H. (2008). Event-related potentials to pitch and rise time change in children with reading disabilities and typically reading children. *Clinical Neurophysiology*, 119 (1), 100–115. doi:10.1016/j.clinph.2007.09.064.

Hämäläinen, J., Leppänen, P. H. T., Torppa, M., Müller, K., & Lyytinen, H. (2005). Detection of sound rise time by adults with dyslexia. *Brain and Language*, 94(1), 32–42.

Hannum, E., & Buchmann, C. (2005). Global educational expansion and socio-economic development: An assessment of findings from the social sciences. *World Development*, 33(3), 333–354.

Hargrave, A. C., & Senechal, M. (2000). A book reading intervention with preschool children who have limited vocabularies: The benefits of regular reading and dialogic reading. *Early Childhood Research Quarterly*, 15(1), 75–90.

Harlaar, N., Trzaskowski, M., Dale, P. S., & Plomin, R. (2014). Word reading fluency: Role of genome-wide single-nucleotide polymorphisms in developmental stability and correlations with print exposure. *Child Development*, 85(3), 1190–1205.

Hatano, G., Kuhara, K., & Akiyama, M. (1981). Kanji help readers of Japanese infer the meaning of unfamiliar words. *The Quarterly Newsletter of the Laboratory of Comparative Human Cognition*, 3, 30–33.

Hayes, J. R. (1996). A new framework for understanding cognition and affect in writing. In C. M. Levy & S. Ransdell (eds), *The science of writing: Theories, methods, individual differences and applications* (pp. 1–28). Mahwah, NJ: Lawrence Erlbaum Associates.

Hayes, J. R., & Flower, L. S. (1980). Identifying the organization of writing processes. In L. Gregg & E. R. Steinberg (eds), *Cognitive processes in writing* (pp. 3–30). Hillsdale, NJ: Lawrence Erlbaum Associates.

Ho, C. S.-H. (2014). Preschool predictors of dyslexia status in Chinese first graders with high or low familial risk. *Reading and Writing*, 27(9), 1673–1701.

Ho, C. S.-H. (1997). The importance of phonological awareness and verbal short-term memory to children's success in learning to read Chinese. *Psychologia*, 40, 211–219.

Ho, C. S.-H., & Bryant, P. (1997a). Learning to read Chinese beyond the logographic phase. *Reading Research Quarterly*, 32, 276–289.

Ho, C. S.-H., & Bryant, P. (1997b). Phonological skills are important in learning to read Chinese. *Developmental Psychology*, 33, 946–951.

Ho, C. S.-H., & Bryant, P. (1999). Different visual skills are important in learning to read English and Chinese. *Educational and Child Psychology*, 16, 4–14.

Ho, C. S.-H., Chan, D. W., Chung, K. K., Lee, S. H., & Tsang, S. M. (2007). In search of subtypes of Chinese developmental dyslexia. *Journal of Experimental Child Psychology*, 97(1), 61–83.

Ho, C. S.-H., Chan, D. W. O., Lee, S. H., Tsang, S. M., & Luan, V. H. (2004). Cognitive profiling and preliminary subtyping in Chinese developmental dyslexia. *Cognition*, 91(1), 43–75.

Ho, C. S.-H., Chan, D. W.-O., Tsang, S.-M., & Lee, S.-H. (2002). The cognitive profile and multiple deficit hypothesis in Chinese developmental dyslexia. *Developmental Psychology*, 38, 543–553.

Ho, C. S.-H., Chow, B. W. Y., Wong, S. W. L., Waye, M., & Bishop, D. V. M. (2012). The genetic and environmental foundation of the simple view of reading in Chinese. *PLoS ONE*, 7(10), e47872. doi:10.1371/journal.pone.0047872.

Ho, C. S.-H., & Lai, D. N.-C. (1999). Naming-speed deficits and phonological memory deficits in Chinese developmental dyslexia. *Learning and Individual Differences*, 11, 173–186.

Ho, C. S.-H., Leung, M. T., & Cheung, H. (2011). Early difficulties of Chinese preschoolers at familial risk for dyslexia: Deficits in oral language, phonological processing skills, and print-related skills. *Dyslexia*, 17(2), 143–164.

Ho, C. S.-H., & Ma, R. N.-L. (1999). Training in phonological strategies improves Chinese dyslexic children's character reading skills. *Journal of Research in Reading*, 22, 131–142.

Ho, C. S.-H., Wong, Y. K., Yeung, P. S., Chan, D. W. O., Chung, K. K. H., Lo, S. C., & Luan, H. (2012). The core components of reading instruction in Chinese. *Reading and Writing*, 25(4), 857–886.

Ho, C. S.-H., Yau, P. W.-Y., & Au, A. (2003). Development of orthographic knowledge and its relationship with reading and spelling among Chinese kindergarten and primary school children. In C. McBride-Chang & H.-C. Chen (eds), *Chinese children's reading development* (pp. 51–72). Westport, CT: Praeger Publishers.

Hoien, T., Lundberg, I., Stanovich, K. E., & Bjaalid, I.-K. (1995). Components of phonological awareness. *Reading and Writing*, 7(2), 171–188.

Holliman, A., Critten, S., Lawrence, T., Harrison, E., Wood, C., & Hughes, D. (2014). Modeling the relationship between prosodic sensitivity and early literacy. *Reading Research Quarterly*, 49(4), 469–482.

Holm, A., & Dodd, B. (1996). The effect of first written language on the acquisition of English literacy. *Cognition*, 59, 119–147.

Hong Kong Education Department. (1996). *Guide to the pre-primary curriculum*. Retrieved from http://www.edb.gov.hk/attachment/en/curriculum-development/major-level-of edu/preprimary/pre-primaryguide-net_en.pdf.

Hoosain, R. (1991). *Psycholinguistic implications for linguistic relativity: A case study of Chinese*. Hillsdale, NJ: Lawrence Erlbaum Associates, Inc.

Hoover-Dempsey, K. V., Battiato, A. C., Walker, J. M. T., Reed, R. P., DeJong, J. M., & Jones, K. P. (2001). Parental involvement in homework. *Educational Psychologist*, 36, 195–209.

Horn, J. L., & Cattell, R. B. (1966). Refinement and test of the theory of fluid and crystallized general intelligences. *Journal of Educational Psychology*, 57, 253–270.

Hu, C. F., & Catts, H. W. (1998). The role of phonological processing in early reading ability: What we can learn from Chinese. *Scientific Studies of Reading*, 2, 55–79.

Hu, W., Lee, H. L., Zhang, Q., Liu, T., Geng, L. B., Seghier, M. L., & Price, C. J. (2010). Developmental dyslexia in Chinese and English populations: Dissociating the effect of dyslexia from language differences. *Brain*, 133(6), 1694–1706.

Huang, H.-S., & Hanley, J. R. (1995). Phonological awareness and visual skills in learning to read Chinese and English. *Cognition*, 54, 73–98.

Huang, H.-S., & Hanley, J. R. (1997). A longitudinal study of phonological awareness, visual skills and Chinese reading acquisition among first graders in Taiwan. *International Journal of Behavioural Development*, 20(2), 249–268.

Huang, Y. M., Liang, T. H., Su, Y. N., & Chen, N. S. (2012). Empowering personalized learning with an interactive e-book learning system for elementary school students. *Educational Technology Research and Development*, 60(4), 703–722.

Hung, D. L., & Tzeng, O. J. L. (1981). Orthographic variation and visual information processing. *Psychological Bulletin*, 90, 377–414.

Ibrahim, R. (2015). How does rapid automatized naming (RAN) correlate with measures of reading fluency in Arabic. *Psychology*, 6(3), 269–277. doi: 10.4236/psych.2015.63027.

Ibrahim, R., Eviatar, Z., & Aharon-Peretz, J. (2002). The characteristics of Arabic orthography slow its processing. *Neuropsychology*, 16(3), 322–326.

Ingulsrud, J. E., & Allen, K. (1999). *Learning to read in China: Sociolinguistic perspectives on the acquisition of literacy*. Lewiston, NY: E. Mellen.

Ise, E., & Schulte-Körne, G. (2010). Spelling deficits in dyslexia: Evaluation of an orthographic spelling training. *Annals of Dyslexia*, 60(1), 18–39.

Jessel, J., Gregory, E., Arhu, T., Kenner, C., & Ruby, M. (2004). Children and their grandparents at home: A mutually supportive context for learning and linguistic development. *English Quarterly*, 36(4), 16–23.

Joly-Pottuz, B., Mercier, M., Leynaud, A., & Habib, M. (2008). Combined auditory and articulatory training improves phonological deficit in children with dyslexia. *Neuropsychological Rehabilitation*, 18(4), 402–429.

Jones, S. M., Brown, J. L., & Lawrence Aber, J. (2011). Two-year impacts of a universal school-based social-emotional and literacy intervention: An experiment in translational developmental research. *Child Development*, 82(2), 533–554.

Juel, C., & Minden-Cupp, C. (2000). Learning to read words: Linguistic units and instructional strategies. *Reading Research Quarterly*, 35(4), 488–492.

Jusczyk, O., & Aslin, R. (1995). Infants' detection of the sound patterns of words in fluent speech. *Cognitive Psychology*, 29, 1–23.

Just, M. A., & Carpenter, P. A. (1992). A capacity theory of comprehension: Individual differences in working memory. *Psychological Review*, 99(1), 122–149.

Justice, L. M., Pence, K., Bowles, R. B., & Wiggins, A. (2006). An investigation of four hypotheses concerning the order by which 4-year-old children learn the alphabet letters. *Early Childhood Research Quarterly*, 21(3), 374–389.

Justice, L. M., Pullen, P. C., & Pence, K. (2008). Influence of verbal and nonverbal references to print on preschoolers' visual attention to print during storybook reading. *Developmental Psychology*, 44(3), 855–866.

Kagitçibasi, C., Sunar, D., & Bekman, S. (2001). Long-term effects of early intervention: Turkish low-income mothers and children. *Applied Developmental Psychology*, 22, 333–361.

Kail, R. (1991). Developmental change in speed of processing during childhood and adolescence. *Psychological Bulletin*, 109, 490–501.

Kail, R. (2000). Speed of information processing: Developmental change and links to intelligence. *Journal of School Psychology*, 38, 51–61.

Kail, R. V., & Ferrer, E. (2007). Processing speed in childhood and adolescence: Longitudinal models for examining developmental change. *Child Development*, 78(6), 1760–1770.

Kail, R. V., McBride-Chang, C., Ferrer, E., Cho, J. R., & Shu, H. (2013). Cultural differences in the development of processing speed. *Developmental Science*, 16(3), 476–483.

Kalindi, S. C. (2015a). Education in sub-Saharan Africa. In J. D. Wright (ed.), *International encyclopedia of the social and behavioral sciences, 2nd edn*, vol. 7 (pp. 198–209). Oxford: Elsevier.

Kalindi, S. C. (2015b). *Parental mediation of word writing in Bemba and English for Zambian children's early literacy skills* (unpublished doctoral dissertation). The Chinese University of Hong Kong, Hong Kong, China.

Kalindi, S. C., McBride, C., Tong, X., Wong, N. L. Y., Chung, K. H. K., & Lee, C.Y. (2015). Beyond phonological and morphological processing: Pure copying as a marker of dyslexia in Chinese but not poor reading of English. *Annals of Dyslexia*. doi: 10.1007/s11881-015-0097-8.

Kang, J.Y. (2012). Do bilingual children possess better phonological awareness? Investigation of Korean monolingual and Korean English bilingual children. *Reading and Writing*, 25(2), 411–431.

Kemp, N. (2009). The spelling of vowels is influenced by Australian and British English dialect differences. *Scientific Studies of Reading*, 13(1), 53–72.

Kendeou, P., Bohn-Gettler, C., White, M. J., & Van Den Broek, P. (2008). Children's inference generation across different media. *Journal of Research in Reading*, 31(3), 259–272.

Kendeou, P., Papadopoulos, T. C., & Kotzapoulou, M. (2013). Evidence for the early emergence of the simple view of reading in a transparent orthography. *Reading and Writing*, 26(2), 189–204.

Kenner, C. (2004). *Becoming biliterate: Young children learning different writing systems*. Sterling, CA: Trentham Books.

Kenner, C., & Gregory, E. (2003). Becoming biliterate. In H. Nigel, J. Larson, & J. Marsh (eds), *Handbook of early childhood literacy* (pp. 178–189). London: SAGE Publications Ltd.

Kenner, C., Ruby, M., Jessel, J., Gregory, E., & Arju, T. (2007). Intergenerational learning between children and grandparents in East London. *Journal of Early Childhood Research*, 5(3), 219–243.

Kessler, B., Pollo, T. C., Treiman, R., & Cardoso-Martins, C. (2013). Frequency analyses of pre-phonological spellings as predictors of success in conventional spelling. *Journal of Learning Disabilities*, 46(3), 252–259.

Keung, Y. C., & Ho, C. S. H. (2009). Transfer of reading-related cognitive skills in learning to read Chinese (L1) and English (L2) among Chinese elementary school children. *Contemporary Educational Psychology*, 34(2), 103–112.

Kieffer, M. J., & Box, C. D. (2013). Derivational morphological awareness, academic vocabulary, and reading comprehension in linguistically diverse sixth graders. *Learning and Individual Differences*, 24, 168–175.

Kim, Y. S. (2007). Phonological awareness and literacy skills in Korean: An examination of the unique role of body-coda units. *Applied Psycholinguistics*, 28(1), 69–94.

Kim, Y. S., Wagner, R. K., & Lopez, D. (2012). Developmental relations between reading fluency and reading comprehension: A longitudinal study from Grade 1 to Grade 2. *Journal of Experimental Child Psychology*, 113(1), 93–111.

Klein, P. K. (2010). *La protection du français au Québec* [The protection of French in Quebec]. Munich: GRIN Publishing.

Klein, R. M. (2002). Observations on the temporal correlates of reading failure. *Reading and Writing*, 15, 207–232.

Ko, H., & Wu, C. F. (2003). The role of character components in reading Chinese. In C. McBride-Chang & H.-C. Chen (eds), *Reading development in Chinese children* (pp. 73–80). Westport, CT: Praeger Publishers.

Koda, K. (2000). Cross-linguistic variations in L2 morphological awareness. *Applied Psycholinguistics*, 21, 297–320.

Kolinsky, R., Morais, J., and Verhaeghe, A. (1994). Visual separability: A study on unschooled adults. *Perception*, 23(4), 471–486.

Ku, Y.-M., & Anderson, R. C. (2001). Chinese children's incidental learning of word meanings. *Contemporary Educational Psychology*, 26, 249–266.

Kuhl, P. K. (2004). Early language acquisition: Cracking the speech code. *Nature Reviews Neuroscience*, 5(11), 831–843.

Kyle, F., Kujala, J., Richardson, U., Lyytinen, H., & Goswami, U. (2013). Assessing the effectiveness of two theoretically motivated computer-assisted reading interventions in the United Kingdom: GG Rime and GG Phoneme. *Reading Research Quarterly*, 48(1), 61–76. doi: 10.1002/rrq.038.

LaBerge, D., & Samuels, S. J. (1974). Toward a theory of automatic information processing in reading. *Cognitive Psychology*, 6, 293–323.

Lai, S. A., Benjamin, R. G., Schwanenflugel, P. J., & Kuhn, M. R. (2014). The longitudinal relationship between reading fluency and reading comprehension skills in second-grade children. *Reading & Writing Quarterly*, 30(2), 116–138.

Lam, S. S. Y., & McBride-Chang, C. (2013). Parent–child joint writing in Chinese kindergarteners: Explicit instruction in radical knowledge and stroke writing skills. *Writing Systems Research*, 5(1), 88–109.

Landsmann, L. T., & Levin, I. (1987). Writing in four- to six-year-olds: Representation of semantic and phonetic similarities and differences. *Journal of Child Language*, 14(1), 127–144.

Lau, D. K. Y., & Leung, M. T. (2004). Development of sub-character processing and the use of orthographical and phonological memories in learning new Chinese characters in primary-school-aged normal readers. *Asia Pacific Journal of Speech, Language and Hearing*, 9(1), 54–61.

Lau, K. L. (2004). Construction and initial validation of the Chinese reading motivation questionnaire. *Educational Psychology*, 24(6), 845–865.

Lavine, L. O. (1977). Differentiation of letter-like forms in prereading children. *Developmental Psychology*, 13, 89–94.

Lee, S.-Y., Stigler, J. W., & Stevenson, H. W. (1986). Beginning reading in Chinese and English. In B. R. Poorman & A. W. Siegel (eds), *Acquisition of reading skills: Cultural constraints and cognitive universals* (pp. 93–115). Hillsdale, NJ: Lawrence Erlbaum Associates.

Lee, S.-Y., Uttal, D. H., & Chen, C. (1995). Writing systems and acquisition of reading in American, Chinese, and Japanese first-graders. In I. Taylor & D. R. Olson (eds), *Scripts and literacy: Reading and learning to read alphabets, syllabaries and characters* (pp. 247–263). Norwell, MA: Kluwer.

Lee, V. E., & Croninger, R. G. (1994). The relative importance of home and school in the development of literacy skills for middle-grade students. *American Journal of Education*, 102, 286–329.

Leek, K. J., Weekes, B. A., & Chen, M. J. (1995). Visual and phonological pathways to the lexicon: Evidence from Chinese readers. *Memory and Cognition*, 23, 468–476.

Lei, L., Pan, J., Liu, H., McBride-Chang, C., Li, H., Zhang, Y., … Shu, H. (2011). Developmental trajectories of reading development and impairment from ages 3 to 8 years in Chinese children. *Journal of Child Psychology and Psychiatry*, 52(2), 212–220.

Leong, C. K. (1997). Paradigmatic analysis of Chinese word reading: Research findings and classroom practices. In C. K. Leong & R. M. Joshi (eds), *Cross-language studies of learning to read and spell: Phonologic and orthographic processing* (pp. 379–418). Dordrecht, Netherlands: Kluwer.

Leong, C. K. (2000). Rapid processing of base and derived forms of words and grades 4, 5 and 6 children's spelling. *Reading and Writing*, 12(3–4), 277–302.

Leong, C. K., Tan, L. H., Cheng, P. W., & Hau, K. T. (2005). Learning to read and spell English words by Chinese students. *Scientific Studies of Reading*, 9(1), 63–84.

Lepola, J., Lynch, J., Laakkonen, E., Silvén, M., & Niemi, P. (2012). The role of inference making and other language skills in the development of narrative listening comprehension in 4–6-year-old children. *Reading Research Quarterly*, 47(3), 259–282.

Leppänen, P. H., Richardson, U., Pihko, E., Eklund, K. M., Guttorm, T. K., Aro, M., & Lyytinen, H. (2002). Brain responses to changes in speech sound durations differ between infants with and without familial risk for dyslexia. *Developmental Neuropsychology*, 22(1), 407–422.

Leseman, P. M., & de Jong, P. F. (1998). Home literacy: Opportunity, instruction, cooperation, and social-emotional quality predicting early reading achievement. *Reading Research Quarterly*, 33(3), 294–318.

Lesgold, A. M., & Welch-Ross, M. (eds) (2012). *Improving adult literacy instruction: Options for practice and research*. Washington, DC: The National Academies Press.

Leventhal, T., & Brooks-Gunn, J. (2003). Children and youth in neighborhood contexts. *Current Directions in Psychological Science*, 12(1), 27–31.

Levin, I., Aram, D., Tolchinsky, L., & McBride, C. (2013). Maternal mediation of writing and children's early spelling and reading: The Semitic abjad versus the European alphabet. *Writing Systems Research*, 5(2), 134–155.

Levin, I., & Korat, O. (1993). Sensitivity to phonological, morphological, and semantic cues in early reading and writing in Hebrew. *Merrill-Palmer Quarterly*, 39(2), 213–232.

Levin, I., Korat, O., & Amsterdam, P. (1996). Emergent writing among Israeli kindergartners: Cross-linguistic commonalities and Hebrew-specific issues. In G. Rijlaarsdam, H. van den Bergh, & M. Couzin (eds), *Theories, models and methodology in writing research* (pp. 398–422). Amsterdam: Amsterdam University Press.

Levin, I., Patel, S., Margalit, T., & Barad, N. (2002). Letter names: Effect on letter saying, spelling, and word recognition in Hebrew. *Applied Psycholinguistics*, 23, 269–300.

Levin, I., Ravid, D., & Rapaport, S. (2001). Morphology and spelling among Hebrew-speaking children: From kindergarten to first grade. *Journal of Child Language*, 28(3), 741–772.

Levin, I., Shatil-Carmon, S., & Asif-Rave, O. (2006). Learning of letter names and sounds and their contribution to word recognition. *Journal of Experimental Child Psychology*, 93(2), 139–165.

Levine, E. R. (1982). What teachers expect of children from single-parent families. Paper presented at the Annual Convention of the American Personnel and Guidance Association, Detroit, MI.

Li, H., Corrie, L. F., & Wong, B. K. M. (2008). Early teaching of Chinese literacy skills and later literacy outcomes. *Early Child Development and Care*, 178(5), 441–459.

Li, H., & Rao, N. (2000). Parental influences on Chinese literacy development: A comparison of preschoolers in Beijing, Hong Kong, and Singapore. *International Journal of Behavioral Development*, 24, 82–90.

Li, H., Shu, H., McBride-Chang, C., Liu, H.Y., & Xue, J. (2009). Paired associate learning in Chinese children with dyslexia. *Journal of Experimental Child Psychology*, 103(2), 135–151.

Li, J. (2005). Mind or virtue: Western and Chinese beliefs about learning. *Current Directions in Psychological Science*, 14(4), 190–194.

Li, T., & McBride-Chang, C. (2014). How character reading can be different from word reading in Chinese and why it matters for Chinese reading development. In X. Chen, Q. Wang, & Y. C. Luo (eds), *Reading development and difficulties in monolingual and bilingual Chinese children* (pp. 49–65). Dordrecht, Netherlands: Springer.

Li, W., Anderson, R. C., Nagy, W., & Zhang, H. (2002). Facets of metalinguistic awareness that contribute to Chinese literacy. In W. Li, J. S. Gaffney, & J. L. Packard (eds), *Chinese children's reading acquisition: Theoretical and pedagogical issues* (pp. 87–106). Boston, MA: Kluwer Academic.

Liberman, A. M., & Mattingly, I. G. (1985). The motor theory of speech perception revised. *Cognition*, 21(1), 1–36.

Liberman, I. Y. (1973). Segmentation of the spoken word and reading acquisition. *Bulletin of the Orton Society*, 23, 65–77.

Liberman, I. Y., Shankweiler, D., Fischer, F. W., & Carter, B. (1974). Explicit syllable and phoneme segmentation in the young child. *Journal of Experimental Child Psychology*, 18, 201–212.

Lie, A. (1991). Effects of a training program for stimulating skills in word analysis in first grade children. *Reading Research Quarterly*, 26(3), 234–250.

Lin, D., McBride-Chang, C., Aram, D., Levin, I., Cheung, R. Y., Chow, Y. Y., & Tolchinsky, L. (2009). Maternal mediation of writing in Chinese children. *Language and Cognitive Processes*, 24(7–8), 1286–1311.

Lin, D., McBride-Chang, C., Aram, D., Shu, H., Levin, I., & Cho, J.-R. (2012). Maternal mediation of word writing in Chinese across Hong Kong and Beijing. *Journal of Educational Psychology*, 104(1), 121–137.

Lin, D., McBride-Chang, C., Shu, H., Zhang, Y., Li, H., Zhang, J., Aram, D., & Levin, I. (2010). Small wins big: Analytic Pinyin skills promote Chinese word reading. *Psychological Science*, 21(8), 1117–1122.

Lin, D., Wong, K. K., & McBride-Chang, C. (2012). Reading motivation and reading comprehension in Chinese and English among bilingual students. *Reading and Writing*, 25(3), 717–737.

Litt, R. A., & Nation, K. (2014). The nature and specificity of paired associate learning deficits in children with dyslexia. *Journal of Memory and Language*, 71(1), 71–88.

Liu, P. D., Chung, K. K. H., McBride-Chang, C., & Tong, X. (2010). Holistic versus analytic processing: Evidence for a different approach to processing of Chinese at the word and character levels in Chinese children. *Journal of Experimental Child Psychology*, 107(4), 466–478.

Liu, W., Shu, H., & Yang, Y. (2009). Speech perception deficits by Chinese children with phonological dyslexia. *Journal of Experimental Child Psychology*, 103(3), 338–354.

Logan, S., Medford, E., & Hughes, N. (2011). The importance of intrinsic motivation for high and low ability readers' reading comprehension performance. *Learning and Individual Differences*, 21(1), 124–128.

Lonigan, C. J., Burgess, S. R., Anthony, J. L., & Barker, T. A. (1998). Development of phonological sensitivity in 2- to 5-year-old children. *Journal of Educational Psychology*, 90(2), 294–311.

Loosli, S. V., Buschkuehl, M., Perrig, W. J., & Jaeggi, S. M. (2012). Working memory training improves reading processes in typically developing children. *Child Neuropsychology*, 18(1), 62–78.

Lott, B. (2001). Low-income parents and the public schools. *Journal of Social Issues*, 57, 247–259.

Lovegrove, W. J., & Williams, M. C. (1993). Visual temporal processing deficits in specific reading disability. In D. M. Willows, R. S. Kruk, & E. Corcos (eds), *Visual processes in reading and reading disabilities* (pp. 311–330). Hillsdale, NJ: Lawrence Erlbaum Associates.

Lu, Z. L., Sperling, A. J., Manis, F. R., & Seidenberg, M. S. (2005). Deficits in forming perceptual templates may underlie the etiology of developmental dyslexia. *Journal of Vision*, 5(8), 808. doi:10.1167/5.8.808.

Lundberg, I. (1994). Reading difficulties can be predicted and prevented: A Scandinavian perspective on phonological awareness and reading. In C. Hulme & M. Snowling (eds), *Reading development and dyslexia* (pp. 180–199). London: Whurr Publishers Ltd.

Lundberg, I. (1999). Learning to read in Scandinavia. In M. Harris & G. Hatano (eds), *Learning to read and write: A cross-linguistic perspective. Cambridge studies in cognitive and perceptual development* (pp. 157–172). New York, NY: Cambridge University Press.

Lundberg, I., Frost, J., & Petersen, O.-P. (1988). Effects of an extensive program for stimulating phonological awareness in preschool children. *Reading Research Quarterly*, 23, 263–284.

Lundberg, I., Olofsson, A., & Wall, S. (1980). Reading and spelling skills in the first school years predicted from phonemic awareness skills in kindergarten. *Scandinavian Journal of Psychology*, 21, 159–173.

Luo, Y. C., Chen, X., & Geva, E. (2014). Concurrent and longitudinal cross-language transfer of phonological awareness and morphological awareness in Chinese-English bilingual children. *Written Language and Literacy*, 27, 89–115.

Lyster, S. A. H. (2002). The effects of morphological versus phonological awareness training in kindergarten on reading development. *Reading and Writing*, 15(3–4), 261–294.

Lyytinen, H., Guttorm, T. K., Huttunen, T., Hämäläinen, J., Leppänen, P. H., & Vesterinen, M. (2005). Psychophysiology of developmental dyslexia: A review of findings including studies of children at risk for dyslexia. *Journal of Neurolinguistics*, 18(2), 167–195.

McBride-Chang, C. (1995). Phonological processing, speech perception, and reading disability: An integrative review. *Educational Psychologist*, 30(3), 109–121.

McBride-Chang, C. (1996). Models of speech perception and phonological processing in reading. *Child Development*, 67(4), 1836–1856.

McBride-Chang, C. (1998). The development of invented spelling. *Early Education and Development*, 9, 147–160.

McBride-Chang, C. (1999). The ABCs of the ABCs: The development of letter name and letter sound knowledge. *Merrill-Palmer Quarterly*, 45, 285–308.

McBride-Chang, C. (2012). Shared-book reading: There is no downside for parents. In S. Suggate & E. Reese (eds), *Contemporary debates in childhood education and development* (pp. 51–58). New York, NY: Routledge.

McBride-Chang, & Chang, L. (1995). Memory, print exposure, and metacognition: Components of reading in Chinese children. *International Journal of Psychology*, 30(5), 607–616.

McBride-Chang, C., Chen, H. C., Kasisopa, B., Burnham, D., Reilly, R., & Leppanen, P. (2012). What and where is the word? *Behavioral and Brain Sciences*, 35(5), 295–296.

McBride-Chang, C., Chow, B. W.-Y., Zhong, Y.-P., Burgess, S., & Hayward, W. (2005). Chinese character acquisition and visual skills in two Chinese scripts. *Reading and Writing*, 18, 99–128.

McBride-Chang, C., & Ho, C. S.-H. (2000a). Developmental issues in Chinese children's character acquisition. *Journal of Educational Psychology*, 92, 50–55.

McBride-Chang, C., & Ho, C. S.-H. (2000b). Naming speed and phonological awareness in Chinese children: Relations to reading skills. *Journal of Psychology in Chinese Societies*, 1(1), 93–108.

McBride-Chang, C., & Kail, R. (2002). Cross-cultural similarities in the predictors of reading acquisition. *Child Development*, 73(5), 1392–1407.

McBride-Chang, C., Lam, F., Lam, C., Chan, B., Fong, C. Y. C., Wong, T. T. Y., & Wong, S. W. L. (2011). Early predictors of dyslexia in Chinese children: Familial history of dyslexia, language delay, and cognitive profiles. *Journal of Child Psychology and Psychiatry*, 52(2), 204–211.

McBride-Chang, C., Lam, F., Lam, C., Doo, S., Wong, S. W., & Chow, Y. Y. (2008). Word recognition and cognitive profiles of Chinese pre-school children at risk for dyslexia through language delay or familial history of dyslexia. *Journal of Child Psychology and Psychiatry*, 49(2), 211–218.

McBride-Chang, C., Lin, D., Liu, P. D., Aram, D., Levin, I., Cho, J. -R., Shu, H., & Zhong, Y. (2012). The ABCs of Chinese: Maternal mediation of Pinyin for Chinese children's early literacy skills. *Reading and Writing*, 25, 283–300.

McBride-Chang, C., Shu, H., Chan, W., Wong, T., Wong, A. M.-Y., Zhang, Y., Pan, J., & Chan, P. (2013). Poor readers of Chinese and English: Overlap, stability, and longitudinal correlates. *Scientific Studies of Reading*, 17(1), 57–70.

McBride-Chang, C., Shu, H., Zhou, A., Wat, C. P., & Wagner, R. K. (2003). Morphological awareness uniquely predicts young children's Chinese character recognition. *Journal of Educational Psychology*, 95(4), 743–751.

McBride-Chang, C., Tong, X., Shu, H., Wong, A. M.-Y., Leung, K., & Tardif, T. (2008). Syllable, phoneme, and tone: Psycholinguistic units in early Chinese and English word recognition. *Scientific Studies of Reading*, 12, 171–194.

McBride-Chang, C., & Treiman, R. (2003). Use of letter names and letter sounds in learning to read English among young Hong Kong Chinese children. *Psychological Science*, 14(2), 138–143.

McBride-Chang, C., Wagner, R. K., Muse, A., Chow, B. W. Y., & Shu, H. U. A. (2005). The role of morphological awareness in children's vocabulary acquisition in English. *Applied Psycholinguistics*, 26(3), 415–435.

McBride-Chang, C., Zhou, Y., Cho, J. R., Aram, D., Levin, I., & Tolchinsky, L. (2011). Visual spatial skill: A consequence of learning to read? *Journal of Experimental Child Psychology*, 109(2), 256–262.

McGee, A., & Johnson, H. (2003). The effect of inference training on skilled and less skilled comprehenders. *Educational Psychology*, 23(1), 49–59.

McLean, G. M., Stuart, G. W., Coltheart, V., & Castles, A. (2011). Visual temporal processing in dyslexia and the magnocellular deficit theory: The need for speed? *Journal of Experimental Psychology*, 37(6), 1957–1975.

McVay, J. C., & Kane, M. J. (2012). Why does working memory capacity predict variation in reading comprehension? On the influence of mind wandering and executive attention. *Journal of Experimental Psychology: General*, 141(2), 302–320.

Magnusson, E., & Naucler, K. (1990). Can preschool data predict language-disordered children's reading and spelling at school? *Folia Phoniatrica*, 42(6), 277–282.

Mahfoudhi, A., Elbeheri, G., Al-Rashidi, M., & Everatt, J. (2010). The role of morphological awareness in reading comprehension among typical and learning disabled native Arabic speakers. *Journal of Learning Disabilities*. doi: 10.1177/0022219409355478.

Mahony, D., Singson, M., & Mann, V. (2000). Reading ability and sensitivity to morphological relations. *Reading and Writing*, 12, 191–218.

Manis, F. R., & Lindsey, K. A. (2010). Cognitive and oral language contributors to reading disabilities in Spanish–English bilinguals. In A. Y. Durgunoglu & C. Goldenberg (eds), *Language and literacy development in bilingual settings* (pp. 280–303). New York, NY: Guilford Press.

Manis, F. R., Seidenberg, M. S., & Doi, L. M. (1999). See Dick RAN: Rapid naming and the longitudinal prediction of reading subskills in first and second graders. *Scientific Studies of Reading*, 3, 129–157.

Manis, F. R., Seidenberg, M. S., Doi, L. M., McBride-Chang, C., & Peterson, A. (1996). On the bases of two subtypes of developmental dyslexia. *Cognition*, 58, 157–195.

Marean, G. C., Werner, L. A., & Kuhl, P. K. (1992). Vowel categorization by very young infants. *Developmental Psychology*, 28, 396–405.

Masgoret, A.-M., & Gardner, R. C. (2003). Attitudes, motivation, and second language learning: A meta-analysis of studies conducted by Gardner and associates. *Language Learning*, 53(1), 123–163.

Mashburn, A. J., Pianta, R. C., Hamre, B. K., Downer, J. T., Barbarin, O. A., Bryant, D., . . . Howes, C. (2008). Measures of classroom quality in prekindergarten and children's development of academic, language, and social skills. *Child Development*, 79(3), 732–749.

Matafwali, B., & Bus, A. G. (2013). Lack of familiarity with the language of instruction: A main cause of reading failure by grades 1 and 2 pupils in Zambia. *Insights on Learning Disabilities*, 10(2), 31–44.

Maurer, U., Bucher, K., Brem, S., & Brandeis, D. (2003). Altered responses to tone and phoneme mismatch in kindergartners at familial dyslexia risk. *NeuroReport*, 14(17), 2245–2250.

Maurer, U., Schulz, E., Brem, S., van der Mark, S., Bucher, K., Martin, E., & Brandeis, D. (2011). The development of print tuning in children with dyslexia: Evidence from longitudinal ERP data supported by fMRI. *NeuroImage*, 57(3), 714–722.

Mayringer, H., Wimmer, H., & Landerl, K. (1998). Phonological skills and literacy acquisition in German. In P. Reitsma & L. Verhoeven (eds), *Problems and interventions in literacy development* (pp. 147–161). Dordrecht, Netherlands: Kluwer Academic.

Melby-Lervåg, M., & Lervåg, A. (2014). Effects of educational interventions targeting reading comprehension and underlying components. *Child Development Perspectives*, 8(2), 96–100.

Melby-Lervåg, M., Lyster, S. A. H., & Hulme, C. (2012). Phonological skills and their role in learning to read: A meta-analytic review. *Psychological Bulletin*, 138(2), 322–352.

Meng, X., Sai, X., Wang, C., Wang, J., Sha, S., & Zhou, X. (2005). Auditory and speech processing and reading development in Chinese school children: Behavioural and ERP evidence. *Dyslexia*, 11(4), 292–310.

Messer, S. (1967). Implicit phonology in children. *Journal of Verbal Learning and Verbal Behavior*, 6, 609–613.

Metsala, J. L. (1997). Spoken word recognition in reading disabled children. *Journal of Educational Psychology*, 89, 159–169.

Metsala, J. L. (1999). Young children's phonological awareness and nonword repetition as a function of vocabulary development. *Journal of Educational Psychology*, 91, 3–19.

Metsala, J. L., Stanovich, K. E., & Brown, G. D. A. (1998). Regularity effects and the phonological deficit model of reading disabilities: A meta-analytic review. *Journal of Educational Psychology*, 90(2), 279–293.

Metsala, J. L., & Walley, A. C. (1998). Spoken vocabulary growth and the segmental restructuring of lexical representations: Precursors to phonemic awareness and early reading ability. In J. L. Metsala & L. C. Ehri (eds), *Word recognition in beginning literacy* (pp. 89–120). London: Lawrence Erlbaum Associates.

Metsala, J. L., & Walley, A. C. (2013). Spoken vocabulary growth and the segmental restructuring of lexical representations: Precursors to phonemic awareness and early reading ability. In J. L. Metsala & L. C. Ehri (eds), *Word recognition in beginning literacy* (pp. 89–120). Abingdon, UK: Routledge.

Miller, K. F. (2002). Children's early understanding of writing and language: The impact of characters and alphabetic orthographies. In W. Li, J. S. Gaffney, & J. L. Packard (eds), *Chinese children's reading acquisition: Theoretical and pedagogical issues* (pp. 17–30). London: Kluwer Academic.

Modin, B., Erikson, R., & Vågerö, D. (2013). Intergenerational continuity in school performance: Do grandparents matter? *European Sociological Review*, 29(4), 858–870.

Mol, S. E., Bus, A. G., de Jong, M. T., & Smeets, D. J. (2008). Added value of dialogic parent-child book readings: A meta-analysis. *Early Education and Development*, 19(1), 7–26.

Molfese, D. L. (2000). Predicting dyslexia at 8 years of age using neonatal brain responses. *Brain and Language*, 72, 238–245.

Moll, L., Diaz, S., Estrada, E., & Lopes, L. (1992). Making contexts: The social construction of lessons in two languages. In M. Savaria-Shore & S. Arvizu (eds), *Cross-cultural literacy: Ethnographies of communication in multi-ethnic classrooms* (pp. 339–366). New York, NY: Garland.

Montsion, J. M. (2014). Chinese ethnicities in neoliberal Singapore? State designs and dialect (ical) struggles of community associations. *Ethnic and Racial Studies*, 37(9), 1486–1504.

Moon, C., Cooper, R. P., & Fifer, W. P. (1993). Two-day-old infants prefer their native language. *Infant Behavior and Development*, 16, 495–500.

Moore, L. C. (2011). Moving across languages, literacies, and schooling traditions. *Language Arts*, 89(2), 288–297.

Morais, J. (1991). Constraints on the development of phonemic awareness. In S. A. Brady & D. P. Shankweiler (eds), *Phonological processes in literacy: A tribute to Isabelle Y. Liberman* (pp. 5–27). Hillsdale, NJ: Lawrence Erlbaum Associates.

Morais, J., Bertelson, P., Cary, L., & Alegria, J. (1986). Literacy training and speech segmentation. *Cognition*, 24(1–2), 45–64.

Morgan, P. L., & Fuchs, D. (2007). Is there a bidirectional relationship between children's reading skills and reading motivation? *Exceptional Children*, 73(2), 165–183.

Morrison, F. J., Connor, C. M., & Hindman, A. (2010). Early schooling and growth of literacy in the transition to school. In D. Aram & O. Korat (eds), *Literacy development and enhancement across orthographies and cultures* (pp. 153–166). New York, NY: Springer.

Morrison, F. J., Smith, L., & Dow-Ehrensberger, M. (1995). Education and cognitive development: A natural experiment. *Developmental Psychology*, 31, 789–799.

Mullis, I. V. S., Martin, M. O., Foy, P., & Drucker, K. T. (2011). *PIRLS 2011 International Results in Reading*. Chestnut Hill, MA: TIMSS & PIRLS International Study Center, Lynch School of Education, Boston College.

Mumtaz, S., & Humphreys, G. W. (2001). The effects of bilingualism on learning to read English: Evidence from the contrast between Urdu–English bilingual and English monolingual children. *Journal of Research in Reading*, 24(2), 113–134.

Muneaux, M., Ziegler, J. C., Truc, C., Thomson, J., & Goswami, U. (2004). Deficits in beat perception and dyslexia: Evidence from French. *NeuroReport*, 15(8), 1255–1259.

Munson, B. (2001). Relationships between vocabulary size and spoken word recognition in children aged 3 to 7. *Contemporary Issues in Communication Science and Disorders*, 28, 20–29.

Nag, S. (2007). Early reading in Kannada: The pace of acquisition of orthographic knowledge and phonemic awareness. *Journal of Research in Reading*, 30(1), 7–22.

Nag S. (2011). The akshara languages: What do they tell us about children's literacy learning? In R. Mishra & N. Srinivasan (eds), *Language-cognition interface: State of the art* (pp. 291–310). Munich: Lincom Europa.

Nagy, W. E., & Anderson, R. C. (1984). How many words are there in printed school English? *Reading Research Quarterly*, 19, 304–330.

Nagy, W. E., & Anderson, R. C. (1999). Metalinguistic awareness and literacy acquisition in different languages. In D. A. Wagner, R. L. Venetzky and B. Street (eds), *Literacy: An international handbook* (pp. 155–160). Boulder, CO: Westview Press.

Nakamoto, J., Lindsey, K. A., & Manis, F. R. (2008). A cross linguistic investigation of English language learners' reading comprehension in English and Spanish. *Scientific Studies of Reading*, 12(4), 351–371.

Nash, H. M., Hulme, C., Gooch, D., & Snowling, M. J. (2013). Preschool language profiles of children at family risk of dyslexia: Continuities with specific language impairment. *Journal of Child Psychology and Psychiatry*, 54(9), 958–968.

Nation, K., Cocksey, J., Taylor, J. S., & Bishop, D. V. (2010). A longitudinal investigation of early reading and language skills in children with poor reading comprehension. *Journal of Child Psychology and Psychiatry*, 51(9), 1031–1039.

Neuman, S. B., & Celano, D. C. (2012). *Giving our children a fighting chance: Poverty, literacy, and the development of information capital*. New York, NY: Teachers College Press.

Nicholson, T. (1999). Reading comprehension processes. In G. B. Thompson & T. Nicholson (eds), *Learning to read: Beyond phonics and whole language* (pp. 127–149). New York, NY: Teachers College Press.

Nicolson, R. I., & Fawcett, A. J. (2011). Dyslexia, dysgraphia, procedural learning and the cerebellum. *Cortex*, 47(1), 117–127.

Nicolson, R. I., Fawcett, A. J., & Dean, P. (2001). Developmental dyslexia: The cerebellar deficit hypothesis. *Trends in Neurosciences*, 24, 508–511.

Niemi, J., Laine, M., & Tuominen, J. (1994). Cognitive morphology in Finnish: Foundations of a new model. *Language and Cognitive Processes*, 9(3), 423–446.

Norton, E. S., Black, J. M., Stanley, L. M., Tanaka, H., Gabrieli, J. D., Sawyer, C., & Hoeft, F. (2014). Functional neuroanatomical evidence for the double-deficit hypothesis of developmental dyslexia. *Neuropsychologia*, 61, 235–246.

Nurmi, J. E., Kiuru, N., Lerkkanen, M. K., Niemi, P., Poikkeus, A. M., Ahonen, T., . . . Lyyra, A. L. (2013). Teachers adapt their instruction in reading according to individual children's literacy skills. *Learning and Individual Differences*, 23, 72–79.

Oakhill, J. V., & Cain, K. (2012). The precursors of reading ability in young readers: Evidence from a four-year longitudinal study. *Scientific Studies of Reading*, 16(2), 91–121.

Oakhill, J., & Garnham, A. (1988). *Becoming a skilled reader*. New York, NY: Basil Blackwell, Inc.

Ogle, L. T., Sen, A., Pahlke, E., Jocelyn, L., Kastberg, D., Roey, S., & Williams, T. (2003). *International comparisons in fourth-grade reading literacy: Findings from the Progress in International Reading Literacy Study (PIRLS) of 2001 (NCES 2003–073)*, US Department of Education, NCES. Washington, DC: US Government Printing Office.

Ojanen, E., Ronimus, M., Ahonen, T., Chansa-Kabali, T., February, P., Jere-Folotiya, J., . . . Lyytinen, H. (2015). GraphoGame: A catalyst for multi-level promotion of literacy in diverse contexts. *Frontiers in Psychology*, 6, 671. doi:10.3389/fpsyg.2015.00671.

Olson, D. R., & Torrance, N. (2001). *Conceptualizing literacy as a personal skill and as a social practice*. In D. R. Olson & N. Torrance (eds), *The making of literate societies* (pp. 3–18). Oxford: Blackwell.

Olson, R. K., Keenan, J. M., Byrne, B., & Samuelsson, S. (2014). Why do children differ in their development of reading and related skills? *Scientific Studies of Reading*, 18(1), 38–54.

Olson, R. K., Wise, B. W., Johnson, M. C., & Ring, J. (1997). The etiology and remediation of phonologically based word recognition and spelling disabilities: Are phonological deficits the 'hole' story? In B. Blachman (ed.), *Foundations of reading acquisition and dyslexia* (pp. 305–326). London: Lawrence Erlbaum Associates.

Omanson, R. C., Warren, W. M., & Trabasso, T. (1978). Goals, inferential comprehension, and recall of stories by children. *Discourse Processes*, 1, 337–354.

Oney, B., & Durgunoglu, A.-Y. (1997). Beginning to read in Turkish: A phonologically transparent orthography. *Applied Psycholinguistics*, 18, 1–15.

Opper, S. (1996). *Hong Kong's young children: Their early development and learning*. Hong Kong: Hong Kong University Press.

Ortiz, C., Stowe, R. M., & Arnold, D. H. (2001). Parental influence on child interest in shared picture book reading. *Early Childhood Research Quarterly*, 16(2), 263–281.

Orton, S. T. (1925). 'Word blindness' in schoolchildren. *Archives of Neurology and Psychiatry*, 14, 581–615.

Packard, J. L. (2000). *The morphology of Chinese: A linguistic and cognitive approach*. Cambridge: Cambridge University Press.

Pak, A. K., Cheng-Lai, A., Tso, I. F., Shu, H., Li, W., & Anderson, R. C. (2005). Visual chunking skills of Hong Kong children. *Reading and Writing*, 18(5), 437–454.

Pan, J., McBride-Chang, C., Shu, H., Liu, H., Zhang, Y., & Li, H. (2011). What is in the naming? A 5-year longitudinal study of early rapid naming and phonological sensitivity in relation to subsequent reading skills in both native Chinese and English as a second language. *Journal of Educational Psychology*, 103(4), 897–908.

Paris, S. G., Lindauer, B. K., & Cox, G. L. (1977). The development of inferential comprehension. *Child Development*, 48, 1728–1733.

Paris, S. G., & Upton, L. R. (1976). Children's memory for inferential relationships in prose. *Child Development*, 47, 660–668.

Paulesu, E., Danelli, L., & Berlingeri, M. (2014). Reading the dyslexic brain: Multiple dysfunctional routes revealed by a new meta-analysis of PET and fMRI activation studies. *Frontiers in Human Neuroscience*, 8, 830. doi: 10.3389/fnhum.2014.00830.

Paulesu, E., Démonet, J. F., Fazio, F., McCrory, E., Chanoine, V., Brunswick, N., . . . Frith, U. (2001). Dyslexia: Cultural diversity and biological unity. *Science*, 291(5511), 2165–2167.

Pellegrini, A., & Gaida, L. (1998). *The development of school-based literacy*. London: Routledge.

Peng, G., Minett, J. W., & Wang, W. S. Y. (2010). Cultural background influences the liminal perception of Chinese characters: An ERP study. *Journal of Neurolinguistics*, 23(4), 416–426.

Pennington, B. F., van Ordern, G. C., Smith, S. D., Green, P. A., & Haith, M. M. (1990). Phonological processing skills and deficits in adult dyslexics. *Child Development*, 61, 1753–1778.

Perfetti, C. A., Beck, I., Bell, L., & Hughes, C. (1987). Phonemic knowledge and learning to read are reciprocal: A longitudinal study of first grade children. *Merrill-Palmer Quarterly*, 33, 283–319.

Perfetti, C. A., & Tan, L. H. (1999). The constituency model of Chinese word identification. In J. Wang, A. W. Inhoff, & H.-C. Chen (eds), *Reading Chinese script: A cognitive analysis* (pp. 115–134). Mahwah, NJ: Erlbaum.

Peterson, R. L., & Pennington, B. F. (2012). Developmental dyslexia. *The Lancet*, 379(9830), 1997–2007.

Pinker, S. (1994). *The language instinct: How the mind creates language*. New York, NY: Morrow.

Pittas, E., & Nunes, T. (2014). The relation between morphological awareness and reading and spelling in Greek: A longitudinal study. *Reading and Writing*, 27(8), 1507–1527.

Plak, R. D., Kegel, C. A., & Bus, A. G. (2015). Genetic differential susceptibility in literacy delayed children: A randomized controlled trial on emergent literacy in kindergarten. *Development and Psychopathology*, 27(1), 69–79.

Pomerantz, E. M., Ng, F. F. Y., Cheung, C. S. S., & Qu, Y. (2014). Raising happy children who succeed in school: Lessons from China and the United States. *Child Development Perspectives*, 8(2), 71–76.

Pomerantz, E. M., Qin, L., Wang, Q., & Chen, H. (2011). Changes in early adolescents' sense of responsibility to their parents in the United States and China: Implications for academic functioning. *Child Development*, 82(4), 1136–1151.

Porpodas, C. D. (1999). Patterns of phonological and memory processing in beginning readers and spellers of Greek. *Journal of Learning Disabilities*, 32, 406–416.

Pounder, A. (2000). *Processes and paradigms in word-formation morphology*. Hawthorne, NY: M. de Gruyter.

Pratt, A., & Brady, S. (1988). Relation of phonological awareness to reading disability in children and adults. *Journal of Educational Psychology*, 80, 319–323.

Pressley, M. (1998). *Reading instruction that works: The case for balanced teaching*. New York, NY: Guilford Press.

Rack, J. P., Snowling, M. J., & Olson, R. K. (1992). The nonword reading deficit in developmental dyslexia: A review. *Reading Research Quarterly*, 27(1), 28–53.

Ramirez, G., Chen, X., Geva, E., & Kiefer, H. (2010). Morphological awareness in Spanish speaking English language learners: Within and cross-language effects on word reading. *Reading and Writing*, 23(3–4), 337–358.

Rao, N., Pearson, E., Cheng, K.-M., & Taplin, M. (2013). *Teaching in primary schools in China and India: Contexts of learning*. New York, NY: Routledge.

Ravid, D., and Schiff, R. (2006). Roots and patterns in Hebrew language development: Evidence from written morphological analogies. *Reading and Writing*, 19, 789–818.

Read, C., Zhang, Y.-N., Nie, H.-Y., & Ding, B.-Q. (1986). The ability to manipulate speech sounds depends on knowing alphabetic writing. *Cognition*, 24, 31–44.

Reese, E. (2012). The tyranny of shared book-reading. In S. Suggate & E. Reese (eds), *Contemporary debates in childhood education and development* (pp. 59–68). New York, NY: Routledge.

Rego, L. L. B. (1999). Phonological awareness, syntactic awareness and learning to read and spell in Brazilian Portuguese. In M. Harris & G. Hatano (eds), *Learning to read and write: A cross-linguistic perspective* (pp. 71–88). Cambridge, MA: Cambridge University Press.

Ren, L., & Hu, G. (2013). A comparative study of family social capital and literacy practices in Singapore. *Journal of Early Childhood Literacy*, 13(1), 98–130.

Reyes, I., & Azuara, P. (2008). Emergent biliteracy in young Mexican immigrant children. *Reading Research Quarterly*, 43, 374–398.

Richards, T. L., Berninger, V. W., Stock, P., Altemeier, L., Trivedi, P., & Maravilla, K. R. (2011). Differences between good and poor child writers on fMRI contrasts for writing newly taught and highly practiced letter forms. *Reading and Writing*, 24(5), 493–516.

Rispens, J. E., McBride-Chang, C., & Reitsma, P. (2008). Morphological awareness and early and advanced word recognition and spelling in Dutch. *Reading and Writing*, 21(6), 587–607.

Rittle-Johnson, B., & Siegler, R. S. (1999). Learning to spell: Variability, choice, and change in children's strategy use. *Child Development*, 70, 332–348.

Rosenthal, R., & Jacobson, L. (1968). *Pygmalion in the classroom*. New York, NY: Holt, Rinehart, Winston.

Rubin, H., & Turner, A. (1989). Linguistic awareness skills in grade one children in a French immersion setting. *Reading and Writing*, 1(1), 73–86.

Sahlberg, P. (2011). The fourth way of Finland. *Journal of Educational Change*, 12(2), 173–185.

Saiegh-Haddad, E., & Geva, E. (2008). Morphological awareness, phonological awareness, and reading in English–Arabic bilingual children. *Reading and Writing*, 21(5), 481–504.

Saiegh-Haddad, E., & Joshi, R. M. (eds) (2014). *Handbook of Arabic literacy*. London: Springer.

Saine, N. L., Lerkkanen, M. K., Ahonen, T., Tolvanen, A., & Lyytinen, H. (2011). Computer assisted remedial reading intervention for school beginners at risk for reading disability. *Child Development*, 82(3), 1013–1028.

Santi, K. L., Francis, D. J., Currie, D., & Wang, Q. (2014). Visual-motor integration skills: Accuracy of predicting reading. *Optometry & Vision Science*. doi: 10.1097/OPX.0000000000000473.

Scanlon, D. M., & Vellutino, F. R. (1997). A comparison of the instructional backgrounds and cognitive profiles of poor, average, and good readers who were initially identified as at risk for reading failure. *Scientific Studies of Reading*, 1(3), 191–215.

Scarborough, H. S. (1989). Prediction of reading disability from familial and individual differences. *Journal of Educational Psychology*, 81(1), 101–108.

Scarborough, H. S. (1990). Antecedents to reading disability: Preschool language development and literacy experiences of children from dyslexic families. In B. F. Pennington (ed.), *Reading disabilities: Genetic and neurological influences* (pp. 31–46). Boston, MA: Kluwer Academic.

Scarr, S., & Ricciuti, A. (1991). What effects do parents have on their children? In L. Okagaki & R. J. Sternberg (eds), *Directors of development: Influences on the development of children's thinking* (pp. 3–23). Hillsdale, NJ: Lawrence Erlbaum Associates.

Schneider, W., Kuspert, P., Roth, E., Vise, M., & Marx, H. (1997). Short- and long-term effects of training phonological awareness in kindergarten: Evidence from two German studies. *Journal of Experimental Child Psychology*, 66(3), 311–340.

Schoonen, R., Gelderen, A. V., Glopper, K. D., Hulstijn, J., Simis, A., Snellings, P., & Stevenson, M. (2003). First language and second language writing: The role of linguistic knowledge, speed of processing, and metacognitive knowledge. *Language Learning*, 53(1), 165–202.

Schreiber, P., & Read, C. (1980). Children's use of phonetic cues in spelling, parsing, and maybe reading. *Bulletin of the Orton Society*, 30, 209–224.

Scribner, S., & Cole, M. (1981). *The psychology of literacy*. Cambridge, MA: Harvard University Press.

Searle, C. (1991). *A blindfold removed: Ethiopia's struggle for literacy*. London: Young World Books.

Segers, E., & Verhoeven, L. (2002). Does speech manipulation make word discrimination easier? In L. Verhoeven, C. Elbro, & P. Reitsma (eds), *Precursors of functional literacy* (pp. 109–118). Amsterdam: John Benjamins Publishing Company.

Seidenberg, M., & Tanenhaus, M. K. (1979). Orthographic effects on rhyme monitoring. *Journal of Experimental Psychology: Human Learning and Memory*, 5, 546–554.

Sénéchal, M., LeFevre, J. A., Thomas, E. M., & Daley, K. E. (1998). Differential effects of home literacy experiences on the development of oral and written language. *Reading Research Quarterly*, 33, 96–116.

Serpell, R. (2001). Cultural dimensions of literacy promotion and schooling. In L. Verhoeven & C. E. Snow (eds), *Literacy and motivation: Reading engagement in individuals and groups* (pp. 243–274). London: Lawrence Erlbaum Associates.

Seymour, P. H., Aro, M., & Erskine, J. M. (2003). Foundation literacy acquisition in European orthographies. *British Journal of Psychology*, 94(2), 143–174.

Seymour, P. H., & Elder, L. (1986). Beginning reading without phonology. *Cognitive Neuropsychology*, 3(1), 1–36.

Seymour, P. H. K., & Porpodas, C. D. (1980). Lexical and non-lexical processing of spelling in dyslexia. In U. Frith (ed.), *Cognitive processes in spelling* (pp. 443–473). London: Academic Press.

Shahar-Yames, D., & Share, D. L. (2008). Spelling as a self-teaching mechanism in orthographic learning. *Journal of Research in Reading*, 31(1), 22–39.

Shamir, A., Korat, O., & Fellah, R. (2012). Promoting vocabulary, phonological awareness and concept about print among children at risk for learning disability: Can e-books help? *Reading and Writing*, 25(1), 45–69.

Shankweiler, D. (1999). Words to meanings. *Scientific Studies of Reading*, 3, 113–127.

Share, D. L. (2008). On the Anglocentricities of current reading research and practice: The perils of overreliance on an 'outlier' orthography. *Psychological Bulletin*, 134(4), 584–615.

Share, D. L., & Gur, T. (1999). How reading begins: A study of preschoolers' print identification strategies. *Cognition and Instruction*, 17, 177–213.

Share, D., & Levin, I. (1999). Learning to read and write in Hebrew. In M. Harris & G. Hatano (eds), *Learning to read and write: A cross-linguistic perspective. Cambridge studies in cognitive and perceptual development* (pp. 89–111). New York, NY: Cambridge University Press.

Sharp, A. C., Sinatra, G. M., & Reynolds, R. E. (2008). The development of children's orthographic knowledge: A microgenetic perspective. *Reading Research Quarterly*, 43(3), 206–226.

Shaywitz, B. A., Shaywitz, S. E., Pugh, K. R., Mencl, W. E., Fulbright, R. K., Skudlarski, P., . . . Gore, J. C. (2002). Disruption of posterior brain systems for reading in children with developmental dyslexia. *Biological Psychiatry*, 52(2), 101–110.

Shen, H. H., & Bear, D. R. (2000). Development of orthographic skills in Chinese children. *Reading and Writing*, 13, 197–236.

Shu, H., & Anderson, R. (1997). Role of radical awareness in the character and word acquisition of Chinese children. *Reading Research Quarterly*, 32, 78–89.

Shu, H., Anderson, R. C., & Zhang, H. (1995). Incidental learning of word meanings while reading: A Chinese and American cross-cultural study. *Reading Research Quarterly*, 30, 76–95.

Shu, H., Chen, X., Anderson, R. C., Wu, N., & Xuan, Y. (2003). Properties of school Chinese: Implications for learning to read. *Child Development*, 74(1), 27–48.

Shu, H., McBride-Chang, C., Wu, S., & Liu, H. (2006). Understanding Chinese developmental dyslexia: Morphological awareness as a core cognitive construct. *Journal of Educational Psychology*, 98(1), 122–133.

Siegel, L. S. (1989). IQ is irrelevant to the definition of learning disabilities. *Journal of Learning Disabilities*, 25, 469–479.

Siegel, L. S., Share, D., & Geva, E. (1995). Evidence for superior orthographic skills in dyslexics. *Psychological Science*, 6, 250–255.

Siegler, R. S. (2000). The rebirth of children's learning. *Child Development*, 71, 26–35.

Silven, M., Niemi, P., & Voeten, M. J. M. (2002). Do maternal interaction and early language predict phonological awareness in 3- to 4-year-olds? *Cognitive Development*, 17, 1133–1155.

Siok, W. T., & Fletcher, P. (2001). The role of phonological awareness and visual-orthographic skills in Chinese reading acquisition. *Developmental Psychology*, 37(6), 886–899.

Siok, W. T., Niu, Z., Jin, Z., Perfetti, C. A., & Tan, L. H. (2008). A structural-functional basis for dyslexia in the cortex of Chinese readers. *Proceedings of the National Academy of Sciences*, 105(14), 5561–5566.

Skibbe, L. E., Connor, C. M., Morrison, F. J., & Jewkes, A. M. (2011). Schooling effects on preschoolers' self-regulation, early literacy, and language growth. *Early Childhood Research Quarterly*, 26(1), 42–49.

Skibbe, L. E., Grimm, K. J., Bowles, R. P., & Morrison, F. J. (2012). Literacy growth in the academic year versus summer from preschool through second grade: Differential effects of schooling across four skills. *Scientific Studies of Reading*, 16(2), 141–165.

Snow, C. (2002). *Reading for understanding: Toward a research and development program in reading comprehension*. Santa Monica, CA: RAND.

Snow, C. E., Burns, M. S., & Griffin, P. (eds) (1998). *Preventing reading difficulties in young children*. Washington, DC: National Academy Press.

Snowling, M. J. (2000). *Dyslexia, 2nd edn*. Malden, MA: Blackwell.

Snowling, M. J., Gallagher, A., & Frith, U. (2003). Family risk of dyslexia is continuous: Individual differences in the precursors of reading skills. *Child Development*, 74(2), 358–373.

Snowling, M. J., & Stackhouse, J. (eds) (2013). *Dyslexia, speech and language: A practitioner's handbook*. Chichester, UK: Whurr Publishers Limited.

Sorhagen, N. S. (2013). Early teacher expectations disproportionately affect poor children's high school performance. *Journal of Educational Psychology*, 105(2), 465–477.

Sprenger-Charolles, L. (2004). Linguistic processes in reading and spelling: The case of alphabetic writing systems: English, French, German, and Spanish. In T. Nunes & P. Bryant (eds), *Handbook of literacy* (pp. 43–65). London: Kluwer.

Sprenger-Charolles, L., & Bonnet, P. (1996). New doubts on the importance of the logographic stages. *Cahiers de Psychologie Cognitive* (Current Psychology of Cognition), 15, 173–208.

Sprenger-Charolles, L., Cole, P., Lacert, P., & Serniclaes, W. (2000). On subtypes of developmental dyslexia: Evidence from processing time and accuracy scores. *Canadian Journal of Experimental Psychology*, 54, 87–103.

Sprenger-Charolles, L., Siegel, L. S., & Bechennec, D. (1997). Beginning reading and spelling acquisition in French: A longitudinal study. In C. A. Perfetti, L. Rieben, & M. Fayol (eds), *Learning to spell: Research theory and practice across languages* (pp. 339–359). London: Lawrence Erlbaum Associates.

Sprenger-Charolles, L., Siegel, L. S., Jimenez, J. E., & Ziegler, J. C. (2011). Prevalence and reliability of phonological, surface, and mixed profiles in dyslexia: A review of studies conducted in languages varying in orthographic depth. *Scientific Studies of Reading*, 15(6), 498–521.

Stage, S. A., Abbott, R. D., Jenkins, J. R., & Berninger, V. W. (2003). Predicting response to early reading intervention from verbal IQ, reading-related language abilities, attention ratings, and verbal IQ-word reading discrepancy: Failure to validate discrepancy method. *Journal of Learning Disabilities*, 36(1), 24–33.

Stahl, S. A., & Murray, B. A. (1994). Defining phonological awareness and its relationship to early reading. *Journal of Educational Psychology*, 86(2), 221–234.

Stanovich, K. E. (1986). Matthew effects in reading: Some consequences of individual differences in the acquisition of literacy. *Reading Research Quarterly*, 21, 360–407.

Stanovich, K. E. (1987). Perspectives on segmental analysis and alphabetic literacy. *Cahiers de Psychologie Cognitive*, 7, 514–519.

Stanovich, K. E. (1993). Introduction. In D. M. Willows, R. S. Kruk, & E. Corcos (eds), *Visual processes in reading and reading disability* (pp. xxi–xxiii). Hillsdale, NJ: Lawrence Erlbaum Associates.

Stanovich, K. E. (2000). *Progress in understanding reading*. London: Guilford Press.

Stanovich, K. E., Siegel, L. S., Gottardo, A., Chiappe, P., & Sidhu, R. (1997). Subtypes of developmental dyslexia: Differences in phonological and orthographic coding. In B. Blachman (ed.), *Foundations of reading acquisition and dyslexia* (pp. 115–142). London: Lawrence Erlbaum Associates.

Stanovich, K. E., West, R. F., & Cunningham, A. E. (1991). Beyond phonological processes: Print exposure and orthographic processing. In S. A. Brady & D. P. Shankweiler (eds), *Phonological processes in literacy: A tribute to Isabelle Y. Liberman* (pp. 219–235). Hillsdale, NJ: Lawrence Erlbaum Associates, Inc.

Stein, J., & Kapoula, Z. (eds) (2012). *Visual aspects of dyslexia*. Oxford: Oxford University Press.

Stevenson, H. W., & Lee, S.-Y. (1996). The academic achievement of Chinese students. In M. Bond (ed.), *The handbook of Chinese psychology* (pp. 124–142). Oxford: Oxford University Press.

Stevenson, H. W., Lee, S. Y., Chen, C., Stigler, J. W., Hsu, C. C., Kitamura, S., & Hatano, G. (1990). Contexts of achievement: A study of American, Chinese, and Japanese children. *Monographs of the Society for Research in Child Development*, 1–119.

Strehlow, U., Haffner, J., Bischof, J., Gratzka, V., Parzer, P., & Resch, F. (2006). Does successful training of temporal processing of sound and phoneme stimuli improve reading and spelling? *European Child & Adolescent Psychiatry*, 15(1), 19–29.

Strong, W. C. (1998). Low expectations by teachers within an academic context. Paper presented at the Annual Meeting of the American Educational Research Association, San Diego, CA.

Strong, G. K., Torgerson, C. J., Torgerson, D., & Hulme, C. (2011). A systematic meta-analytic review of evidence for the effectiveness of the 'Fast ForWord' language intervention program. *Journal of Child Psychology and Psychiatry*, 52(3), 224–235.

Sulpizio, S., Burani, C., & Colombo, L. (2015). The process of stress assignment in reading aloud: Critical issues from studies on Italian. *Scientific Studies of Reading*, 19(1), 5–20.

Sun-Alperin, M. K., & Wang, M. (2011). Cross-language transfer of phonological and orthographic processing skills from Spanish L1 to English L2. *Reading and Writing*, 24(5), 591–614.

Taboada, A., Tonks, S. M., Wigfield, A., & Guthrie, J. T. (2009). Effects of motivational and cognitive variables on reading comprehension. *Reading and Writing*, 22(1), 85–106.

Tabors, P. O., & Snow, C. E. (2001). Young bilingual children and early literacy development. In S. B. Neuman & D. K. Dickinson (eds), *Handbook of early literacy research* (pp. 159–178). New York, NY: Guilford Press.

Takacs, Z. K., Swart, E. K., & Bus, A. G. (2014). Can the computer replace the adult for storybook reading? A meta-analysis on the effects of multimedia stories as compared to sharing print stories with an adult. *Frontiers in Psychology*, 5, 1366. doi: 10.3389/fpsyg.2014.01366.

Talcott, J. B., Gram, A., van Ingelghem, M., Witton, C., Stein, J. F., & Toennessen, F. E. (2003). Impaired sensitivity to dynamic stimuli in poor readers of a regular orthography. *Brain and Language*, 87(2), 259–266.

Tallal, P. (1980). Auditory temporal perception, phonics and reading disabilities in children. *Brain and Language*, 9, 182–198.

Tallal, P., Miller, S. L., Bedi, G., Byma, G., Wang, X., Nagarajan, S. S., . . . Merzenich, M. M. (1996). Language comprehension in language-learning impaired children improved with acoustically modified speech. *Science*, 271(5245), 81–84.

Tallal, P., Miller, S. L., Jenkins, W. M., & Merzenich, M. M. (1997). The role of temporal processing in developmental language-based learning disorders: Research and clinical implications. In B. Blachman (ed.), *Foundations of reading acquisition and dyslexia* (pp. 49–66). London: Lawrence Erlbaum Associates.

Tan, L. H., Spinks, J. A., Eden, G. F., Perfetti, C. A., & Siok, W. T. (2005). Reading depends on writing, in Chinese. *Proceedings of the National Academy of Sciences of the United States of America*, 102(24), 8781–8785.

Tan, L. H., Spinks, J. A., Feng, C.-M., Siok, W. T., Perfetti, C. A., Xiong, J., & Gao, J.-H. (2003). Neural systems of second language reading are shaped by native language. *Human Brain Mapping*, 18(3), 158–166.

Tardif, T. (1996). Nouns are not always learned before verbs: Evidence from Mandarin speakers' early vocabularies. *Developmental Psychology*, 32(3), 492–504.

Tardif, T. (2006). The importance of verbs in Chinese. In P. Li, L.-H. Tan & E. Bates (eds), *Handbook of East Asian psycholinguistics,* vol. 1: *Chinese Psycholinguistics* (pp.124–135). London: Cambridge University Press.

Taylor, I., & Taylor, M. M. (1995). *Writing and literacy in Chinese, Korean and Japanese.* Philadelphia, PA: John Benjamins.

Temple, E. (2002). Brain mechanisms in normal and dyslexic readers. *Current Opinion in Neurobiology*, 12, 178–183.

Temple, E., Deutsch, G. K., Poldrack, R. A., Miller, S. L., Tallal, P., . . . & Gabrieli, J. D. (2003). Neural deficits in children with dyslexia ameliorated by behavioral remediation: Evidence from functional MRI. *Proceedings of the National Academy of Sciences*, 100(5), 2860–2865.

Temple, E., Poldrack, R. A., Salidis, J., Deutsch, G. K., Tallal, P., Merzenich, M. M., & Gabrieli, J. D. (2001). Disrupted neural responses to phonological and orthographic processing in dyslexic children: An fMRI study. *NeuroReport*, 12(2), 299–307.

Terry, N. P. (2006). Relations between dialect variation, grammar, and early spelling. *Reading and Writing*, 19, 907–931.

Tesman, J. R., & Hills, A. (1994). Developmental effects of lead exposure in children. *Social Policy Report, Society for Research in Child Development*, 8, 1–16.

Tibi, S., & McLeod, L. (2014). The development of young children's Arabic language and literacy in the United Arab Emirates. In E. Saiegh-Haddad & R. M. Joshi (eds), *Handbook of Arabic literacy* (pp. 303–321). New York, NY: Springer.

Tolchinsky-Landsmann, L., & Levin, I. (1985). Writing in preschoolers: An age-related analysis. *Applied Psycholinguistics*, 6, 319–339.

Tong, X., Deacon, S. H., & Cain, K. (2014). Morphological and syntactic awareness in poor comprehenders: Another piece of the puzzle. *Journal of Learning Disabilities*, 47(1), 22–33.

Tong, X., & McBride, C. (2014). Chinese children's statistical learning of orthographic regularities: Positional constraints and character structure. *Scientific Studies of Reading*, 18(4), 291–308.

Tong, X., & McBride-Chang, C. (2010). Developmental models of learning to read Chinese words. *Developmental Psychology*, 46(6), 1662–1676.

Tong, X., McBride-Chang, C., Shu, H., & Wong, A. M. (2009). Morphological awareness, orthographic knowledge, and spelling errors: Keys to understanding early Chinese literacy acquisition. *Scientific Studies of Reading*, 13(5), 426–452.

Tong, X., Mo, J., Shu, H., Zhang, Y., Chan, S., & McBride-Chang, C. (2014). Understanding Chinese children's complex writing: Global ratings and lower-level mechanical errors. *Writing Systems Research*, 6(2), 215–229.

Tong, X., Tong X., & McBride-Chang, C. (2013). A tale of two writing systems: Double dissociation and metalinguistic transfer between Chinese and English word reading among Hong Kong children. *Journal of Learning Disabilities*. doi: 10.1177/0022219413492854.

Tops, W., Callens, C., van Cauwenberghe, E., Adriaens, J., & Brysbaert, M. (2013). Beyond spelling: The writing skills of students with dyslexia in higher education. *Reading and Writing*, 26(5), 705–720.

Torgesen, J. K., Wagner, R. K., & Rashotte, C. A. (1997). Approaches to the prevention and remediation of phonologically based reading disabilities. In B. Blachman (ed.), *Foundations of reading acquisition and dyslexia* (pp. 287–304). London: Lawrence Erlbaum Associates.

Trehub, S. E., & Rabinovitch, M. S. (1972). Auditory-linguistic sensitivity in early infancy. *Developmental Psychology*, 6, 74–77.

Treiman, R. (1997). Spelling in normal children and dyslexics. In B. Blachman (ed.), *Foundations of reading acquisition and dyslexia* (pp. 191–218). London: Lawrence Erlbaum Associates.

Treiman, R. (2006). Knowledge about letters as a foundation for reading and spelling. In Joshi, R. M. & Aaron, P. G. (eds), *Handbook of orthography and literacy* (pp. 581–599). New York, NY: Routledge.

Treiman, R., & Barry, C. (2000). Dialect and authography: Some differences between American and British spellers. *Journal of Experimental Psychology: Learning Memory and Cognition*, 26, 1423–1430.

Treiman, R., Berch, D., & Weatherston, S. (1993). Children's use of phoneme–grapheme correspondences in spelling: Roles of position and stress. *Journal of Educational Psychology*, 85(3), 466–477.

Treiman, R., & Bourassa, D. C. (2000). The development of spelling skill. *Topics in Language Disorders*, 20, 1–18.

Treiman, R., & Broderick, V. (1998). What's in a name: Children's knowledge about the letters in their own name. *Journal of Experimental Child Psychology*, 70, 97–116.

Treiman, R., & Cassar, M. (1997). Spelling acquisition in English. In C. A. Perfetti, L. Rieben, & M. Fayol (eds), *Learning to spell: Research theory and practice across languages* (pp. 61–80). Mahwah, NJ: Lawrence Erlbaum Associates.

Treiman, R., & Kessler, B. (2013). Learning to use an alphabetic writing system. *Language Learning and Development*, 9(4), 317–330.

Treiman, R., & Kessler, B. (2014). *How children learn to write words.* New York, NY: Oxford University Press.

Treiman, R., Levin, I., & Kessler, B. (2007). Learning of letter names follows similar principles across languages: Evidence from Hebrew. *Journal of Experimental Child Psychology*, 96(2), 87–106.

Treiman, R., & Rodriguez, K. (1999) Young children use letter names in learning to read words. *Psychological Science*, 10, 334–338.

Treiman, R., Sotak, L., & Bowman, M. (2001). The roles of letter names and letter sounds in connecting print and speech. *Memory & Cognition*, 29, 860–873.

Treiman, R., Stothard, S. E., & Snowling, M. J. (2012). Instruction matters: Spelling of vowels by children in England and the US. *Reading and Writing*, 26(3), 473–487.

Treiman, R., Tincoff, R., Rodriguez, R., Mouzaki, A., & Francis, D. J. (1998). The foundations of literacy: Learning the sounds of letters. *Child Development*, 69, 1524–1540.

Treiman, R., & Yin, L. (2011). Early differentiation between drawing and writing in Chinese children. *Journal of Experimental Child Psychology*, 108(4), 786–801.

Treiman, R., & Zukowski, A. (1991). Levels of phonological awareness. In S. A. Brady & D. P. Shankweiler (eds), *Phonological processes in literacy: A tribute to Isabelle Y. Liberman* (pp. 97–117). Hillsdale, NJ: Lawrence Erlbaum Associates.

Tsai, K.-C., & Nunes, T. (2003). The role of character schema in learning novel Chinese characters. In C. McBride-Chang & H.-C. Chen (eds), *Reading development in Chinese children* (pp. 109–126). Westport, CT: Praeger Publishers.

Tse, S. K., Chan, W. S., Ho, W. K., Law, N. W. Y., Lee, T., Shek, C., . . . Yu, F. Y. (1995). *Chinese language education for the 21st century: A Hong Kong perspective.* Hong Kong: The University of Hong Kong.

Tsui, A. B. M., & Tollerson, J. W. (2003). *Medium of instruction policies: Which agenda? Whose agenda?* Mahwah, NJ: Lawrence Erlbaum Associates, Inc.

Tunmer, W. E. (2014). How cognitive science has provided the theoretical basis for resolving the 'great debate' over reading methods in alphabetic orthographies. In S. Cooper & K. Ratele (eds), *Psychology serving humanity: Proceedings of the 30th International Congress of Psychology,* vol. 2: *Western psychology* (pp. 228–239). Hove: Psychology Press.

Tzeng, O. J. L., & Hung, D. L. (1988). Cerebral organization: Clues from scriptal effects on lateralization. In I.-M. Liu, H.-C. Chen, & M. J. Chen (eds), *Cognitive aspects of the Chinese language* (pp. 119–139). Hong Kong: Asian Research Service.

UNESCO. (2000). *National Literacy Policies (China).* Retrieved from: http://www.accu.or.jp/litdbase/policy/chn/index.htm.

UNICEF. (2001). *The state of the world's children 2001.* Retrieved from: http://www.unicef.org/sowc01/.

UNICEF. (2014). *State of the world's children 2014 in numbers: Every child counts: Revealing disparities, advancing children's rights.* New York, NY: UNICEF. Retrieved from: http://www.unicef.org/gambia/SOWC_report_2014.pdf.

Uno, A., Wydell, T. N., Haruhara, N., Kaneko, M., & Shinya, N. (2009). Relationship between reading/writing skills and cognitive abilities among Japanese primary-school children: Normal readers versus poor readers (dyslexics). *Reading and Writing*, 22(7), 755–789.

US Department of Education, National Center for Education Statistics. (2014). *The Condition of Education 2014* (NCES 2014–083), Status Dropout Rates.

Vacca, J. L., Vacca, R. T., & Gave, M. K. (2000). *Reading and learning to read*. New York, NY: Longman.

Valenzuela, M. (1997). Maternal sensitivity in a developing society: The context of urban poverty and infant chronic under-nutrition. *Developmental Psychology*, 33, 845–855.

van der Leij, A., van Bergen, E., van Zuijen, T., de Jong, P., Maurits, N., & Maassen, B. (2013). Precursors of developmental dyslexia: An overview of the longitudinal Dutch dyslexia programme study. *Dyslexia*, 19(4), 191–213.

van Dijken, M. J., Bus, A. G., & de Jong, M. T. (2011). Open access to living books on the internet: A new chance to bridge the linguistic gap for at-risk preschoolers? *European Journal of Special Needs Education*, 26(3), 299–310.

van Goch, M. M., McQueen, J. M., & Verhoeven, L. (2014). Learning phonologically spe-cific new words fosters rhyme awareness in Dutch preliterate children. *Scientific Studies of Reading*, 18(3), 155–172.

Varnhagen, C. K., McCallum, M., & Burstow, M. (1997). Is children's spelling naturally stage-like? *Reading and Writing*, 9(5–6), 451–481.

Vellutino, F. R., Scanlon, D. M., & Chen, R. S. (1994). The increasingly inextricable rela-tionship between orthographic and phonological coding in learning to read: Some reservations about current methods of operationalizing orthographic coding. In V. W. Berninger (ed.), *The varieties of orthographic knowledge* (pp. 47–112). Boston, MA: Kluwer Academic.

Vellutino, F. R., Steger, J. A., Kaman, M., & De Setto, L. (1975). Visual form perception in deficient and normal readers as a function of age and orthographic-linguistic familiarity. *Cortex*, 11(1), 22–30.

Vellutino, F. R., Steger, J. A., Moyer, B. M., Harding, S. C., & Niles, C. J. (1977). Has the per-ceptual deficit hypothesis led us astray? *Journal of Learning Disabilities*, 10, 54–64.

Venezky, R. (1970). *The structure of English orthography*. The Hague: Mouton & Co.

Verhoeven, L., & van Leeuwe, J. (2008). Prediction of the development of reading compre-hension: A longitudinal study. *Applied Cognitive Psychology*, 22(3), 407–423.

Vernon-Feagans, L. (1996). *Children's talk in communities and classrooms*. Cambridge, MA: Blackwell.

Vygotsky, L. S. (1978). *Mind in society: The development of higher mental processes*. Cambridge, MA: Harvard University Press. (Original works published 1930, 1933, and 1935).

Wade-Woolley, L., & Heggie, L. (2015). Implicit knowledge of word stress and derivational morphology guides skilled readers' decoding of multisyllabic words. *Scientific Studies of Reading*, 19(1), 21–30.

Wagemaker, H., Taube, K., Munck, I., Kontogiannopoulou-Polydorides, G., & Martin, M. (1996). *Are girls better readers?* Amsterdam: IEA.

Wagner, D. A. (1993). *Literacy, culture and development*. New York, NY: Cambridge University Press.

Wagner, R. K., & Barker, T. A. (1994). The development of orthographic processing ability. In V. W. Berninger (ed.), *The varieties of orthographic knowledge,* vol. 1: *Theoretical and develop-mental issues. Neuropsychology and cognition*, vol. 8 (pp. 243–276). New York, NY: Kluwer Academic/Plenum.

Wagner, R. K., Puranik, C. S., Foorman, B., Foster, E., Wilson, L. G., Tschinkel, E., & Kantor, P. T. (2011). Modeling the development of written language. *Reading and Writing*, 24(2), 203–220.

Wagner, R. K., & Torgesen, J. (1987). The nature of phonological processing and its causal role in the acquisition of reading skills. *Psychological Bulletin*, 101, 192–212.

Wagner, R. K., Torgesen, J. K., Rashotte, C. A., Hecht, S. A., Barker, T. A., Burgess, S. R., & Garon, T. (1997). Changing relations between phonological processing abilities and word-level reading as children develop from beginning to skilled readers: A 5-year longitudinal study. *Developmental Psychology*, 33(3), 468–479.

Waldron, S., Kemp, N., Plester, B., & Wood, C. (2015). Texting behavior and language skills in children and adults. In L. D. Rosen, N. A. Cheever, & L. M. Carrier (eds), *The Wiley handbook of psychology, technology, and society* (pp. 232–249). Chichester, UK: John Wiley & Sons Ltd.

Wang, J. H. Y., & Guthrie, J. T. (2004). Modeling the effects of intrinsic motivation, extrinsic motivation, amount of reading, and past reading achievement on text comprehension between US and Chinese students. *Reading Research Quarterly*, 39(2), 162–186.

Wang, L. (2008). The marginality of migrant children in the urban Chinese educational system. *British Journal of Sociology of Education*, 29(6), 691–703.

Wang, M., & Arciuli, J. (2015). Introduction to the special issue. Phonology beyond phonemes: Contributions of suprasegmental information to reading. *Scientific Studies of Reading*, 19(1), 1–4.

Wang, M., Cheng, C., & Chen, S. W. (2006). Contribution of morphological awareness to Chinese–English biliteracy acquisition. *Journal of Educational Psychology*, 98(3), 542–553.

Wang, M., & Geva, E. (2003). Spelling performance of Chinese children using English as a second language: Lexical and visual-orthographic processes. *Applied Psycholinguistics*, 24(1), 1–25.

Wang, M., Ko, I. Y., & Choi, J. (2009). The importance of morphological awareness in Korean-English biliteracy acquisition. *Contemporary Educational Psychology*, 34(2), 132–142.

Wang, M., Park, Y., & Lee, K. R. (2006). Korean–English biliteracy acquisition: Cross-language phonological and orthographic transfer. *Journal of Educational Psychology*, 98(1), 148–158.

Wang, M., Perfetti, C. A., & Liu, Y. (2005). Chinese–English biliteracy acquisition: Cross language and writing system transfer. *Cognition*, 97(1), 67–88.

Wang, Q., & Ng, F. F. Y. (2012). Chinese students' implicit theories of intelligence and school performance: Implications for their approach to schoolwork. *Personality and Individual Differences*, 52(8), 930–935.

Wang, Q., & Pomerantz, E. M. (2009). The motivational landscape of early adolescence in the United States and China: A longitudinal investigation. *Child Development*, 80(4), 1272–1287.

Wang, S., & Gathercole, S. E. (2013). Working memory deficits in children with reading difficulties: Memory span and dual task coordination. *Journal of Experimental Child Psychology*, 115(1), 188–197.

Wang, Y., & McBride, C. (2015). Character reading and word reading in Chinese: Unique correlates for Chinese kindergarteners. *Applied Psycholinguistics*. doi: 10.1017/S014271641500003X.

Wang, Y., McBride-Chang, C., & Chan, S. (2014). Correlates of Chinese kindergarteners' word reading and writing: The unique role of copying skills? *Reading and Writing*, 27(7), 1281–1302.

Waters, G. A., & Caplan, D. (1996). The measurement of verbal working memory capacity and its relation to reading comprehension. *Quarterly Journal of Experimental Psychology: Human Experimental Psychology*, 49A, 51–79.

Weiner, B. (1985). An attributional theory of achievement motivation and emotion. *Psychological Review*, 92, 548–573.

Wells, G. (1985). *Language development in the preschool years*. New York, NY: Cambridge University Press.

Werker, J. F., & Tees, R. C. (1984). Cross-language speech perception: Evidence for perceptual reorganization during the first year of life. *Infant Behavior and Development*, 7, 49–63.

Werker, J. F., & Tees, R. C. (1999). Influences on infant speech processing: Toward a new synthesis. *Annual Review of Psychology*, 50, 509–535.

White, T. G., Power, M. A., & White, S. (1989). Morphological analysis: Implications for teaching and understanding vocabulary growth. *Reading Research Quarterly*, 24(3), 283–304.

Whitehurst, G. J., Epstein, J. N., Angell, A. L., Payne, A. C., Crone, D. A., & Fischel, J. E. (1994). Outcomes of an emergent literacy intervention in Head Start. *Journal of Educational Psychology*, 86, 542–555.

Whitehurst, G. J., & Lonigan, C. J. (1998). Child development and emergent literacy. *Child Development*, 69, 848–872.

Whitehurst, G. J., Zevenbergen, A. A., Crone, D. A., Schultz, M. D., Velting, O. N., & Fischel, J. E. (1999). Outcomes of an emergent literacy intervention from Head Start through second grade. *Journal of Educational Psychology*, 91, 261–272.

Wigfield, A., & Guthrie, J. T. (1997). Relations of children's motivation for reading to the amount and breadth of their reading. *Journal of Educational Psychology*, 89(3), 420–432.

Williams, C. L. (1980). The transfer of reading skills between first and second language in bilingual junior high students of Spanish origin. *Dissertation Abstracts International*, 41(6-A), 2434.

Willows, D. M., & Geva, E. (1995). What is visual in orthographic processing. In V. W. Berninger (ed.), *The varieties of orthographic knowledge,* vol. 2: *Relationships to phonology reading and writing* (pp. 355–376). London: Kluwer Academic.

Willows, D. M., Kruk, R. S., & Corcos, E. (1993). Are there differences between disabled and normal readers in their processing of visual information? In D. M Willows, R. S. Kruk, & E. Corcos (eds), *Visual processes in reading and reading disabilities* (pp. 265–285). Hillsdale, NJ: Lawrence Erlbaum Associates, Inc.

Wimmer, H. (1996). The early manifestation of developmental dyslexia: Evidence from German children. *Reading and Writing*, 8, 171–188.

Wimmer, H., & Hummer, P. (1990). How German-speaking first graders read and spell: Doubts on the importance of the logographic stage. *Applied Psycholinguistics*, 11, 349–368.

Wimmer, H., Mayringer, H., & Landerl, K. (2000). The double-deficit hypothesis and difficulties in learning to read a regular orthography. *Journal of Educational Psychology*, 92, 668–680.

Wimmer, H., Mayringer, H., & Raberger, T. (1999). Reading and dual-task balancing: Evidence against the automatization deficit explanation of developmental dyslexia. *Journal of Learning Disabilities*, 32, 473–478.

Windfuhr, K. L., & Snowling, M. J. (2001). The relationship between paired associate learning and phonological skills in normally developing readers. *Journal of Experimental Child Psychology*, 80, 160–173.

Windsor, J. (2000). The role of phonological opacity in reading achievement. *Journal of Speech, Language and Hearing Research*, 43, 50–61.

Wise, B. W., & Olson, R. K. (1995). What computerized speech can add to remedial reading. In A. Syrdal, R. Bennett, & S. Greenspan (eds), *Applied speech technology* (pp. 583–592). Boca Raton, FL: CRC Press.

Wolf, M. (1997). A provisional, integrative account of phonological and naming-speed deficits in dyslexia: Implications for diagnosis and intervention. In B. A. Blachman (ed.), *Foundations of reading acquisition and dyslexia: Implications for early intervention* (pp. 67–92). Mahwah, NJ: Lawrence Erlbaum Associates.

Wolf, M., Barzillai, M., Gottwald, S., Miller, L., Spencer, K., Norton, E., ... Morris, R. (2009). The RAVE-O intervention: Connecting neuroscience to the classroom. *Mind, Brain, and Education*, 3(2), 84–93.

Wolf, M., & Bowers, P. G. (1999). The double-deficit hypothesis for the developmental dyslexias. *Journal of Educational Psychology*, 91(3), 415–438.

Wolf, M., & Katzir-Cohen, T. (2001). Reading fluency and its intervention. *Scientific Studies of Reading*, 5, 211–239.

Wong, S. W., McBride-Chang, C., Lam, C., Chan, B., Lam, F. W., & Doo, S. (2012). The joint effects of risk status, gender, early literacy and cognitive skills on the presence of dyslexia among a group of high-risk Chinese children. *Dyslexia*, 18(1), 40–57.

Wong-Fillmore, L. (1992). Against our best interest: The attempts to sabotage bilingual education. In J. Crawford (ed.), *Language loyalties: A source book on the official English controversy* (pp. 367–375). Chicago: University of Chicago Press.

Woo, E. Y., & Hoosain, R. (1984). Visual and auditory functions of Chinese dyslexics. *Psychologia: An International Journal of Psychology in the Orient*, 27(3), 164–170.

Worden, P. E., & Boettcher, W. (1990). Young children's acquisition of alphabet knowledge. *Journal of Reading Behavior*, 22(3), 277–295.

Wouters, P., van Nimwegen, C., van Oostendorp, H., & van der Spek, E. D. (2013). A meta-analysis of the cognitive and motivational effects of serious games. *Journal of Educational Psychology*, 105(2), 249–265.

Wright, S., Fugett, A., & Caputa, F. (2013). Using e-readers and internet resources to support comprehension. *Educational Technology & Society*, 16(1), 367–379.

Wu, Q., Palinkas, L. A., & He, X. (2011). Social capital in promoting the psychosocial adjustment of Chinese migrant children: Interaction across contexts. *Journal of Community Psychology*, 39(4), 421–442.

Wu, X., Anderson, R. C., Li, W., Chen, X., & Meng, X. (2002). Morphological instruction and teacher training. In W. Li, J. S. Gaffney, & J. L. Packard (eds), *Chinese children's reading acquisition* (pp. 157–173). London: Kluwer Academic.

Wu, X., Li, W., & Anderson, R. C. (1999). Reading instruction in China. *Journal of Curriculum Studies*, 31, 571–586.

Wydell, T. N., & Butterworth, B. (1999). A case study of an English–Japanese bilingual with monolingual dyslexia. *Cognition*, 70(3), 273–305.

Wydell, T. N., & Kondo, T. (2003). Phonological deficit and the reliance on orthographic approximation for reading: A follow-up study on an English–Japanese bilingual with monolingual dyslexia. *Journal of Research in Reading*, 26(1), 33–48.

Wysocki, K., & Jenkins, J. R. (1987). Deriving word meanings through morphological generalization. *Reading Research Quarterly*, 22(1), 66–81.

Yan, C. M. W., McBride-Chang, C., Wagner, R. K., Zhang, J., Wong, A. M., & Shu, H. (2012). Writing quality in Chinese children: speed and fluency matter. *Reading and Writing*, 25(7), 1499–1521.

Yang, L., Guo, J., Richman, L., Schmidt, F., Gerken, K. C., & Ding, Y. (2013). Visual skills and Chinese reading acquisition: A meta-analysis of correlation evidence. *Educational Psychology Review*, 25(1), 115–143.

Yang, W. E., & Zhou, W. (2008). What accounts for Chinese-American children's high academic performance: A literature review of parental influences and home environment. *Gifted Education International*, 24(1), 88–104.

Yao, S., & Liu, J. (1998). Economic reforms and regional segmentation in rural China. *Regional Studies*, 32, 735–746.

Yelland, G. W., Pollard, J., & Mercuri, A. (1993). The metalinguistic benefits of limited contact with a second language. *Applied Psycholinguistics*, 14, 423–444.

Yildiz, M., Yildirim, K., Ates, S., Rasinski, T., Fitzgerald, S., & Zimmerman, B. (2014). The relationship between reading fluency and reading comprehension in fifth grade Turkish students. *International Journal of School & Educational Psychology*, 2(1), 35–44.

Yin, L., & McBride, C. (2015). Chinese kindergartners learn to read characters analytically. *Psychological Science*, 26(4), 424–432.

Yin, L., & Treiman, R. (2013). Name writing in Mandarin-speaking children. *Journal of Experimental Child Psychology*, 116(2), 199–215.

Yip, M. J. W. (2002). *Tone*. New York, NY: Cambridge University Press.

Zevenbergen, A. A., & Whitehurst, G. J. (2003). Dialogic reading: A shared picture book reading intervention for preschoolers. In A. van Kleeck, S. A. Stahl, & E. B. Bauer (eds), *On reading books to children: Parents and teachers* (pp. 177–200). Mahwah, NJ: Lawrence Erlbaum Associates.

Zhang, J., Anderson, R. C., Li, H., Dong, Q., Wu, X., & Zhang, Y. (2010). Cross-language transfer of insight into the structure of compound words. *Reading and Writing*, 23(3–4), 311–336.

Zhang, J., & McBride-Chang, C. (2010). Auditory sensitivity, speech perception, and reading development and impairment. *Educational Psychology Review*, 22(3), 323–338.

Zhang, J., & McBride-Chang, C. (2014). Auditory sensitivity, speech perception, L1 Chinese, and L2 English reading abilities in Hong Kong Chinese children. *Developmental Psychology*, 50(4), 1001–1013.

Zhang, J., McBride-Chang, C., Wagner, R. K., & Chan, S. (2014). Uniqueness and overlap: Characteristics and longitudinal correlates of native Chinese children's writing in English as a foreign language. *Bilingualism: Language and Cognition*, 17(2), 347–363.

Zhang, J., McBride-Chang, C., Wong, A. M. Y., Tardif, T., Shu, H., & Zhang, Y. (2014). Longitudinal correlates of reading comprehension difficulties in Chinese children. *Reading and Writing*, 27(3), 481–501.

Zhang, Y., Tardif, T., Shu, H., Li, H., Liu, H., McBride-Chang, C., . . . Zhang, Z. (2013). Phonological skills and vocabulary knowledge mediate socioeconomic status effects in predicting reading outcomes for Chinese children. *Developmental Psychology*, 49(4), 665–671.

Zhang, Y., Zhang, L., Shu, H., Xi, J., Wu, H., Zhang, Y., & Li, P. (2012). Universality of categorical perception deficit in developmental dyslexia: An investigation of Mandarin Chinese tones. *Journal of Child Psychology and Psychiatry*, 53(8), 874–882.

Zhong, Y., McBride-Chang, C., & Ho, C. S.-H. (2002). A study of the relation between phonological and orthographic processing and Chinese character reading of bilingual children in Hong Kong. *Psychological Science China*, 25(2), 173–176.

Zhou, Y. L., McBride-Chang, C., Fong, C. Y. C., Wong, T. T. Y., & Cheung, S. K. (2012). A comparison of phonological awareness, lexical compounding, and homophone training for Chinese word reading in Hong Kong kindergartners. *Early Education & Development*, 23(4), 475–492.

Zhou, Y., McBride-Chang, C., Law, A. B. Y., Li, T., Cheung, A. C. Y., Wong, A. M. Y., & Shu, H. (2014). Development of reading-related skills in Chinese and English among Hong Kong Chinese children with and without dyslexia. *Journal of Experimental Child Psychology*, 122, 75–91.

Ziegler, J. C., & Goswami, U. (2005). Reading acquisition, developmental dyslexia, and skilled reading across languages: A psycholinguistic grain size theory. *Psychological Bulletin*, 131(1), 3–29.

INDEX